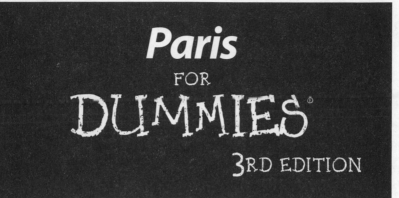

Paris

FOR

DUMMIES®

3RD EDITION

by Cheryl A. Pientka

WILEY

Wiley Publishing, Inc.

Paris For Dummies, 3rd Edition

Published by
Wiley Publishing, Inc.
111 River St.
Hoboken, NJ 07030-5774
www.wiley.com

For general information on our other products and services, please contact our Customer Care Department within the U.S. at 800-762-2974, outside the U.S. at 317-572-3993, or fax 317-572-4002.

For technical support, please visit www.wiley.com/techsupport.

Wiley also publishes its books in a variety of electronic formats. Some content that appears in print may not be available in electronic books.

Library of Congress Control Number: 2005921456

ISBN: 0-7645-7630-5

Manufactured in the United States of America

10 9 8 7 6 5 4 3 2 1

3B/QS/QT/QV/IN

WILEY

About the Authors

Cheryl A. Pientka is a literary scout and freelance writer. She is the coauthor of both *Frommer's Paris From $80 a Day* and *France For Dummies,* and a contributor to *Frommer's Europe on $70 a Day.* A graduate of Columbia University Graduate School of Journalism and the University of Delaware, she lives in New York when she can't be in Paris.

Sean Stevens (a contributing writer) studied art history, then followed the family calling into politics before finding his passion in the restaurant world. When not in New York working for world-renowned chefs, he splits his free time between Paris and Delaware.

Dedication

CAP: To the memory of my father, Philip E. Pientka.

S.S. To Nellie, Lou and Johnny for nurturing the adventure in my heart.

Authors' Acknowledgments

CAP: A big *merci* to: my mother for all her support, and to my mom, Alicia Patterson Giesa, to Amy Lyons, Aliyah Vinikoor, and Sophia Seidner; to *Bonjour Paris*'s Karen Fawcett, *Parler Paris*'s Adrian Leeds, and to John and Mimi Forde. Thanks also to Caren Lissner, John, Claire, Eric, Tyler, Andy, Gramps and Grandmother, Barbara Tolley, Allison Heiny, Jayne Pliner, Gloria Fleming, the dog owners on the Great Hill, and the staff and volunteers at Animal Haven shelter in Flushing, Queens, for their terrific work — and for Josie.

SS: With heartfelt thanks to Mom and Mike; Shannon, Lisa, Lily and Carter; Brock and Alex; Chris Biddle, Frank Everett, and Marc Koutoufaris, Grandmom Isaacs and my pals in San Clemente.

Publisher's Acknowledgments

We're proud of this book; please send us your comments through our Dummies online registration form located at www.dummies.com/register/.

Some of the people who helped bring this book to market include the following:

Editorial

Editors: Kathleen A. Dobie, Project Editor; Amy Lyons, Development Editor

Cartographer: Roberta Stockwell

Editorial Manager: Michelle Hacker

Editorial Supervisor: Carmen Krikorian

Editorial Assistant: Nadine Bell

Senior Photo Editor: Richard Fox

Cover Photos: Front cover photo © Terry Vine/Getty Images; back cover photo © Sitki Tarlan/Panoramic Images

Cartoons: Rich Tennant, www.the5thwave.com

Composition

Project Coordinator: Ryan Steffen

Layout and Graphics: Lauren Goddard, Barry Offringa, Jacque Roth, Julie Trippetti

Proofreaders: Leeann Harney, Jessica Kramer, TECHBOOKS Production Services

Indexer: TECHBOOKS Production Services

Publishing and Editorial for Consumer Dummies

Diane Graves Steele, Vice President and Publisher, Consumer Dummies

Joyce Pepple, Acquisitions Director, Consumer Dummies

Kristin A. Cocks, Product Development Director, Consumer Dummies

Michael Spring, Vice President and Publisher, Travel

Kelly Regan, Editorial Director, Travel

Publishing for Technology Dummies

Andy Cummings, Vice President and Publisher, Dummies Technology/General User

Composition Services

Gerry Fahey, Vice President of Production Services

Debbie Stailey, Director of Composition Services

Contents at a Glance

Maps at a Glance

Table of Contents

Introduction

. . . .

*W*hy is it so easy to fall in love with this particular city? After all, the Parisians have a notorious reputation for snobbishness and rudeness (though these days it's nearly unfounded). They don't clean up after their dogs. The place is expensive. But once you have a taste of the way the French live a typical day, you may find yourself waxing poetic about the luxury of lingering at a café under an awning with just a small cup of espresso and a book. The history! The culture — you can visit a museum a day for a year and still not see all of them! And the beauty — from the curved beaux-arts apartment buildings with iron balconies dripping with flowers, graceful bridges arching over the Seine, and eye-pleasing formal gardens balanced by no-less tended but more natural parks, to the paintings and sculptures in the museums, to exquisite displays in store windows. If you've never been to Paris, you may find your heart stolen by one of the world's most legendary cities.

If this is your first visit or if you haven't been to Paris in a dog's age, you're in for some changes. First of all, forget that stereotype about rude Parisians; the city is much, much friendlier. It seems the majority of people now is willing to try out their English to help visitors, and service at stores and in restaurants can be downright warm when visitors take the time to acknowledge storekeepers and waiters with a pleasant *bonjour*. Monuments have been restored: The gold leaf on the Opéra Garnier's exterior is positively sparkling, and its interior (with a Marc Chagall mural) glows from its million-dollar scrubbing. This city noted for past glories has also entered the 21st century at full speed. People tap on their laptops at the many wi-fi spaces around the city, they talk on the tiniest, most advanced cell phones you've ever seen. The Métro's Meteor line drives itself. Architecture has a decidedly futuristic flair: The buildings of the Cité des Sciences et de l'Industrie, a park and museum complex, include a huge sphere on which movies are shown, and the giant Bibliothèque Nationale de François Mitterand is shaped to resemble an open book.

Paris is an eternal source of discovery. Even a familiar walk will yield surprises — an unexpected passage that veers off the main road into a park, or an unusual building, or a cluster of houses containing some half-forgotten history from centuries past. Paris is more than a city; it's an encounter. Every visitor, from package-tour traveler to lone backpacker, experiences Paris's glory in an individual and unique way. Perhaps the city will get in your heart, too, and you'll be itching to return before you even depart.

About This Book

Consider this a textbook of sorts that you don't have to read from front to back, and certainly one you won't be tested on! Basically *Paris For Dummies,* 3rd Edition presents you with to-the-point information on Paris that's fun and easy to access. I explain very basic information about the city for readers who have never visited, but I also include points of interest for the seasoned traveler.

Please be advised that travel information is subject to change at any time — and this is especially true of prices. I therefore suggest that you write or call ahead for confirmation when making your travel plans. The authors, editors, and publisher cannot be held responsible for the experiences of readers while traveling. Your safety is important to us, however, so we encourage you to stay alert and be aware of your surroundings. Keep a close eye on cameras, purses, and wallets, all favorite targets of thieves and pickpockets.

Conventions Used in This Book

Paris For Dummies is a reference book, meaning you may read the chapters in any order you want. I use some standard listings for hotels, restaurants, and sights. These listings enable you to open the book to any chapter and access the information you need quickly and easily.

In this book, I include lists of hotels, restaurants, and attractions. As I describe each, I often include abbreviations for commonly accepted credit cards. Take a look at the following list for an explanation of each:

> AE: American Express
>
> DC: Diners Club
>
> DISC: Discover
>
> MC: MasterCard
>
> V: Visa

I divide the hotels into two categories — my personal favorites and those that don't quite make my preferred list but still get my hearty seal of approval. Don't be shy about considering these runner-up hotels if you're unable to get a room at one of my favorites or if your preferences differ from mine — the amenities that the runners-up offer and the services that each provides make all these accommodations good choices to consider as you determine where to rest your head at night.

I also include some general pricing information to help you as you decide where to unpack your bags or dine on the local cuisine. I use a system of euros and dollar signs to show a range of costs for one night in a hotel (the price refers to a double-occupancy room) in Chapter 9 or

Dummies Post-it® Flags

As you read this book, you'll find information that you'll want to reference as you plan or enjoy your trip — whether it be a new hotel, a must-see attraction or a must-try walking tour. Mark these pages with the handy Post-it® Flags included in this book to help make your trip planning easier!

a meal at a restaurant (included in the cost of each meal is soup or salad, an entrée, dessert, and a non-alcoholic drink) in Chapter 10.

I include the Paris *arrondissements,* or administrative districts, in each address to give you a better idea of where each place is located. Paris is divided into 20 arrondissements, which spiral out like a snail shell from the first arrondissement in the very center of Paris (abbreviated *1er*), to the 20th on the outer edges of the city (abbreviated *20e*). The arrondissement number appears after the street address in each citation in this book. For example, "123 bd. St-Germain, 6e," indicates the building numbered 123 on the boulevard St-Germain is in the 6th arrondissement. To get an idea of where each arrondissement is located, consult the "Paris at a Glance" map in Chapter 1. Street abbreviations used throughout the book include not only *bd.* (boulevard), but also *rue* (street), *av.* (avenue), *place* (square), *bis* (an odd term generally meaning an address between two buildings), *Ter* (terrace), or *quai* (quay or riverbank).

To help you orient yourself, I also give the nearest Métro (subway) stop for all destinations (for example: Métro: Pont Marie).

Although exchange rates can and do fluctuate daily, the price conversions in this book were calculated at the rate of one euro (the local currency) to $1.15 U.S. dollar. For more information about the euro, see Chapter 4.

Foolish Assumptions

As I wrote this book, I made some assumptions about you and your needs as a traveler. Here's what I assumed about you:

- ✔ You may be an experienced traveler who hasn't had much time to explore Paris and wants expert advice when you finally do get a chance to enjoy that particular locale.

- ✔ You may be an inexperienced traveler looking for guidance when determining whether to take a trip to Paris and how to plan for it.

- ✔ You're not looking for a book that provides all the information available about Paris or that lists every hotel, restaurant, or attraction available to you. Instead, you're looking for a book that focuses on the places that give you the best or most unique experience in Paris.

If you fit any of this criteria, *Paris For Dummies* gives you the information you're looking for!

How This Book Is Organized

Paris For Dummies is divided into seven parts and two appendixes. If you read the parts in sequential order, they can guide you through all the advance planning aspects of your trip and then get you off and running while you're in the City of Light.

Part I: Introducing Paris

You get a best-of overview of the city, some basic history and architecture, and you find out what Paris has to offer at different times of the year.

Part II: Planning Your Trip to Paris

These chapters give you the nitty-gritty of trip planning, with the answers to questions such as: Should I use a travel agent or go it alone? Is travel insurance a good idea? These chapters touch on everything you need to consider before planning a trip. I give you hints on developing a realistic budget, and tell you about a host of options available to travelers with special needs or interests.

Part III: Settling into Paris

What kind of accommodations should you use in Paris? Why don't you have to pay full price at hotel chains? Some of the city's best moderately priced hotels (with a few super-budget and some deluxe resorts thrown in for good measure), are listed here, as well as advice on how to tie up those frustrating last-minute details that can unnerve the most seasoned of travelers.

Get oriented in Paris in no time. You get tips on everything from navigating your way through customs to getting to your hotel from the airport to discovering Paris neighborhood by neighborhood. You find out how to use the city's terrific transportation system, why you shouldn't rent a car here, and what to know when you hail a cab. You make sense of the euro, and find out where to turn if your wallet gets stolen.

Paris is known for its fine food, and Chapter 10 helps you choose some of the best restaurants for your taste and budget. I list everything from moderately priced to haute cuisine restaurants, so you can discover that a fine meal is truly an art in itself. I also reserve a chapter to provide you with street food and light fare options for those occasions when you don't have the time, or the desire, for a full-course meal.

Part IV: Exploring Paris

This part has everything you need to know about Paris's top sights — how to get to them, how much they cost, and how much time to devote to them, as well as handy indexes by sight, type, and neighborhood to make them easier to find. There are kid- and teen-specific sights, as well as information on orientation and other tours, a shopper's guide to Paris, three recommended itineraries, and five great day trips if you're in the mood to get out of town.

Part V: Living It Up after Dark: Paris Nightlife

Nothing is more beautiful than Paris at night when the city's monuments are lit up like a stage set where anything can happen. This part gives you all the information you need about seeing plays, opera, ballet, and live music as well as which nightclubs and bars are fun. It's honest about whether those spectacles for which Paris has come to be known — the cabarets — are truly worth it. You uncover how to find out what's going on and where you can get reduced-rate tickets. You even get the low-down on how Parisians dress for a visit to a classy bar.

Part VI: The Part of Tens

What *For Dummies* book would be complete without a Part of Tens? Included is a quick collection of fun tidbits: what to do on a rainy day, and recommendations for the best place to relax with a picnic — a very Parisian pastime!

Part VII: The Appendixes

In back of this book, I include two appendixes. Appendix A is a Quick Concierge that contains lots of handy information you may need when traveling in Paris: phone numbers and addresses of emergency personnel, area hospitals, and pharmacies; lists of local newspapers and magazines; protocol for sending mail and finding taxis; and more. Check out this appendix when searching for answers to lots of little questions that may come up as you travel. You can find Quick Concierge easily because it's printed on yellow paper.

Appendix B is a glossary of English-to-French translations of basic vocabulary and health, travel, and (of course) shopping terms.

Icons Used in This Book

The little pictures in the margins are meant to draw your attention to especially useful text. Explanations of what each icon means follow.

Keep an eye out for the Bargain Alert icon as you seek out money-saving tips and/or great deals.

Best of the Best icon highlights the best Paris has to offer in all categories — hotels, restaurants, attractions, activities, shopping, and nightlife.

 You see this icon whenever something needs your particular attention. When you need to be aware of a rip-off, an overrated sight, a dubious deal, or any other trap set for unsuspecting travelers, this icon alerts you to that fact. These hints also offer the lowdown on the quirks, etiquette, and unwritten rules of the area so you can avoid looking like a tourist and, instead, be treated more like a local.

 This icon is a catchall for any special hint, tip, or bit of insider's advice that can help make your trip run more smoothly. Really, the point of a travel guide is to serve as one gigantic tip, but this icon singles out those nuggets of knowledge you may not have run across before or of which you can make immediate use.

 This icon, in addition to flagging tips and resources of special interest to families, points out the most child-friendly hotels, restaurants, and attractions. If you need a baby sitter at your hotel, a welcoming relaxed atmosphere at a restaurant, or a dazzling site that delights your child, look for this icon. Information is included regarding larger, family-sized rooms at hotels and restaurants that serve meals that go easy on your little ones' tummies.

 Sometimes a great hotel, restaurant, or attraction may be a bit out of the center or require a bit of effort to get to. This icon alerts you to these secret finds, and you can rest assured, no spots are included that aren't truly worth the energy. This icon also signifies any resource that's particularly useful and worth the time to seek out.

Where to Go from Here

To Paris! The City of Light is for everyone, and *Paris For Dummies* shows you just how accessible it can be. Included is a selective list of some of the best hotel, dining, and touring options along with insider info to help you make informed decisions. Follow the advice laid out here, and you'll want to return to Paris again and again. As author Honoré de Balzac once said that in Paris there will always remain an undiscovered place, an unknown retreat, and something unheard of.

Part I
Introducing Paris

"I know it's a wedding present from your niece, I just don't know why you had to wear it to the Louvre."

In this part . . .

Are you a stranger to Paris? Or has it been a loooong time since you last visited? Then (re)introduce yourself to the city and whet your appetite to find out more about it. In Chapter 1, you get an overview of Paris and learn about the best the city has to offer. Chapter 2 gives you a crash course in Paris's history and architecture, briefly introduces you to French cuisine, soothes any worries you may have about the language, and recommends some great books and movies to enhance your understanding of the city. In Chapter 3, the pros and cons of the seasons as well as a Paris calendar of events helps you decide the perfect time for your visit.

Chapter 1

Discovering the Best of Paris

* *

In This Chapter

▶ Unveiling Paris's best sights
▶ Discovering Paris's best accommodations for every price range
▶ Endulging in glorious food, the best bars, a shopping nirvana, and the best culture, parks and gardens

* *

Congratulations on choosing to visit one of the most beautiful and magical cities on the planet! With so much to do and see, you're probably wondering what you should do first, and frankly, what's a waste of time. You may be concerned that you don't speak French, and that a language barrier may prevent you from doing some of the things you'd like. If this is your first visit to Paris, you know you want to taste the delicious food for which the country is renowned. But facing the choice of so many different types of French cuisine — Provençal, Lyonnaise, Corsican, Alsatian, Basque, classic, and more — might be enough to make you want to stick to tried-and-true McDo (pronounced mac *doh*; French for McDonald's) and just have a cup of wine with your fries.

Take it easy. Know up front that, much as you'd like, you simply won't be able to do, see, and taste it all. Avoid the Griswold syndrome (think of the family in the movie *European Vacation* who rush to see all of Paris and suffer the consequences!), and take in what could be Paris's greatest attraction of all: a way of life in which relaxing in a cafe and watching the world go by are natural parts of the day. Bring a phrase book, but keep in mind that Parisians are much more eager to speak English with visitors than they were even a few years ago, especially with those visitors who make an effort to try speaking French first. After you realize that you don't have to tour to exhaustion, you can appreciate Paris the way it was intended to be enjoyed — in parks, on bridges, and along streets meant for strolling and exploring.

You'll discover that the **Louvre** Museum is as incredible as its reputation and that the views from the **Eiffel Tower** are stunning — but did you know that the views from the terrace of department store **Samaritaine**

Paris at a Glance

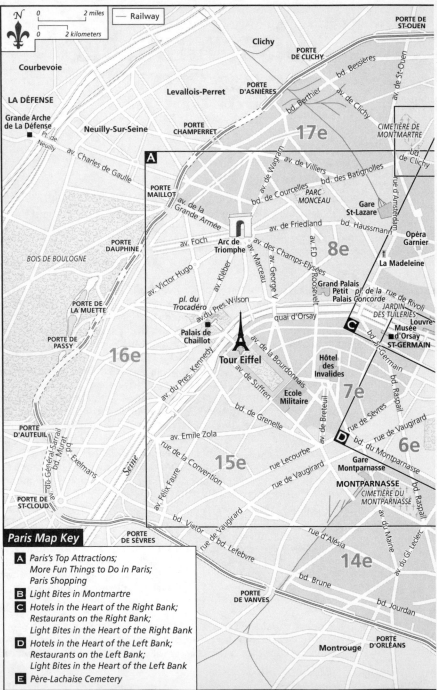

Paris Map Key

A Paris's Top Attractions;
More Fun Things to Do in Paris;
Paris Shopping

B Light Bites in Montmartre

C Hotels in the Heart of the Right Bank;
Restaurants on the Right Bank;
Light Bites in the Heart of the Right Bank

D Hotels in the Heart of the Left Bank;
Restaurants on the Left Bank;
Light Bites in the Heart of the Left Bank

E Père-Lachaise Cemetery

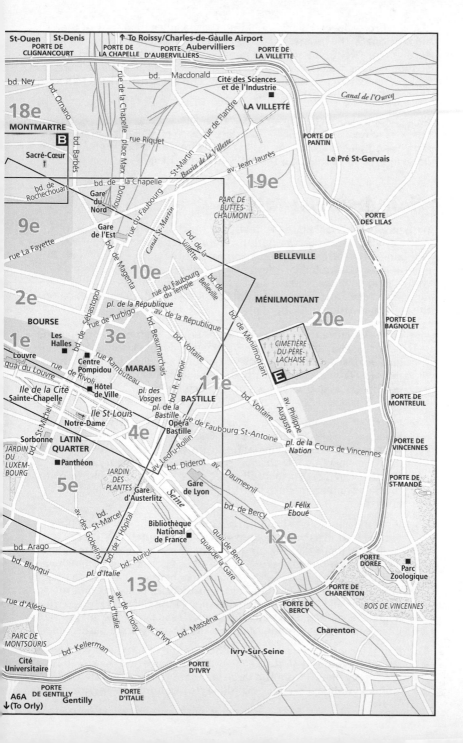

also are pretty spectacular? You'll find that taking a **boat tour of the Seine** is one of the best ways to see Paris, but rowing a boat in the **Bois de Boulogne's Grand Lac** can be much more personal. Whatever you do, you'll quickly discover that Paris (see the "Paris at a Glance" map) is more of an experience than merely a city, and each visitor experiences it in an entirely individual way.

 This chapter is designed as an at-a-glance reference to the absolute best — the Best of the Best — that Paris has to offer. Each of these experiences and places are discussed in detail later in the book; you can find them in their indicated chapter, marked with a Best of the Best icon.

The Best Accommodations

With more than 2,200 places to rest your head in Paris — chain hotels, deluxe, palace-like accommodations, hotels that cater to business travelers, budget hotels, and mom-and-pop establishments — it's difficult to narrow things down to just a few. But the hotels here are the hotels to which, in my opinion, you'll want to return on your next visit (because no one can see Paris just once!). See Chapter 9 for more information on the accommodations I list here.

✔ **Hôtel Minerve** (5e) is a welcoming budget, kid-friendly hotel in the Latin Quarter. Rooms are decent-sized and have wood-beamed ceilings, exposed stone walls, carved mahogany wood furnishings, and ten have large balconies with a table and chairs overlooking rue des Ecoles, just around the corner from the Cluny Museum, a true Paris treasure.

✔ For a just a few more euros, you can stay at the pretty **Hôtel de Seine** (6e) in St-Germain-des-Près. Each room is distinctly decorated with either French provincial furniture and flowered wall-paper or Provence-inspired jewel-toned paint and Louis XVI-era reproductions. Located on a street full of art galleries, it's a few blocks from the Seine and the pedestrian bridge Pont des Arts that leads to the Louvre.

✔ Have the autonomy of an apartment with the amenities of a hotel at the **Citadines Préstige Haussmann Aparthotel** (8e). Part of a chain, Citadines Haussmann has 24-hour reception desks, satellite TV, and housekeeping services, as well as kitchenettes with dishware (if you prepare only a few of your dinners here you can save a bundle on your dining budget). Located near Galeries Lafayette and Au Printemps and within walking distance of the Champs-Elysées, the Madeleine church, and parc Monceau, this is one of the chain's most luxurious featuring rare wood furnishings and granite bathrooms.

✔ Celebrate special occasions and bask in the privacy of the gorgeous deluxe **Pavillon de la Reine** (4e) right off place des Vosges. Rooms are simply divine: from the large standard rooms decorated with gingham wallpaper and Louis XIII-style furniture, to superior duplex rooms in which modern beds are located in a loft above a cozy sitting room with comfortable chairs and couches, to suites with four-poster beds and beamed ceilings opening onto the courtyard. You'll find all amenities here. For these prices you can have the extravagant splendor of one of Paris's palace hotels, but Pavillon de la Reine's intimate surroundings are just as appealing.

The Best Food

Mmmmmmm — Paris has some of the world's best restaurants and some of the tastiest regional dishes on the planet. It's no question that one of the greatest things about visiting Paris is finding out for yourself what a high-quality meal *à la française* can be. The following list contains some of my favorite restaurants (the information in parentheses indicates the arrondissement in which each establishment is located). See Chapter 10 for more information on the restaurants listed here.

✔ **Ze Kitchen Galerie (6e):** This art gallery and kitchen serving melt-in-your-mouth Asian-inspired dishes has become so popular that First Lady Laura Bush even paid it a visit. The menu is broken down into four parts: soup, raw (usually fish), pasta, and grilled (*à la plancha*), and the innovative combination of flavors and the trendy atmosphere makes this restaurant a memorable one.

✔ **L'Ébauchoir (12e):** A mural pays homage to the workers of the neighborhood in this well-worth-the-search restaurant in a part of the Bastille often overlooked by tourists. The superb yet homey food harkens back to the neighborhood's working-class roots.

✔ **Le Cinq (8e):** This three-Michelin-starred restaurant in the Four Seasons George V is truly extraordinary from exquisite pull-out-all-the-stops food to its award winning sommelier and fantastic wine cellar. Dining here is a sumptuous experience!

✔ **Chainterelle (5e):** The owners try mightily to make you feel as if you're visiting their home in the Auvergne, the rugged, pastoral south-central region of France. Little fonts contain essential oils made from native plants; a sound system incorporates native bird-song, rain, and church bells; and the door even says "moo" when you walk in. The peasant food is hearty and delicious; there's even a terrific vegetarian cheese, mushroom, and egg tart on the menu.

✔ **L'Atelier de Joël Robuchon (7e):** You can't make reservations at this, one of Paris's hottest restaurants, so get there right as it opens for simple, exquisite French and Asian fusion food where the ingredients are the real stars. Seating is at a 40-person sushi bar that wraps around the open kitchen to give diners a "behind the line" experience. The food here is absolutely divine; the chef was France's most famous before he retired in the late 1990s. This restaurant is his first post-retirement effort — which has truly paid off!

The Best Sights

For most people, the real reason for visiting Paris is to see the quintessentially French attractions for which the city is known. Are the sights really as great as returning travelers say? Yes, yes, and yes. Here are just a few of the best. See Chapter 11 for more information on the sights listed here.

- ✔ The **Eiffel Tower** graces the city skyline with its lacy presence and twinkles for ten minutes each hour at night with some 30,000 bulbs installed in 2003. Upon its completion in 1889, it was the tallest human-built structure in the world. People have climbed it, bungee-jumped from it, and cycled down the tower's steps, but hopefully you'll be content just to enjoy its views!

- ✔ Take a **tour boat down the Seine** and see the towers of Notre-Dame highlighted against the sky; at night, lights from bridges older than the United States cast reflections in the water. English-language commentary is included.

- ✔ **The Musée d'Orsay** is the world's best-renovated train station! Take a moment at the top of the central staircase to envision where trains once pulled into the station under the curved roof. Then enjoy this wonderful museum's real claim to fame — its unsurpassed collection of Impressionist masterpieces (and a terrific collection of Art Nouveau pieces).

- ✔ When you catch your first glimpse of the nearly 900-year-old **Cathédrale de Notre-Dame,** it just may take your breath away. Flying buttresses lend a graceful air to what would otherwise be an imposing structure. Play Quasimodo and climb to the top of the bell tower (get there early — the lines grow huge from late morning through closing) or marvel at the gorgeous rose windows and reflect on its history that included crusaders praying here before leaving for the holy wars, Napoléon crowning himself and his wife emperor and empress of France, and General de Gaulle rushing here to give thanks after the liberation of Paris.

- ✔ The **Arc de Triomphe** is the largest triumphal arch in the world, commissioned by Napoléon to honor his army and its 128 victorious battles, but the real reason people visit is for the view — one that takes in the Eiffel Tower. From the top, 162 feet up, you can see in a straight line the Champs-Elysées, the obelisk in the place de la Concorde, the Louvre, and the Grande Arche de la Défense in St-Denis, a giant open cube built to be the modern equivalent to this arch.

- ✔ Every phase of Picasso's prolific 75-year career is represented at the **Musée Picasso,** which includes more than 200 paintings, nearly 160 sculptures, 88 ceramics, and more than 3,000 prints and drawings. All of it is housed in a beautiful 17th-century mansion deep in the Marais, one of Paris's best neighborhoods.

✔ The **Musée Nationale d'Auguste Rodin** has to be one of Paris's most relaxing museums. After taking in the sensual sculptures displayed in the beautiful former convent, stroll through the gardens here to see more of the legendary artist's masterpieces like *The Thinker* and *The Gates of Hell.*

The Best Parks and Gardens

From flowers, plants, and city views to puppet shows, pony rides, and museums, Paris has parks for every taste and interest. Here are some of its best. Chapter 11 has more information

✔ The **Jardin des Tuileries** (1er) is Paris's most visited park and a great place to rest your feet and catch some rays on conveniently placed wrought-iron chairs surrounding the garden's fountains. In keeping with the French style of parks, trees are planted according to an orderly design and the sandy paths are arrow straight. During the summer, a carnival features an enormous Ferris wheel (with great views of the city), a log flume, fun house, arcade-style games, and snacks.

✔ Relax with Parisians in their most beloved park, the **Jardin du Luxembourg** in the Latin Quarter. Children love it for its playground, pony rides, puppet theater, and the Fontaine de Médicis where they can sail toy boats. You can make use of tennis and boules courts (*boules* is a French game similar to lawn bowling and the Italian *bocce* in which players try to be the first to roll their balls closest to the small object ball called the *cochonnet)* or appreciate the art exhibited on the wrought iron fence at the garden's northwestern entrance near boulevard St-Michel and rue de Médicis.

✔ **Parc de la Villette** (19e) is a modern park with a series of theme gardens, including an exotic bamboo garden and a garden featuring steam and water jets. Scattered throughout the park are playgrounds and other attractions — this is a must-visit if you've spent time at the huge children's science complex, **Cité des Sciences et l'Industrie.**

✔ Located in the Bois de Boulogne on Paris's western edge, the **Parc de la Bagatelle** (16e) is perhaps the city's loveliest park, known for its flower and thematic gardens. A water lily pond pays homage to a certain famous painter (think Monet), and you can visit a chateau and an *orangerie* (a hothouse where oranges and other tropical fruit are grown) where Chopin concerts are held during the summer. But the highlight is the rose garden with 10,000 roses of 1,200 varieties, most of them peaking in June.

✔ **Parc Monceau** in Paris's upscale 8th arrondissement, was one of *Remembrance of Things Past* author Marcel Proust's favorite haunts. In the 19th century, he strolled among such oddities as the Dutch windmill, a Roman temple, a covered bridge, a waterfall, a farm, medieval ruins, a pagoda, and Paris's largest tree, an Oriental plane — all still here.

✔ Rock formations and grottoes in the tranquil **Parc de Belleville** (20e) are still around from the days when the hill was a strategic point for fighting Attila the Hun. Watch the sun set over western Paris and take in the wonderful (free!) views of the city. Topped by the **Maison de l'Air,** a museum with displays devoted to the air that we breathe, you can enjoy fountains, a children's play area, and an open-air theater with rock concerts during the summer.

The Best Shopping

An upswing in France's economy and a favorable euro-to-dollar rate has seen many new stores open and others expand. The city has a well-deserved reputation as a bastion of over-the-top luxury. All you have to do to understand why is head for the 8th arrondissement. But discount, re-sale, and overstock stores also abound. Whenever I'm in Paris, a visit to the following stores is a must. See Chapter 12 for more information on the stores listed here.

✔ **Monoprix** is a reasonably-priced department store with branches around the city that has stylish and reasonably-priced clothing and is also great for accessories, low-priced cosmetics, lingerie, and housewares. Many locations also have large grocery stores. The one at 52 av. du Champs-Elysées (8e) is chock-full of goodies.

✔ **Le Bon Marché** (6e) is Paris's only Left Bank department store. Elegant, but small enough to be manageable, much of the store's merchandise is exquisite; The third floor is particularly renowned for its large shoe selection and lingerie department (where dressing rooms have phones to summon your salesperson!).

✔ Although it isn't cheap, Le Bon Marché's next-door grocery store, **Le Grand Epicerie** (6e) is one of the best luxury supermarkets in Paris and a great place to look for gourmet gifts such as olive oils, home-made chocolates, or wine. It makes for wonderful one-stop picnic shopping, too, offering a wide array of prepared foods and cheeses.

✔ Bi-level gift shop **La Chaise Longue** (3e) is simply bursting at the seams with cool gifts such as silver cufflinks in the shape of computer mice, dinnerware, designer teapots, three-dimensional picture frames, and glasses, among many, many other things. It's reasonably priced and open on Sunday.

✔ **Du Pareil au Même** is *the* store to buy clothes for every child on your list — clothes are practical, *très mignons* (very cute), and very reasonably priced.

✔ **Déhillerin** is for amateur and professional chefs alike — filled with high-quality copper cookware, glasses, dishes, china, gadgets, utensils, ramekins, and pots — all at a discount.

The Best of Culture

With more than 100 theaters, competing opera houses, ballet at the **Opéra Garnier** and chamber music concerts in many churches, getting "cultured" is not a problem in Paris. Even if your French is rusty or not up to par, many avant-garde productions and English-language theaters serve as alternatives to French-language plays. In this section, I list some of the best places to see theater, watch a ballet, or hear a symphony. See Chapter 15 for more information.

✔ You can see dazzling performances by the national opera and ballet troupes that perform at both the radiant **Palais Garnier** (9e) and the ultramodern **Opéra National de Bastille** (11e). The Palais Garnier conducts more ballet performances, and the Opéra Bastille puts on more opera.

✔ A good mix of modern and classic tragedies and comedies comes alive in wonderful performances in the **Salle Richelieu** of the **Comédie-Française,** 2 rue de Richelieu, 1er.

✔ For popular, contemporary plays, the **Théâtre National de Chaillot,** place du Trocadéro (16e) is your place.

✔ Whatever your choice of the classic arts — opera, ballet, concerts, recitals — you'll find it performed at the **Châtelet, Théâtre Musical de Paris** (1er) by local and international performers of the highest caliber.

✔ For comedy in English, try **Laughing Matters,** in the historic Hôtel du Nord (10e). This company is thriving, and the lineups are always terrific, featuring award-winning comics from the United States, the United Kingdom, Ireland, and Australia.

✔ More than a dozen Parisian churches regularly schedule relatively inexpensive organ recitals and concerts. The most glorious, where the music is nearly outdone by the glorious stained glass windows, is **Sainte-Chapelle** (4e).

The Best Clubs

Paris is a perpetual party, and each neighborhood makes a different contribution to the nightlife scene. Listed here are some of the best places to dance the night away. See Chapter 16 for more information.

✔ **Barrio Latino** (11e) has three bars, private areas where you can see (but not be seen), a lounge complete with pool table, a second floor restaurant serving Latino food, a top-floor private club with a kitschy Che Guevara mural, and energetic Latin music that sets everyone to dancing. It's pure fun!

✔ **Batofar** (13e), an Irish light ship docked right in the Seine, is one hot, sweaty, and ultimately fun time right on the Seine, with all types of music represented, from drum-and-bass to British pop.

✔ **Elysée Montmartre** (18e) serves the dual function of disco and major concert hall, and is home to twice-monthly nights that pull in more than 1,000 clubbers. Dance music is usually house; the monthly *bals musettes* (dances) usually have live local bands.

✔ **Le Wax**'s (11e) decor is very *Clockwork Orange,* with plastic bubbles on the walls, yellow plastic couches, and lots of crimson and orange. The music is house, and best of all, it's free.

✔ **La Nouvelle Java** (10e) is where Edith Piaf made her debut and is said to be the oldest club in Paris. Here you dance with a diverse crowd of Cuban and Brazilian music lovers.

✔ **La Locomotive** (18e) is a huge, tri-level space where people dance to rock, heavy metal, and techno. Check out the basement, the coolest of the three levels, where you can see the remnants of an old railway line.

✔ **Rex** (2e) opened in 1992 and is still going strong. It has been one of the most popular clubs — if not *the* club — for house and techno music with Paris's best sound system and its most famous DJ, Laurent Garnier.

✔ **Le Pulp** (2e) is one of Paris's hippest lesbian clubs where all are welcome. Reminiscent of a 19th-century French music hall, this venue is très cool, with all types of cutting-edge music.

Chapter 2

Digging Deeper into Paris

. . . .

In This Chapter

▶ Discovering the rich history of Paris

▶ Admiring the city's architecture

▶ Enjoying the local cuisine

▶ Getting to know the local language

▶ Previewing the city in books and movies

. . . .

Consider this chapter a cultural course in a nutshell, filling you in on the city's history, the basics of French architecture, the art of the meal, and why the French language is nothing to be afraid of. Plus, you get your pre-trip homework assignment — reading wonderful books and watching great movies!

History 101: The Main Events

The Parisii tribe on the **Ile de la Cité** (one of two islands in the Seine around Central Paris — these days, Notre-Dame sits on Ile de la Cité) settled Paris in the third century B.C. Peaceful fishermen, they traded with other tribes along the river and with travelers on the main north-south trading road that connected the Mediterranean with northern Europe. Unfortunately, the road made attacking the Parisii all too convenient for invaders. The first and most successful were Romans led by Julius Caesar in 52 B.C. During their 500-year stay, the settlement became known as Lutetia Parisiorum (*Lutèce* in French). You can still see their public baths at the **Musée National du Moyen Age/Cluny Museum** in the **Latin Quarter.**

Years of barbarian invasions eventually weakened Rome's hold over the territory. Around A.D. 350, Attila the Hun, on his way to sack Paris, changed course at the last minute, purportedly answering the prayers of a young girl named Geneviève. She became the patron saint of Paris. In the 400s, Franks from the east successfully wrested control away from the Romans. In 508, Clovis, king of the Franks, chose Paris as his capital. It was abandoned as a capital 250 years later only to regain that status in 987 when Hugues Capet was proclaimed king of France. Celebrating the city's importance, two Gothic masterpieces, the cathedrals of **Notre-Dame** and **Sainte-Chapelle,** were built on the Ile de la Cité. Across the river, on the **Left Bank, Sorbonne University** was born. Under Louis XIV, who ruled for 72 years, the monarchy's power reached its height, supported by heavy taxes. Although he added monuments and splendor to the city, the Sun King moved his court to Versailles, alienating the citizenry and preparing the way for the French Revolution.

On July 14, 1789, a mob stormed the **Bastille** prison, which held many who were out of favor with French royalty. To most French citizens at the time, the Bastille was a sign of much that was wrong with the monarchy, and the attack on the Bastille came to represent the end of the monarchy. Three days later at the Hôtel de Ville, **Louis XVI** was forced to kiss the new French tricolor. On July 14, 1790, the Festival of the Federation was celebrated on the Champs de Mars, and an estimated 300,000 attended a Mass at which the king swore an oath of loyalty to the constitution. Still, radical factions grew. On August 10, 1792, revolutionary troops joined a Parisian mob storming the **Tuileries Palace,** where the king lived and took him prisoner. In 1793, he and **Queen Marie Antoinette** were beheaded in the place de la Concorde. At this time, Maximilien **Robespierre** was elected leader of the Committee of Public Safety, which conducted witch hunts for those it deemed counterrevolutionaries. This became known as the Reign of Terror. Between September, 1793, and February, 1794, 238 men and 31 women were tried and executed for crimes against the state. Nearly 5,500 more awaited trial in prisons until Robespierre's arrest in July 1794 He was executed the same month.

A reaction ushered in the Directory, the last stage of the French revolution, in which five directors shared power and governed France over the next four years. But Napoléon staged a coup in 1799, turning the country into a dictatorship. Five years later, in 1804, at Notre-Dame, Napoléon crowned himself emperor and his wife, Joséphine, empress. He then embarked on a series of military campaigns against surrounding countries until his defeat at Waterloo in 1815. During his reign, he gave Paris many of its most grandiose monuments, notably the **Arc de Triomphe** and the **Bourse,** but his greatest gift was starting the **Louvre** on course to becoming an art museum, in part, by displaying the art he had "acquired" in his many campaigns, which became the core of the museum's collection.

The look that most of us associate with Paris was created in the 19th century. Napoléon landscaped the view from the Louvre, extending the perspective past the Tuileries and the place de la Concorde to the Champs-Elysées and the Arc de Triomphe and built fountains, cemeteries, and the arcades along the rue de Rivoli. From 1852 to 1870, Napoléon's nephew, Napoléon III, reshaped Paris with the aid of Baron Haussmann, razing entire neighborhoods in favor of boulevards, avenues, and 24 parks.

The **Eiffel Tower** (La Tour Eiffel), built only as a temporary structure for the 1889 World's Fair, was allowed to remain standing as the tallest structure in the world at the time. Paris opened its first Métro line in 1900, and by the turn of the 20th century, had thousands of restaurants and 27,000 cafes, about 150 of which held concerts with dancing, called cafe concerts.

In the years that followed, Paris witnessed two world wars with more than ten million military casualties, nearly one million Jews losing their lives, and four years of German occupation. Tens of thousands of soldiers died fighting the end of French colonial rule around the world.

In 1968, students took to the streets of Paris, rebelling against France's antiquated educational system among a host of other causes, including the rights of workers (this period of time is known in France as *Mai 1968*). De Gaulle's government tried to quash the strikes with police action, but only succeeded in making the situation worse. Young people hurled paving stones at police in street battles, and ten million French workers througout the country went on strike. This nearly led to the collapse of the government, and De Gaulle called for new elections. Almost as quickly as the student and worker revolution started, it was over by June 1968 when voters elected an even stronger De Gaulle administration. DeGaulle, himself, resigned in 1969. The government flirted unsuccessfully with socialism in the 1980s and ended the decade with a great celebration of democracy: the bicentennial of the French Revolution and the centennial of the Eiffel Tower.

Former Paris Mayor **Jacques Chirac** was elected president in 1995 on his promise to jump-start the economy, but growth remained stagnant, and the president was forced to share power with Prime Minister Lionel Jospin, after the leader of the opposition called for elections in 1997. Facing rising gas prices, escalating crime, anti-Semitic vandalism, and a lack of interest in the 2002 presidential elections, Jospin lost his prime minister's seat, sending extremist Jean-Marie Le Pen into the presidential race against Chirac. French citizens took to the streets in protest, and Chirac won by a landslide. Jospin retired from politics.

One of the biggest events in 2003 was a terrible summer heat wave that left more than 15,000 mostly elderly people dead throughout the country. Many of the dead were left alone while family members went on vacation, and as a result, the whole French system of priorities was thrown into question. The year 2003 also saw the largest rise in anti-Semitic crimes since WWII, an increase that has only extended into 2004, even as the government vows to punish perpetrators aggressively. Finally, Chirac's opposition to the U.S.–led war on Iraq in 2003 severely affected tourism (who can forget "freedom fries"?), with some sources reporting a 30% decline in tourist revenues from 2002. A strong euro played a part in the drop in tourism, and the euro has grown even stronger since then, making the City of Light a very expensive destination these days.

Building Blocks: Local Architecture

First-time visitors to Paris are struck by the graceful curves and balconies of the city's gorgeous apartment buildings, many of which were built during the reign of Napoléon III in the mid-1800s. In a city bursting with architectural treasures, these are but some of the newest. In addition to the mixture of styles associated with the 19th and 20th centuries, many architectural eras are represented in Paris, among them the Ancient Roman, Romanesque, Gothic, Renaissance, classical (classicism), and rococo periods. You see artifacts from Paris's founding in the third century B.C. by a tribe of fisherman, as well as such modern-day projects as the Centre Georges Pompidou.

Paris's important architectural periods are outlined here:

- ✔ **Ancient Roman (125 B.C.– A.D. 450):** After Julius Caesar conquered the island of Lutétia, his legions began using bricks and concrete in building and introduced the load-bearing arch, which led to the construction of stronger bridges and doorways. You can see examples of excavated Roman ruins at the **Crypte Archéologique** (see Chapter 11), about 200 feet directly in front of the entrance of Notre-Dame. The ruins of ancient Roman baths are in the cellar at the **Cluny Museum** (also in Chapter 11), a former private residence that was built around and on top of the ruins.

- ✔ **Romanesque (800–1100):** Characterized by arches and curves, thick walls with small windows, huge piers to hold up the roof, simple geometric arrangements, and painting in decorative hues. The architects during this period built large churches; none survive intact in Paris; all were improved upon with different architectural styles or rebuilt. **St-Germain-des-Près** is a Romanesque building with a Gothic interior. **St-Julien-le-Pauvre** was originally a Romanesque church, but later Gothic additions obscure the original details.

- ✔ **Gothic (1100–1500):** Known for its slender vertical piers and counterbalancing buttresses and for vaulting and pointed arches that allow for taller and thinner structures, the interiors of which force the eyes upward. Windows with stained glass were constructed so that most of the illiterate population could understand the stories told in each pane. Gargoyles (drain spouts), spires, flying buttresses, rose windows, and choir screens were all features of the Gothic church. The best examples are **Notre-Dame,** of course, and the **Cathédrale de Notre-Dame de Chartres** (Chapter 14 describes this cathedral in more detail).

- ✔ **Renaissance (1500–1630):** This architectural style is characterized by harmonious form, mathematical proportion, and a unit of measurement based on the human scale. Roofs became steeply pitched, and dormer windows were built taller, using stone. The mansions surrounding the **Place des Vosges** are all Renaissance, as is the **Hôtel Carnavalet,** home to the **Musée Carnavalet.**

- ✔ **Classicism (1630–1800):** In this school, the emphasis was on form, simplicity, proportion, and restraint, influenced by the architecture of ancient Greece and Rome. Exteriors in the classical style may feature Doric, Corinthian, and Ionic columns, low and simple dormer windows, mansard roofs (having two slopes on all sides with the lower slope steeper than the upper, invented by François Mansard), and simple proportions, the interiors of classical buildings went over the top. This interior style is known as **rococo**, derived from the words *rocaille* (rock) and *coquille* (shell), delicate decorative motifs that appeared along with scrolls, branches of leaves, flowers, and bamboo stems. The best example of classicism and rococo is **Versailles** (see Chapter 14). The **Louvre** is also a classical tour de force.

✔ **Nineteenth century (1800–1889):** This style began with *neoclassicism,* a return to the majesty of past civilizations, and an adoption of classical forms and styles. Examples include the **Arc de Triomphe** and the **Madeleine.** The **Second Empire** brought wide boulevards lined with six-story apartment buildings with balconies, and mansard roofs with dormer windows. The **Third Republic**'s industrial age produced glass and steel structures; the most famous are the **Eiffel Tower** and **Sacré-Coeur.**

✔ **Art Nouveau (1890–1914:** This period saw the end of the 19th century and continued into the 20th with beautiful renderings of plants and flowers in wrought iron (**Abbesses Métro station entrance**), stained glass, wood, tile, and hand-painted wallpapers (for a wonderful introduction to Art Nouveau, visit the middle floor of the **Musée d'Orsay**; see Chapter 11).

✔ **Twentieth century (1900–1999):** This style may be defined by late President François Mitterand's *grands projets* (grand projects), most of which were controversial when completed. Richard Rogers' and Renzo Piano's **Centre Georges Pompidou** (see Chapter 11), with its "guts on the outside" architecture, horrified Parisians, as did I.M. Pei's glass pyramids at the Louvre, but residents have slowly come to accept them. The four looming towers shaped like open books that comprise Mitterand's last project, the Bibliothèque Nationale de France, are another story; the building, which is still suffering from the occasional technological glitch, has gotten little respect since its opening in the late 1990s. You may recall that the Parisians initially hated the Eiffel Tower, too; Now where would they be without it?

A Taste of Paris: The Local Cuisine

Parisians are on an eternal quest for the perfect meal, and what wonderful meals they have to choose from — regional French, three-star haute cuisine, North African *couscouseries,* tasty crepes sold from street vendors, and more. During the last decade, the city witnessed the rise of *baby bistros,* restaurants opened by celebrity chefs and their talented young apprentices offering simpler and less expensive meals than those served at their deluxe establishments. Also in vogue is a back-to-Grandmère's-kitchen approach featuring chefs turning out homey meals such as *blanquette de veau* (veal stew in white sauce), *cassoulet* (meat-and-vegetable casserole), and *confit de canard* (duck preserved and cooked in its own fat until it's so tender it falls off the bone). Asian influences are also in vogue; witness the success of William LeDeuil's **Ze Kitchen Galerie.** I talk in more depth about dining in Paris in Chapter 10.

A glossary good enough to eat

Use this helpful guide when you're trying to decide what to order and how you want it cooked.

General Terms

compris (comb-*pree;* included)
déjeuner (*day*-zhu-nay; lunch)
dîner (*dee*-nay; dinner)
petit déjeuner (pet-*tee day*-zhu-nay; breakfast)
ménu dégustation (meh-*noo* day-goo-*stah*-sion; sampler, or tasting, menu)
prix fixe (pree-feeks; set price)
supplément (sup-play-*mahn;* extra charge)

Les Entrées (layz ahn-trays; appetizers)

charcuterie (shar-koot-*ree;* assorted cold cuts)
crudités (kroo-dee-*tay;* assorted raw vegetables)
foie gras (fwah grah; goose liver paté)
saumon fumé (soh-*moh* foo-may; smoked salmon)
soupe à l'oignon (soop-ah-lowh-*yon;* onion soup)
soupe à pistou (soop-ah-pees-*too;* vegetable soup with pesto)
velouté (vay-loot-*ay;* cream-based soup)
vichyssoise (vee-shee-*swahz;* cold leek and potato soup)
salade composée (sa-*lad com*-poh-zay; mixed salad)
salade de chèvre chaud (sa-*lad* deh-shev-rah-*sho;* salad with warm goat cheese on croutons)
salade gesiers (sa-*lad* zheh-shee-*air;* salad with sautéed chicken gizzards)
salade landaise (sa-*lad* lahn-*dehs;* salad containing duck breast, duck liver, and duck gizzards)

salade de Niçoise (sa-*lad* nee-*shwahz;* salad with tuna, canned corn, anchovies, and potato)

Boeuf (bewf; beef)

bavette (bah-*vet;* flank steak)
chateaubriand (cha-tow-bree-*ahn;* porterhouse)
contre-filet (*kahn*-trah-fee-lay; filet steak)
côte de boeuf (cote dah bewf; T-bone)
entrecôte (ahn-trah-*cote;* rib-eye)
faux-filet (foe-fee-*lay;* sirloin)
filet mignon (fee-*lay* mee-*nyahn;* tenderloin)
langue de boeuf (lahng dah bewf; tongue)
onglet (ahn-*glay;* hanger steak)
pavé (pah-*vay;* thick steak; *literally:* paving stone)
queue de boeuf (kyew dah bewf; oxtail)
rôti de boeuf (*roe*-tee dah bewf; roast beef)
steak haché (stake *ha*-shay; minced meat or hamburger)
steak tartare (stake tar-*tar;* a lean cut of beef minced and served raw — a high-quality dish prepared by experts, people rarely get sick from eating this)
tournedo (*tor*-nay-doe; small tender filet usually grilled or sautéed)
veau (voe; veal)

Other Meats

agneau (ah-*nyoe;* lamb)
gigot (*gee*-joe; leg — usually of lamb)
jambon (zhahm-*bon;* ham)

médaillon (meh-dah-ee-*on;* medallions — beef, veal, lamb)
merguez (mare-*gay;* spicy sausage)
porc (pork; pork)
saucisses/saucisson (soh-*sees,* soh-see-*sohn;* sausage/little sausage)

Volailles (voe-lie; fowl)

blanc de volaille (blahn dah voe-*lai;* chicken breast)
caille (kaih; quail)
canard (kah-*nahr;* duck)
dinde (dand; turkey)
magret de canard (mah-*gret* dah kah-*nahr;* duck breast)
oie (wah; goose)
pigéon (pee-jee-*ohn;* game pigeon)
pintade (pan-*tahd;* guinea fowl)
poulet (*poo*-lay; chicken)

Fruits de Mer (free duh mair; seafood)

bar (bar; bass)
coquilles St-Jacques (*koe*-kee san-*jahk;* scallops)
crevettes (kreh-*vet;* shrimp)
daurade (doe-*rahd;* sea bream)
homard (oe-*mahr;* lobster)
huîtres (wee-*tra;* oysters)
langoustine (lang-oo-*steen;* crayfish)
morue/cabillaud (moh-*roo*/ka-bee-*oh;* cod)
moules (mool; mussels)
poissons (pwah-*son;* fish)
raie (ray; skate)
rascasse (ras-*kass;* scorpion fish)
rouget (roo-*zhay;* red mullet)
saumon (soh-*moh;* salmon)
thon (than; tuna)
truite (trweet; trout)

Les Légumes (lay lay-goom; vegetables)

artichault (ar-tee-*show;* artichoke)
asperge (as-*pearzh;* asparagus)
aubergine (oe-bur-*zheen;* eggplant)
champignons/cèpes/truffes/girolles (sham-pee-*nyahn*/sep/troof/*gee*-roll; mushrooms)

choucroute (shoo-*kroot;* sauerkraut)
choux (shoo; cabbage)
choux de bruxelles (shoo dah broo-*zells;* brussels sprouts)
courgette (kore-*zhette;* zucchini)
épinard (ay-pee-*nahr;* spinach)
haricots (ahr-ee-*koe;* beans)
haricots verts (*ahr*-ee-koe-vair; string beans)
oignons (wah-*nyoh;* onions)
petits pois (*pet*-tee pwah; peas)
poireaux (pwah-*roe;* leeks)
poivron rouge (pwah-vrah-*roozh;* red pepper)
poivron vert (pwah-vrah *vair;* green pepper)
pomme de terre (pum dah *tair;* potato)
pommes frites (*pum freet;* french fries)
riz (*ree;* rice)
tomate (toe-*maht;* tomato)

Les Fruits (lay free; fruit)

abricot (*ah*-bree-koh; apricot)
ananas (a-*na*-nas; pineapple)
banane (bah-*nan;* banana)
cerise (sair-*ees;* cherry)
citron (see-*troh;* lemon)
citron vert (see-troh-*vair;* lime)
fraise (frayz; strawberry)
framboise (frahm-*bwahz;* raspberry)
myrtille (meer-*teel;* blueberry)
pamplemousse (pahm-pull-*moos;* grapefruit)
pêche (pehsh; peach)
poire (pwahr; pear)
pomme (pum; apple)
prune (proon; plum)
pruneau (proo-*noh;* prune)
raisin (rah-*zeen;* grape)
raisin sec (rah-zeen-*sek;* raisin)

Les Desserts (lay day-sair; desserts)

Charlotte (shar-*lote;* molded cream ringed with a biscuit)
clafoutis (clah-foo-*tee;* thick batter filled with fruit and fried)
crème brûlée (krem broo-*lay;* creamy custard with caramel topping)

fromage blanc (froe-*mahzh* blahn; smooth cream cheese)

gâteau (gah-*toe;* cake)

glace (glahs; ice cream)

marquise (mar-*keez;* light, mousse-like cake)

mousse au chocolat (moos oh shok-*lah;* chocolate mousse)

tarte aux (tart oh; pie)

tarte tatin (tart ta-*ta;* caramelized upside-down apple pie)

vacherin (*vahsh*-reh; cake of layered meringue, fruit, and ice cream)

Preparation Methods

à l'ail (ah lai; with garlic)

à point (ah pwahn; medium)

au four (oh fore; baked)

béarnaise (bare-*nayse;* hollandaise sauce with tarragon, vinegar, and shallots)

bechamel (beh-sha-*mel;* white sauce made with onions and nutmeg)

bien cuit (byen kwee; well done).

beurre blanc (bur blahn; white sauce made with butter, white wine, and shallots)

bleu (bluh; very rare)

bordelaise (bore-dah-*lays;* brown meat stock made with red wine, mushrooms, shallots, and beef marrow)

bouilli (bwee-*ee;* boiled)

bourguignon (bore-gee-*nyoh;* brown meat stock flavored with red wine, mushrooms, and onions)

confit (kahn-*fee;* meat — usually duck or goose — cooked in its own fat)

consommé (kahn-soe-*may;* clear broth)

coulis (koo-*lee;* any nonflour sauce, purée, or juice)

en croûte (ahn *kroot;* in a pastry crust)

cru (kroo; raw)

diable (dee-*ah*-blah; brown sauce flavored with cayenne pepper, white wine, and shallots)

estouffade (ay-too-*fahd;* meat that has been marinated, fried, and braised)

farci (fahr-*see;* stuffed)

feuilleté (fwee-eh-*tay;* in puff pastry)

fumé (*foo*-may; smoked)

gratiné (*grah*-tee-nay; topped with browned bread crumbs or cheese)

grillé (*gree*-ay; grilled)

hollandaise (ahl-lan-*dehs;* white sauce with butter, egg yolks, and lemon juice)

lyonnais (lee-ohn-*nay;* with onions)

marinière (mar-ee-*nyair;* steamed in garlicky wine stock)

meunière (moo-*nyur;* fish rolled in flour and sautéed)

en papillote (ohn pah-pee-*oat;* cooked in parchment and opened at the table — usually fish)

parmentier (pahr-men-tee-*ay;* with potato)

Provençal (pro-ven-*saw;* tomato-based sauce, with garlic, olives, and onions)

rôti (*roe*-tee roasted)

saignant (sen-*yahn;* rare)

terrine (tuh-*reen;* cooked in an earthenware dish)

Salivating over French cooking

Even with English translations, confronting a French menu can be a daunting experience. Dishes that have been familiar to French people since childhood are often unknown to outsiders. The following list is a user's guide to typical French dishes that you're likely to encounter.

✔ **Andouillette** (ahn-dwee-*et*): A sausage of pork organs encased in intestines. Andouillette has a strong flavor with a distinct aftertaste and is usually grilled and served with mustard and French fries. Look for the A.A.A.A.A. label — the Association Amicale des

Authentiques Amateurs d'Andouillettes (Association of Real Andouillette Lovers) stamps it on the best andouillettes.

✔ **Blanquette de veau** (blahn-*ket* duh voe): Veal cooked in a white stew that includes eggs and cream.

✔ **Boeuf Bourguignon** (buhf bor-gee-*nyon*): Beef cooked with red burgundy wine, mushrooms, and onions.

✔ **Boudin** (boo-*dan*): A rich sausage made from pig's blood, usually combined with *créme fraîche,* onions, and eggs. More elaborate versions may feature a touch of garlic or chestnuts. The dish is often served with sautéed apples or mashed potatoes, which enhance the slightly sweet taste of the sausage.

✔ **Boudin blanc** (boo-*dan* blahn): A white sausage made from veal, chicken, or pork.

✔ **Bouillabaisse** (*bwee*-ah-bess): A fish stew from the Mediterranean that includes assorted shellfish and white fish accompanied by croutons, grated cheese, and *rouille,* a mayonnaise made with garlic.

✔ **Brandade** (brahn-*dahd*): Salt cod (*morue*) soaked in cold water, shredded, and cooked with garlic, olive oil, milk, and potato. It has the look and consistency of mashed potatoes but tastes like salted fish. A green salad makes a good accompaniment.

✔ **Carpaccio** (car-*pahsh*-shyow): Thinly sliced, cured raw beef or tuna.

✔ **Cassoulet** (cass-oo-*lay*): A rich stew made of white beans, dry sausage, onion, duck, prosciutto, herbs, carrots, and tomatoes. It's cooked slowly and usually served in a ceramic bowl or pot. Absolutely delicious, but heavy; don't plan any serious physical exertions after eating — digestion will be enough.

✔ **Cervelles** (suhr-vel): Pork or sheep brains.

✔ **Cheval** (sheh-vahl): Horse meat.

✔ **Choucroute** (shoo-*kroot*): Sauerkraut cooked with juniper berries and wine, served with an assortment of pork cuts, usually including brisket, pork shoulder, ham, frankfurters, or spicy sausage. It goes well with boiled potatoes and is served with mustard.

✔ **Confit de canard** (con-*fee* duh can-*ahr*): A duck leg cooked and preserved in its own fat. The fatty skin is usually salty, but the meat underneath is tender and juicy. Mashed potatoes make a good side dish.

✔ **Cuisses des grenouilles** (cwees day gren-*wee*): Frogs' legs.

✔ **Escargots** (es-car-*go*): Snails.

✔ **Foie** (fwah): Liver.

✔ **Gesiers** (jeh-*zyay*): Gizzards; very good in salads.

✔ **Lapin à la moutarde** (la-*pan* ah la moo-*tard*): Rabbit cooked with mustard, créme fraîche, and sometimes white wine. The mustard perks up the rabbit meat, which has a mild flavor.

✔ **Lièvre** (lee-*yevr*): Hare.

✔ **Magret de canard** (mah-*greh* duh can-*ahr*): The sliced breast of a fattened duck, sautéed and sometimes served with a green peppercorn sauce. The result more closely resembles red meat than poultry. As with any meat, specify how you want it cooked.

✔ **Pieds de cochon** (pyay duh coh-*shon*): Pig's feet.

✔ **Plateau de fruits de mer** (plah-*toe* duh free duh mair): A variety of raw and cooked seafood served on ice. You usually find two kinds of oysters — flat, round *belon,* and larger, crinkly *creuse.* Both types are cultivated, not harvested. The oysters are eaten with lemon or red-wine vinegar and accompanied by thin slices of buttered rye bread. In addition to various kinds of shrimp, clams, and mussels, you also see periwinkles (*bulots*) (edible marine snails), which are eaten with mayonnaise.

✔ **Pot-au-feu** (*pot*-oh-fuh): A hearty dish of boiled vegetables and beef that sometimes includes the marrow bone. Scrape out the marrow, spread it on toast, and sprinkle it with salt. Sometimes the broth is served first, followed by the vegetables and beef. Mustard is the preferred condiment.

✔ **Ris de veau** (ree duh voe): The thymus gland of a calf (a white meat) sautéed in a butter and cream sauce. It has a delicate, pleasant taste but is high in cholesterol.

✔ **Rognons** (*ron*-yawn): Kidneys.

✔ **Tête de veau** (tet duh voe): Calf's head.

Words to the Wise: The Local Language

Parisians are much, much more willing to speak English than ever before — especially to visitors who do them the courtesy of trying to speak a few phrases of French. You often find that you can't even complete a sentence in French before you're answered in English. Don't be afraid of saying you don't understand French (*Je ne comprenne pas;* juh neh cohm-*prenne* pah); you will save yourself, and the person with whom you are conversing, a lot of time, and get help that much faster.

Phrases to remember are the essential *Parlez-vous Anglais* (par-lay voo zahn-glay; do you speak English?); the common courtesy phrase of *Bonjour madame/monsieur* (bohn-*joor* mad-am, mis-*yoo*) when you enter a store or place of business; and *au revoir madame/monsieur* (oh-*vwah*) when you leave. This book, too, has an extensive glossary of words and phrases (See Appendix B for "A Glossary of French Words and Phrases") that anticipate nearly every situation.

Background Check: Recommended Books and Movies

Compiled here is a list of books and movies to help prepare you for your trip.

Books

One of the best parts of planning a trip to Paris is reading about the experiences of travelers who fell under the city's spell, or the doings of a particular French person, or the efforts of those who try to figure out just what it is that makes France such a peculiar culture but such a wonderful place to visit. The following list provides just a sample of books that will get you longing to be there, already!

- ✔ *Almost French: Love and a New Life in Paris* by Sarah Turnbull (Gotham Books). An Australian journalist falls for a Frenchman, moves to Paris to be with him, and finds herself trying to adjust to a city that is infamously chilly to new residents.

- ✔ *C'est La Vie: An American Conquers the City of Light, Begins a New Life, and Becomes — Zut Alors — Almost French* by Suzy Gershman (Viking). Frommer's (a Wiley company) *Born to Shop* author Gershman had long planned to retire in France with her husband. But when he dies of an unexpected illness, she moves to Paris alone to try to work through her grief. This is the deliciously chatty chronicle of her first year in Paris, a memoir of the dizzying delights and maddening frustrations inherent in learning to be a Parisian.

- ✔ *The Flâneur* by Edmund White (Bloomsbury). Edmund White, who lived in Paris for 16 years, wanders through the streets and avenues and along the quays, taking readers into parts of Paris virtually unknown to visitors — and to many Parisians.

- ✔ *French Toast: An American in Paris Celebrates the Maddening Mysteries of the French* by Harriet Welty Rochefort (Thomas Dunne Books). Part memoir, part guide by an Iowan who picked up and moved to Paris more than 20 years ago, this book sheds light on why the French do things the way they do, and how you can, too, while you're there.

- ✔ *Paris to the Moon* by Adam Gopnik (Random House). The often humorous and tender account of the five years *New Yorker*-writer Gopnik spent in Paris with his wife and young son.

- ✔ *The Piano Shop on the Left Bank: Discovering a Forgotten Passion in a Paris Atelier* by Thad Carhart (Random House). Carhart notices an unassuming piano shop while walking his children to school one day. He eventually gains entry into a new world of the piano — its art and history — and rediscovers the forgotten joys of playing the piano.

✔ *Savoir Flair* by Polly Platt (Culture Crossings Ltd.). Cultural do's and don'ts by an American who has lived in Paris since 1967. This guide is simply essential!

✔ *Sixty Million Frenchmen Can't Be Wrong* by Jean-Benoit Nadeau and Julie Barlow (Sourcebooks). Two Canadian journalists who move to France on a two-year fellowship deconstruct French ideas about land, food, privacy, and language. The authors weave together the threads of French society to give readers an understanding of France and the French.

✔ *A Year in the Merde* by Stephen Clarke (Bloomsbury USA). A young Englishman arrives to set up some English tearooms in Paris and writes a laugh-out-loud account of the pleasures and perils of being a Brit in France.

Movies

With so many wonderful French films to choose from, it's difficult to cull this down into a small list. Except for *The Triplets of Belleville,* these films take place in Paris, and their shots of this beautiful city should only increase your anticipation of visiting.

✔ *Au Bout de Souffle (Breathless):* In this classic by Jean-Luc Godard, a small-time gangster kills a cop, then flees to Paris to get enough money together to leave the country with his girlfriend. Wonderful shots of Paris in the late 1950s.

✔ *Before Sunset:* This sequel to *Before Sunrise* takes place nine years after a young French woman and an American man meet on a train. Now they reconnect in Paris. This is shot all over the city.

✔ *Gigi:* This 1958 Lerner and Loewe musical set in Paris at the turn of the 20th century follows a young girl as she is groomed into a would-be courtesan (based on a story by the French author Colette).

✔ *Jules et Jim:* In François Truffaut's new wave classic, two best friends fall in love with the same woman in 1912 Paris. Breathtaking!

✔ *The Fabulous Destiny of Amélie Poulain:* It's hard to tell who the star is in this movie about a young woman trying to do good, actress Audrey Tautou or the city of Paris.

✔ *The Triplets of Belleville:* This fabulous animated film is about what happens when gangsters kidnap a Tour de France racer and his grandmother goes in search of him with the help of a musical trio — the Triplets of Belleville. Though it doesn't take place in Paris, it's a terrific introduction to the country and fun to watch with your kids. There isn't much talking, either, so not a lot of sub-titles to decipher.

✔ *Zazie Dans le Metro:* In Louis Malle's very funny 1962 film, a young girl is foisted on her unwilling transvestite uncle, and they have a series of madcap adventures in Paris.

Chapter 3

Deciding When to Go

● ●

In This Chapter
▶ Choosing the best season to visit
▶ Finding events that suit your interests

● ●

*I*n this chapter, I list the pros and cons of each season to help you decide when you can make the most of your visit to Paris. Also compiled here is a calendar of the most memorable events in Paris; you may want to consider planning your trip to coincide with one of the festivals, sporting events, or celebrations.

Revealing the Secret of the Seasons

Paris is beautiful at any time of year, but most residents find Paris ideal in spring and autumn, when weather is kind, crowds are reasonably sized, and Parisian life runs at a steady hum. In winter, there are plenty of things to do inside: You can fill an entire trip with visits just to the Louvre, and don't forget the January sales. In summer, you can bask in daylight that lasts until 10 p.m. Just remember that timing your visit to Paris depends on what kind of experience you want to have.

Table 3-1 presents average temperature by month in Paris to help you plan your trip. (In Paris, temperatures are reported in Celsius.)

Table 3-1	Average Daytime Temperatures for Paris											
	Jan	Feb	Mar	Apr	May	June	July	Aug	Sep	Oct	Nov	Dec
Fahrenheit (F)	38°	39°	46°	51°	58°	64°	74°	76°	61°	53°	45°	40°
Celsius (C)	3°	4°	8°	11°	14°	18°	28°	29°	16°	12°	7°	6°

Singing in spring

Spring in Paris brings some beautifully clear, fresh days. The parks and gardens of Paris (and those at Versailles, Fontainebleau, and at Claude Monet's home, Giverny — see Chapter 14) burst with colorful, fragrant blooms. Crowds of visitors don't kick in until July summer vacation (except during the spring fashion shows in March), so lines are relatively short at the top sightseeing attractions, and airfares have yet to reach their summertime highs.

But keep in mind that April in Paris is *not* as temperate as Cole Porter, who loved Paris in the springtime, would have you believe. In fact, Paris weather can be very similar to that in London: It's fickle. Pack for warm, cold, wet, dry, and every other eventuality; in other words, bring layers and don't even *think* about coming without an umbrella. Also, nearly every Monday in May is a holiday in France— stores are closed, the Métro runs on a holiday schedule, and other venues are affected.

Wandering through summer

Long and sultry days are summer's hallmark — 6 a.m. sunrises and 10 p.m. sunsets — so you're afforded additional hours to wander and discover. You can find discounts of 30 percent to 50 percent in most stores during July, one of the two big months for shopping sales (the other is January). Hotel room rates are less expensive in July and August, considered the low season, and during August, parking is free in most of the city.

But remember that an influx of tourists during the summer means long lines at museums and other sites. The weather also is capricious: You may have a week of rain and 55-degree temperatures, followed by days of cloudless skies and dry heat.

Because most Parisians take their vacations in August, the city is wonderfully tranquil in some places and devoid of life in others. Although the entire city doesn't exactly shut down in August, some shops and restaurants close for the entire month. The city's cultural calendar slows down, and you may have to walk an extra block or two to find an open shop or newsstand. And if you go to Paris in August with thoughts of practicing your French, think again. French may be the language you're least likely to hear in August.

Featuring fall

Paris crackles back to life starting the first week of September, a time typically known as *la rentrée* (the return). This season is one of the most exciting times of the year, when important art exhibitions open along with trendy new restaurants, shops, and cafes. By the middle of September, airfares drop from summertime highs. And with daytime temperatures in the 60s and 70s and nights in the 50s, the weather is pleasant.

Keep in mind, however, that finding a hotel at the last minute in the fall can be difficult due to the number of business conventions and trade shows that take place in the city, including the October fashion shows. Be sure to book ahead.

Transportation strikes of varying intensities traditionally occur during the fall. Some go virtually unnoticed by the average traveler, but others can be giant hassles.

Coasting through winter

You can find great airfare deals during the winter; Airlines and tour operators often offer unbeatable prices on flights and package tours. Lines at museums and other sights are mercifully short. And, if shopping is your bag, you can save up to 50% during the sales in January.

But remember that although Paris winters may appear mild on paper, in reality, residents know that they are gray (sometimes the sun doesn't shine for weeks), dreary, and bone-chillingly damp. And look out for those winds that lash up and down the city's grand boulevards. Bring a warm, preferably waterproof, coat.

Perusing a Calendar of Events: A Paris Calendar

When you arrive, check with the **Paris Tourist Office** (☎ 08-92-68-30-00 at a charge of 0.34€ per minute, www.parisinfo.com) and buy *Pariscope, L'Officiel des Spectacles* for dates, places, and other up-to-date information. Or, if you pass by an English-language bookstore or bar, pick up a copy of the English-language *Paris Free Voice*. For a refresher course in the ways and means of Paris addresses, see the Introduction.

In the next sections, I list attractions month by month.

January

A big, noisy parade on New Year's Day makes even the mildest hangover throb, but grin and bear **La Grande Parade de Montmartre** for the fun and flash — today Paris is more Rose Bowl than City of Lights. Watch the majorettes, high school bands, and elaborate floats traverse the city streets. The parade begins at 2 p.m. (so you *can* sleep in) in the place Pigalle, 18e (the 18th *arrondissement,* or neighborhood), and ends at the place Jules-Joffrin, 18e. January 1.

The **Fête des Rois** is the celebration of the Feast of the Three Kings, and custom dictates the wearing of gold paper crowns to celebrate. The main object of celebration is a flaky almond-paste-filled pie that conceals a ceramic charm (so watch your teeth). According to custom, whoever finds the charm becomes king or queen for the day, is entitled to wear the crown, and has free reign, as it were, in his or her choice of a consort. The pie with the charm is available at all *pâtisseries* (dessert shops). January 6.

La Mairie de Paris Vous Invite au Concert features a two-week, two-people-for-the-price-of-one special admission to a variety of jazz and classical concerts across the city. Mid-January.

An annual **Commemorative Mass for Louis XVI** attracts a full turnout of aristocrats, royalists, and even some far-right types. At the Chapelle Expiatoire, 29 rue Pasquier, 8e. Sunday closest to January 21.

Though Paris's Chinatown in the 13e seems like a dull neighborhood populated by cement high-rises, you can easily find good street life and many excellent restaurants, especially during the **Chinese New Year Festival.** Residents go all out for the parade, featuring dragons, dancers, and fireworks. Depending on the Chinese calendar, the holiday falls between January 21 and February 19 Twice a year, in January and September, more than 40,000 buyers make their way to the **Ready-to-Wear Fashion Shows** in the Salon International de Prêt-à-Porter (Parc des Expositions, 15e; Métro: Balard or Porte de Versailles). The exposition hall at the Porte de Versailles hosts shows of the new clothing lines from some 1,200 designers. Admission for non-trade visitors is around 23€ ($26). Invitation-only fashion shows are also held at the major design houses. End of January.

February

Foire à la Feraille de Paris is the yearly antiques and secondhand fair that takes place in the Parc Floral de Paris in the Bois de Vincennes (12e). Contact one of the branches of the Paris Tourist Office for exact dates. Branches are

- ✔ The Opéra-Grands-Magasins Welcome Center, 11 rue Scribe, 9e, open Monday to Saturday 9:00 a.m. to 6:30 p.m. (Métro: Chausée d'Antin or Opéra; RER: Auber)

- ✔ The Welcome kiosk beneath the modern glass roofed terminal of the Gare du Nord, 18 rue Dunkerque, 10e, open 7 days a week from 8 a.m. to 6 p.m. (Métro and RER: Gare du Nord)

- ✔ The Gare de Lyon Welcome Center, 20 bd. Diderot, 12e, open Monday to Saturday 8 a.m. to 6 p.m. (Métro and RER: Gare de Lyon)

- ✔ 21 place du Tertre, 18e, open daily 10 a.m. to 7 p.m. (Métro: Abbesses)

- ✔ Carrousel du Louvre, beneath the Pyramide, 99, rue de Rivoli, 1er, open daily 10 a.m. to 7 p.m. (Métro: Palais Royal/Musée du Louvre)

- ✔ Eiffel Tower between the north and east pillars; open daily 11:00 a.m. to 6:40 p.m. (Métro: Bir Hakeim; RER: Champ-de-Mars–Tour Eiffel)

The country fair comes to Paris during the **Salon de l'Agriculture.** Hundreds of farmers display animals and produce and win prizes for the biggest and best at this country fair in the heart of the city. Regional food stands offer tastes from all parts of France, and the atmosphere is friendly and quintessentially French at the Parc des Expositions de Paris, Porte de Versailles, 15e. For more information, call the Parc des Expositions information line at ☎ **01-43-95-37-00** or the Paris Tourist Office. Admission is 10€ ($11.50) adults; 6€ ($6.90) children and students. Last week of February to first week of March.

March

In **La Passion à Ménilmontant,** professional actors and residents of the neighborhood perform the Passion play (the events leading up to and including the Crucifixion of Christ) for a month around Easter. The play is staged at the Théâtre de Ménilmontant in the 20e. The event is a local tradition that's been observed since 1932. Admission 9€–20€ ($10–$23). Call ☎ **01-46-36-98-60** or 01-46-36-03-43 for schedule. Mid-March to mid-April.

Parisians know that spring's around the corner when the **Foire du Trône,** a tacky and fun annual carnival, comes to town. Visitors can take a trip up on the Ferris wheel and other rides, try their hand at games, buy hokey souvenirs, and sample fairground food. The fair is located at the Pelouse de Reuilly in the Bois de Vincennes (Métro: Porte Dorée, Porte de Charenton or Liberté). Late March to end of May.

April

You can follow the archbishop of Paris as he performs **Le Chemin de la Croix (the Stations of the Cross)** from the square Willette in Montmartre up the steps to the basilica of Sacré-Coeur where he leads prayers to commemorate the Passion and Crucifixion of Jesus Christ. Good Friday, 12:30 p.m. (March or April.)

One of the most popular athletic events of the year, the **Paris Marathon** has runners sprinting past a variety of the city's most beautiful monuments. Held on a Sunday, the marathon attracts enthusiastic crowds. Call the Paris Tourist Office for exact dates. Mid-April.

The huge annual fair, **Foire de Paris** is a great place to bargain hunt and people watch, and signals the start of spring with hundreds of stands selling good-priced food and wine, and a variety of clothing and household goods. The fair takes place at the Parc des Expositions, Porte de Versailles. Late April to early May.

The **Grandes Eaux Musicales** and **les Fêtes de Nuit de Versailles** bring the sounds of classical music to life at the magnificent fountains in the gardens of the Château de Versailles every Sunday from mid-April to mid-October, and every Saturday and national holiday from June through August. Even better are the Grandes Fêtes, spectacular sound-and-light shows with fireworks that take place one Saturday in June, three Saturdays in July, one Saturday in August, and two Saturdays in September. These events are held at the Château de Versailles,

Versailles. Log on to www.chateauversailles.fr for more information. (See Chapter 14 for tour companies that go to Versailles.)

May

Banks, post offices, and most museums are closed for **May Day,** May 1, the French version of Labor Day, but you can watch a workers' parade that traditionally ends at the place de la Bastille. May 1.

Staged annually since 1924, the **Vintage Car Rally,** is an array of antique cars that makes its way through the streets of Montmartre starting at 10 a.m. in rue Lépic and ending at the place du Tertre. Sunday closest to May 15.

During **Les Cinq Jours Extraordinaire** (five extraordinary days), the shops in the rue du Bac, de Lille, de Beaune, des St-Pères, and de l'Université, and on the quai Voltaire, feature a free open house focusing on a special object chosen according to the annual theme. The whole quarter takes on a festive ambience, red carpets line the streets, and plants and flowers decorate shop fronts. Third week of May.

Tickets are hard to come by for the **French Open,** Paris's biggest tennis event. The French Open is played in the Stade Roland Garros in the Bois de Boulogne on the western edge of the city. Unsold tickets — those not reserved for corporate sponsors — go on sale two weeks before the competition starts. The stadium is at 2 av. Gordon Bennett, 16e. Call the French Federation of Tennis at the stadium for more information (☎ 01-47-43-48-00) or visit the Web site at www.frenchopen.com. Last week in May and first week in June.

June

The Orangerie museum in the beautiful Bagatelle gardens on the edge of the Bois de Boulogne is the backdrop for the **Festival Chopin à Paris,** a much-loved annual series of daily piano recitals. Mid-June to mid-July (Métro: Porte Maillot, then take bus 244.)

The entire country becomes a concert venue in celebration of the first day of summer, and this musical day is called the **Fête de la Musique.** You can hear everything from classical to hip-hop for free in squares and streets around Paris. A big rock concert usually happens in the place de la République and a fine classical concert generally takes place in the gardens of the Palais-Royal. June..

One of the most distinguished aviation events in the world is **the Paris Air Show,** which takes place in odd-numbered years at Le Bourget Airport just outside Paris. Visitors can check out the latest aeronautic technology on display. Call the Paris Tourist Office for more information.

Art exhibits, concerts, and a fantastic parade are staged in the Marais, the boulevard St-Michel, and in other Paris streets to celebrate **Gay Pride.** Call the Centre Gai et Lesbien for dates at ☎ 01-43-57-21-47. Late June.

July and August

Citywide festivities begin on the evening of July 13 for **Bastille Day,** the celebration of French independence. Street fairs, pageants, feasts, and free *bals* (dances) are open to everyone at fire stations all over the city. (Some of the best *bals* are in the fire stations on the rue du Vieux-Colombier near the place St-Sulpice, 6e; the rue Sévigné, 4e; and the rue Blanche, near place Pigalle, 9e.) Although the *bals* are free, drinks cost.

On July 14, a big military **parade** starts at 10 a.m. on the Champs-Elysées; get there early if you hope to see anything. A sound-and-light show with terrific fireworks can be seen that night at the Trocadéro. Rather than face the crowds, many people watch the fireworks from the Champs de Mars across the river, from hotel rooms with views, or even from the hill on rue Soufflot, in front of the Panthéon. July 13 and 14.

Contemporary music, dance, and film are the bills of fare at outside venues around the city for the celebration of **Paris, Quartier d'Été** (Paris, summer neighborhood). The outdoor movies shown on a giant screen at Parc de la Villette (Métro: Porte de la Villette) are particularly popular. July 14 to August 15.

A smash success when it was started in 2002 by Paris Mayor Bertrand Delanoë, **Paris Plage,** a month-long festival that turns a bit of the Right Bank into the Riviera is now a permanent event. From mid-July to mid-August, the city closes off 3½ kilometers (2 miles) of its quays between the Pont Henri IV and the quai des Tuileries so that people can enjoy the same activities they would at the beach — all but swimming in the swift and dangerous Seine (a pool was added between pont Marie and pont Sully in 2004). There are three "beaches" made from sand, grass, or wooden planks, palm trees and wooden lounge chairs, snack bars, cafés, a climbing wall, trampolines, an area to play boules, and even old-time dance halls known as *guinguettes.* Concerts are organized by the electronics store Fnac, and there are dance and comedy performances as well. If you plan to visit Paris in mid-July, make sure you bring a bathing suit!

The most famous bicycle race in the world, the **Tour de France** always ends in Paris on the Champs-Elysées. For a number of years, spectators along the route have watched Texan Lance Armstrong take on the best in the world, and in 2004, they toasted his unprecedented sixth consecutive victory. You need a special invitation for a seat in the stands near place de la Concorde, but you can see the cyclists farther up the Champs-Elysées and, depending on the route (which changes each year), elsewhere in the city, too. Check the newspapers the day before or log on to www.letour.com. Last Sunday in July.

The **Fête de l'Assomption** celebrates the journey of Mary, Jesus's mother, to Heaven after her death. Church services at Notre-Dame are the most popular and colorful on this important French holiday (many stores are closed, and transportation runs on a holiday schedule), and banners are draped over the church's towers to celebrate the day. August 15.

September

One of the largest and most prestigious antiques shows in the world, the **Biennale des Antiquaires,** opens to the public in even-numbered years in the Cour Carée du Louvre, the underground exhibition space connected to the museum. For more information, contact the Paris Tourist Office. Early September.

Off-limits palaces, churches, and other official buildings throw open their doors to the public for two days during **Les Journées de Patrimoine** (the days of Patrimony). Long lines can put a damper on your sightseeing, so plan what you want to see and show up early (with a good book, just in case). Get a list and a map of all the open buildings from the Paris Tourist Office. Weekend closest to September 15.

The Festival d'Automne, an arts festival around Paris, is recognized throughout Europe for its innovative programming and the high quality of its artists and performers. Obtain programs through the mail so that you can book ahead for events you don't want to miss. Write to the Festival, 56 rue de Rivoli, 75001 Paris.

The second of two annual **Ready-to-Wear Fashion Shows** takes place in September (see the previous entry under "January").

October

Celebrate the harvest of the wine produced from Montmartre's one remaining vineyard, Clos Montmartre, and watch as the wine is auctioned off at high prices to benefit local charities during **Fêtes des Vendanges à Montmartre.** (A word of advice: *Don't* bid! The wine isn't very good.) Locals dress in period costumes, and the streets come alive with music. First or second Saturday of October.

One of the largest contemporary art fairs in the world, the FIAC **(Foire Internationale d'Art Contemporain)** has stands from more than 150 galleries, half of them foreign. As interesting for browsing as for buying, the fair takes at the Parc des Expositions, Porte de Versailles, 15e; Métro: Balard or Porte de Versailles. Admission is 14€ ($16). For more information, call **08-92-69-26-94.** Mid- to late October.

November

Many of the city's major museums celebrate the art of photography during **Mois de la Photo** (the month of the photo) with shows. Check listings in the weekly guide *Pariscope*. All month.

The French commemorate those who died fighting in both World Wars with a wreath-laying ceremony at the Arc de Triomphe, and veterans sell poppy corsages in memory of **Armistice Day.** November 11.

The sooner you drink **Beaujolais Nouveau** the better, and wine bars and cafés are packed for the just-after-midnight public release of the fruity red wine. It takes place the third Thursday (technically early Friday morning) in November.

The annual **Lancement des Illuminations des Champs-Elysées** (lighting of the avenue's Christmas lights) makes for a festive evening, with jazz concerts and an international star to push the button that lights up the avenue. For more information, call the Paris Tourist Office. Late November.

December

Each year a different foreign city installs a life-size Christmas manger scene (**La Crèche sur le Parvis**) in the plaza in front of the Hôtel de Ville (City Hall). The crèche is open daily from 10 a.m. to 8 p.m. December 1 to January 3.

Part II
Planning Your Trip to Paris

The 5th Wave   By Rich Tennant

"And how shall I book your flight to Paris – First Class, Coach, or Medieval?"

In this part . . .

*L*ook no further than these chapters to help you plan everything for your trip — from where to stay and how much to spend to traveling successfully with children to what to do if your wallet has been stolen. Chapter 4 tells you what to expect in each expense category, so you can plan a workable budget. Chapter 5 gets you to Paris, whether it be by plane, train, automobile, or hovercraft and discusses the pros and cons of package tours. Chapter 6 takes into account special interests and gives advice to families, seniors, disabled persons, and gay men and lesbians. And in Chapter 7, you get some advice about those last-minute details that can frustrate even the most frequent flyer.

Chapter 4

Managing Your Money

In This Chapter
▶ Developing a workable budget
▶ Cutting costs — but not the fun
▶ Handling money
▶ Dealing with a lost or stolen wallet

*B*eing reasonable is the key to budgeting a trip to Paris. A good way to figure out a budget is to mentally walk through the trip, from the moment you leave to the minute you get back home, and don't forget to figure in your transportation to and from the airport. Then add in the flight cost (see Chapter 5 for tips on how to fly to Paris for less), the price of getting from the Charles-de-Gaulle or Orly airport to your hotel, your hotel rate per day, meals, public transportation costs, admission prices to museums and the theater, and other entertainment expenses. Add another 15% to 20% to the total for good measure.

Planning Your Budget

Cities rarely are cheap or expensive across the board; Paris tends to be pricey for dining but reasonable for accommodations, so booking a good hotel shouldn't be a problem. The following list offers guidelines for what you're likely to spend while in Paris. The rate of exchange at press time was 1€ = $1.15.

✔ **Lodging:** Before you start shelling out money for lodging, think about how much time you'll actually spend in your room. For between 60€ and 80€ ($69–$92), you can rent a clean, functionally furnished hotel room with a private bathroom and cable TV. This type of budget room is comfortable, has the basic furnishings and decor; the drawbacks are thin yet serviceable towels and thin bars of soap.

If you're feeling extravagant and willing to spend 200€ ($230) or more to live in luxury, upper-tier hotels offer more services, such as room service, air conditioning, and toiletries.

✔ **Transportation:** The Paris Métro has been the model for subways around the world since its inauguration in 1900. Simply put, the

Métro is one of the best transit systems around in terms of price and efficiency. Getting across town in less than a half hour is no problem, and the cost is lower when you purchase one of several available discount tickets or a *carnet* (booklet) of ten tickets. (See Chapter 8 for options and prices.)

If you rent a car, expect your heart to be in your throat the entire time you drive in Paris — unless, of course, you thrive on labyrinthine one-way streets, a dearth of parking spaces, hellish traffic, and driving among what are statistically the worst drivers in Europe. If you want to rent a car to see other parts of France or make a day-trip outside of Paris, rent on your way out of the city. (See Chapter 7 for addresses and phone numbers of car rental agencies in Paris.)

✔ **Restaurants:** The French consider dining out one of the finer joys in life, and they pay for it. You can expect to do the same. An average Parisian dining experience — a three-course dinner in a popular eatery — runs about 40€ to 60€ ($46–$69) per person.

You can find restaurants serving satisfying two-course meals for as little as 18€ ($21) and wonderful ethnic food and sandwich shops that help you save even more money. Dining reasonably in Paris isn't impossible when you know where to look. Chapter 10 helps you discover just that.

✔ **Attractions:** Entry fees to museums and other sights can add up quickly; after referring to the money-saving advice in Chapter 11, make a list of must-dos to get a feel for how much money to set aside.

✔ **Shopping:** Paris is a shoppers' paradise, and French shopkeepers arrange their wares in such enticing window displays that they'll have you *faites du leche-vitrines* (licking the windows). You can find some great deals during the semiannual sales in January and July, but remember that a steep 19.6% tax (value-added tax, abbreviated VAT or TVA) is added to most goods. If you live outside the European Union, you're usually entitled to get back part of the tax, if you meet certain requirements. See Chapter 12 for more information.

✔ **Nightlife:** Don't forgo the spectacles at the Lido or Moulin Rouge if you've always wanted to see them — just know beforehand that you'll be charged a small fortune for entry and alcoholic beverages. Plan on seeing the show without dinner and exit with a wallet that isn't quite as light as it otherwise would be. Budget big, too, especially when you plan to visit clubs and other nightspots; nightclubs usually have covers (though the first drink is generally included) and bars are not cheap.

Table 4-1 gives you approximate prices for some common expenses, listed in euro, U.S. dollars, and British pounds.

Table 4-1	What Things Cost in Paris		
Expense	Euro	U.S. Dollars	Pounds Sterling
Taxi from Charles-de-Gaulle Airport to the city center (depending on traffic)	40€	$46	£29
Taxi from Orly Airport to the city center	35€	$40	£25
Public transportation for an average trip on Métro within the city (from a Métro *carnet* of 10)	1€	$1.15	£.71
Telephone card for public phones	7.50€	$8.60	£5.35
Glass of wine	3€	$3.45	£2.15
Coca-Cola (at a café)	3.35€	$3.85	£2.40
Cup of coffee	3€	$3.45	£2.15
Roll of ASA 100 color film, 36 exposures	10€	$12	£7.15
Admission to the Louvre	9.60€	$11	£6.90
Movie ticket	8.35–9.15€	$9.60–$11	£6–£6.55
Concert ticket (at the Opera Garnier)	5.10–45€	$5.86–$51	£3.65–£32

Cutting Costs

One of the primary ways to save money at the outset is by booking a package tour. For many destinations, you can book airfare, hotel, ground transportation, and even some sightseeing just by making one call to a travel agent or searching the Internet, for a lot less than if you tried to put the trip together yourself. (See Chapter 5 for specific companies to call.) The following list offers additional cost-cutting strategies for various expenses:

✔ **Food and drink:**

- Make lunch your main meal. Many restaurants offer great deals on a fixed-price (*prix fixe*) lunch. After two or three courses at midday, you won't want a big dinner.

- Try the ethnic neighborhoods. You can get terrific Chinese and Vietnamese foods in the 13th arrondissement between the place d'Italie and the Porte de Choisy; and the 10e, 18e, and 20e have restaurants with North African, Turkish, Vietnamese, and Thai menus. Couscous is on the menu at many restaurants and usually is an inexpensive offering.

- Keep in mind that the *plat du jour* (daily special) usually is the cheapest main dish at a budget restaurant.

- Remember that wine is cheaper than soda. Some mineral waters, likewise, are less expensive than others. Ask for tap water (*une carafe d'eau,* oon kar-*ahf* doh), which is free.

- If you're just having drinks or coffee, do it standing at the bar. You pay twice as much when you're seated at a table.

- Know the tipping rules. Most restaurants include the gratuity in the bill. Look for *service compris* on your bill, which means 15% has been added already. It is customary to leave extra; 5% if the service was good.

✔ **Lodging:**

- Book your hotel room early. Rooms at the best prices fill up quickly.

- Negotiate the room price, especially in the low season. Ask for a discount if you're a student or older than 60; ask for a discount when you're staying three days or more.

- Reserve a room with a kitchen. It may not seem like much of a vacation if you cook your own meals and wash your own dishes, but you can save a lot of money by not eating in restaurants three times a day. Even if you make only breakfast and pack an occasional bag lunch, you can save a little extra cash for souvenirs and gifts for your family and friends back home. And you won't need to fret over a hefty room-service bill.

- Try renting an apartment. Renting a Paris apartment can be surprisingly cheap, and apartment rental services flourish online. You save money by eating more meals in the apartment, and you experience a little of what it's like to live like a resident of Paris. (See Chapter 9 for specific rental agencies.)

✔ **Shopping and entertainment:**

- For discounts on fashion, try the rue St-Placide in the 6e arrondissement. You find plenty of overstock and *dégriffe* (clothes with labels removed) items on this street near the Bon Marché department store. Stylish inexpensive clothes also can be found at Monoprix stores located all over the city.

- Whenever you plan to visit two or three museums a day, buy the *Carte Musées et Monuments* (*Museums and Monuments*) *Pass.* The pass is good at major museums and tourist sites (except the Eiffel Tower) and costs 18€ ($21) for one day, 36€

($41) for three days, and 54€ ($62) for five days. It's a great deal if you plan to visit a lot of museums. See Chapter 11 for more information.

- Take advantage of the reduced admission fees at museums. The reduced prices usually apply after 3 p.m. (at the Louvre, it's after 6 p.m.) and all day Sunday. Remember that on the first Sunday of every month, admission to national museums is free.

- Buy half-price theater and other performance tickets. You can find same-day half-price tickets at one of the kiosks by the Madeleine or at the Gare Montparnasse. The kiosks are little huts with panels indicating whether the performance is sold out (symbolized by a little red man) or if tickets are still available (a little green man). (See Chapter 15 for more information.)

- Avoid going to clubs on weekends. Some clubs are cheaper than others, and some are cheaper during the week. Many clubs allow women in free up to a certain time.

✔ **Transportation:**

- Fly during the week rather than on weekends. Many airlines charge less if you fly on weekdays.

- Travel during the *off season* (also called the *low season*), the period from approximately October to April.

- Take the cheapest way into the city from the airport. You can save around 32€ ($37) by taking a train or bus instead of a cab from Roissy–Charles-de-Gaulle Airport and about 26€ ($30) from Orly.

  Making use of this tip dictates that you pack light so that you don't need a taxi to carry your load and can handle it yourself.

- Use the bus or Métro or walk.

  Buy a *carnet* of ten Métro tickets at a time. A single ticket costs €1.40 ($1.60), but one ticket from a €10.50 ($12) carnet costs €1.05 ($1.20). Better yet, if you know you're going to be in Paris from two to five consecutive days, buy a *Paris Visite pass,* which is good for unlimited subway and bus travel. A one-day Paris Visite card costs €8.35 ($9.60), two-day €13.70 ($15.75), three-day €18.25 ($21), and five-day €26.65 ($30.65).

Finally, in general, always ask for discount rates. Membership in AAA, frequent-flyer plans, trade unions, AARP, or other groups may qualify you for savings on car rentals, plane tickets, hotel rooms, even meals. Ask about everything; you may be pleasantly surprised.

Handling Money

The euro, the new single European currency, became the official currency of France and 11 other participating countries on January 1, 1999, but didn't go into general circulation until January 1, 2002. The old currency, the French franc, disappeared into history on March 1, 2002. Exchange rates of participating countries are locked into a common currency fluctuated against the dollar.

For more details on the euro, officially abbreviated as *EUR* and symbolized by €, check out www.europa.eu.int/euro.

Converting to euro

In converting prices to U.S. dollars, I used a conversion rate of 1€ = $1.15. For up-to-the minute exchange rates between the euro and the dollar, check the currency converter Web site at www.xe.com/ucc.

At this writing, £1 equals approximately 1.65€, and £1 = approximately $1.40. These were the rates of exchange used to calculate the values in Table 4-1.

You can withdraw euros at any ATM in Paris, and ATMs are everywhere and open 24 hours. Find them outside nearly every bank, in major department stores, airports, and train stations. If you want a list of ATMs that accept MasterCard or Visa cards before you leave home, ask your bank, or print out lists from the following sites: www.visa.com or www.mastercard.com. MasterCard and/or Cirrus cards can be used at any ATM which displays the MasterCard and/or Cirrus marks. Visa and/or Plus can also be used at ATMs displaying Visa and Plus signs.

Keep in mind you won't be able to check your balance or transfer funds, so keep track of your withdrawals while you travel.

 Finally, remember that every time you withdraw cash from an ATM, your bank hits you with a fee, sometimes as much as $5. Check how much your bank charges before leaving home. On top of this fee, the bank from which you withdraw cash may also include its own fee. Thus, taking out larger amounts of money every two to three days makes more sense than more frequent withdrawals of smaller denominations. Likewise, remember that your bank places a limit on the amount of money you can take out per day, usually between 300€ and 500€ ($345–$575).

 If you need to withdraw more than your bank's limit, visit any Parisian bank where a teller can swipe your ATM card for the amount you need, as long as the amount doesn't surpass the Parisian bank's own limit. Approach the bank's information desk first to explain in English what you need done.

Pulling out your plastic: Using credit cards

Master Card and Visa are accepted at nearly any establishment that takes credit cards in Paris. But, American Express and Diner's Club aren't widely accepted at small restaurants, shops, or budget hotels in Paris or the rest of the country.

Remember that you pay interest on cash advances on your credit card from the moment you receive the cash. And, many credit-card companies now tack on additional fees for foreign currency transactions — sometimes up to 4%, on top of the 1% service charge that MasterCard and Visa charges. If you don't know how much your credit card charges for currency conversion, contact a company representative. If the rate isn't acceptable, consider switching cards — MBNA America (☎ 800-421-2110; www.mbna.com), a Delaware-based credit-card issuer, charges nothing for currency conversion.

Going the way of the dinosaur: The extinction of traveler's checks

These days, there's no need to waste valuable time standing in long lines at the American Express office or in search of *bureaux de change* to cash traveler's checks. Simply use your ATM card to withdraw the money you need. Relatively few banks in Paris exchange currency or cash traveler's checks, preferring to send visitors to bureaux de change in touristy areas that charge a hefty fee.

You can cash traveler's checks at **American Express,** 11 rue Scribe (9e) ☎ 01-47-77-70-00 (Métro: Auber or Opéra); **Travelex,** 194 rue de Rivoli (1er), ☎ 01-42-60-37-61 (Métro: Tuileries) or **Global Change,** 99 rue de Rivoli, Galerie du Carrousel du Louvre (1er), ☎ 01-40-20-09-42.

Dealing with a Lost or Stolen Wallet

In the unlikely event that your wallet or purse is lost or stolen, be sure to block charges against your credit card account immediately. Every credit card company has an emergency international number that you can call if your wallet or purse is stolen. The company may be able to wire you a cash advance off your credit card immediately, and in many places, can deliver an emergency credit card in a day or two. Call ☎ 0-800-90-11-79 if you've lost or had your **Visa** card stolen. **American Express** card and traveler's check holders in France can call ☎ 336-393-1111 for money and lost card emergencies. For **MasterCard,** call ☎ 0800-90-13-87.

If your traveler's checks are lost or stolen, you need to be able to report exactly which checks are gone in order to get them replaced. The check issuer can tell you where to pick up the new checks.

If your purse or wallet gets stolen, the police aren't likely to recover it for you. However, contact the police anyway and file a police report — you may need it for credit-card or insurance purposes later.

Here's what to do if you've been pickpocketed: First, make a police report as soon as possible. There are three or four police stations (*commissariats*) in each arrondissement (the train stations also have small police stations). Go to the station closest to where the crime took place. If you were robbed in the subway, however, you can go to any police station. You will receive a *Récépissé de Déclaration de Perte ou de Vol* (receipt for declaration of loss or theft). If you have lost your passport, identification documents, and/or valuables, you are given separate receipts — one for your papers (*pièces d'identité*) and one for your valuables. The police receipts are sometimes necessary in applying for the replacement of airline tickets, INTERAIL passes (Europass and Eurail), passports, and traveler's checks or for supporting insurance claims.

The report must be made in person and most police stations have English-speaking personnel. Call the U.S. Embassy's **Office of American Services** (☎ **01-43-12-45-18** or 01-43.12-45-01; (www.amb-usa.fr/consul/guideoas/lostfound.pdf) for assistance in interpreting if you have difficulty making yourself understood.

Finally, you can visit the Lost and Found office, run by the French police, to verify whether your belongings were returned: **Centre des Objets trouvés de la Prefecture de Police de Paris,** 36 rue des Morillons, 75015, ☎ **08-21-00-25-25;** Métro: Convention; open Monday, Wednesday, and Friday 8:30 a.m. to 5:00 p.m. and Tuesday and Thursday 8:00 a.m. to 8:00 p.m.

Chapter 5

Getting to Paris

. . . .

In This Chapter

▶ Finding out which airlines fly to Paris
▶ Getting the best fare
▶ Arriving by train or ferry
▶ Deciding on a package tour

. . . .

*T*hese days, the Internet with its online travel agents, airline, lodging, and car rental Web sites — and plenty of information about your destination — has drastically changed travel planning. You still need to decide what kind of travel best suits you. In this chapter, I tell you how to get to Paris simply and easily and be an expert in no time.

Flying to Paris

Paris has two major airports: Charles de Gaulle and Orly. Charles de Gaulle is the larger, busier, and more modern airport, commonly known as CDG and sometimes called Roissy–Charles de Gaulle. It's located 14½ miles (23km) northeast of downtown Paris. Orly Airport is located 8½ miles (14km) south of the city. Web sites and phone numbers for the major airlines serving Paris are in the list that follows. These sites offer schedules, flight bookings, and package tours; Most have Web pages where you can sign up for e-mail alerts that list weekend deals and other late-breaking bargains.

Who flies there from the United States and Canada:

✔ **Air Canada** (☎ 800-630-3299; www.aircanada.ca) flies from Halifax, Montréal, Toronto, and Vancouver.

✔ **Air France** (☎ 800-237-2747; www.airfrance.com) flies from Atlanta, Boston, Chicago, Cincinnati, Houston, Los Angeles, Miami, New York, Philadelphia, and Washington, D.C.

✔ **Air Tahiti Nui** (☎ 877-824-4846; www.airtahitinui-usa.com) flies from Los Angeles.

✔ **American Airlines** (☎ 800-433-7300; www.aa.com) flies from Boston, Chicago, Dallas, Los Angeles, New York, and Miami.

✔ **British Airways** (☎ 800-247-9297; www.ba.com) flies from Atlanta, Baltimore, Boston, Charlotte, Chicago, Cincinnati, Detroit, Houston, Los Angeles, Miami, Orlando, Philadelphia, Phoenix, Newark, New York, San Diego, San Francisco, Tampa, and Washington, D.C.

✔ **Continental Airlines** (☎ 800-523-3273; www.continental.com) flies from Houston and Newark.

✔ **Delta Air Lines** (☎ 800-221-1212; www.delta.com) flies from Atlanta, Cincinnati, and New York and shares flights with Air France from Los Angeles, Philadelphia, and San Francisco.

✔ **Iceland Air** (☎ 800-223-5500; www.icelandair.com) flies from Baltimore, Boston, Minneapolis, and New York.

✔ **Northwest/KLM** (☎ 800-225-2525; www.nwa.com) flies from Detroit, Memphis, and Minneapolis.

✔ **United Airlines** (☎ 800-864-8331; www.united.com) flies from Chicago, Los Angeles, San Francisco, and Washington, D.C.

✔ **US Airways** (☎ 800-428-4322; www.usairways.com) flies from Charlotte, Philadelphia, and Pittsburgh.

✔ **Virgin Atlantic** (☎ 800-862-8621; www.virginatlantic.com) flies from Los Angeles, Las Vegas, Boston, New York, Newark, Washington, D.C., Orlando and Miami. You land in London and are transferred to an inter-European airline, usually British Midland, to Paris.

Who flies there from the United Kingdom:

✔ **Air France** (☎ 0845 359 1000; www.airfrance.com/uk) flies from London and Manchester.

✔ **British Airways** (☎ 0870 850 9 850; www.ba.com) flies from Edinburgh, Glasgow, London, and Manchester.

✔ **British Midland** (☎ 0870 6070 222; www.flybmi.com) flies from Leeds, London, and Manchester.

✔ **easyJet** (☎ 0871 7 500 100. www.easyjet.com) flies from Aberdeen, Belfast, Bristol, Inverness, Glasgow, Edinburgh, New Castle, Liverpool, East Midlands, London, Stansted, and Luton.

Who flies there from Australia and New Zealand (actually, these airlines fly to Paris only from Australia):

✔ **Qantas** (☎ 13-13-13 anywhere in Australia; www.qantas.com.au) flies from Sydney.

✔ **Singapore Airlines** (check the Web site for phone booking from your particular city: www.singaporeairlines.com) flies from Sydney and Auckland.

Getting the best deal on your airfare

Competition among the major U.S. airlines is unlike that of any other industry. Every airline offers virtually the same product (basically, a coach seat is a coach seat is a . . .), yet prices can vary by hundreds of dollars.

Business travelers who need the flexibility to buy their tickets at the last minute and change their itineraries at a moment's notice — and who want to get home before the weekend — pay (or at least their companies pay) the premium rate, known as the *full fare.* But if you can book your ticket far in advance, stay over Saturday night, and are willing to travel midweek (Tuesday, Wednesday, or Thursday), you can qualify for the least expensive price — usually a fraction of the full fare. On most flights, even the shortest hops within the United States, the full fare is close to $1,000 or more, but a 7- or 14-day advance purchase ticket may cost less than half of that amount. Obviously, planning ahead pays.

The airlines also periodically hold sales, in which they lower the prices on their most popular routes. These fares have advance purchase requirements and date-of-travel restrictions, but you can't beat the prices. As you plan your vacation, keep your eyes open for these sales, which tend to take place in seasons of low travel volume — November 1st to December 1st and January to April. You almost never see a sale around the peak summer vacation months of July and August, or around Thanksgiving or Christmas, when many people fly, regardless of the fare they have to pay.

Consolidators, also known as *bucket shops,* negotiate bulk quantities of airline tickets and sell them at a discount. They are great sources for international tickets, although they usually can't beat the Internet on fares within North America. Start by looking in Sunday newspaper travel sections; their ads are usually formatted to look like classified ads. U.S. travelers should focus on the *New York Times, Los Angeles Times,* and *Miami Herald.*

Bucket-shop tickets are usually nonrefundable or rigged with stiff cancellation penalties, often as high as 50% to 75% of the ticket price, and some put you on charter airlines with questionable safety records.

Several reliable consolidators are worldwide and available on the Net. **STA Travel** (☎ 800-781-4040; www.statravel.com), the world's leader in student travel, offers good fares for travelers of all ages. **ELTExpress** (☎ 800-TRAV-800; www.flights.com) started in Europe and has excellent fares worldwide, but particularly to that continent. **Flights.com** also has local Web sites in 12 countries. **FlyCheap** (☎ 800-FLY-CHEAP; www.1800flycheap.com) is owned by package-holiday megalith MyTravel. **Air Tickets Direct** (☎ 800-778-3447; www.airticketsdirect.com) is based in Montreal and leverages the currently weak Canadian dollar for low fares.

Booking your ticket online

The big three online travel agencies, **Expedia** (www.expedia.com), **Travelocity** (www.travelocity.com), and **Orbitz** (www.orbitz.com) sell most of the air tickets bought on the Internet. (Canadian travelers should try www.expedia.ca and www.travelocity.ca; U.K. residents can go for expedia.co.uk and opodo.co.uk.) Each has different business deals with the airlines and may offer different fares on the same flights, so shopping around is wise. Expedia and Travelocity will also send you an **e-mail notification** when a cheap fare becomes available to your favorite destination.

Of the smaller travel agency Web sites, **SideStep** (www.sidestep.com) receives good reviews from users. It's a browser add-on that purports to "search 140 sites at once," but in reality only beats competitors' fares as often as other sites do.

Great **last-minute deals** are available through free weekly e-mail services provided directly by the airlines. Most of these deals are announced on Tuesday or Wednesday and must be purchased online. Most are only valid for travel that weekend, but some (such as Southwest's) can be booked weeks or months in advance. Sign up for weekly e-mail alerts at airline Web sites or check mega-sites that compile comprehensive lists of last-minute specials, such as **Smarter Living** (smarterliving.com). For last-minute trips, www.site59.com in the U.S. and www.lastminute.com in Europe often have better deals than the major-label sites.

If you're willing to give up some control over your flight details, use an *opaque fare service* such as **Priceline** (www.priceline.com) or **Hotwire** (www.hotwire.com). Both offer rock-bottom prices in exchange for travel on a mystery airline at a mysterious time of day, often with a mysterious change of planes en route. The mystery airlines are all major, well-known carriers. But your chances of getting a 6 a.m. or 11 p.m. flight are pretty high. Hotwire tells you flight prices before you buy; Priceline usually has better deals than Hotwire, but you have to play their "name our price" game. *Note:* In 2004, Priceline added non-opaque service to its roster. You now have the option to pick exact flights, times, and airlines from a list of offers — or opt to bid on opaque fares as before.

Great last-minute deals are also available directly from the airlines themselves through a free e-mail service called *E-savers.* Each week, the airline sends you a list of discounted flights, usually leaving the upcoming Friday or Saturday and returning the following Monday or Tuesday. You can sign up for all the major airlines at one time by logging on to **Smarter Living** (www.smarterliving.com), or you can go to each individual airline's Web site. Airline sites also offer schedules, flight booking, and information on late-breaking bargains.

Arriving by Other Means

If you're arriving in Paris by **train** from northern Germany, Belgium, or London, you disembark in the **Gare du Nord.** Trains from Normandy come into the **Gare St-Lazare,** in Northwest Paris by Galeries Lafayette and Opéra Garnier. Trains from western France (Brittany, Chartres, Versailles, Bordeaux) head to the **Gare de Montparnasse** in the 14e; those from the southwest (the Loire Valley, Pyrénées, Spain) arrive at the **Gare d'Austerlitz** near the Jardin des Plantes, 13e. Those from the south and southeast (the Riviera, Lyon, Italy, Geneva) pull in at the **Gare de Lyon.** Trains coming from Alsace and eastern France, Luxembourg, southern Germany, and Zurich arrive at the **Gare de l'Est.** All train stations connect to Métro stations with the same name. All Paris train stations are located within the first 15 arrondissements, and are easily accessible.

Buses connect Paris to most major European cities. European Railways operates **Europabus** and **Eurolines.** The companies don't have American offices, so you must make bus transportation arrangements after arriving in Europe. In Great Britain, contact Eurolines (☎ 08-705-143-219). In Paris, contact Eurolines (Gare Routière Internationale Paris Galliéni, 28 av. du Général-de-Gaulle, 93541 Bagnolet; ☎ 08-92-89-90-91 at .34€/min). International buses pull into the **Gare Routière Internationale** (International Bus Terminal) in the suburb of Bagnolet, just across the *périphérique* (ring road) from the Galliéni Métro station. To go into Paris proper, take Line 3 and change buses according to your final destination.

About a dozen companies run **hydrofoil, ferry,** and **hovercraft** across the English Channel, or *La Manche* ("the sleeve," pronounced la mahnsh), as the French say. Services operate daily and most carry cars. Hovercraft and hydrofoils make the trip in about 40 minutes; the shortest ferry route between Dover and Calais is about 1½ hours. The major routes are between Dover and Calais and Folkestone and Boulogne (about 12 trips a day). Depending on weather conditions, prices and timetables can vary. It's important to make reservations because ferries are crowded.

In the United Kingdom, contact **Hoverspeed** (☎ 0870/240 8070; www.hoverspeed.com). Special fares, such as a three-day round trip from Dover to Calais for £49 ($81), are offered frequently, and change just as often.

The **Channel Tunnel** (Chunnel) opened in 1994, and the popularity of its Eurostar train service has had the happy effect of driving down prices on all cross-channel transport. This remarkable engineering feat means that if you hop aboard Le Shuttle in Britain, you can be eating a meal in France two hours later. You can purchase tickets in advance or at the tollbooth. Eurostar tickets start at $90 USD one way off season if you book seven days in advance. Prices rise in April and in June. Eurostar transports *passengers only* (no vehicles) between London or Ashford in Kent and Paris, Brussels, Lille and beyond. For more information on

Eurostar, including online booking, go to www.eurostar.com. For special packages information in the U.S., call Britrail (☎ 1-866-BRIT-RAIL; www.britrail.net) which often offers roundtrip London to Paris (via Eurostar) specials starting at $369 USD.

A separate company known as **Eurotunnel** (☎ 08-05-35-35-35 in the U.K.; www.eurotunnel.com) can transport passengers with their cars between Folkestone in the United Kingdom and Calais in France. Car prices start at £19 for a roundtrip day trip and rise to £413 for a roundtrip journey longer than five days. One-way prices start at £162.

Joining an Escorted Tour

As the most inclusive kind of travel, an *escorted tour* spells out nearly everything in advance: your flights, your hotels, your meals, your sightseeing itineraries, and your costs. It's the least independent way to travel, but some travelers find escorted tours liberating — no hassles with public transportation, no deciphering maps, and the comfort of knowing what you're getting. Others fervently despise escorted group tours, because they feel as if they're being herded from one sight to the next, missing the element of surprise and individuality that independent travel affords.

On escorted tours, the tour company takes care of all the details, and tells you what to expect at each leg of your journey. You know your costs up front, and you don't get many surprises. Escorted tours can take you to the maximum number of sights in the minimum amount of time with the least amount of hassle.

 If you decide to go with an escorted tour, I strongly recommend purchasing travel insurance, especially if the tour operator asks to you pay up front. But don't buy insurance from the tour operator! If the tour operator doesn't fulfill its obligation to provide you with the vacation you paid for, there's no reason to think that they'll fulfill their insurance obligations either. Get travel insurance through an independent agency. (I tell you more about the ins and outs of travel insurance in Chapter 7.)

When choosing an escorted tour, along with finding out whether you have to put down a deposit and when final payment is due, ask a few simple questions before you buy:

- ✔ **What is the cancellation policy?** Can they cancel the trip if they don't get enough people? How late can you cancel if you are unable to go? Do you get a refund if you cancel? If they cancel?

- ✔ **How jam-packed is the schedule?** Does the tour schedule try to fit 25 hours into a 24-hour day, or does it give you ample time to relax by the pool or shop? If getting up at 7 a.m. every day and not returning to your hotel until 6 or 7 p.m. at night sounds like a grind, certain escorted tours may not be for you.

✔ **How large is the group?** The smaller the group, the less time you spend waiting for people to get on and off the bus. Tour operators may be evasive about this, because they may not know the exact size of the group until everybody has made reservations, but they should be able to give you a rough estimate.

✔ **Is there a minimum group size?** Some tours have a minimum group size, and may cancel the tour if they don't book enough people. If a quota exists, find out what it is and how close they are to reaching it. Again, tour operators may be evasive in their answers, but the information may help you select a tour that's sure to happen.

✔ **What exactly is included?** Don't assume anything. You may have to pay to get yourself to and from the airport. A box lunch may be included in an excursion but drinks may be extra. Beer may be included but not wine. Find out how much flexibility you have: Can you opt out of certain activities, or does the bus leave once a day, with no exceptions? Are all your meals planned in advance? Can you choose your entree at dinner, or does everybody get the same chicken cutlet?

Depending on your recreational passions, I recommend one of the following tour companies:

✔ **The French Experience,** 370 Lexington Ave., Suite 812, New York, NY 10017 (☎ 212-986-3800; www.frenchexperience.com), offers several fly/drive programs through different regions of France (the quoted price includes airfare and a rental car). You can specify the type and price level of hotels you want. The agency arranges the car rental in advance, and the rest is up to you. Some staff can seem unfriendly, but persevere for good deals.

✔ **American Express Vacations** (☎ 800-241-1700; www.american expressvacations.com), is perhaps the most instantly recognizable tour operator in the world. Its offerings in Paris and the rest of Europe are probably more comprehensive than those of any other company and include package tours and independent stays.

Choosing a Package Tour

For lots of destinations, package tours can be a smart way to go. In many cases, a package tour that includes airfare, hotel, and transportation to and from the airport costs less than the hotel alone on a tour you book yourself. That's because packages are sold in bulk to tour operators, who resell them to the public. It's kind of like buying your vacation at a buy-in-bulk store — except the tour operator is the one who buys the 1,000-count box of garbage bags and resells them 10 at a time.

Package tours can vary as much as those garbage bags, too. Some offer a better class of hotels than others; others provide the same hotels for lower prices. Some book flights on scheduled airlines; others sell charters. In some packages, your choice of accommodations and travel days may be limited. Some let you choose between escorted vacations and independent vacations; others allow you to add on just a few excursions or escorted day trips (also at discounted prices) without booking an entirely escorted tour.

To find package tours, check out the travel section of your local Sunday newspaper or the ads in the back of national travel magazines such as *Travel & Leisure, National Geographic Traveler,* and *Condé Nast Traveler.* **Air France Holidays** (☎ 800-2-FRANCE; www.airfranceholidays.com) has France-specific package tours; their four-day, three-night Summer Getaway special starts at $399 and includes air and hotel fare, breakfast, and a Seine River cruise. **Liberty Travel** (call ☎ 888-271-1584 to find the store nearest you; www.libertytravel.com) is one of the biggest packagers in the Northeast, and usually boasts a full-page ad in Sunday papers.

Another good source of package deals is the airlines themselves. Most major airlines offer air/land packages, including **American Airlines Vacations** (☎ 800-321-2121; www.aavacations.com), **Delta Vacations** (☎ 800-221-6666; www.deltavacations.com), **Continental Airlines Vacations** (☎ 800-301-3800; www.covacations.com), and **United Vacations** (☎ 888-854-3899; www.unitedvacations.com). Several big **online travel agencies** — Expedia, Travelocity, Orbitz, Site59, and Lastminute.com — also do a brisk business in packages. If you're unsure about the pedigree of a smaller packager, check with the Better Business Bureau in the city where the company is based, or go online at www.bbb.org. If a packager won't tell you where it's based, don't fly with them.

Chapter 6

Catering to Special Travel Needs or Interests

● ●

In This Chapter

▶ Traveling with the brood
▶ Getting discounts for seniors
▶ Locating wheelchair-accessible attractions and accommodations
▶ Identifying resources for gay and lesbian travelers

● ●

*F*rance ranks among the most visited of all tourist destinations, and more resources than ever make it available — and enjoyable — to all. How-to guides, tour companies for disabled travelers, and English-speaking baby sitters are only some of the ways that travelers with special needs are making the most of Paris these days. This chapter discusses those resources and others.

Taking the Family Along

Don't let anyone talk you out of taking your kids to Paris. The City of Light is full of attractions worthy of your children's attention, and they only benefit from the experience! Parks and playgrounds abound, as do kid-specific sights and museums, interesting boat rides, and bike tours. And you're less than an hour away from Disneyland Paris. Paris is just as safe as, if not safer than, most big American cities. Though taking your children thousands of miles away may seem at times like an insurmount-able challenge, it can be immensely rewarding, giving you new ways of seeing the world through smaller pairs of eyes.

Familyhostel (☎ 800-733-9753; www.learn.unh.edu/familyhostel) takes the whole family, including kids ages 8 to 15, on moderately priced domestic and international learning vacations. Lectures, field trips, and sightseeing are guided by a team of academics.

You can find good family-oriented vacation advice on the Internet from sites like the **Family Travel Forum** (www.familytravelforum.com), a comprehensive site that offers customized trip planning; **Family Travel**

Network (www.familytravelnetwork.com), an award-winning site that offers travel features, deals, and tips; **Traveling Internationally with Your Kids** (www.travelwithyourkids.com) was started by parents whose daughters were born abroad and is a clearinghouse for information on traveling (and living abroad) with your children from those who have been there; and **Family Travel Files** (www.thefamilytravel files.com), which offers an online magazine and a directory of off-the-beaten-path tours and tour operators for families.

If you plan your trip well in advance, your kids may get a kick out of learning the language from one of the many French-language instructional videotapes on the market.

Books like Ludwig Bemelmans's *Madeline* series, Albert Lamorisse's *The Red Balloon,* and Kay Thompson's *Eloise in Paris* are great for kids under eight years of age. Look for them at your local library or bookstore or order them from the Librairie de France in New York (☎ 212-581-8810; Fax: 212-265-1094). Older teens may appreciate Ernest Hemingway's *A Moveable Feast* (Scribner paperback reissue), Victor Hugo's *Les Misérables,* Mark Twain's *Innocents Abroad,* and Rose Tremain's *The Way I Found Her* (Washington Square Press paperback reprint).

Children younger than 18 are admitted free to France's national museums (although not necessarily to Paris's city museums), and some attractions offer a lower rate for families of four or more. When purchasing tickets, ask if there is a family rate (*carte famille nombreus,* pronounced kart fam-ee nohm-*brooz*).

If your children are younger than 12, and you're traveling by rail through France, check out the **Carte Enfant Plus,** a children's rail pass. It's available at any SNCF (French National Railroads) station or, for non-Americans, online at www.sncf-voyages.com. (Unfortunately, SNCF does not sell directly to North Americans, who have to purchase these cards at a French train station), the pass offers a 50% discount for the child and up to four adult travel companions on non-TGV (Train Grand Vitesse, France's high-speed train) mainline trains in off-peak periods, and 25% off on TGV trains (except overnight trains) and mainline trains during peak travel times. The pass costs 55€ ($63), and you can reserve it online right before you leave and pick it up at any Paris train station within the time limit (usually two days). Similarly, a discount travel card is available for those aged 12 to 25 called **Carte 12–25.** For 43€ ($50), a cardholder is entitled to 50% discounts on all non-TGV rail services (except overnight services) and couchette berths on non-TGV mainline services at all times. A guaranteed 25% reduction is available on all TGV rail services (except overnight services) and couchette berths on non-TGV mainline services at all times where no seats are available at the 50% reduction rate. A passport photo must be presented when applying for these cards. *Note:* To find out where to buy these passes within the train station, go to the Acceuil (Welcome) information kiosk and have an English-speaking representative direct you.

If you're traveling with a baby, you can arrange ahead of time for such necessities as a crib and bottle warmer at your hotel, and, if you're driving, a car seat (small children are prohibited from riding in the front seat). Find out whether your hotel stocks baby food; if not, take some with you for your first day but then plan to buy some. Plenty of choices are available, from Nestlé to Naturalia.

Transportation in Paris isn't as stroller-friendly as in the United States. Be prepared to lift your child out of the stroller when boarding buses, climbing up and down stairs, and/or walking long distances in some Métro subway stations. The upside of all of this is that once you get to your destination, you and your child can stroll and play in some of the world's prettiest parks and gardens.

And when you need some kid-free time, consider one of the following agencies that employ English-speaking baby sitters: **Allo Maman Dépannage,** 38 rue Greuze, 16e (☎ 01-47-55-15-75), or **Kid Services,** (☎ 08-20-00-02-30). Specify when calling that you need a sitter who speaks English. Also, try the **American Church**'s basement bulletin board where English-speaking (often American) students post notices offering baby-sitting services. The church is located at 65 quai d'Orsay, 7e (☎ 01-45-62-05-00; Métro: Invalides).

The books *Family Travel* (Lanier Publishing International) and *How to Take Great Trips with Your Kids* (The Harvard Common Press) are full of good, general advice that can apply to travel anywhere. Another reliable tome with a worldwide focus is *Adventuring with Children* (Foghorn Press).

You can also check out *Family Travel Times,* published six times a year by **Travel with Your Children,** 40 Fifth Ave., Seventh floor, New York, NY 10011 (☎ 212-477-5524; www.familytraveltimes.com). It includes a weekly call-in service for subscribers. Subscriptions are $39 a year. A free publication list and a sample issue are available on request.

Finally, a word of advice: Although French people love kids and welcome them just about anywhere, they expect them to be well mannered. Proper behavior is expected everywhere, but especially in restaurants and museums. French children are taught at an early age to behave appropriately in these settings, and French adults expect the same from your kids.

Making Age Work for You: Tips for Seniors

Mention that you're a senior citizen when you first make your travel reservations; you may be entitled to some discounts before you even get to Paris. When you arrive in Paris, don't be shy about asking for senior discounts, and always carry a form of identification that shows your date of birth.

People over the age of 60 qualify for reduced admission to theaters, museums, and other attractions and for other travel bargains like the **Carte Senior,** which entitles holders to 50% discounts on TGV rail services (except overnight services) and couchette berths on non-TGV mainline services, subject to seating availabilities. There is 25% off all TGV rail services (except overnight services) and couchette berths on non-TGV mainline services at all times, where no seats are available at the 50% reduction. The Carte Senior also triggers some discounts on admission to museums and historic sites. It's valid for one year, costs 45€ ($52), and you can buy it at any SNCF (train) station. You have to present a passport photo when applying for these cards. *Note:* To find out where to buy these passes within the train station, go to the Acceuil (Welcome) information kiosk, where an English-speaking representative will direct you.

Membership in certain organizations can qualify you for some discounts. Be sure to bring whatever membership card the organization issues. If you're over 50, consider joining **AARP,** 601 E St. NW, Washington, DC 20049 (☎ **800-424-3410;** www.aarp.org), for discounts on hotels, airfares, and car rentals. As a member, you're eligible for a wide range of special benefits, including *Modern Maturity* magazine and a monthly newsletter.

Hundreds of travel agencies specialize in senior travel, one of which is Grand Circle. Although many of the vacations are of the tour-bus variety, which may cramp the style of an independent senior, one bonus is that free trips are often thrown in for organizers of groups of 20 or more. Obtain travel information from **SAGA International Holidays,** 222 Berkeley St., Boston, MA 02116 (☎ **800-343-0273;** www.sagaholidays.com), which offers inclusive tours and cruises for those 50 and older.

Recommended publications offering travel resources and discounts for seniors include: the quarterly magazine *Travel 50 & Beyond* (www.travel50andbeyond.com); *101 Tips for Mature Travelers,* available from Grand Circle Travel (☎ **800-221-2610** or 617-350-7500; www.gct.com); and *Unbelievably Good Deals and Great Adventures That You Absolutely Can't Get Unless You're Over 50* (McGraw-Hill), by Joan Rattner Heilman.

Accessing Paris: Advice for Travelers with Disabilities

Unfortunately, the features that make Paris so beautiful — uneven cobblestone streets, quaint buildings with high doorsills from the Middle Ages, and twisting lanes too narrow and traffic-clogged to simultaneously admit pedestrians and autos — also make using a walker or a wheelchair a nightmare. According to French law, newer hotels with three stars or more are required to have at least one wheelchair-accessible guest room. Most of the city's older, budget hotels, which are exempt from the law, occupy buildings with winding staircases, or elevators smaller than phone booths, and generally aren't good choices for travelers with disabilities.

And, similar to the way it is for people with babies in strollers, Paris's public transportation system isn't the most accessible to folks with mobility problems. Few Métro stations have elevators, most feature long tunnels, and some have wheelchair-unfriendly moving sidewalks and staircases. Escalators often lead to flights of stairs, and many times when you climb a flight of stairs, you're faced with another set of stairs leading down. Currently, wheelchair lifts aren't standard equipment on city buses, and the buses don't kneel closer to the curb to make that first step any lower.

However, line 14 of the Métro is wheelchair accessible, and so are the stations at Nanterre-Université, Vincennes, Noisiel, Saint-Maur-Créteil, Torcy, Auber, Cité-Universitaire, Saint-Germain-en-Laye, Charles-de-Gaulle–Étoile, Nanterre-Ville, and several others. Bus 91, which links the Bastille with Montparnasse, is wheelchair accessible, and so are new buses on order. Some high-speed and intercity trains are equipped for wheelchair access, and a special space is available in first class (at the price of a second-class ticket) for wheelchairs, although you must reserve well in advance.

Don't let these inconveniences change your mind about visiting Paris. Before your trip to Paris, contact the **French Government Tourist Office** for the publication (with an English glossary) *Touristes Quand Même,* which provides an overview of facilities for the disabled in the French transportation system and at monuments and museums in Paris and the provinces. Their Web site (www.paris-touristoffice.com) also provides a list of everything from tour guides to parks with disabled access to organizations for disabled persons to specialized transport.

 You can get a list of hotels in France that meet the needs of disabled travelers by writing to **L'Association des Paralysés de France** (The Association of the Paralyzed of France), 2217 rue de Père Guérion bd. Auguste-Blanqui, 75013 Paris (☎ **01-40-78-69-00;** Web site in French: www.apf.asso.fr).

You can contact the **Groupement pour l'Insertion des Personnes Handicapées Physiques** (Help for the Physically Handicapped), Paris Office, 10 rue de Georges de Porto Riche, 75014 Paris (☎ **01-43-95-66-36**) and **Les Compagnons du Voyage** of the RATP (Paris public transporta-tion) (☎ **01-53-11-11-12;** Web site in French: www.ratp.fr) for help in planning itineraries using public transportation.

A good English-language guide for disabled travelers is *Access in Paris,* which you can obtain by calling ☎ **44-20-1250-3222** or writing to **RADAR,**

Unit 12, City Forum, 250 City Road, London EC1V 8AF. It costs £13.95 (approximately $9.50).

Check out *A World of Options,* a 658-page book of resources for disabled travelers that covers everything from biking trips to scuba outfitters around the world. At press time, MIUSA was running a clearance special for the book for just $18. You can order it from **Mobility International USA,** P.O. Box 10767, Eugene, OR 97440 (☎ **541-343-1284,** voice and TYY; www.miusa.org). Another place to try is **Access-Able Travel Source** (www.access-able.com), a comprehensive database of travel agents who specialize in disabled travel and a clearinghouse for information about accessible destinations around the world.

Many travel agencies offer customized tours and itineraries for travelers with disabilities. **Flying Wheels Travel** (☎ **507-451-5005;** www.flying wheelstravel.com) offers escorted tours and cruises that emphasize sports and private tours in minivans with lifts. **Access-Able Travel Source** (☎ **303-232-2979;** www.access-able.com) offers extensive access information and advice for traveling around the world with disabilities. **Accessible Journeys** (☎ **800-846-4537** or 610-521-0339) addresses the needs of wheelchair travelers and their families and friends.

Organizations that offer assistance to disabled travelers include the **MossRehab** (www.mossresourcenet.org), which provides a library of accessible-travel resources online; **SATH** (Society for Accessible Travel and Hospitality) (☎ **212-447-7284;** www.sath.org; annual membership fees: $45 adults, $30 seniors and students), an educational nonprofit membership organization whose mission is to raise awareness of the needs of all travelers with disabilities, remove physical and attitudinal barriers to free access and expand travel opportunities in the United States and abroad. SATH offers a wealth of travel resources for all types of disabilities and informed recommendations on destinations, access guides, travel agents, tour operators, vehicle rentals, and companion services, and includes *Open World Magazine* (subscription: $13 per year, $21 outside the United States); and the **American Foundation for the Blind** (AFB) (☎ **800-232-5463;** www.afb.org), a referral resource for the blind or visually impaired that includes information on traveling with guide dogs.

For more information specifically targeted to travelers with disabilities, the community Web site **iCan** (www.icanonline.net/channels/ travel/index.cfm) has destination guides and several regular columns on accessible travel. Also check out the quarterly magazine **Emerging Horizons** ($14.95 per year, $19.95 outside the United States; www.emerginghorizons.com); **Twin Peaks Press** (☎ **360-694-2462**), offers books for travelers with special needs.

Following the Rainbow: Resources for Gay and Lesbian Travelers

They don't call it *Gay Paree* for nothing. Everyone from hotel clerks to servers treats same-sex couples with polite indifference. Oscar Wilde and James Baldwin lived here, and Gertrude Stein settled here with Alice B. Toklas. France is one of the world's most tolerant countries toward gays and lesbians. It has no laws that discriminate against them. Technically, sexual relations are legal for consenting partners ages 16 and older.

Paris's gay center is the Marais, which stretches from the Hôtel de Ville to the place de la Bastille. The biggest concentration of gay bookstores, cafes, bars, and clothing boutiques is here, and so is the best source of information on Parisian gay and lesbian life — the **Centre Gai et Lesbien,** 3 rue Keller, 11e (☎ 01-43-57-21-47; Métro: Bastille). The center is a source of information, and members of its staff coordinate the activities and meetings of gay people around the world. The center is open daily from 2 to 8 p.m.

Another helpful source is **La Maison des Femmes,** 163 rue Charenton, 12e (☎ 01-43-43-42-13; Métro: Charonne), which has a cafe and a feminist library for lesbians and bisexual women. Meetings about everything from sexism to working rights and informal dinners and get-togethers all take place here. Call Monday, Wednesday, or Friday from 3 to 8 p.m. for more information.

Gay magazines that focus mainly on cultural events include *Illico* (free in gay bars) and *e.m@le* (available free at bars and bookstores). *Lesbia* is available for women. You can find these and others at Paris's largest and best-stocked gay bookstore, **Les Mots à la Bouche,** 6 rue Ste-Croix-la-Bretonnerie, 4e (☎ 01-42-78-88-30; Métro: Hôtel-de-Ville). Open 11 a.m. to 11 p.m. Monday through Saturday and 3 to 8 p.m. Sunday, the store carries French- and English-language publications.

For advice on HIV issues, call **F.A.C.T.S.** (☎ 01-44-93-16-32) from 6 to 10 p.m. Monday, Wednesday, and Friday. The acronym stands for Free Aids Counseling Treatment and Support, and the English-speaking staff provides counseling, information, and doctor referrals.

The International Gay and Lesbian Travel Association (IGLTA) (☎ 800-448-8550 or 954-776-2626; www.iglta.org) is the trade association for the gay and lesbian travel industry, and offers an online directory of gay- and lesbian-friendly travel businesses; go to their Web site and click on Members.

Many agencies offer tours and travel itineraries specifically for gay and lesbian travelers. **Above and Beyond Tours** (☎ 800-397-2681; www.abovebeyondtours.com) is the exclusive gay and lesbian tour operator for United Airlines. **Now, Voyager** (☎ 800-255-6951;

www.nowvoyager.com) is a well-known San Francisco-based gay-owned and -operated travel service.

The following travel guides are available at most travel bookstores and gay and lesbian bookstores, or you can order them from **Giovanni's Room** bookstore, 1145 Pine St., Philadelphia, PA 19107 (☎ **215-923-2960;** www.giovannisroom.com); *Frommer's Gay & Lesbian Europe* (Wiley), an excellent travel resource (www.frommers.com); *Out and About* (☎ **800-929-2268** or 415-644-8044; www.outandabout.com), which offers guidebooks and a newsletter ($20/yr; 10 issues) packed with solid information on the global gay and lesbian scene; *Spartacus International Gay Guide* (Bruno Gmünder Verlag; www.spartacusworld.com/gay uide/) and *Odysseus* (Odysseus Enterprises, www.odyusa.com/html/ trvlguide.html), both good, annual English-language guidebooks focused on gay men; and the *Damron* guides (www.damron.com), with separate, annual books for gay men and lesbians.

Chapter 7

Taking Care of the Remaining Details

● ●

In This Chapter

▶ Dealing with passports

▶ Discovering why you don't need to rent a car in Paris

▶ Understanding travel and medical insurance

▶ Guarding your health while traveling

▶ Keeping in touch via e-mail and cellphone

▶ Preparing to go through airline security

● ●

*S*ometimes it seems that the planning for a trip abroad lasts longer than the actual trip itself. This chapter advises and helps you organize those innumerable loose ends and last-minute tasks.

Getting a Passport

A valid passport is the only legal form of identification accepted around the world. You can't cross an international border without it. Getting a passport is easy, but the process takes some time. For an up-to-date country-by-country listing of passport requirements around the world, go to the "Foreign Entry Requirement" Web page of the U.S. State Department at http://travel.state.gov.

Applying for a U.S. passport

If you're applying for a first-time passport, follow these steps:

1. Complete a **passport application** in person at a U.S. passport office; a federal, state, or probate court; or a major post office. To find your regional passport office, either check the **U.S. State Department** Web site, http://travel.state.gov/passport/index.html, or call the **National Passport Information Center** (☎ 877-487-2778) for automated information.

2. Present a **certified birth certificate** as proof of citizenship. (Bringing along your driver's license, state or military ID, or social security card is also a good idea.)

3. Submit **two identical passport-sized photos,** measuring 2-x-2 inches in size. You often find businesses that take these photos near a passport office. *Note:* You can't use a strip from a photo-vending machine because the pictures aren't identical.

4. Pay a **fee.** For people 16 and over, a passport is valid for ten years and costs $85. For those 15 and under, a passport is valid for five years and costs $70.

Allow plenty of time before your trip to apply for a passport; processing normally takes three weeks but can take longer during busy periods (especially spring).

If you have a passport in your current name that was issued within the past 15 years (and you were over age 16 when it was issued), you can renew the passport by mail for $55. Whether you're applying in person or by mail, you can download passport applications from the U.S. State Department Web site at http://travel.state.gov/passport/index. html. For general information, call the **National Passport Agency** (☎ 202-647-0518). To find your regional passport office, either check the U.S. State Department Web site or call the **National Passport Information Center** toll-free number (☎ 877-487-2778) for automated information.

Applying for other passports

The following list offers more information for citizens of Australia, Canada, New Zealand, and the United Kingdom:

- ✔ **Australians** can visit a local post office or passport office, call the **Australia Passport Information Service** (☎ 131-232 toll-free from Australia), or log on to www.passports.gov.au for details on how and where to apply.

- ✔ **Canadians** can pick up applications at passport offices throughout Canada, post offices, or from the central **Passport Office, Department of Foreign Affairs and International Trade,** Ottawa, ON K1A 0G3 (☎ 800-567-6868; www.ppt.gc.ca). Applications must be accompanied by two identical passport-sized photographs and proof of Canadian citizenship. Processing takes five to ten days if you apply in person, or about three weeks by mail.

- ✔ **New Zealanders** can pick up a passport application at any New Zealand Passports Office or download it from their Web site. For information, contact the **Passports Office** or check out their Web site. Contact the **Passports Office** at ☎ 0800-225-050 in New Zealand or 04-474-8100 or log on to www.passports.govt.nz.

✔ **United Kingdom** residents can pick up applications for a standard ten-year passport (five-year passport for children under 16) at passport offices, major post offices, or a travel agency. For information, contact the **United Kingdom Passport Service** (☎ **0870-521-0410;** www.ukpa.gov.uk).

 Always keep a photocopy of the inside page of your passport with your picture packed separately from your wallet or purse. In the event your passport is lost or stolen, the photocopy can help speed up the replacement process. When traveling in a group, never let one person carry all the passports. If the passports are stolen, obtaining new ones can be much more difficult, because at least one person in a group needs to be able to prove his or her identity to identify the others.

If you're a U.S. citizen and either lose or have your passport stolen in Paris, go to the Consulate of the American Embassy at 2 rue St. Florentin, 1er (☎ **01-43-12-22-22;** Métro: Concorde). Canadians in the same circumstances need to visit the Consulate of the Canadian Embassy, 35 av. Montaigne, 8e (☎ **01-44-43-29-00;** Métro: Franklin-D-Roosevelt or Alma Marceau). Australians must go to the Ambassade d'Australie at 4 rue Jean-Rey, 15e (☎ **01-40-59-33-00;** Métro: Bir-Hakeim). New Zealanders need to visit the New Zealand Embassy, 7 *Ter* rue Léonard de Vinci, 16e (☎ **01-45-01-43-43,** ext. 280, from 9 a.m. to 1 p.m.; Métro: Victor-Hugo).

Renting a Car in Paris — Not

Extreme sports aficionados, this is for you. In the 1998 movie, *Ronin,* starring Robert De Niro, a former U.S. intelligence agent tries to track down a mysterious package wanted by both the Irish and the Russians. Naturally, there's a car chase, and this one is edge of the seat: The bad guys in a BMW are fleeing from the good guys in a Mercedes through the center of Paris. The BMW speeds through traffic the wrong way with the Mercedes in hot pursuit, and after nearly ten nail-biting minutes, one of the cars flips over (I won't tell you which one) in a flaming crash. To the uninitiated, simply driving a car in Paris makes you feel like you're in this Paris chase. Why? Parisian drivers are ruthlessly aggressive. Traffic is dense. Roundabouts pop up everywhere, and cars seem to hurtle at you from the left — no better example than the circle called Étoile that surrounds the Arc de Triomphe, where cars enter and exit from *12 different locations* at high speeds. Parking is difficult, both in terms of finding a space and the size of the spaces available. Most hotels, except luxury ones, don't have garages. And if you drive to Paris from somewhere else and get on the limited-access roadway called the *périphérique* that circles the city, you'll find that its exits aren't numbered. Because the Paris Métro is one of the world's best urban transportation systems, having a car in Paris seems highly unnecessary. Even the day-trips described in Chapter 14 are easily accessible by public transportation.

If you must drive in Paris, make sure that you have a copilot helping you navigate the streets. Children, by law, are required to sit in the back, and backseat passengers must wear seat belts. And remember that the majority of rentals available in France (and, indeed, most of Europe) have manual (stick-shift) transmissions. In fact, if you request an automatic transmission, you'll probably end up paying more for the car.

When you rent a car, try doing so for three days or more because the cost usually works out to be less per day than renting for one day, with unlimited mileage thrown in. Reserve before you leave home (make sure to print out your reservation!), and keep in mind that government taxes are calculated at an eye-popping 20.6% of the total contract, collision damage insurance tacks on 15€ to 20€ ($17–$23) per day, gas is very expensive, and a surcharge of about 15€ ($17) is assessed if you pick up the car at the airport.

Car rental agencies in Paris include

- ✔ **Avis,** gare d'Austerlitz, 13e (☎ **01-45-84-22-10;** www.avis.com). A compact car, such as a Renault Megane, that seats four runs about 70€ ($80) per day unlimited mileage before tax.

- ✔ **Europcar,** 60 bd Diderot, 12e (☎ **08-25-35-23-52**/.15€ per minute; www.europcar.fr). A compact four-door with air conditioning, such as the Volkswagen Golf, costs 83€ ($95) per day with limited miles before tax.

- ✔ **Hertz France,** gare de l'Est, 10e (☎ **01-42-05-50-43;** www.hertz.com). A compact car such as a Renault Megane costs about 88€ ($101.20) per day with limited mileage but with all taxes.

- ✔ **National,** gare de Lyon, 12e (☎ **01-40-04-90-04;** www.nationalcar.com). A economy four-door car that seats four, such as an Opel Corsa, costs about 59€ ($68) per day unlimited mileage before tax.

The major highways (*autoroutes*) to Paris are the **A1** from the north (the United Kingdom and Belgium); the **A13** from Normandy and other points in northwest France; the **A109** from Spain and the southwest; the **A7** from the Alps, the Riviera, and Italy; and the **A4** from eastern France. At the beginning and end of long weekends, school breaks, and August summer vacations, these roads become parking lots.

Playing It Safe with Travel and Medical Insurance

Three kinds of travel insurance are available: trip-cancellation insurance, medical insurance, and lost luggage insurance. The cost of travel insurance varies widely, depending on the cost and length of your trip, your age and health, and the type of trip you're taking, but expect to pay between 5% and 8% of the vacation itself.

✔ **Trip-cancellation insurance** helps you get your money back if you have to back out of a trip, if you have to go home early, or if your travel supplier goes bankrupt. Allowed reasons for cancellation can range from sickness to natural disasters to the State Department declaring your destination unsafe for travel. (Insurers usually won't cover vague fears, though, as many travelers who tried to cancel their trips in October 2001 because they were wary of flying discovered.)

A good resource is **Travel Guard Alerts,** a list of companies considered high-risk by Travel Guard International (www.travelinsured.com) that you can read about on the Web site. Protect yourself further by paying for the insurance with a credit card — by law, consumers can get their money back on goods and services not received if they report the loss within 60 days after the charge is listed on their credit card statement.

Note: Many tour operators, particularly those offering trips to remote or high-risk areas, include insurance in the cost of the trip or can arrange insurance policies through a partnering provider, a convenient and often cost-effective way for the traveler to obtain insurance. Make sure the tour company is a reputable one, however: Some experts suggest you avoid buying insurance from the tour or cruise company you're traveling with, saying it's better to buy from a third-party insurer than to put all your money in one place.

✔ Most health plans (including Medicare and Medicaid) do not provide **medical insurance** coverage for travel overseas, and the ones that do often require you to pay for services up front and reimburse you only after you return home. Even if your plan does cover overseas treatment, most out-of-country hospitals make you pay your bills up front, and send you a refund only after you return home and file the necessary paperwork with your insurance company. As a safety net, you may want to buy travel medical insurance, particularly if you're traveling to a remote or high-risk area where emergency evacuation is a possible scenario. If you require additional medical insurance, try **MEDEX Assistance** (☎ 410-453-6300; www.medexassist.com) or **Travel Assistance International** (☎ 800-821-2828; www.travelassistance.com; for general information on services, call the company's Worldwide Assistance Services, Inc., at ☎ 800-777-8710).

✔ **Lost luggage insurance** is not necessary for most travelers. On international flights (including U.S. portions of international trips), baggage coverage is limited to approximately $9.07 per pound, up to approximately $635 per checked bag. If you plan to check items more valuable than the standard liability, see if your valuables are covered by your homeowner's policy, get baggage insurance as part of your comprehensive travel-insurance package or buy Travel Guard's "BagTrak" product. Don't buy insurance at the airport, as it's usually overpriced. Be sure to take any valuables or irreplaceable items with you in your carry-on luggage, as many valuables (including books, money, and electronics) aren't covered by airline policies.

If your luggage is lost, immediately file a lost-luggage claim at the airport, detailing the luggage contents. For most airlines, you must report delayed, damaged, or lost baggage within 4 hours of arrival. The airlines are required to deliver luggage, once found, directly to your house or destination free of charge.

For more information on travel insurance, contact one of the following recommended insurers: **Access America** (☎ 866-807-3982; www.access america.com); **Travel Guard International** (☎ 800-826-4919; www.travelguard.com); **Travel Insured International** (☎ 800-243-3174; www.travelinsured.com); **Travelex Insurance Services** (☎ 888-457-4602; www.travelex-insurance.com); and **InsuranceToGo.com** (☎ 877-598-8646; www.insurancetogo.com).

Staying Healthy When You Travel

Getting sick will ruin your vacation, so I *strongly* advise against it (of course, last time I checked, the bugs weren't listening to me any more than they probably listen to you). The French government pays 70% of the cost of doctor visits, and its national health insurance covers 99% of France's population. Visitors needing medical care in France find that same-day appointments are easily made, and patient fees are relatively inexpensive. Patients almost always have to pay up front, unless they're citizens of European Union countries with reciprocal medical arrangements. U.S. health insurance companies usually reimburse you for most of the cost of treating illnesses in foreign countries; make sure to keep all your receipts.

If you do get sick, ask the concierge at your hotel to recommend a local doctor — even his or her own doctor, if necessary. You can also call SOS Medecins (☎ 01-47-07-77-77), a 24-hour service. Ask for an English-speaking doctor. The **Centre Médicale Europe,** 44 rue d'Amsterdam, 9e (☎ 01-42-81-93-33), is another good and efficient option. It has a host of specialists, and foreigners pay about 25€ ($29) for a consultation. If you're in urgent need of a dentist, try **SOS Urgences Stomatologique Dentaire,** 87 bd. Port-Royal (☎ 01-43-36-36-00).

Talk to your doctor before leaving on a trip if you have a serious and/ or chronic illness. For conditions such as epilepsy, diabetes, or heart problems, wear a **MedicAlert identification tag** (☎ 888-633-4298; www.medicalert.org), which immediately alerts doctors to your condition and gives them access to your records through Medic Alert's 24-hour hotline. Contact the **International Association for Medical Assistance to Travelers (IAMAT)** (☎ 716-754-4883 or, in Canada, 416-652-0137; www.iamat.org) for tips on travel and health concerns in the countries you're visiting, and lists of local, English-speaking doctors. The United States **Centers for Disease Control and Prevention** (☎ 800-311-3435; www.cdc.gov) provides up-to-date information on health hazards by region or country and offers tips on food safety.

Avoiding economy-class syndrome

Deep vein thrombosis, or as it's know in the world of flying, *economy-class syndrome,* is a blood clot that develops in a deep vein. Symptoms include leg pain or swelling, or even shortness of breath. This potentially deadly condition can be caused by sitting in cramped conditions — such as an airplane cabin — for too long.

During a flight (especially a long-haul flight), get up, walk around, and stretch your legs every 60 to 90 minutes to keep your blood flowing. Other preventative measures include frequent flexing of the legs while sitting, drinking lots of water, and avoiding alcohol and sleeping pills.

If you have a history of deep vein thrombosis, heart disease, or any other condition that puts you at high risk, some experts recommend wearing compression stockings or taking anticoagulants when you fly; always ask your physician about the best course for you.

Staying Connected by Cellphone or E-mail

The three letters that define much of the world's **wireless capabilities** are GSM (Global System for Mobiles), a big, seamless network that makes for easy cross-border cellphone use throughout Europe and dozens of other countries worldwide. In the United States, T-Mobile, AT&T Wireless, and Cingular use this quasi-universal system; in Canada, Microcell and some Rogers customers are GSM, and all Europeans and most Australians use GSM.

If your cellphone is on a GSM system, and you have a world-capable multiband phone such as many Sony Ericsson, Motorola, or Samsung models, you can make and receive calls across civilized areas on much of the globe, from Andorra to Uganda. Just call your wireless operator and activate *international roaming* on your account. Unfortunately, per-minute charges can be high — usually $1 to $1.50 in Western Europe and up to $5 in places like Russia and Indonesia.

That's why it's important to buy an *unlocked* world phone from the get-go. Many cellphone operators sell *locked* phones that restrict you from using any other removable computer memory phone chip card (called a **SIM card**) other than the ones they supply. Having an unlocked phone allows you to install a cheap, prepaid SIM card (found at a local retailer) in your destination country. (Show your phone to the salesperson; not all phones work on all networks.) You get a local phone number — and much, much lower calling rates. Getting an already locked phone unlocked can be a complicated process, but it can be done; just call your cellular operator and say you're going abroad for several months and want to use the phone with a local provider.

For many, **renting** a phone is a good idea. (Even owners of cellphones with international calling capabilities have to rent new phones if they're traveling to non-GSM regions, such as Japan or Korea.) Although you can rent a phone from any number of overseas sites, including kiosks at airports and at car rental agencies, I suggest renting the phone before you leave home. One good place is www.roadpost.com. You can rent a phone from them that starts at $79 for basic service for up to 30 days. The phone comes with your own number, voice mail, call forwarding, adaptors and accessories for your travel destinations, and free 24/7 technical support. When you return home, just ship the phone back to Road Post in the pre-paid envelope they provide. You can give loved ones and business associates your new number, make sure the phone works, and take the phone wherever you go — especially helpful for overseas trips through several countries, where local phone-rental agencies often bill in local currency and may not let you take the phone to another country.

In France, phone rental isn't cheap. You usually pay $40 to $50 per week, plus airtime fees of at least a dollar a minute. One option is www.mobirent.fr, a French company that specializes in phone rental and will deliver to your lodging. The phone and its accessories are accompanied by one of three pricing plans: first class, business class, or economy. Economy rates are 52€ ($60) for 90 minutes of calling in France, 162€ ($186) for 90 minutes of calls to North America, and 243€ ($279) for 90 minutes of calls to the rest of the world. With rates like this, it may be more prudent to just buy a cellphone in France. For around $100, you get a phone and accessories, and some free minutes. Cellphone stores abound in Paris: the biggest are **SFR** (there's a branch at 87 rue de Sèvres, 6e, Métro: Vaneau), **France Télécom** (a central location is 46 bis rue de Louvre, 1e, Métro: Les Halles), and **Bouygues Télécom** (33 rue de Rivoli, 4e, Métro: Hôtel de Ville). You can also ask about rental policies at these stores.

Accessing the Internet Away from Home

Travelers have any number of ways to check their e-mail and access the Internet on the road. Of course, using your own laptop — or even a PDA (personal digital assistant) or electronic organizer with a modem — gives you the most flexibility. But even if you don't have a computer, you can still access your e-mail and even your office computer from cybercafes.

It's hard nowadays to find a city that *doesn't* have a few cybercafes. Although there's no definitive directory for cybercafes — they are independent businesses, after all — three places to start looking are at www.cybercaptive.com and www.cybercafe.com.

Aside from formal cybercafes, most **youth hostels** nowadays have at least one computer you can use to get on the Internet. And most **public libraries** across the world offer Internet access free or for a small charge. You can always find a cybercafe near a college; in France the Latin Quarter abounds with them around rue des Écoles and boulevard St-Michel. Try the 24-hour **XS Arena St. Michel** at 53 rue de la Harpe, 5e (☎ **01-44-07-38-39**). More centrally located, in Forum des Halles, is **Cybercafé de Paris,** 15 rue Halles, 1e, (☎ **01-42-21-13-13**). Avoid **hotel business centers** unless you're willing to pay exorbitant rates.

Most major airports now have **Internet kiosks** scattered throughout their gates. These kiosks, which you also see in shopping malls, hotel lobbies, and tourist information offices around the world, give you basic Web access for a per-minute fee that's usually higher than cybercafe prices. The kiosks' clunkiness and high price mean they should be avoided whenever possible.

To retrieve your e-mail, ask your **Internet Service Provider** (ISP) if it has a Web-based interface tied to your existing e-mail account. If your ISP doesn't have such an interface, you can use the free **mail2web** service (www.mail2web.com) to view and reply to your home e-mail. For more flexibility, you may want to open a free, Web-based e-mail account with **Yahoo! Mail** (http://mail.yahoo.com). (Microsoft's Hotmail is another popular option, but Hotmail has severe spam problems.) Your home ISP may be able to forward your e-mail to the Web-based account automatically.

If you need to access files on your office computer, look into a service called **GoToMyPC** (www.gotomypc.com). The service provides a Web-based interface for you to access and manipulate a distant PC from anywhere — even a cybercafe — provided your target PC is on and has an always-on connection to the Internet (such as with Road Runner cable). The service offers top-quality security, but if you're worried about hackers, use your own laptop rather than a cybercafe computer to access the GoToMyPC system.

If you're bringing your own computer, the buzzword in computer access to familiarize yourself with is **wi-fi** (wireless fidelity) — more and more hotels, cafes, and retailers are signing on as wireless hotspots from where you can get high-speed connection without cable wires, networking hardware, or a phone line. You can get Wi-fi connection one of several ways. Many laptops sold in the last year have built-in Wi-fi capability (an 802.11b wireless Ethernet connection). Mac owners have their own networking technology, Apple AirPort. For those with older computers, an 802.11b/**wi-fi card** (around $50) can be plugged into your laptop.

You sign up for wireless access service much as you do cellphone service, through a plan offered by one of several commercial companies that make wireless service available in airports, hotel lobbies, and coffee shops, primarily in the United States (followed by the United Kingdom and Japan). **T-Mobile Hotspot** (www.t-mobile.com/hotspot) serves up wireless connections at more than 1,000 Starbucks coffee shops nationwide and at the seven Starbucks locations in Paris, including the newest at 91 bd. St-Germain, 6e, Métro: Odéon). **Boingo** (www.boingo.com) and

Wayport (www.wayport.com) have networks in airports and high-class hotel lobbies. IPass (www.ipass.com) providers also give you access to a few hundred wireless hotel lobby setups. Best of all, you don't need to be staying at the Four Seasons to use the hotel's network; just set yourself up on a nice couch in the lobby. The companies' pricing policies can be complicated, with a variety of monthly, per-connection, and per-minute plans, but in general you pay around $30 a month for limited access — and as more and more companies jump on the wireless bandwagon, prices are likely to get more competitive.

Some companies provide **free wireless networks** in cities around the world. To locate these free hotspots, go to www.personaltelco.net/index.cgi/WirelessCommunities.

If wi-fi is not available at your destination, most business-class hotels throughout the world offer dataports for laptop modems, and a few thousand hotels in the United States and Europe now offer free high-speed Internet access using an Ethernet network cable. You can bring your own cables, but most hotels rent them for around $10. **Call your hotel in advance** to see what your options are.

In addition, major Internet Service Providers (ISP) have **local access numbers** around the world, allowing you to go online by simply placing a local call. Check your ISP's Web site or call its toll-free number and ask how you can use your current account away from home, and how much it will cost. If you're traveling outside the reach of your ISP, the **iPass** network has dial-up numbers in most of the world's countries. You have to sign up with an iPass provider, who then tells you how to set up your computer for your destination(s). For a list of iPass providers, go to www.ipass.com and click on <u>Individuals Buy Now</u>. One solid provider is **i2roam** (☎ **866-811-6209** or 920-235-0475; www.i2roam.com).

Keeping Up with Airline Security Measures

With the federalization of airport security, security procedures at U.S. airports are more stable and consistent than ever. Generally, you'll be fine if you arrive at the airport **one hour** before a domestic flight and **two hours** before an international flight; if you show up late, tell an airline employee to get whisked to the front of the line (usually).

Bring a **current, government-issued photo ID** such as a driver's license or passport. Keep your ID at the ready to show at check-in, the security checkpoint, and sometimes even the gate. (Children under 18 do not need government-issued photo IDs for domestic flights, but they do for international flights to most countries.)

In 2003, the Transportation Security Administration (TSA) phased out **gate check-in** at all U.S. airports. And **e-tickets** have made paper tickets nearly obsolete. If you have an e-ticket, you can beat the ticket-counter lines by using airport **electronic kiosks** or even **online check-in** from your home computer. Online check-in involves logging on to your airline's Web site, accessing your reservation, and printing out your boarding pass — and the airline may even offer you bonus miles to do so! If you're using a kiosk at the airport, bring the credit card you used to book the ticket or your frequent-flier card. Print out your boarding pass from the kiosk and simply proceed to the security checkpoint with your pass and a photo ID. If you're checking bags or looking to snag an exit-row seat, you can do so using most airline kiosks. Even the smaller airlines are employing the kiosk system, but always call your airline to make sure these alternatives are available. **Curbside check-in** is also a good way to avoid lines, although a few airlines still ban curbside check-in; call before you go.

Security checkpoint lines are getting shorter than they were during 2001 and 2002, but some doozies remain. If you have trouble standing for long periods of time, tell an airline employee; the airline will provide a wheelchair. Speed up security by not wearing metal objects such as big belt buckles. If you have metallic body parts, a note from your doctor can prevent a long chat with the security screeners. Keep in mind that only ticketed passengers are allowed past security, except for folks escorting disabled passengers or children.

Federalization has stabilized what you can carry on and what you can't. The general rule is that sharp things are out, nail clippers are okay, and food and beverages must be passed through the X-ray machine — but that security screeners can't make you drink from your coffee cup. Bring food in your carry-on rather than checking it, as explosive-detection machines used on checked luggage have been known to mistake food (especially chocolate, for some reason) for bombs. Travelers in the United States are allowed one carry-on bag, plus a personal item such as a purse, briefcase, or laptop bag. Carry-on hoarders can stuff all sorts of things into a laptop bag; as long as it has a laptop in it, it's still considered a personal item. The TSA has issued a list of restricted items; check its Web site (www.tsa.gov/public/index.jsp) for details.

Airport screeners may decide that your checked luggage needs to be searched by hand. You can now purchase luggage locks that allow screeners to open and re-lock a checked bag if hand-searching is necessary. Look for Travel Sentry certified locks at luggage or travel shops and Brookstone stores (you can buy them online at www.brookstone.com). These locks, approved by the TSA, can be opened by luggage inspectors with a special code or key. For more information on the locks, visit www.travelsentry.org. If you use something other than TSA-approved locks, your lock will be cut off your suitcase if a TSA agent needs to hand-search your luggage.

Part III
Settling into Paris

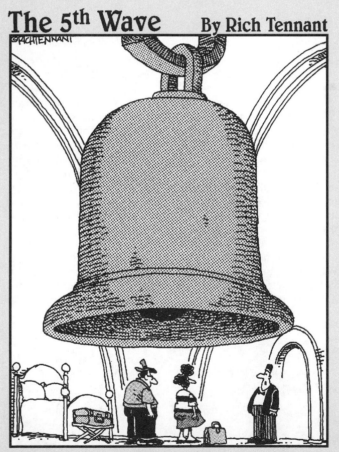

The 5th Wave   By Rich Tennant

"Welcome to the Hotel d'Notre Dame. If there's anything else I can do for you, please don't hesitate to ring."

In this part . . .

This section helps you go from point A to point B without wasting time and money. Better yet, it suggests great places to stay, and tells you all you want to know about eating French style, then directs you to some memorable eateries. Chapter 8 guides you from the airport to your hotel, describes the most popular neighborhoods, and tells you where to go for information after you're in Paris. Need to know how to get around by subway, taxi, bus, and on foot? Read Chapter 9 and prepare to start zipping around the city in no time. Chapter 10 proves that Paris is indeed a feast with an overview of the local dining scene, advice on how to trim the fat from your food budget, and recommendations for some of the best restaurants, brasseries, cafes, wine bars, tea salons, and sandwich places in the city. A handy index cross-references all the dining establishments by neighborhood, price, and type.

Chapter 8

Arriving and Getting Oriented

● ●

In This Chapter

▶ Passing through passport control and Customs

▶ Securing transportation to your hotel

▶ Discovering Paris by neighborhood

▶ Getting information on Paris in Paris

▶ Navigating the city

● ●

*T*he Paris experience begins for most on the plane, where announce-ments are made in English and French. For others it begins at the airport — with bi- and tri-lingual signs directing you to passport control and baggage claim. The smell of cigarettes. Free luggage carts! Horrendous lines at passport control (see the first section for an expla-nation). Little dogs peek out of bags or prance at the end of leashes. People dress more formally than at home. It all may seem a little aston-ishing, especially when you arrive at the spaceship-like Charles de Gaulle Aérogare 1 with its pod-like terminals and extra long corridors — usually at some ungodly early morning hour. But, the important thing is you've arrived! Now you can move on to the first item of the day — getting from the airport to your hotel.

Navigating Your Way through Passport Control and Customs

Most visitors to Paris land at Charles de Gaulle Airport, the larger, busier, and more modern airport, commonly known as CDG and some-times called Roissy–Charles de Gaulle. Nearly all direct flights from North America land at Charles de Gaulle. Bilevel Terminal 1 (Aérogare 1) is the older and smaller of the two terminals and is used by foreign air-lines. Narrow escalators and moving sidewalks connect its pod-like cement terminals. The bright and spacious Terminal 2 (Aérogare 2) is divided into halls A through F and is used by Air France, domestic and intra-European airlines, and some foreign airlines, including Air Canada.

Hall 2E, however, has been closed since May 2004, when it collapsed due to architectural flaws less than a year after opening for service. This has caused delays as flights (mostly Air France) scheduled to land here have had to be redirected to other terminals or, in some cases, to nearby airports. You may find long lines at Passport Control and elsewhere as staff handle the Terminal 2E overflow. Keep this in mind for your return journey and arrive early if you leave France out of Charles de Gaulle.

A free shuttle bus (*navette*) connects Terminal 1 and 2. Signs in French and English in both terminals direct you to Customs, baggage claim, and transportation to the city. Staff at information desks also are on hand to answer questions.

Two lines are set up for passport control, one for European Union nationals and the other for everyone else. These lines can move quite quickly or horrendously slowly; it usually depends on the clerk checking your passport and riffling through your luggage.

When passing through Customs, keep in mind that restrictions are different for citizens of the European Union than they are for citizens of non-EU countries. As a non-EU national, you can bring in 200 cigarettes or 100 cigarillos or 50 cigars or 250 grams of smoking tobacco duty-free. You can also bring in two liters of wine and one liter of alcohol of more than 38.80 proof. In addition, you can bring in 50 grams of perfume, a quarter-liter of toilet water, 500 grams of coffee, and 100 grams of tea. Travelers 15 years old and older can also bring in 171€ ($197) in other goods; for those 14 years of age and younger, the limit is 85.75€ ($99). (See Chapter 12 for what you're allowed to bring home.) Because you probably aren't going to need to make a claim, you should be waved through by an officer pretty quickly. Customs officers do, however, pull random travelers over to check luggage. Whenever that happens to you, don't be offended; be polite and as helpful as you can, and if you don't speak French, let them know by saying, "Je ne parle pas français" (zhe ne *parl* pah frahn-*say)*.

 Regardless of the terminal, you need euro to get from the airport into Paris. You can find ATMs in the arrival areas of the airports along with *bureaux de change,* where you can exchange dollars for euro, but you're better off buying and bringing 200€ from your bank at home. Airport ATMs are notorious for being broken when you need them most, and the airport bureaux de change are just as notorious for their bad rates of exchange.

Making Your Way to Your Hotel

You can travel to and from the airports by several different means, and the amount of text here notwithstanding, they're all easy!

If you fly into Charles de Gaulle

Charles de Gaulle Airport (CDG) is located 14½ miles (23km) northeast of downtown Paris. Transportation into the city is plentiful.

Taking a taxi

Probably the easiest, but certainly not the cheapest, mode of transportation to your hotel from the airport is by **taxi**. A cab into town from Charles de Gaulle takes 40 to 50 minutes, depending on traffic, and costs about 50€ ($57.50) from 7 a.m. to 8 p.m., and about 40 percent more at other times. Taxi drivers are required to turn the meter on and charge the price indicated plus 0.90€ ($1.05) for each piece of luggage stowed in the trunk. If your French is poor or nonexistent, writing down the name and full address of your hotel is a good idea. The five-digit postal code is the most important morsel of information, because it tells the driver to the arrondissement where to take you. Check the meter before you pay — rip-offs of arriving tourists are not uncommon. Whenever you strongly think that you may have been overcharged, demand a receipt (*un reçu, ray*-soo), which drivers are obligated to provide, and contact the Paris Préfecture of Police (☎ **01-53-71-53-71**).

The taxi stands at Charles de Gaulle:

- ✔ **CDG Terminal 1:** Exit 16, arrivals level

- ✔ **CDG Terminals 2A and 2C:** 2A Exit 6, 2C Exit 6

- ✔ **CDG Terminals 2B and 2D:** 2B Exit 8, 2D Exit 8

- ✔ **CDG Terminal 2F:** Exit 0.10, arrivals level

Taking a shuttle

If you don't want to schlep your bags through Paris's streets and Métro stations, taking an airport shuttle is definitely the way to go. Although more expensive than airport buses and trains, shuttles are much cheaper and roomier than taxis. And you can reserve a seat in advance and pay by credit card. **World Shuttle,** 13 rue Voltaire, 94400 Vitry-sur-Seine (☎ **01-46-80-14-67;** www.world-shuttles.com) costs 25€ ($29) for one person, 17€ ($20) per person for two or more from Charles de Gaulle and Orly. Before 5:30 a.m., it's 70€ ($81) for two to four people.

PariShuttle, 128 bis av. Paris, 94800 Villejuif (☎ **01-53-39-18-18;** www.parishuttle.com) offers a similar service. While you wait for your bags, call PariShuttle's toll-free number to confirm pickup (☎ **08-00-63-34-40**). You're picked up in a minivan at Orly or Charles de Gaulle and taken to your hotel for 25€ ($29) for one person, 18€ ($21) per person for groups of two to four people, and 15€ ($17) per person for five to eight people. The cost for children aged three to ten is 10€ ($12).

Riding the rails

A good option when you're not overloaded with baggage and want to keep your expenses down is to take the suburban commuter train to the Métro. **RER** (Réseau Express Régional) **Line B** stops near Terminals 1 and 2. Easy, cheap, and convenient, you can ride both to and from the airport from 5 a.m. to midnight Monday through Friday, and 7 a.m. to 9 p.m. weekends.

Free shuttle buses connect terminals CDG 1 and CDG 2 to the RER train station. You can pick up the free shuttle bus at:

- ✔ **CDG Terminal 1:** Follow RER signs to exit on arrivals level

- ✔ **CDG Terminal 2A:** Exit A8

- ✔ **CDG Terminal 2B:** Exit B6

- ✔ **CDG Terminal 2C:** Exit C8

- ✔ **CDG Terminal 2D:** Exit D6

- ✔ **CDG Terminal 2F:** Exit 2.06

You can also take a walkway to the RER station — ask an airport employee or look for the round RER logo. (RER is pronounced air-uh-air in French.)

Buy the **RER** ticket, which costs 7.85€ ($9) for adults, 5.55€ ($6.40) for children, at the RER ticket counter and hang onto it in case of ticket inspection. (You can be fined if you can't produce your ticket for an inspector.) In any case, you need your ticket later to get off the RER system and onto the Métro.

Depending where your hotel is located, you exit either on the Right or the Left Bank. From the airport station, trains depart about every 15 minutes for the half-hour trip into town and stop on the **Right Bank** at Gare du Nord and Châtelet–Les Halles, and on the **Left Bank** at St-Michel, Luxembourg, Port-Royal, and Denfert-Rochereau, before heading south out of the city.

Boarding the bus

A bus is better than the RER if

- ✔ You're heading into Paris during off-peak driving hours, and you're not in a hurry.

- ✔ Your hotel is located near one of the drop-off points. *Note:* The bus is most convenient for the hotels I recommend in the 2e and 8e arrondissements. If you're staying outside these arrondissements, you can take a taxi from the shuttle drop-off point or board the closest subway if you aren't loaded down with luggage. If a bus isn't convenient, check out the door-to-door airport shuttle services in the earlier "Taking a shuttle" section.

If your hotel is located on the **Right Bank,** in the **8e, 16e,** or **17e** arrondissements, take **Air France coach Line 2,** which stops at rue Gouvion Saint-Cyr at Porte Maillot before ending up at 1 av. Carnot at place Charles de Gaulle–Étoile, the name for the huge traffic roundabout at the Arc de Triomphe. The bus costs 10€ ($12) one-way and runs every 15 minutes from 5:40 a.m. to 11:00 p.m. (from 6 a.m. to 11 p.m. back to the airport). You needn't have flown on an Air France flight to use the service, and tickets are available right on the bus. The trip from the airport into the city and vice versa takes about 40 minutes in light traffic, such as on weekend mornings. During weekday morning rush hour, however, the same trip can take twice as long, if not longer. Pick up the coach from:

- ✔ **CDG Terminal 1:** Exit 34, arrivals level

- ✔ **CDG Terminals 2A and 2C:** Exit 5

- ✔ **CDG Terminals 2B and 2D:** Exit 6

- ✔ **CDG Terminal 2F:** Exit 0.07, arrivals level

If your hotel is located on the **Right Bank** near the **Bastille** (11e or 12e) or on the **Left Bank** in **Montparnasse** (14e), take the **Air France Line 4** coach, which stops at boulevard Diderot in front of the Gare de Lyon before ending up on rue du Commandant Mouchotte near the back of the Gare de Montparnasse. The bus costs 11.50€ ($13) one-way and runs every 30 minutes from 7:00 a.m. to 9:30 p.m. both to and from the airport. It takes about 50 minutes to get from the airport into the city in light traffic. Catch this coach from:

- ✔ **CDG Terminal 1:** Exit 34, arrivals level

- ✔ **CDG Terminals 2A and 2C:** Exit 2 from Terminal 2C

- ✔ **CDG Terminals 2B and 2D:** Exit 2 from Terminal 2B

- ✔ **CDG Terminal 2F:** Exit 0.07, arrivals level

Take the **Roissybus** if your hotel is on the **Right Bank** near the **Opéra** (2e or 9e). It costs 8.30€ ($9.55) and leaves every 15 minutes from the airport between 6 a.m. and 11 p.m. (from 5:45 a.m. to 11:46 p.m. back to the airport). The drop-off point is on rue Scribe, a block from the **Opéra Garnier** near American Express. You can get to your destination in 45 to 50 minutes in regular traffic. Buy your tickets in the small office next to where the bus is parked. Pick up this coach from:

- ✔ **CDG Terminal 1:** Exit 30, arrivals level

- ✔ **CDG Terminals 2A and 2C:** Exit 9 from Terminal 2A

- ✔ **CDG Terminals 2B and 2D:** Exit 11 from Terminal 2D

- ✔ **CDG Terminal 2F:** Exit 0.08, arrivals level

If you fly into Orly

Orly Airport, 8½ miles (14km) south of the city, has two terminals — **Ouest** (West) and **Sud** (South) — and English speakers find the terminals easy to navigate. French domestic flights land at Orly Ouest, and intra-European and intercontinental flights land at Orly Sud. Shuttle buses connect these terminals, and other shuttles connect them to Charles de Gaulle every 30 minutes or so. A tourist information desk is conveniently located on the arrivals level of both terminals.

Like Charles de Gaulle Airport, two lines are set up for passport control; one for European Union nationals, one for visitors carrying passports from all other countries, and you should be waved through Customs. (See the previous section, "Navigating Your Way through Passport Control and Customs" for information about what you can bring into France.)

Taking a taxi

A cab from Orly into Paris costs about 25€ to 30€ ($29–$35), depending on traffic, and takes anywhere from 25 minutes to an hour. The taxi stand at Orly Sud is just outside Exit L; at Orly Ouest it's at Exit I. The same advice as when taking a taxi from Charles de Gaulle holds true here: Write down the full name and address of your hotel for the driver. And remember that cabs charge 0.90€ ($1.05) for each piece of luggage put in the trunk.

Busing is best — sometimes

Take the **Air France coach Line 1** if your hotel is located on the **Left Bank** near Les Invalides (7e). Buses leave Orly Sud at Exit K, Platform 6 and Orly Ouest at Exit D, arrivals level every 12 to 15 minutes. The trip takes 30 minutes and costs 5.80€ ($6.70). You can request that the bus stop at Montparnasse-Duroc (14e).

The cheapest trip into town is on the **Jetbus.** You take this bus from Orly to Métro station Villejuif–Louis Aragon in south Paris (13e). It costs 5.15€ ($6) for the 15-minute journey. Beginning at 6:34 a.m., the bus leaves every 15 minutes from Orly Sud, Exit H, and Platform 2 and from Orly Ouest at Exit C on the arrivals level. The bus departs Paris for Orly from 6:15 a.m. to 10:15 p.m. An **Orly bus** also operates from 6 a.m. to 11:30 p.m. from Exit J, arrivals level at Orly Ouest, and from Exit H Platform 4 at Orly Sud to the Left Bank's Denfert-Rochereau station. It costs 5.80€ ($6.70) for the 25-minute journey. It departs Paris for Orly from 5:35 a.m. to 11:00 p.m.

Taking the train

You can take the **RER C line,** but it's a bit of a hassle. You catch a free shuttle bus from Exit G, Platform 1 at Orly Sud and Exit G on the arrivals level at Orly Ouest to the **Rungis** station, where RER C trains leave every 15 minutes for **Gare d'Austerlitz** (13e). A one-way fare is 5.50€ ($6.30), 3.35€ ($3.85) for children four to ten years old. The trip into the city takes 30 minutes, making various stops along the Seine on the **Left Bank.**

If you're staying on the **Right Bank,** you can take the **Orlyval/RER B line** to **Antony** Métro station. From Orly Sud, the train departs from Exit K near the baggage-claim area; from Orly Ouest, it leaves from an area between Exit W and Terminal 1 on the departures level. You connect at the **Antony** RER station where you board the RER B train to Paris. Hold onto the ticket because you will need it to get into the Métro/RER system. A trip to the Châtelet station on the Right Bank takes about 30 minutes and costs 8.85€ ($10) for adults, 4.40€ ($5.05) for children. Once in Paris, the train stops at **Denfert-Rochereau, Port-Royal, Luxembourg,** and **St-Michel** on the Left Bank, and then crosses to the Right Bank for stops at **Châtelet** and **Gare du Nord.**

Figuring Out the Neighborhoods

You arrive at your hotel, check in, and maybe unpack a little. But taking a nap prolongs your jet lag. So, go out and act like a Parisian by having a cup of coffee at a cafe before getting ready to explore. *Note:* Those little shots of espresso you get in Paris cafes have less caffeine than a mug of American-style coffee or a cup of tea, so ask for the more American style *café allongé* (al-lohn-*jay*).

The Seine River divides Paris into two halves: the **Right Bank** (*Rive Droite*) on the north side of the river and the **Left Bank** (*Rive Gauche*) on the south side of the river. The larger Right Bank is where you find the city's business sector, stately monuments, and high-fashion industry. The Left Bank has the publishing houses, universities, and a reputation as bohemian because students, philosophers, and creative types have been congregating here for centuries. Two of the city's tallest monuments are on the Left Bank — the **Tour Montparnasse** (that lonely tall black building hovering on the edge of the city) and the **Eiffel Tower. Sacré Coeur,** the white wedding-cake of a basilica (church) on the hill overlooking Paris, is considered to be on the Right Bank, and so are **Notre-Dame** and **Sainte-Chapelle,** although neither is technically on any bank. They're actually islands in the Seine.

The city is divided into 20 numbered *arrondissements* (municipal districts). And although visitors tend to think of Paris in terms of neighborhood names, Parisians think of the city in terms of arrondissement numbers. For example, ask a home-towner where he works, and he's more likely to say "in the 5th" and not "in the Latin Quarter." The layout of these districts follows a distinct pattern. The first (abbreviated 1er for *premiere*) arrondissement is the dead center of Paris, comprising an area around Notre-Dame and the Louvre. From there, the rest of the districts spiral outward, clockwise, in ascending order. The lower the arrondissement number, the more central the location. To get a better idea of what I'm talking about, consult the "Paris Neighborhoods" map.

Arrondissement numbers are key to locating an address in Paris. And this book lists addresses the way they appear in Paris, with the

Paris Neighborhoods

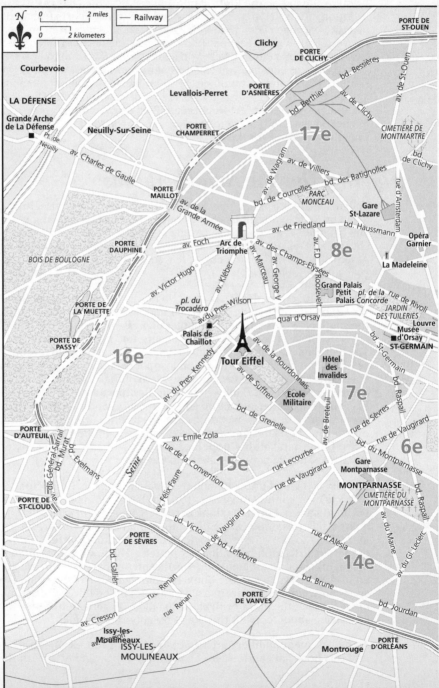

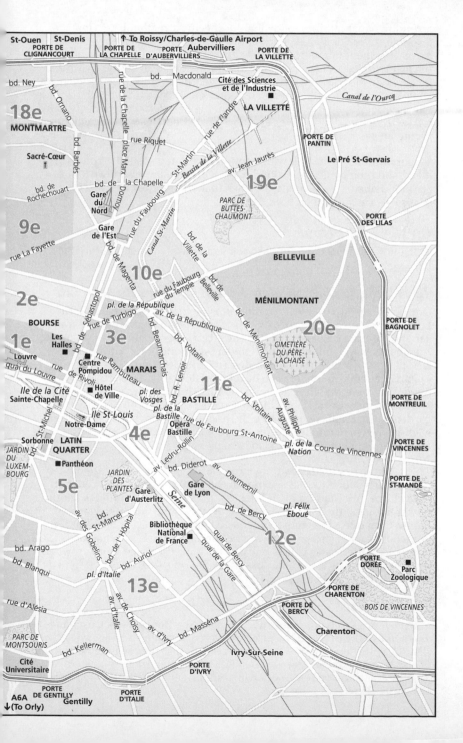

arrondissement number following the specific street address (for instance, 29 rue de Rivoli, 4e, is in the fourth arrondissement). Arrondissement numbers are noted on street signs and are indicated by the last two digits of the postal code. For instance, an address with a postal code of 75007 is located in the seventh arrondissement. Once you know in which arrondissement an address is located, finding that spot is much easier. Numbers on buildings running parallel to the Seine usually follow the course of the river east to west. On north-south streets, numbering begins at the river.

Neighborhoods in the following sections are listed first by arrondissement, and then by neighborhood name. Only the better-known arrondissements — meaning the ones that you're most likely to stay in or visit — are mentioned here.

On the Right Bank

The following are the neighborhoods you're likely to visit on the Right Bank.

1er: Musée du Louvre/Palais-Royal/Les Halles/Ile de la Cité

One of the world's greatest art museums (some say *the* greatest), the **Louvre,** still lures all visitors to Paris to the 1er arrondissement. You can see the contrast between many of the city's elegant addresses along the rue de Rivoli and arched arcades under which all kinds of touristy junk is sold. Walk through the **Jardin des Tuileries,** the most formal garden of Paris, and take in the classic beauty, opulence, and wealth of the **place Vendôme,** which is home to the Ritz Hotel. Browse the arcaded shops and view the striped columns and seasonal art on display in the garden of the **Palais Royal,** once the home to Cardinal Richelieu. The slightly seedy **Forum des Halles,** an above- and below-ground shopping and entertainment center, is also here.

This arrondissement tends to be crowded, and hotel prices are higher during Paris's high tourist season (in early fall) because the area is so convenient. Aristocratic town houses, courtyards, and antiques shops, flower markets, the **Palais de Justice, Notre-Dame Cathedral** and **Sainte-Chapelle,** (the chapel built in 1243 for St. Louis, famous for its gorgeous stained glass windows) are also part of the 1er on Ile de la Cité, an island in the Seine. This is one of Paris's prettiest and most crowded neighborhoods, as is its sister island, Ile St-Louis (see "4e: Ile St-Louis/ Centre Pompidou" below).

2e: La Bourse

Often overlooked by tourists, the 2e houses the **Bourse** (stock exchange), and some of the pretty 19th-century covered shopping passageways. The district, lying between the Grands Boulevards and the rue Etienne Marcel, is also home to the **Sentier** area, where the garment trade is located, and wholesale fashion outlets abound. Sex shops and prostitutes line parts of the rue St-Denis.

3e: Le Marais

Le Marais (translated as "the swamp") is one of Paris's hippest neighborhoods, and one of the city's most popular attractions, the **Musée Picasso**, and one of the more interesting museums, **Musée Carnavalet,** are located here. Paris's old Jewish neighborhood is located around the rue des Rosiers, and the rue Vieille-du-Temple is home to numerous gay bars and boutiques.

4e: Ile St-Louis/Centre Pompidou

Aristocratic town houses, courtyards, and antiques shops, the **Brasserie Ile-St-Louis** (a historic brasserie with literary associations), **Berthillon** (reputed to be Paris's best ice cream), the **Centre Georges Pompidou museum,** and the **place des Vosges** make up the 4e arrondissement which is partly on the Ile St-Louis and partly in the Marais district. The area around the Centre Pompidou is one of Paris's more eclectic; you see everyone from pierced and Goth-style art students to chic Parisians sipping coffee at Café Beaubourg to tourists buying football shirts from one of the many souvenir stores.

8e: Champs-Elysées/Madeleine

The 8e is the heart of the Right Bank, and its showcase is the **Champs-Elysées.** The Champs stretches from the **Arc de Triomphe** to the city's oldest monument, the Egyptian obelisk on **place de la Concorde.** The fashion houses, the most elegant hotels, expensive restaurants and shops, and the most fashionably attired Parisians are here.

9e: Opéra Garnier/Pigalle

Everything, from the **Quartier de l'Opéra** (the neighborhood around the Opéra Garnier) to the strip joints of **Pigalle,** falls within the 9e, which was radically altered by Baron Haussmann's 19th-century redevelopment projects; his Grands Boulevards radiate through the district. You'll probably pay a visit to the 9e to shop at its famous department stores **Au Printemps** and **Galeries Lafayette.** Try to visit the **Opéra Garnier** (Paris Opera House), which recently reopened after an expensive restoration, worth a visit for its gorgeously restored ceiling by Marc Chagall.

10e: Gare du Nord/Gare de l'Est

In the movie *Amélie,* the young heroine likes to skip stones on the Canal St-Martin in the newly hip neighborhood of the same name with a burgeoning night scene, located here. Though most of this arrondissement is dreary (**Gare du Nord** and **Gare de l'Est** are two of the city's four main train stations), the canal's **quai de Valmy** and **quai de Jemmapes** are scenic, tree-lined promenades. The classic movie *Hotel du Nord* was also filmed here.

11e: Opéra Bastille

The 11e has few landmarks or famous museums, but the area has become a mecca for hordes of young Parisians looking for casual, inexpensive nightlife. Always crowded on weekends and in summer, the overflow retires to the steps of the **Opéra Bastille,** where inline skaters and skateboarders skate and teens flirt.

16e: Trocadéro/Bois de Boulogne

This area of Paris is where the moneyed people live. Highlights include the **Bois de Boulogne** (the huge wooded park on Paris's western edge), the **Jardin du Trocadéro** (known for its famous fountains bordering the Eiffel Tower), the **Musée de Balzac,** the **Musée Guimet** (famous for its Asian collections), and the **Cimetière de Passy,** resting place of Manet, Talleyrand, Giraudoux, and Debussy. One of the largest arrondissements, the 16e is known today for its exclusivity, its BCBG residents (*bon chic bon genre,* or yuppie), its upscale rents, and some rather posh (and, according to its critics, rather smug) residential boulevards. The arrondissement includes what some visitors consider the best place in Paris from which to view the Eiffel Tower, the **place du Trocadéro.**

18e: Montmartre

The **Moulin Rouge,** the **Basilica of Sacré-Coeur** (the white domed structure on a hill overlooking Paris), and the **place du Tertre** (the square filled with restaurants behind it) are only some of the attractions in this outer arrondissement. Take a walk through the winding old streets here, and you feel transported into another era. The **Bateau-Lavoir,** Picasso's first studio in Paris, is also here. The city's most famous flea market, **Marché aux Puces de la Porte de St-Ouen,** is nearby in the 20e.

On the Left Bank

The following are neighborhoods you're likely to visit on the Left Bank.

5e: Latin Quarter

Bookstores, schools, churches, nightclubs, student dives, Roman ruins, publishing houses, and expensive boutiques characterize this district, which is called *Latin* because students and professors at the Sorbonne, located here, once spoke Latin exclusively. Stroll along **quai de Montebello,** inspecting the inventories of the *bouquinistes* (booksellers), and wander the shops in the old streets of rue de la Huchette and rue de la Harpe (but don't eat here; you can find much better places). The 5e also stretches down to the **Panthéon,** and to the steep cobblestone rue Mouffetard behind it, where you can visit one of the city's best produce markets, eat at a variety of ethnic restaurants, or raise a glass in très cool Café Contrescarpe.

6e: St-Germain and the Luxembourg Gardens

The art school that turned away Rodin, the **École des Beaux-Arts,** is here, and so are some of the chicest designers around. But the secret of the district lies in discovering its narrow streets and hidden squares. Everywhere you turn here, you encounter famous historical and literary associations. For instance, the restaurant **Brasserie Lipp** is where

Hemingway lovingly recalls eating potato salad in *A Moveable Feast,* and the **Café les Deux Magots** is depicted in the movie adaptation of Hemingway's *The Sun Also Rises.* The 6e takes in the **rue de Fleurus** where Gertrude Stein lived with Alice B. Toklas, and down the street is the wonderful **Luxembourg Gardens,** probably local residents' most loved park. (Try to find the Statue of Liberty in the garden.)

7e: Near the Eiffel Tower and Musée d'Orsay

The city's most famous symbol, the **Eiffel Tower,** dominates the 7e, and part of the **St-Germain** neighborhood is here, too. The **Hôtel des Invalides,** which contains **Napoléon's Tomb** and the **Musée de l'Armée,** is also in the 7e, in addition to the **Musée Rodin** and the **Musée d'Orsay,** the world's premier showcase of 19th-century French art and culture. The Left Bank's only department store, **Le Bon Marché,** is also located here, and so is a warren of streets along which beautiful shoes, clothing, and objects for the home are sold.

13e: Butte-aux-Cailles and Chinatown

Although high-rises dominate much of 13e, a nightlife scene has emerged on the dance barges along the **quai Tolbiac** (where the new **Bibliothèque François Mitterand** sits) and in the cozy network of winding streets that make up the **Butte-aux-Cailles** (literally hill of pebbles) neighborhood. The 13e has also become a lively hub for Paris's Asian community with Vietnamese and Chinese restaurants along **avenue d'Ivry** and **avenue de Choisy** next to stores selling all kinds of items from France's former colonies in Southeast Asia. The Chinese New Year Parade takes place here in late January or February.

14e: Montparnasse

Montparnasse is the former stomping ground of the *lost generation* — writers Gertrude Stein, Ernest Hemingway, Edna St. Vincent Millay, Ford Madox Ford, and other American expatriates gathered here in the 1920s. After World War II, it ceased to be the center of intellectual life in Paris, but the memories linger. Some of the world's most famous literary cafés, including **La Rotonde, Le Select, Le Dôme,** and **La Coupole,** are in the northern end of this large arrondissement, near the Rodin statue of Balzac at the junction of boulevard Montparnasse and boulevard Raspail. Some of those same literary giants (most notably Jean-Paul Sartre and Simone de Beauvoir) are buried nearby, in the Cimitière du Montparnasse. At its southern end, the arrondissement contains pleasant residential neighborhoods filled with well-designed apartment buildings, many built between 1910 and 1940.

Finding Information after You Arrive

The Office de Tourisme et des Congrès de Paris is no longer headquartered on the Champs-Elysées, but has branches throughout the city at the following locations *Note:* These centers are closed on May 1.

✔ **The Opéra-Grands-Magasins Welcome Center,** 11 rue Scribe, 9e,
open Monday to Saturday 9 a.m. to 6:30 p.m. (Métro: Chausée
d'Antin or Opéra; RER: Auber)

✔ **The welcome kiosk beneath the modern glass roofed terminal of
the Gare du Nord,** 18 rue Dunkerque, 10e, open seven days a week
from 8 a.m. to 6 p.m. (Métro and RER: Gare du Nord)

✔ **The Gare de Lyon Welcome Center,** 20 bd. Diderot, 12e, open
Monday to Saturday 8 a.m. to 6 p.m. (Métro and RER: Gare de Lyon)

✔ **21 place du Tertre,** 18e, open daily 10 a.m. to 7 p.m. (Métro:
Abbesses)

✔ **Carrousel du Louvre, beneath the Pyramide,** 99 rue de Rivoli, 1er,
open daily 10 a.m. to 7 p.m. (Métro: Palais Royal/Musée du Louvre)

✔ **Eiffel Tower between the North and East pillars** open daily 11 a.m.
to 6:40 p.m. (Métro: Bir Hakeim, RER: Champ-de-Mars/Tour Eiffel)

Getting Around Paris

Probably your best introduction to Paris, and to the way the city is laid
out, is from the north tower at Notre-Dame. You can see the magnificent
cathedral from many parts of the city, and a visit helps you get oriented.
From the cathedral, you see that the river Seine is actually Paris's most
important "street."

By Métro

The best way to get around Paris is to walk, but for longer distances
the Métro, or subway, rules. The **Métropolitain** is fast, safe, and easy to
navigate. Open from 5:45 a.m. to 12:45 a.m., it's an efficient and cheap
way to get around. The only times you may want to avoid it are the
hours between 7 to 10 a.m. and 6 to 8 p.m. — in other words, rush hour.
Operated by the RATP (Régie Autonome des Transports Parisiens), the
Métro has a total of 16 lines and more than 360 stations, making it likely
that one is near your destination. The Métro is connected to the suburban commuter train, the **Réseau Express Régional** (RER), which connects
downtown Paris with its airports and suburbs.

You can recognize a Métro station either by an elegant Art Nouveau gate-
way reading *Métropolitain* or by a big yellow *M* sign. Unless otherwise
marked, all Métro stations have a ticket booth, where you purchase a
single ticket (1.40€/$1.60) or a group of ten tickets called a *carnet* (kar-
nay; 10.50€/$12) from an attendant or, in most stations, from a machine
that accepts only bills and coins (no credit cards). Every Métro stop has
maps of the system; you can get portable maps by asking at a ticket
booth for *une carte* (oon kart). Near the exits, you usually can find a
plan du quartier, a very detailed pictorial map of the streets and buildings surrounding the station, with all exits marked. A good idea is to
consult the *plan du quartier* before you exit the system, especially at very

large stations. You may want to use a different exit to reach the other side of a busy street or wind up closer to your destination.

Navigating the Métro is easy, and you'll be a pro in no time. Here's what you do:

1. **Use the Métro map on the Cheat Sheet at the front of this book to figure out which station is closest to you.**

   For example, if you want to go to the Louvre and are in your hotel in the Latin Quarter, say the Familia, check the listing in this book for your hotel. The book tells you that your nearest Métro station, or your starting point, is Jussieu. Look at the Métro map on the Cheat Sheet at the front of this book for the line that the Jussieu station is on. (Each end of the lines on the Métro map is marked with the number of the line.) The Jussieu station is on Line 7.

2. **Look for your destination station.**

   In the example, you look for the Louvre. You see that the Louvre has two stops: the Palais Royal-Musée du Louvre station on Line 7 and the Louvre Rivoli station on Line 14. Choose the Palais-Royal Musée du Louvre station, and you won't have to change trains.

3. **Enter the Métro system through a turnstile with two ticket slots.**

   With the magnetic strip facing down, insert your ticket into the nearer slot. Your ticket pops out of the second slot. Remove it, and either walk through a set of rubberized doors that briskly open on each side or push through a turnstile.

   Keep your ticket with you until you exit the station. At any point while in you're the Métro, an inspector may ask to see your ticket again. If you fail to produce it, you're subject to a steep fine. When you ride the RER, you must keep your ticket because you have to insert it in a turnstile when you exit the station.

4. **Make sure you're going in the right direction.**

   When you're past the entrance, look at your subway map and trace the line past your destination to its end. The station's name at the end of the line is the name of the subway train on which you'll be traveling; in the case of Line 7 the train is La Corneuve. To get back to your hotel from the Louvre, you take the train going in the opposite direction, marked Villejuif Louis Aragon and exit at the Jussieu station.

5. **Enter the train and exit at the station you want.**

   Blue signs reading *Sortie* mark all exits.

See? Pretty easy! Suppose, however, that the Métro line nearest to you doesn't directly go to your destination. For example, you want to go to the Arc de Triomphe from Jussieu, and the stop is Charles de Gaulle–Étoile. Find the Charles de Gaulle–Étoile stop on the Métro map. You see that you can reach Charles de Gaulle–Étoile on Line 6 or Line 1. But you're on Line 7. You have to change trains. Changing trains is called a *correspondance,* or transfer.

To make a transfer (correspondance), follow these steps:

1. **Figure out which transfer station you need.**

   On your map, blank white circles indicate where a number of lines intersect. These circles are *transfer stations,* where you can change subway trains.

   To figure out where you need to change from the 7 train to Line 1 or Line 6 (to get from Jussieu to the Arc de Triomphe), use the map to see where Line 7 intersects with Line 1 and with Line 6. Line 7 and Line 6 intersect at Stalingrad, opposite from where you want to go. But Line 7 and Line 1 intersect at Concorde, very close to Charles de Gaulle–Étoile. This is the train you want to take. To make sure you go in the right direction on Line 1, look on your map for the name of the station at the very end past Charles de Gaulle–Étoile. It's called Grande Arche de la Défense, and this is the name of the train you want to ride.

2. **Look for a bright orange *Correspondance* sign above the platform at the transfer station.**

   Beneath it is a white sign that has the number of the line you can transfer to in a circle (in the example, Line 1).

3. **Follow the direction the sign indicates for the line you want.**

   You eventually come to two stairwells leading to the platforms. Navy blue signs mark this area, indicating the train's direction and listing all the stops the train makes. Make sure you choose the stairwell leading to the train going in the direction you want — in the example, you want the train to Grande Arche de la Défense, so that you can exit at Charles de Gaulle–Étoile.

 The distances between platforms at the *correspondance* (transfer) stations can be very long. You may climb stairs, walk a short distance, only to descend stairs to walk some more. Châtelet is particularly long. Some lines are connected by moving sidewalks that seem to do nothing but make a very long walk a little less long. For those with limited mobility, take the bus or a cab.

The Métro connects with the suburban commuter train, the RER, in several stations in the city. The RER operates on a zone fare system, but Métro tickets are valid on it in the city. You probably won't go past the first two zones, unless you visit Disneyland on the A4 or Versailles on the C5. When you ride the RER, keep your ticket because you need to insert it into a turnstile to leave the station.

The doors on most Métro cars don't open automatically. You must lift a door handle or press a button to get on and off.

Anyone who has ever been crushed on a Paris subway at rush hour can attest that commuters don't easily give up their places. If you step out of the train to let someone off, you may just be giving others on the platform the chance to squeeze in before you. Be polite, but stand your ground.

After the subway shuts down around 1 a.m., the RATP operates **Noctambuses** that run on the hour from 1:30 a.m. to 5:30 a.m. from Châtelet-Hôtel de Ville, but they don't cover every arrondissement. Check the maps at the entrance to Métro stations to determine if a Noctambus services your destination. (If your hotel isn't in a Noctambus zone, consult the sidebar "Top taxi stands" later in this chapter for the one nearest you and queue up with all the others who are trying to get home.) The bus has a distinctive yellow-and-black owl symbol, and tickets cost 2.70€ ($3.10).

Buying the best travel pass

The RATP (Paris's public transportation agency) offers a variety of travel cards that you can purchase in larger Métro stations. You simply show your card to bus conductors and Métro ticket booth personnel when you get on.

✔ **Carte Orange:** The weekly or monthly passes are inexpensive — 15.40€ ($18) for a week's unlimited travel or 50.40€ ($58) for a month's pass. Bring a photo of yourself to a Métro ticket booth in one of the larger stations, such as Châtelet, Monday through Wednesday mornings when the carte is on sale. The monthly card is only sold the first two days of the month.

✔ **Mobilis:** This pass is good for unlimited travel on subway and bus lines (except to and from the airports) for one day. The cost is 5.30€ ($6). If you will be hopping on and off subways for more than one day, you may want to try one of the other passes.

✔ **Paris Visite:** This pass is good for unlimited travel for one, two, three, or five days. Though it has discounts for some museums and monuments, check the brochure to make sure you want to see the listed sites. Otherwise, the Paris Visite card turns out to be more expensive than a Carte Orange or a one-day Mobilis pass. A one-day Paris Visite card costs 8.35€ ($9.60), two-day 13.70€ ($16), three-day 18.25€ ($21), and five-day 26.65€ ($31).

✔ **Paris l'Open Tour:** This pass is good for one or two days of unlimited travel around Paris on special open-air buses. You can get on and off whenever you like. It's a bit pricey at 25€ ($29) for one day and 28€ ($32) for two days, but it's a good way to get to know Paris.

A ten-ticket *carnet* good for the Métro and on buses is a good deal for 10.50€ ($12) because a single ticket costs 1.40€ ($1.60). You can purchase a *carnet* at all Métro stations as well as *tabacs* (cafes and kiosks that sell tobacco products). The heavily publicized **Paris Visite** card, which starts at 8.35€ ($9.60) a day offers free or reduced entry to some minor attractions and free souvenirs from others in addition to unlimited travel on Métro and buses, but make sure the attractions that interest you are included on the list (ask for it at the ticket window first) or visit the Paris Visite Web site before you leave home (www.ratp.fr/ ParisVisite/Eng/index.htm).

How long do you plan to be in Paris? If you plan to use public transportation frequently, consider buying the **Carte Orange.** The weekly or monthly pass is inexpensive — 13.75€ ($16) for a week's unlimited travel (*coupon hebdomadair,* koo-*poh* eb-*doh*-muh-dare) or 46€ ($53) for a month's pass (*coupon mensue* koo-*poh men*-soo-ell) covering the first 20 arrondissements. The only catch is that you must supply a passport-sized photo of yourself. Bring one from home or visit a photo booth at one of the many Monoprix stores, major Métro stations, department stores, or train stations, where you can get four black-and-white pictures for less than 5€ ($5.75). The weekly Carte Orange is on sale Monday through Wednesday morning and is valid through Sunday, but the monthly card is only sold the first two days of the month.

For more information on the city's public transportation, call the RATP's English information line (0.34€/minute, ☎ **08-92-68-41-14;** www.ratp.fr).

By bus

The bus system is convenient and can be an inexpensive way to sightsee without wearing out your feet. Most Parisian buses run from 6:30 a.m. to 8:30 p.m.; a few run until 12:30 a.m. Each bus shelter has a route map, which you want to check carefully. Because of the number of one-way streets, the bus is likely to make different stops depending on its direction. Main stops are written on the side of the buses with the endpoint shown on the front above the driver. Furthermore, the back of every bus shelter has posted large bus maps and smaller maps inside the shelter showing the specific bus route. Métro tickets are valid for bus travel, and although you can buy single tickets from the conductor, you can't buy ticket packages (*carnets*) on the bus.

Board at the front of the bus. If you have a single-trip ticket, insert it into the slot in the small machine right behind the driver. The machine punches your ticket and pops it back out. If you have a pass, show it to the driver. To get off at the next stop, press one of the red buttons on the safety poles; the *arrêt demandé* (stop requested) sign above the driver lights up.

The downside of taking the bus is that it often gets mired in heavy Parisian traffic, so I don't recommend it if you're in a hurry. And, like

Keeping the picks out of your pockets

Over the past few years, petty crime has been making a comeback in Paris, a city that is otherwise relatively safe. Anywhere where you find a high concentration of tourists, you also find pickpockets — including in the Métro, hovering around the lines outside the Eiffel Tower and Notre-Dame, and in the church and its bell tower. Keep an eye out for little bands of scruffy children, who often surround you, distract you, and make off with your belongings.

Your best bet is to use common sense. Be aware of the people around you at all times. Get a money belt. Women wear purses diagonally across the body with the flap facing the body. Make sure zipper purses are closed at all times. (In fact, zippered purses aren't recommended.) See Chapter 4 for what to do if you get pickpocketed.

the Métro, avoid the bus during rush hours when it seems *le monde* (the world) is sharing the bus with you.

Bus routes great for sightseeing include:

- ✔ **Bus 69:** Eiffel Tower, Invalides, Louvre, Hôtel de Ville, place des Vosges, Bastille, Père-Lachaise Cemetery

- ✔ **Bus 80:** Department stores on boulevard Haussmann, Champs-Elysées, Ave. Montaigne *haute couture* shopping, Eiffel Tower

- ✔ **Bus 96:** St-Germain-des-Prés, Musée de Cluny, Hôtel de Ville, place des Vosges

By taxi

You have three ways to get a taxi in Paris, and I rank them in order of how successful they are.

- ✔ The best way to find a cab is by **phoning Alpha Taxis** (☎ 01-45-85-85-85) or **Taxis G7** (☎ 01-47-39-47-39). Keep in mind, however, that phoning ahead is more expensive because the meter starts running as soon as the driver commences the journey to get you.

- ✔ You can also **wait at a taxi stand** (*station de taxis;* see the nearby "Top taxi stands" sidebar); a blue Taxi sign denotes the stands. Depending on the time of day, however, you may wait in a long line of people, or a very limited number of cabs stop.

- ✔ Finally, you can **hail a cab,** as long as you're not within 200 feet of a taxi stand. Look for a taxi with its white light illuminated, which means the cab is available. An orange light means the cab is occupied or on the way to a pickup. You may get a cab driver who refuses to take you to your destination; by law, a driver can do this only during his or her last half-hour at work. Be prepared, as well, for the selective vision of drivers, especially when you hail a cab. Don't be surprised to see a free taxi or two pass you by.

Top taxi stands

Go to the following locations within each arrondissement to find the most convenient taxi stands. *Place* indicates a square, *pont* is a bridge, and *hôpital* is a hospital.

1er Arrondissement

Métro Concorde

Place André Malraux

Place du Châtelet

2e Arrondissement

Place de l'Opéra

3e Arrondissement

Métro Rambuteau

Square du Temple

4e Arrondissement

Métro St-Paul

5e Arrondissement

Place des Gobelins

Place Maubert

Place Monge

Place St-Michel

Pont de la Tournelle

6e Arrondissement

Métro Mabillon

Métro Port-Royal

Métro St-Germain

7e Arrondissement

Métro Bac

27 bd. La Tour-Maubourg

Métro La Tour-Maurbourg

Métro Solferino

Place de l'Ecole Militaire

Tour Eiffel (Eiffel Tower)

8e Arrondissement

Av. de Friedland

Place de l'Alma

Place de la Madeleine

Place des Ternes

Rond Point des Champs-Elysées

9e Arrondissement

Métro Richelieu-Drouout

Place d'Estienne d'Orves

Square de Montholon

10e Arrondissement

Métro Goncourt

11e Arrondissement

Métro Faidherbe-Chaligny

Métro Goncourt

Place de la Bastille

Place de la Nation

Place de la République

Place Léon Blum

12e Arrondissement

Hôpital Trousseau

Château de Vincennes (Bois de Vincennes)

Porte Dorée

13e Arrondissement

Métro Glacière

Porte d'Italie

Hôpital Pitié-Salpétrière (bd. de l'Hôpital)

14e Arrondissement

Métro Plaisance

Porte d'Orléans

Place Denfert-Rochereau

Porte de Vanves

15e Arrondissement

Métro Bir-Hakeim

Métro LaMotte-Piquet Grenelle

Métro Convention

Place Balard

Place de Breteuil

16e Arrondissement

Métro Muette

Métro Passy

Maison de la Radio

Place d'Iéna

Place du Trocadero

12 place Victor Hugo

Gare Henri Martin

17e Arrondissement

Métro Brochant

Métro Villiers

Place Charles de Gaulle

Porte de Clichy

Porte de Saint-Ouen

18e Arrondissement

Métro Lamarck-Calaincourt

Métro Porte de la Chapelle

Place Blanche

Place de la Clichy

Place Jules Joffrin

Place du Tertre

Porte de Clignancourt

19e Arrondissement

Métro Stalingrad

Métro Botzaris

Porte de Lilas

Porte de Pantin

Porte de la Villette

Église de Belleville

20e Arrondissement

Métro Ménilmontant

Métro Père-Lachaise

Métro Porte de Montreuil

Métro Pyrénées

For one to three people, the fare in Paris proper is around 2€ to 3€ ($2.30 to $3.45); the rate per kilometer is 0.60€ ($.70) from 7 a.m. to 7 p.m. (otherwise known as Rate A); otherwise, it's 1€ to 2€ ($1.15 to $2.30) (Rate B). You pay a 0.70€ ($.81) supplement for taxi stands at train stations and at the Air France shuttle-bus terminals, as well as 0.90€ ($1.05) for each piece of luggage weighing more than 5kg. If the driver agrees to do so, it's 1.50€ ($1.70) for transporting a fourth person. Common practice is to tip your driver 10 to 15 percent on longer journeys when the fare exceeds 15€ ($17); otherwise round up the charge and give the driver the change.

By car

Streets are narrow, parking is next to impossible, and nerve, skill, ruthlessness, and a knowledgeable copilot are required if you insist on driving in Paris. I *strongly* recommend that you don't. (If you must drive in Paris, do it in August when residents are away on vacation, and traffic is lighter.)

A few tips: Get an excellent street map and ride with another person; traffic moves so lightning-fast you don't have time to think at intersections. For the most part, you must pay to park in Paris. Depending on the neighborhood, expect to pay 1.80€ ($2.10) to 2.30€ ($2.65) an hour for a maximum of two hours. Place coins in the nearest meter, which issues you a ticket to place on your dashboard. You can also buy parking cards at the nearest *tabac* (tobacco shop) for meters that accept only parking cards. Parking is free on Sundays, holidays, and for the entire month of August.

Drivers and all passengers must wear seat belts. Children under 12 must ride in the back seat. Drivers are supposed to yield to the car on the right, except where signs indicate otherwise, as at traffic circles.

 Watch for the *gendarmes* (police officers), who lack patience and who consistently contradict the traffic lights. Horn blowing is frowned upon except in emergencies. Flash your headlights instead.

By bicycle

The banks of the Seine are closed to cars and open to pedestrians and cyclists March to November each Sunday from 10 a.m. to 5 p.m. It may not make much of a dent in the air quality, but bicycling is a fun and healthy way to spend a Sunday afternoon.

City planners have been trying to encourage more cycling by setting aside 62 miles of bicycle lanes throughout Paris. The main routes run north-south from the Bassin de La Villette along the Canal St-Martin through the Left Bank and east-west from Château de Vincennes to the Bois de Boulogne and its miles of bike lanes. The RATP (which runs the city's buses and subways) in partnership with the mayor's office rents bikes through its *Roue Libre* program. To rent a bike, you need to put down a 150€ ($173) deposit per bike by traveler's check or with cash and show a passport or driver's license (credit card deposits were not accepted when I visited). Costs are 7€ ($8.05) per weekday, 15€ ($17) for five days, 30€ ($35) for the week. On weekends you'll pay 4€ (4.60) per hour, 10€ ($12) for a half day, 15€ ($17) 9 a.m.–5 p.m. and 25€ ($29) for the weekend. A Roue Libre location is at 1 passage Mondétour, in front of 120 de la rue Rambuteau, 1er (☎ 08-10-44-15-34; Métro: Les Halles); open daily 9 a.m.–7 p.m. Roue Libre also gives 24€ ($28), three-hour guided tours of Paris (see Chapter 11.)

For more information and a bike map, pick up the *Plan Vert* from the tourist office. (For bike tours of the city, see Chapter 11.)

Paris à pied (On foot)

Paris is one of the prettiest cities in the world for strolling, and getting around on foot is probably the best way to really appreciate the city's character. The best walking neighborhoods are **St-Germain-des-Prés** on the Left Bank and the **Marais** on the Right Bank, both of which are filled with romantic little courtyards, wonderful boutiques, and congenial cafes and watering holes. The **quays of the Seine,** as well as its bridges, are also lovely, especially at sunset when the sun fills the sky with a pink glow that's reflected on the water. And try not to miss the pretty **Canal St-Martin** with its arched bridges and locks in the 10e, featured in the movies *Amélie* and *Hôtel du Nord* or the tiny streets off the Montmartre *butte* (hill).

Take special care when crossing streets, even when you have the right of way. The number-one rule of the road in France is that whoever is coming from the right side has the right of way. Drivers often make right turns without looking, even when faced with pedestrians at crosswalks. And don't ever attempt to cross a traffic circle if you're not on a crosswalk. The larger roundabouts, such as the one at the Arc de Triomphe, have pedestrian tunnels.

Chapter 9

Checking in at Paris's Best Hotels

- -

In This Chapter

▶ Getting the best room at the best rate
▶ Trying to find a place to stay without a reservation
▶ Reviewing Paris's favorite accommodations
▶ Locating hotels by neighborhood and price

- -

*P*art of the fun of traveling is waking up in a new place with so much to explore! If this is your first trip to Paris, your expectations about what a hotel room should look like may be based on what you have seen in your own country. For those visiting from North America, one important thing to know is that rooms in Paris tend to be smaller than they are in hotels in North America, even in expensive places (unless you opt for a modern chain hotel, which can lack charm). Parisian doubles are almost never big enough to hold two queen-sized beds, and the space around the bed usually isn't big enough for more than a desk and perhaps a chest of drawers. The story is the same in London, Rome, and most other continental capitals where buildings date back two, three, four, or more centuries, when dimensions — and people! — were smaller.

Parisian hotels also vary widely in their plumbing arrangements. Some units come equipped with only a sink; others may also have a toilet and either a shower or tub. Private bathrooms with tubs often have handheld shower devices, and some shower stalls don't have curtains — so pay attention where you aim. The trend is toward renovating small hotels by installing a small shower, toilet, and sink in each room, but don't count on having all these amenities in your room unless you're in a pricier hotel.

Acoustics tend to be unpredictable in old Parisian hotels. Your quarreling neighbors may compete with street noise for the prize of most annoying, so bring earplugs for the neighbors, or ask for a room in the rear of the hotel to avoid the street noise. Another point to remember: Most budget hotels in Paris don't have air conditioning, but fortunately, their solid stone walls tend to keep out the summer heat.

Getting to Know Your Options

More than 2,200 hotels are located in Paris — chain hotels, deluxe palace-like accommodations, hotels that cater to business travelers, budget hotels, and mom-and-pop establishments.

The French government grades hotels with a star system, ranging from one star for a simple inn to four stars for a deluxe hotel. Moderately priced hotels usually get two or three stars. This system is based on a complex formula of room sizes, facilities, plumbing, elevators, dining options, renovations, and so on.

To find the hotel that's right for you, you need to weigh five variables: price, location, room size, amenities, and — the least tangible, but perhaps most desired of them all — a charming Parisian ambience. If the first variable, price, poses no problem, then you can have it all: great location, huge room, super perks, and sumptuous surroundings. Most travelers, however, need to make some compromises.

Before committing to a hotel, however, keep in mind that Paris offers additional options for lodging — renting an apartment, for example. Nothing beats living in Paris as a Parisian. In your own **apartment,** you can conduct cooking experiments, taste fine wines that would be too expensive in a restaurant, and entertain new friends. Although the daily rate can be higher than a budget hotel, the room will be larger, you can save money on meals, and in the end, you may end up paying the same rate you would for room and board at a hotel — or less.

The most practical way to rent an apartment is through an agency. Most agencies require a seven-day minimum stay and offer discounts for longer stays. I've found that apartments vary quite a bit in size, location, and amenities. At the bottom end — for about 100€ ($115) per day — you'll find yourself in either a small, centrally located studio, or a larger studio in an *arrondissement* (neighborhood) a bit far from the center of Paris. Studio apartments usually feature a convertible couch, an armchair or two, a bathroom with a tub or shower, and a tiny kitchenette with a refrigerator, stove, coffeemaker, and maybe a microwave. Dishes, cutlery, pots and pans, telephone, TV, iron, vacuum cleaner, linen, and sometimes a washing machine are also provided. Pay a bit more — 150€ ($173) per day — and you get a more centrally located one-bedroom apartment. As with anything else, higher prices pay for larger, more luxurious spaces.

You can find many rental agencies online and comparison shop among them. Companies offering attractive apartments at reasonable prices are **Apartment Living in Paris** (www.apartment-living.com), which is run by two French real estate brokers, and **Lodgis Solutions** (www.lodgis.com). **Paris Vacation Rentals** (www.rentals-paris.com) is an agency that deals in short-term rental of upscale apartments at very good prices. More expensive is **New York Habitats** (www.newyorkhabitat.com), a New York real estate brokerage that rents Paris flats as a sideline.

Bonjour Paris (www.bonjourparis.com) has reviews and information about apartment rental agencies.

Keep in mind that this is a short-term apartment rental. You have to sign a contract and put down a security deposit, which may not be refunded if you damage the apartment in any way.

If the agency offers optional gift baskets or transportation to and from the airport, you're better off refusing. The gift basket usually contains items you can buy more cheaply at the grocery store, and the transportation is usually twice as much as a cab.

If you bring the kids with you to Paris, your best option may be the *aparthotel,* a hybrid between an apartment and a hotel where you can have the autonomy of an apartment with some of the amenities of a hotel. You book an aparthotel just like you do any other hotel, through its Web site or phone number. And, like hotels, they have 24-hour reception desks, satellite TV, housekeeping services, kitchenettes, and laundry. For a family of four, a one-bedroom apartment is a good-value alternative to two double rooms in a cheap hotel. And if you use your kitchenette to prepare even half of your own meals in Paris, you can reap huge savings on your dining bill.

Finding the Best Room at the Best Rate

The *rack rate* is the maximum rate a hotel charges for a room. It's the rate you get if you walk in off the street and ask for a room for the night. But you often don't have to pay it! This section gives tips on finding the best rooms in Paris at the best rate.

Finding the best rate

At chain hotels (especially the American ones) and other luxury hotels, you can often get a good deal simply by asking for a discounted rate. Your odds of getting a reduced rate improve drastically if you're staying for more than a few nights.

Keep in mind that bartering for a cheaper room isn't the norm at Paris's budget hotels. Small and privately owned; these establishments post their rates in the reception area and may not be willing to negotiate. To be fair, they may not be able to afford to let rooms go for less.

Room rates change with the seasons as occupancy rates rise and fall. In Paris, summer is low season. Yes, you're reading that correctly: Room rates tend to be lower in July and August, which is typically when the French flee the big cities for the beaches and the mountains. November and December are also low season, but early fall is high season, with October, in particular, heavy on conventioneers, making it difficult to find a room. If a hotel is close to full, it's less likely to extend discount rates; if it's close to empty, it may be willing to negotiate.

Prices for the hotels recommended here are designated with dollar signs; Table 9-1 explains how this works. In a nutshell, the more dollar signs you see, the more expensive the hotel. The number of dollar signs corresponds to the hotel's rack rates (full rate) from the cheapest double room in low season to the most expensive in high season. The most noticeable difference between budget hotels and the most expensive hotels is better amenities and services, followed by a more luxurious decor. None of the recommended hotels listed in this chapter is a dump; the places are decent and reputable. Naturally, the luxury level in a 1,000€ ($1,150) room is substantially higher than in a 100€ one ($115).

Table 9-1		Key to Hotel Prices
Dollar Sign(s)	*Price Range*	*What to Expect*
$	Less than 75€ ($86)	These accommodations are relatively simple and inexpensive. Rooms are likely to be small, and televisions are not necessarily provided. Parking is not provided but is rather catch-as-you-can on the street.
$$	76€–150€ ($86–$173)	A bit classier, these mid-range accommodations offer more room, more extras (such as irons, hair dryers, and a trouser press), and a more convenient location than the preceding category.
$$$	151€–300€ ($116–$230)	Higher-class still, these accommodations begin to look plush. Think chocolates on your pillow, a classy restaurant, room service, and maybe a view of the Eiffel Tower or another landmark.
$$$$	Above 300€ ($345)	These top-rated accommodations come with luxury amenities such as on-premise spas, deluxe toiletries, Web access, CD players, multi-starred gourmet restaurants with room service, views, robes — frankly nearly every luxury you can imagine — but you pay through the nose for 'em.

Room prices are subject to change without notice, so the rates quoted in this book may be different than the actual rate you receive when you make your reservation. Be sure to mention membership in AAA, AARP, frequent-flyer programs, and any other corporate rewards programs you belong to when making your reservation at a chain hotel. You never know when it may be worth a few dollars off your room rate. Family-run establishments rarely have arrangements with large organizations.

Keep this advice in mind when you're trying to save money on a room:

- A **travel agent** may be able to negotiate a better price at top hotels than you can get yourself. (The hotel gives the agent a discount for steering business its way.)

- Always ask if the hotel offers any **weekend specials,** which typically require you to stay two nights (either Friday and Saturday or Saturday and Sunday). In Paris, you can find this kind of deal from September through March at almost all price levels.

- A *forfait* (*fohr*-feh) is a discount that requires you to stay a certain number of nights — perhaps a minimum of three or five. Sometimes something else is thrown in — like a bottle of champagne — to sweeten the deal. If you're going to be in Paris for more than three days, always ask if there's a *forfait* and then pick the hotel with the best deal.

- Don't forget about **package deals** (see Chapter 5) that include airfare, hotel, and transportation to and from the airport.

- Look on the **Internet** for deals (see below).

Surfing the Web for hotel deals

Although the major travel booking sites (such as Travelocity, Orbitz, Expedia, and Cheap Tickets; see Chapter 5 for details) offer hotel booking, using a site devoted primarily to lodging can be best, because you may find properties that aren't listed on more general online travel agencies. **The Paris Tourist Office** (www.parisinfo.com) gives detailed information on hotels and other lodging it sanctioned by the Paris Convention and Visitor's Bureau and provides links to accommodation reservation centers (but the Web site doesn't tell you about special rates). Some lodging sites specialize in a particular type of accommodation, such as bed-and-breakfast accommodations, which you won't find on the more mainstream booking services. Others offer weekend deals on major chain properties that cater to business travelers and have more empty rooms on weekends. Therefore, checking out some of the online lodging sites, many of which offer discounts, is in your best interest.

Hotel Discounts (www.hoteldiscounts.com), a service of the Hotel Reservations Network (HRN), offers bargain room rates at hotels in more than two-dozen U.S. and international cities. HRN pre-books blocks of rooms in advance, so sometimes it has rooms — at discount rates — at hotels that otherwise are considered sold out. **TravelWeb** (www.travel web.com) lists more than 16,000 hotels worldwide, focusing on chains such as Hyatt and Hilton, and you can book almost 90% of these online. **France Hotels Online** (www.france-hotel-online.com) offers detailed listings of independent hotels, apartments, and bed-and-breakfasts according to budget and neighborhood. **All Hotels on the Web** (www.all-hotels.com) lists tens of thousands of lodgings throughout the world. (The hotels on this site pay a fee to be listed.) **Places to Stay** (www.placestostay.com) lists inns, B&Bs, resorts, hotels, and properties you may not find anywhere else.

Arriving Without a Reservation

If you arrive in Paris without a reservation, you have two choices. You can pick up a phone and start dialing (after you purchase a phone card for public phones at the nearest *tabac,* a cafe or kiosk that sells tobacco products). Or you can walk in to one of the branches of the **Office de Tourisme de Paris** and let the multilingual staff make you a reservation. Staff at three of the Office's six branches make reservations (*Note:* These centers are closed on May 1.):

- ✔ The **Opéra-Grands-Magasins** welcome center, 11 rue Scribe, 9e, open Mon–Sat 9 a.m.–6:30 p.m. (Métro: Chausée d'Antin or Opéra; RER: Auber)

- ✔ The welcome kiosk beneath the modern glass roofed terminal of the **Gare du Nord,** 18 rue Dunkerque, 10e, open 7 days a week from 8 a.m.–6 p.m. (Métro and RER: Gare du Nord)

- ✔ The welcome kiosk at the **Gare de Lyon,** 20 bd. Diderot, 12e, open Mon-Sat 8 a.m.–6 p.m. (Métro and RER: Gare de Lyon)

Hotels with unsold rooms offer them through the Office de Tourisme at rock-bottom prices, so you may get a 3-star hotel at a 2-star price. For a fee, the staff will make a reservation for you on the same day that you want a room. The charge is 1.20€ ($1.40) for hostels and *foyers* (usually dormitories in universities for student travelers), and beyond that depends on the French government's star ratings. The tourism office charges 3.05€ ($3.50), for 1-star hotels, 3.80€ ($4.40) for 2-star hotels, and 6.10€ ($7) for 3-star hotels.

Note that during the summer season, you'll have to wait in a long line, and you aren't guaranteed a room.

Paris's Best Hotels

There are more than 2,200 hotels in Paris ranging from small alcove singles in historic buildings to the deluxe new Hilton on the Champs-Elysées that anticipates a traveler's every need. But only 47 are described here.

Hotels in the Heart of the Right Bank (1-4, 8-12, & 16-18)

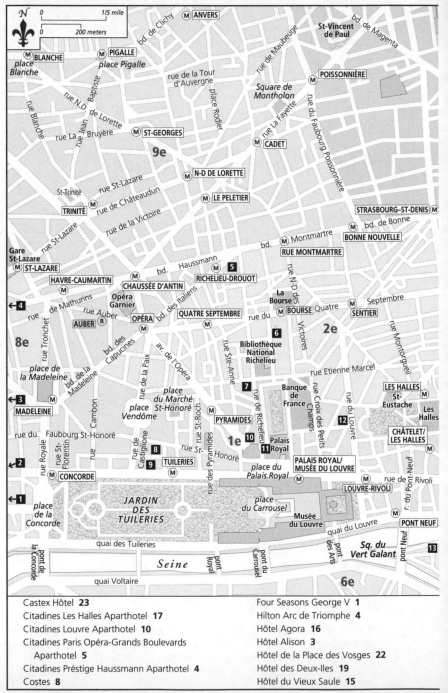

Castex Hôtel **23**	Four Seasons George V **1**
Citadines Les Halles Aparthotel **17**	Hilton Arc de Triomphe **4**
Citadines Louvre Aparthotel **10**	Hôtel Agora **16**
Citadines Paris Opéra-Grands Boulevards	Hôtel Alison **3**
Aparthotel **5**	Hôtel de la Place des Vosges **22**
Citadines Préstige Haussmann Aparthotel **4**	Hôtel des Deux-Iles **19**
Costes **8**	Hôtel du Vieux Saule **15**

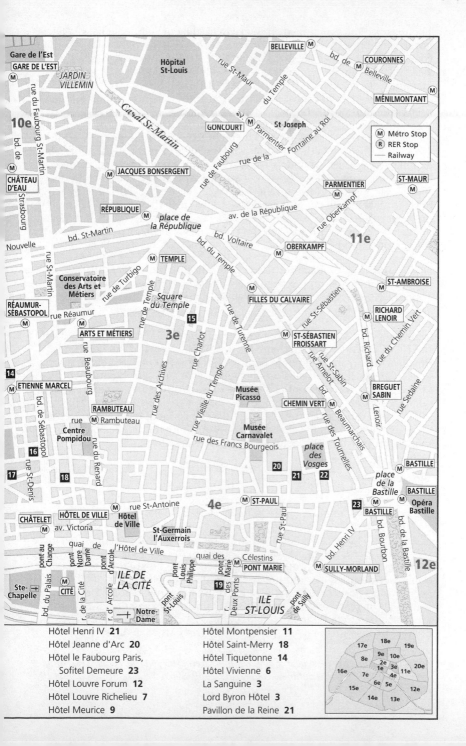

The reason? You don't need an overwhelming, encyclopedic list of all the hotels, just ones that are right for you, and an equally right backup in case your first choice is booked solid. In compiling this list, the first step was considering the typical traveler's wish list. And for most of you, the main priority is location. Thus, the first criterion, though ruthless, was simple: **If a hotel isn't located in the first eight arrondissements, it isn't recommended in this book.**

The second concern was price. The most expensive category listed here, $$$$, contains hotels that cost more than 300€ ($345) a night, which is expensive by nearly anyone's standards. Only a few hotels described here fall into the $$$$ category because most travelers are on a budget. (For a complete rundown on the $ system, see Table 9-1.) Three-quarters of the hotels in this chapter rent doubles for less than 150€ ($173) night but nevertheless give you comfort, some nice amenities, and that *frisson* of Parisian character for which the city's hotels are known. And none of the hotels listed here is a dive.

Finally, a variety of neighborhoods between the first and eighth arrondissements is represented here with a nice range of styles from conservative to trendy. The aim? I want to make sure that everyone is accounted for, regardless of budget, taste, or style of travel.

In this chapter, two maps pinpoint the locations of the hotels: "Hotels in the Heart of the Right Bank" and "Hotels in the Heart of the Left Bank." Reviews are arranged alphabetically for easy reference. Hotels that are especially good for families are designated with the kid-friendly icon. Listed immediately beneath the name of the hotel is the neighborhood in which it's located and the number of dollar signs corresponding to the hotel's rack rates, from the cheapest double room in low season to the most expensive in high season. At chapter's end are indexes of accommodations by price and neighborhood for easy reference.

Castex Hôtel
$$ Le Marais (4e)

Less than five minutes from one of Paris's most famous brasseries, Bofinger, the Castex is a popular budget classic, near *everything* in the Marais. Each large room has a writing table or a desk and chair; some have views overlooking the courtyard. The front of the building was undergoing a renovation that the proprietor expected to be finished by fall 2004, so construction noise should not be a problem for visitors in 2005. Staff is friendly and accommodating. Rooms don't have televisions, but you can watch TV or read the papers in the TV salon. Reserve at least a month in advance. The Café de la Poste is located just a few doors away at 13 rue Castex, to ease just-arrived travelers into the Paris cafe lifestyle.

See map p. 110. 5 rue Castex. ☎ *01-42-72-31-52. Fax: 01-42-72-57-91.* www.castex hotel.com. *Métro: Bastille or Sully-Morland. Rates: 95€–115€ ($109–$132) single; 120€–140€ ($138–$161) double; 190€–220€ ($219–$253) triple/quad. Breakfast 10€ ($12). AE, DC, MC, V.*

Citadines Les Halles Aparthotel
$$–$$$ Louvre (1er)

Staying here is like living in your own high-rise apartment in Paris. Studios and one-bedrooms have fully equipped kitchenettes, and services include a 24-hour reception desk, satellite TV, air conditioning, housekeeping, baby-equipment rental, and laundry facilities. The Les Halles neighborhood is a bit rough at night, so if you're a single traveler, this hotel may not be the best bet.

See map p. 110. 4 rue des Innocents (100 yards from the Forum des Halles). ☎ 01-40-39-26-50. www.citadines.com. *Métro: Les Halles. Rates: 159€ ($185) per night for 1–6 days, 144€ ($167) 7–29 days for a 2-person studio; 252€ ($290) per night for 1–6 days, 227€ ($261) 7–29 days 4-person (1 bedroom) apt. AE, MC, V.*

Citadines Louvre Aparthotel
$$$ Louvre (1er)

This seven-story aparthotel is in a terrific location in an upscale and pretty neighborhood just opposite the Comédie-Française and next to the Jardin du Palais-Royal. It has several studios (each with a double fold-out sofa) and apartments equipped for travelers with disabilities. Studios and one-bedrooms (a separate bedroom with two single beds and pull-out double sofa) have fully equipped kitchenettes, and services include a 24-hour reception desk, satellite TV, air conditioning, housekeeping, baby equipment rental, and laundry facilities. Rent well in advance.

See map p. 110. 8 rue de Richelieu (1 block north of the Louvre). ☎ 01-55-35-28-00. www.citadines.com. *Métro: Palais-Royal or Pyramides. Rates: 197€ ($227) per night for 1–6 days, 173€ ($199) 7–29 days for a 2-person studio; 300€ ($345) per night 1–6 days, 270€ ($311) 7–29 days for a 4-person (1 bedroom) apt. AE, MC, V.*

Citadines Paris Opéra-Grands Boulevards Aparthotel
$$$–$$$$ Opéra (2e)

Around the corner from the Opéra Comique and the Comédie-Française and near the Grands Boulevards, this five-story aparthotel is the most centrally located in the Citadines chain. It's located in a peaceful passage, and rooms come with fully equipped kitchenettes; available services include a 24-hour reception desk, satellite TV, air conditioning, baby-equipment rental, dry cleaning, laundry facilities, housekeeping, bar, billiards table, and fitness center. A one-bedroom apartment here (two single beds in the bedroom, a double pull-out couch) can be a good alternative to renting two rooms in a cheap hotel because cooking in the kitchenette saves on your dining costs.

See map p. 110. 18 rue Favart. ☎ 01-40-15-14-00. www.citadines.fr. *Métro: Richelieu-Drouot. Rates: 190€ ($219) per night 1–6 days, 170€ ($196) 7–29 days for a 2-person studio; 274€ ($315) 1–6 days, 240€ ($276) per night 7–29 days for a 3-person duplex (1 bedroom) apt.; 300€ ($345) per night 1–6 days, 274€ ($315) 7–29 days 4-person (1 bedroom) apt. AE, MC, V.*

Hotels in the Heart of the Left Bank (5-7 & 13-14)

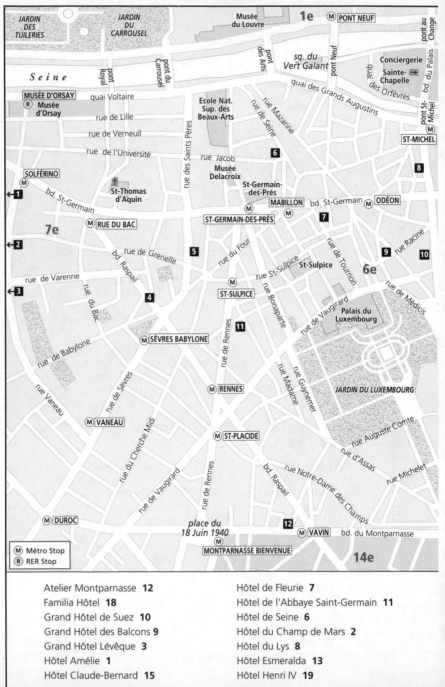

(M) Métro Stop
(R) RER Stop

Atelier Montparnasse **12**
Familia Hôtel **18**
Grand Hôtel de Suez **10**
Grand Hôtel des Balcons **9**
Grand Hôtel Lévêque **3**
Hôtel Amélie **1**
Hôtel Claude-Bernard **15**

Hôtel de Fleurie **7**
Hôtel de l'Abbaye Saint-Germain **11**
Hôtel de Seine **6**
Hôtel du Champ de Mars **2**
Hôtel du Lys **8**
Hôtel Esmeralda **13**
Hôtel Henri IV **19**

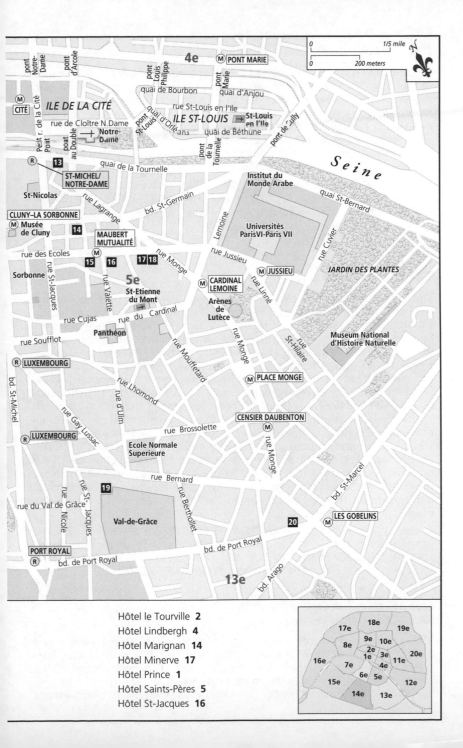

0   1/5 mile

0   200 meters

4e

M PONT MARIE

pont Notre-Dame

pont d'Arcole

pont Louis Philippe

pont Marie

quai de Bourbon

quai d'Anjou

M CITÉ

rue de la Cité

ILE DE LA CITÉ

rue St-Louis en l'Ile

ILE ST-LOUIS

St-Louis en l'Ile

Petit r. de la Cité Pont

rue de Cloître N.Dame

quai d'Orléans

Notre-Dame

pont au Double

pont St-Louis

quai de Béthune

port de Sully

Seine

R **13**

quai de la Tournelle

pont de la Tournelle

ST-MICHEL/ NOTRE-DAME

Institut du Monde Arabe

quai St-Bernard

St-Nicolas

rue Lagrange

bd. St-Germain

Lemoine

CLUNY–LA SORBONNE

M Musée de Cluny

14

MAUBERT MUTUALITÉ

Universités Paris VI-Paris VII

rue Cuvier

rue des Ecoles

15 M **16**

17 18

rue Monge

rue Jussieu

M JUSSIEU

JARDIN DES PLANTES

Sorbonne

rue St-Jacques

5e

rue Valette

St-Etienne du Mont

M CARDINAL LEMOINE

rue Linné

rue Cujas

rue du Cardinal

Arènes de Lutèce

rue St-Hilaire

Museum National d'Histoire Naturelle

rue Soufflot

Panthéon

rue Mouffetard

rue Monge

R LUXEMBOURG

M PLACE MONGE

bd. St-Michel

rue Lhomond

rue d'Ulm

CENSIER DAUBENTON M

rue Gay Lussac

rue Monge

R LUXEMBOURG

rue Brossolette

Ecole Normale Superieure

rue Bernard

rue Nicole

rue St-Jacques

19

rue Berthollet

bd. St-Marcel

rue du Val de Grâce

Val-de-Grâce

20 M

LES GOBELINS

PORT ROYAL

R

bd. de Port Royal

bd. de Port Royal

13e

bd. Arago

Hôtel le Tourville **2**
Hôtel Lindbergh **4**
Hôtel Marignan **14**
Hôtel Minerve **17**
Hôtel Prince **1**
Hôtel Saints-Pères **5**
Hôtel St-Jacques **16**

17e   18e   19e
8e   9e 10e
2e
16e   1e 3e 11e   20e
7e   4e
15e   6e 5e   12e
14e   13e

Citadines Préstige Haussmann Aparthotel
$$$$ Champs-Elysées (8e)

Located near Galeries Lafayette and Au Printemps and in walking distance of the Champs-Elysées, the Madeleine Church, and parc Monceau, this seven-story aparthotel is one of Citadines chain's most luxurious. Studios and apartments are more expensive but also more spacious and luxurious — featuring rare wood furnishings and granite bathrooms. Services and amenities include a 24-hour reception desk, satellite TV, air conditioning, baby-equipment rental, dry cleaning, laundry facilities, housekeeping, bar, and fitness center.

See map p. 110. 129–131 bd. Haussmann. ☎ *01-56-88-61-00.* www.citadines.fr. *Métro: Miromesnil. Rates: 210€ ($242) per night 1–6 days, 144€ ($166) 7–29 days for a 2-person studio; 252€ ($299) per night 1–6 days, 227€ ($261) 7–29 days for a 4-person apt. AE, MC, V.*

Familia Hôtel
$–$$ Latin Quarter (5e)

You can tell that this hotel is a labor of love for its owners the Gaucherons; they've made it the prettiest it can be. Flowers spill out of window boxes; the stone walls in some of the bedrooms have been painstakingly restored or have had provincial-inspired wallpaper added. In other rooms, artists from l'École des Beaux-Arts (Paris's best art school) have painted sepia-toned murals of Parisian scenes. The cozy lobby exudes the atmosphere of a tiny castle with rich tapestries, a winding staircase, and frescoed walls. Some rooms have balconies (numbers 22, 23, 52, 53, 61, 62, 65) with captivating views of the Latin Quarter. From the fifth and sixth floors, you can see Notre-Dame. Bathrooms are small but modern and tiled. All rooms have cable TV and hair dryers. The staff understands what it's like to travel with children and tries to provide kid-friendly services (such as bottle heating) and larger rooms for the weary traveler who requests ahead. Take note that most rooms in the hotel are on the small side, and the least expensive doubles in the corners are tiny. No air conditioning is provided, and remember that it can get hot in Paris heat waves. The Jardin des Plantes is down the street.

See map p. 114. 11 rue des Écoles. ☎ *01-43-54-55-27. Fax: 01-43-29-61-77.* www.hotel-paris-familia.com. *Métro: Cardinal Lemoine or Jussieu. Rates: 70€–91€ ($81–$105) single; 81€–111€ ($93–$128) double; 145€ ($167) quad; 101€ ($116) single or double with balcony. Breakfast 6€ ($6.90). AE, DC, MC, V.*

Four Seasons George V
$$$$ Champs-Elysées (8e)

This is one of Paris's truly legendary palace hotels. When the Four Seasons bought the slightly decaying George V in the late 1990s, they restored fixtures such as the Murano chandeliers and Louis XIV tapestries, yet added modern touches, too. From the elegant light-wood-and-marble lobby opening onto an outside marble courtyard decorated with bright blue awnings and umbrellas, to the cascading displays of fresh flowers, to the friendly welcome of the team of concierges, you'll wake up happy to be staying here. The 245 rooms, separated from the public corridors by their own hallways for more peace and quiet, start at 450 square feet, are decorated in Louis XVI–style furniture, have marble bathrooms, and enjoy the latest technology, including dual phone lines, high-speed Internet access, 51-channel TV with a wireless infrared keyboard, stereo system, and VCR. The Honeymoon Suite has three terraces, and other suites offer a stone's-throw view of the Eiffel Tower — some from their bathtubs. Amenities include the signature Four Season mattresses (930 coils instead of the industry-standard 800), a spa (with its own elevator) offering 24-hour massages and a huge pool, an American bar, and a multi-starred gourmet restaurant, Le Cinq (reviewed in Chapter 10).

See map p. 110. 31 av. George V, 1½ blocks from the Champs-Elysées. ☎ *01-49-52-70-00. Fax: 01-49-52-70-10. Métro: George V. Rates: 680€–890€ ($782–$1,024) double; 1,250€–9,000€ ($1,438–$10,350) suite. Continental breakfast 32€ ($37); American breakfast 43€ ($50). AE, DC, MC, V.*

Grand Hôtel des Balcons
$$–$$$ St-Germain-des-Prés (6e)

Steps from Théâtre de l'Odéon is this gracious and comfortable hotel with balconied rooms, modern light oak furnishings, bright fabrics, 19th-century stained-glass windows, and Art Nouveau lobby furnishings (look for the voluptuous statue of Venus in the breakfast room). Although most rooms and their wrought-iron balconies are small, clever use of space allows for large closets and full-length mirrors. Bathrooms are also small but well designed and come equipped with a clothesline. The higher-priced doubles, triples, and quads are big and luxurious; some have double-sink bathrooms. Free tea and coffee are available in the lounge; all rooms have satellite television and Internet access. If you're celebrating your birthday while in Paris, treat yourself to a stay here; the breakfast buffet (which includes sausage and eggs) is free for the birthday boy or girl. The Jardin du Luxembourg is a five-minute walk south.

See map p. 114. 3 rue Casimir Delavigne. ☎ *01-46-34-78-50. Fax: 01-46-34-06-27. www.balcons.com. Métro: Odéon. RER: Luxembourg. Rates 80€–120€ ($92–$138) single; 100€–150€ ($115–$173) double; 180€ ($207) triple. Buffet breakfast 10€ ($12), free on your birthday. AE, DC, MC, V.*

Grand Hôtel de Suez
$–$$ Latin Quarter (5e)

If you want to stay in the Latin Quarter, you can't beat this location. Guests return for the hotel's 49 good-sized rooms at great prices. Beds are firm, storage space is ample, and the modern bathrooms have hair dryers. Décor is typical modern hotel: a comfortable mirrored lobby furnished with couches and art nouveau lamps, rooms with striped or flowered bedspreads and curtains with color-coordinated artwork and blonde furniture. Each room has satellite TV with 30 channels and an Internet connection.

But you may want to keep the windows to the street-side balconies shut — the Boulevard St-Michel is as noisy as a carnival way past midnight on weekends. The hotel is in a great location near Musée de Cluny, Jardin du Luxembourg, and the Panthéon. The Seine and Notre-Dame are a ten-minute walk away. The hotel also has a high-speed Internet access terminal.

See map p. 114. 31 bd. St-Michel. ☎ *01-53-10-34-00. Fax: 01-40-51-79-44.* www.hotel desuez.fr. *Métro: St-Michel. Rates: 75€–105€ ($86–$121) single; 85€–110€ ($98–$127) double; 115€–130€ ($132–$150) triple. Breakfast 3€ ($3.45). AE, DC, MC, V.*

Grand Hôtel Lévêque
$ Eiffel Tower (7e)

This 1930s–era hotel has been newly renovated with an elevator — and air conditioning! It's just three blocks from the Eiffel Tower on a colorful pedestrian street with the bustling Rue Cler market, bakeries, restaurants, wine shops, and florists. The lobby has a comfortable lounge area with plush circular sofas, a soda- and ice-dispenser, and the daily newspaper. Rooms are snug, with just enough space to be comfortable, and have new, if not inspired, decorations. The bathrooms are small but in excellent condition, and each room has a satellite TV, hair dryer, Internet access, and ceiling fan. Staff members are very friendly and helpful, and if you ask, they may be able to give you a higher-priced room on the fifth floor with a balcony and partial view of the Eiffel Tower. This hotel fills up fast, so book well in advance. Street-side rooms (which have good views) cost a little more than interior rooms.

See map p. 114. 29 rue Cler (where rue Cler meets rue de Grenelle). ☎ *01-47-05-49-15. Fax: 01-45-50-49-36.* www.hotel-leveque.com. *Métro: École-Militaire or Latour-Maubourg. Rates: 56€ ($64) single room without bathroom; 86€–91€ ($90–$105) double bed with bathroom; 86€–106€ ($90–$122) twin beds with bathroom; 122€ ($140) triple with bathroom. Breakfast 8€ ($9.20). AE, MC, V.*

Hôtel Agora
$–$$ Louvre (1er)

Don't worry about the ugly entryway here; it's a disguise for a very good find. This two-star hotel on a busy pedestrian street near Les Halles has a traditional French air once you mount a curved staircase (those with baggage will breathe a sigh of relief that after the initial climb an elevator leads from reception to upper floors) to its eclectic reception area. Rooms have antique furniture, marble mantelpieces, floral prints, and old-fashioned wallpapers. The windows are double-glazed, thankfully, which helps muffle the outside noise. Fifth-floor rooms have balconies with views of the impressive St-Eustache Church.

See map p. 110. 7 rue de la Cossonnerie. ☎ *01-42-33-46-02. Fax: 01-42-33-80-99. Métro: Châtelet. Rates: 78€–103€ ($90–$118) single; 96€–131€ ($110–$151) double; 146€ ($170) triple. Breakfast 8€ ($9.20). AE, MC, V.*

Hôtel Alison
$$ Madeleine (8e)

Located between the Madeleine and the Elysée Palace and near the Champs-Elysées and rue Faubourg St-Honoré, this hotel has a retro 1970s ambience that still manages to be perfectly in tune with the classy neighborhood. The large, well-appointed rooms are furnished in modern style, with black furniture and light walls. Inside the rooms have plenty of storage space, a safe, minibar, trouser press, satellite TV, Internet access, and double-glazed windows. Hair dryers and Roger & Gallet toiletries grace gleaming, tiled bathrooms with wall-mounted showers. You can relax on low, orange-leather couches in the plush lobby or enjoy a drink in the vaulted brick lounge.

See map p. 110. 21 rue de Surène. ☎ *01-42-65-54-00. Fax: 01-42-65-08-17.* www. hotel-alison.com. *Métro: Madeleine or Concorde. Rates: 78€–140€ ($90–$161) single; 110€–140€ ($126–$161) double; 125€–140€ ($144–$161) twin beds; 160€ ($184) triple; 215€–280€ ($247–$322) for two adjoining rooms. Breakfast 8€ ($9.20). AE, DC, MC, V.*

Hôtel Amélie
$ Eiffel Tower (7e)

This is a modest 16-room hotel bedecked with blooming flowers in brimming pots at each window. The renovated rooms are small with tiny closets, but the white-tiled bathrooms offer hair dryers and good-quality toiletries. The location is excellent for seeing such 7th Arrondissement sights as the Eiffel Tower and Napoleon's Tomb, yet the atmosphere is peaceful, almost serene. There is no elevator. The owners often have special summer promotions; in summer 2004 rooms were 7€–10€ ($8.05–$12) off low-season rates.

See map p. 114. 5 rue Amélie. ☎ *01-45-51-74-75. Fax: 01-45-56-93-55. www.*hotel amelie.fr. *Métro: Latour-Maubourg. Rates: 75€–82€ ($86–$94) single; 85€–92€ ($98–$106) double with shower; 93€–100€ ($107–$115) double with bath; 95€–102€ ($109–$117) twin beds. Breakfast: 7€ ($8.05) free. Check Web site for special offers in July and August. AE, DC, MC, V.*

Hôtel Claude-Bernard
$$–$$$ Latin Quarter (5e)

This highly recommended hotel keeps very high standards and wins much repeat business. It features a lobby bar (but it's not manned by a regular bartender; you have to ask at reception if you want to be served), a lounge area with comfortable chairs and a two-person elevator. The decently sized rooms have tasteful wallpaper, sleek bathrooms, minibars, satellite TV, decorative balconies with flowers, and often a well-preserved piece of antique furniture. Some particularly attractive suites come with couches and armchairs. A sauna is available for guests to use, and all rooms are air-conditioned. Nearby is the Panthéon, the Sorbonne, and the fantastic Cluny Museum.

See map p. 114. 43 rue des Écoles. ☎ *01-43-26-32-52. Fax: 01-43-26-80-56.* www. hotelclaudebernard.com. *Métro: Maubert-Mutualité. Rates: 89€–131€ ($102–$150) single; 115€–149€ ($132–$171) double; 135€–185€ ($155–$213)triple; 245€ ($282) suite for 1–4 persons. Continental breakfast 7.90€ ($9.10). AE, DC, MC, V.*

Hôtel de Fleurie
$$$–$$$$ St-Germain-des-Prés (6e)

The Marolleau family has owned this superb hotel since 1988 and earned many repeat visitors. Just off place Odéon on a pretty side street, the Fleurie has all the comforts, including air conditioning, marble bathrooms with heated towel racks, quality toiletries, Oriental carpets, high-speed Internet connections, and satellite TV. The jewel-toned rooms are small but comfortable, and all are furnished in a modern or classic style with such touches as fresh flowers, pretty gingham curtains, and wood-paneled accents. Book at least six weeks in advance for one of the *chambres familiales* — two connecting rooms with two large beds in each room. A continental breakfast is served in the cozy vaulted stone cellar dining room. The staff is friendly, and the hotel is in a superb location near the church of St-Germain-des-Prés; the historic Café de Flore, Café les Deux Magots, and Brasserie Lipp; and a few blocks from the Seine and the Jardin du Luxembourg. The hotel was offering a special promotion at the time of this writing: Stay for four nights, including a Sunday, and get one night free. The owners often offer such special promotions as 10% off a two-consecutive-nights stay if booked through the hotel's Web site.

See map p. 114. 32–34 rue de Grégoire-de-Tours. ☎ *01-53-73-70-00. Fax: 01-53-73-70-20.* www.fleurie-hotel-paris.com. *Métro: Odéon. Rates: 130€–145€ single ($150–$167); 165€–185€ ($190–$213) double with queen-size bed; 240€–265€ ($276–$305) deluxe rooms (large room with two twin beds or one king-size bed); 290€–325€ ($333–$374) family suite. Breakfast 10€ ($12); 5€ ($5.75) for children under 12. AE, DC, MC, V.*

Hôtel de l'Abbaye Saint-Germain
$$$–$$$$ St-Germain-des-Prés (6e)

This former convent is a popular stop for travelers on a budget who have a taste for chic surroundings. You enter through a courtyard and check in at the reception desk, which is in the convent's original vault. Some of the 42 rooms and two- and four-bedroom suites have their original oak ceiling beams, and 19th-century–style furnishings and damask upholstery; all are air-conditioned, with hair dryers, and satellite TV. The rooms are a good size by Paris standards, and the suites are absolutely spacious. Some first-floor rooms open onto a vine-covered terrace; late Italian actor Marcello Mastroianni preferred Room 3. Rooftop suites have terraces. In summer you can eat breakfast — included in the price of your room — in the flower-filled courtyard; in winter, you can lounge in front of the lobby fireplace. The hotel provides a money-changing service.

See map p. 114. 10 rue Cassette, 4 short blocks from the northwest corner of the Jardin du Luxembourg. ☎ *01-45-44-38-11. Fax: 01-45-48-07-86.* www.hotel-abbaye.com.

Métro: St-Sulpice. Rates: 211€–313€ ($243–$360) double room; 393€ ($452) suite; 449€ ($516) duplex suite. AE, MC, V.

Hôtel de la Place des Vosges
$$–$$$ Le Marais (4e)

The entrance to the place des Vosges is only steps away from this hotel which used to be the stables of King Henri IV. Now the exposed stone walls and beamed ceilings complement a plush, antiques-filled lobby. The small rooms with beamed ceilings, firm beds, and tiled bathrooms are well-maintained, though a renovation is planned for the near future. All rooms have TVs (suspended by a chain from the ceiling), desks, and hair dryers, but there is a lack of storage space. The larger top-floor room (number 10) has a pretty view over the Right Bank and a Jacuzzi, but the elevator stops a floor down, which is a consideration if you have a lot of luggage.

See map p. 110. 12 rue de Birague. ☎ *01-42-72-60-46. Fax: 01-42-72-02-64.* www. hotelplacedesvosges.com. *Métro: Bastille. Rates: 105€–120€ ($121–$138) single, double, or twin beds with shower or bath; 205€–250€ ($236–$288) top-floor room with shower, bath, or Jacuzzi. Breakfast 7€ ($8.05). MC, V.*

Hôtel des Deux-Îles
$$–$$$ Ile St-Louis (4e)

With only 17 double rooms, this appealing hotel is superbly located on the Ile St-Louis (practically in Notre-Dame's backyard). The owners are interior decorators, and it shows; the rooms have exposed oak ceiling beams and provincial upholstery, and the lobby is a warm and cozy gem with fresh flowers and bamboo furniture. Off the lobby is a garden that some of the rooms overlook and a basement breakfast room with a fireplace. Although amenities include bathrooms, hair dryers, cable TV, and air conditioning, rooms run from tiny to small, so if you have a large amount of luggage, you may want to look elsewhere. Paris's best ice cream shop, Berthillon (closed in August), is just around the corner, and you can find Berthillon ice cream in nearby brasseries, too. So much is nearby — the Memorial de la Déportation, which commemorates the French Jews sent to Auschwitz; Sainte-Chapelle; the Conciergerie; and the bird and flower markets on Ile de la Cité, to name a few — you may not know where to begin. *Hint:* Start early in the morning with Notre-Dame.

See map p. 110. 59 rue St-Louis-en-l'Ile. ☎ *01-43-26-13-35. Fax: 01-43-29-60-25.* www. deuxiles-paris-hotel.com. *Métro: Pont Marie. Rates: 140€ ($161) single with shower; 158€ ($182) double or twin beds. Breakfast 10€ ($11.50). AE, V.*

Hôtel du Champ de Mars
$–$$ Eiffel Tower (7e)

This 25-room hotel is like a country house tucked away on a colorful street near the Eiffel Tower, and it's a bargain that's hard to beat. The proprietors, the Gourdals, have decorated the rooms with flowered drapes, fabric-covered headboards, throw pillows, and cushioned high-backed seats. There is satellite TV, and bathrooms have hair dryers, large towels, and good lighting; those with tubs have wall-mounted showers. A cozy breakfast room is located in the remodeled basement. Reserve at least four months in advance. In the summer, the two best rooms are on the ground floor and open onto the leafy courtyard; they stay cool despite the lack of air conditioning. A grocery store is two doors down for travelers needing provisions at 27 rue Cler, and the rue Cler outdoor market (open Tuesday-Sunday mornings) is right around the corner.

See map p. 114. 7 rue du Champ de Mars. ☎ *01-45-51-52-30. Fax: 01-45-51-64-36. E-mail:* reservation@hotel-du-champ-de-mars.com. www.hotel-du-champ-de-mars.com. *Métro: École-Militaire. RER: Pont de l'Alma. Rates: 70€–76€ ($81–$87) single with shower; 76€ ($87) double; 80€ ($92) twin beds; 96€ ($110) triple. Breakfast 6.50€ ($7.50). AE, MC, V.*

Hôtel du Lys
$$ St-Germain-des-Prés (6e)

Housed in a 17th-century mansion with its original tall casement windows, Hôtel du Lys is the perfect place for a romantic tryst on a budget. The homey, intimate rooms are decorated in floral wallpaper with exposed-beam high ceilings. Rooms feature double glazing to keep out the noise, and rooms 19 and 22 have balconies. People with disabilities need to heed the lack of an elevator, and the staircase, although historic, is narrow. The Lys is just a few blocks from the Seine and Notre-Dame in an area that gets quite crowded in summer; fortunately, a room here is a haven.

See map p. 114. 23 rue Serpente. ☎ *01-43-26-97-57. Fax: 01-44-07-34-90. Métro: St-Michel or Odéon. Rates: 95€ ($109) single; 110€ ($127) double; 125€ ($144) triple. Rates include breakfast. MC, V.*

Hôtel du Vieux Saule
$–$$ Le Marais/Bastille (3e)

This hotel in the Marais near place de la République offers not only air conditioning but a free sauna, too. The cheerful, but small, rooms have tiled bathrooms, hair dryers, safes, double-glazed windows, luggage racks, satellite TV, trouser presses, and even small irons and ironing boards. The rooms on the fifth floor tend to be bigger. Breakfast is a buffet served in the original 16th-century cozy vaulted cellar accessed by a winding staircase (no elevator).

See map p. 110. 6 rue de Picardie. ☎ *01-42-72-01-14. Fax: 01-40-27-88-21.* www.hotelvieuxsaule.com. *Métro: République. Rates: 76€–91€ ($87–$105) single with shower; 136€–161€ ($156–$185) double with shower or tub; 121€–136€ ($139–$156) deluxe double. Parking garage 12€ ($14) for 12 hours. Buffet breakfast 9€ ($10). AE, DC, MC, V.*

Hôtel Esmeralda
$-$$ Latin Quarter (5e)

This hotel is a favorite of many travelers, and you may have to book as far in advance as three months. However, if you prefer hotels with such amenities as satellite TV and free toiletries, then the Esmeralda is probably not for you. It's off-beat and ramshackle with creaky wood floors and cramped hallways (and even dusty in some places), but its superior location steps from the Seine and Notre-Dame and its prices — a budget traveler's dream — just can't be beat. There is an old, winding wooden staircase (no elevator) and outstanding views of Notre-Dame and the Seine from the hotel's front rooms. East rooms overlook St-Julien-le-Pauvre and square Viviani. Shabby-chic velvet coverings and antique furniture create a homey warmth that almost makes up for the disappointingly dark rear rooms. The front rooms with a view have modern bathrooms with tubs, and some are exceptionally large, making them perfect for travelers with children.

See map p. 114. 4 rue St-Julien-le-Pauvre. ☎ *01-43-54-19-20. Fax: 01-40-51-00-68. Métro: St-Michel. Rates: 35€ ($40) single with sink; 65€ ($75) single or double with bathroom; 85€ ($98) double with view of Notre-Dame; 110€ ($126) triple; 120€ ($138) quad. Breakfast 6€ ($6.90). Shower 2€ ($2.30) per person. No credit cards.*

Hôtel Henri IV
$ Louvre (1er)

This place is old. It doesn't have an elevator; only five rooms have showers or baths, only two have toilets, and none have phones. But this super-budget hotel is one of Europe's most famous and nearly always is full. It occupies a dramatic location on place Dauphine — the northernmost tip of Ile de la Cité, across the river from St-Germain and the Louvre and a few steps from Pont-Neuf. The 17th-century building houses cozy rooms that are past their prime, though many find them romantically evocative (others think they're just rundown). Each room has a sink, but guests share the spotless toilets and showers on each of the five floors. One of the communal bathrooms has an enormous tub, and a few rooms have beautiful views of place Dauphine. All in all, staying here is an adventure. Book far in advance.

See map p. 114. 25 place Dauphine. ☎ *01-43-54-44-53. Métro: Pont Neuf. Rates: 25€–28€ ($29–$32) single with sink; 56€ ($64) single with shower; 32€ ($37) double with sink; 42€–45€ ($48–$52) double with shower but no toilet; 55€–69€ ($63–$79) double with toilet and bath or shower; 50€–62€ ($58–$71) triple. No credit cards. Breakfast is included.*

Hôtel Jeanne d'Arc
$-$$ Le Marais (4e)

Reserve well in advance for this great budget hotel on a pretty little street just off the place St-Catherine. An ongoing renovation to this 18th-century building has toned down some of the surrealistic touches of local artists. Soft tangerine colored wallpaper now decorates the halls of the ground floor, except for the fresh white dining area with billowing white curtains and the blue sitting area directly down the hall from the entrance. Reception is through a door on the right where I was delighted to see hanging on the wall the hotel's signature mosaic mirror tribute to French pride. There is new carpeting up to the first floor, and fish-themed paintings hang near every landing. Rooms are small to decent-sized with large windows, card-key access, and large bathrooms, but storage space is a bit cramped. Other room features include direct-dial telephones, cable TV, and bedside tables. If a view is important, make sure you request one because some rooms don't have one. The hotel is in the center of the Marais, and it can be a little noisy, but you're near the Musée Picasso, place des Vosges, and the Bastille, and the fabulous Au Bistro de la Place cafe is in the square next door.

See map p. 110. 3 rue de Jarente. ☎ 01-48-87-62-11. Fax: 01-48-87-37-31. www.hotel jeannedarc.com. *Métro: St-Paul or Bastille. Rates: 57–80€ ($65–$92) single; 80€–95€ ($92–$109) double; 112€ ($129) triple; 140€ ($161) quad. Breakfast 6€ ($6.90). MC, V.*

Hôtel le Faubourg Paris, Sofitel Demeure
$$$$ Champs-Elysées (8e)

If you want a luxurious but cozy place to stay near the Jardins des Tuileries, the Louvre, and Place Vendôme shopping, Le Faubourg is the spot. Opened in 1999, Le Faubourg is comprised of two buildings — one 18th-century, the other 19th-century and formerly the offices of *Marie Claire* magazine (reflected in the décor: a mix of contemporary and classic styles, with feng shui touches). The 174 rooms are decently sized, and all are comfortable and quiet. In fact, the short-stay, one-person Classic rooms are small without being the least bit claustrophobic. If you want a specific feature — a balcony, a view, high ceilings — be sure to ask when booking your room. All rooms include Sofitel's cloud-like MyBed and thoughtful touches such as bottles of Evian, Lenôtre chocolates, a card of recommended jogging routes in the nearby gardens, and Roger & Gallet toiletries (suites and the apartment kick it up a notch with Hermès toiletries), satellite television with pay movies and Nintendo, air conditioning, CD players, dataports, minibars, and hairdryers. The hotel is frequented primarily by business travelers, including fashionistas in town for the biannual shows, but celebrity guests like David Bowie and Plácido Domingo seem to appreciate Le Faubourg's low-key, high-quality accommodations and the relaxed, personalized service. Complimentary coffee is served in the library every morning, and Bar30 has live music Monday through Saturday from 7 p.m. till 1:30 a.m. Plans are afoot to convert the fitness center into a spa in 2005. Be sure to ask about packages and special rates in July and August, when business is a bit slower. Babysitting is available.

See map p. 110. 15 rue Boissy d'Anglas, 75008 Paris. ☎ 800/SOFITEL or 01-44-94-14-00. www.sofitel.com. *Métro: Concorde. 420€–525€ ($483–$604) single; 480€–600€ ($552–$690) double; 555€–1,213€ ($638–$1,395) suite; 2,000€–2,500€ ($2,300–$2,875) apartment. Breakfast 23€ ($26). AE, MC, V. Parking 25€ ($29).*

Hôtel le Tourville
$$–$$$ Eiffel Tower (7e)

This splendid restored mansion, located just steps behind Les Invalides, can be addictive. You receive almost all the amenities of a pricier hotel — Roger & Gallet toiletries, hair dryers, air conditioning, chic decor with antiques — for manageable prices. Rooms are decorated in soft yellows, pink, or sand, with crisp white damask upholsteries, antique bureaus and lamps, fabulously mismatched old mirrors, and marble bathrooms. Rooms also have satellite TV, hair dryers, and 24-hour room service. You may want to ask for one of the four magnificent rooms with walk-out vine-draped terraces or a junior suite with whirlpool bath. The staff is wonderfully helpful. A grocery store a few doors down is open until 10 p.m., and a tabac is right next door.

See map p. 114. 16 av. de Tourville. ☎ *01-47-05-62-62. Fax: 01-47-05-43-90. Métro: École-Militaire. Rates: 182€ standard double; 254€ ($292) superior double; 291€ ($335) double with private terrace; 400€ ($460) junior suite. Breakfast 12€ ($14). AE, DC.*

Hôtel Lindbergh
$$ St-Germain-des-Prés (7e)

Aviation-themed photos add a tasteful touch to the decor at this pretty hotel named for the American aviator. The standard rooms are simple and delightful, with colorful bedspreads and matching bathrooms. The deluxe rooms have floor-length draperies, fabric headboards, and color-coordinated cushioned seats. The garnet-toned lobby is inviting; you can chat there with the friendly owners who like to talk about their collections of photos that include Charles Lindbergh in his plane, Lindbergh standing with Louis Blériot (the first man to fly across the English Channel), and Lindbergh with Antoine de Saint-Exupéry, the pilot author of *Le Petit Prince*. The hotel is right at the edge of the St-Germain-des-Prés shopping district, and Au Bon Marché department store, with its terrific L'Épicerie supermarket, is only a few short blocks away. The Musée Rodin is within walking distance. Those with energy can hoof the long blocks over to the Eiffel Tower; otherwise catch bus number 69 from nearby rue du Bac to the Champ du Mars.

See map p. 114. 5 rue Chomel. ☎ *01-45-48-35-53. Fax: 01-45-49-31-48.* www.hotel lindbergh.com. *Métro: Sèvres-Babylone. Rates: 95€ ($109) double with shower; 95€–108€ ($109–$124) double (or twin beds) with shower and bath; 112€–156€ ($129–$179) larger double for 1–4 people. Breakfast 8€ ($9.20). AE, MC, V.*

Hôtel Louvre Forum
$ Louvre (1er)

For a truly central, reasonably priced hotel just steps from the Louvre, this comfortable modern hotel is difficult to beat. The brightly colored rooms have tiled bathrooms (with hair dryers) and furniture that includes writing tables, lamps, and chairs. Each room has a small armoire with hanging space and shelves; however, the rooms on the lower floors are a bit cramped. The lobby features a mural of the neighborhood, which is only a short walk from the elegant Palais Royal and the Louvre.

See map p. 110. 25 rue du Bouloi. ☎ *01-42-36-54-19. Fax: 01-42-36-66-31.* www. paris-hotel-louvre-forum.com. *Métro: Louvre-Rivoli. Rates: 75€ ($86) single; 85€ ($98) double with shower; 95€ ($109) double with full bath. Continental breakfast 9€ ($10). AE, DC, MC, V.*

Hôtel Louvre Richelieu
$–$$ Louvre (1er)

This is a very basic hotel with good-sized rooms and a great location — halfway between the Louvre and the Opéra. Enter through a corridor with restored stone walls; the pleasant reception area and lobby are on the second floor. The two-bed double rooms are dark, but spacious with high ceilings. Each room has a writing table, a small closet, and a suitcase rack. The lack of an elevator here means that you may want to book elsewhere if you're loaded down with luggage. Reserve at least two weeks in advance for summer. A bakery is right next door.

See map p. 110. 51 rue de Richelieu. ☎ *01-42-97-46-20. Fax: 01-47-03-94-13.* www. louvre-richelieu.com. *Métro: Palais-Royal–Musée du Louvre, Pyramides. Rates: 60€ ($69) single with toilet; 84€ ($97) single with bathroom; 72€ ($83) double with toilet; 84€ ($97) double with bathroom; 88€ ($101) twin with bathroom; 108€ ($124) triple with bathroom; 124€ ($143) quad with bathroom. Breakfast 6€ ($6.90) MC, V.*

Hôtel Marignan
$–$$ Latin Quarter (5e)

It's plain and unassuming on the outside, but owners Paul and Linda Keniger have invested much time and energy in their hotel and have many repeat customers. They welcome families, don't mind if you bring your own food into the dining room, and they even make the kitchen available during the low season. You also have a washer-dryer and iron at your disposal. Signs in English recommend neighborhoods to visit and tours to take, and you can always ask one of the Kenigers for recommendations. The hotel is very close to the Sorbonne — it's around the corner from the Panthéon, near the outdoor green market on rue Mouffetard — and its good rates attract students. Rooms fill up quickly in July and August, so if you plan to travel then, book well in advance.

See map p. 114. 13 rue du Sommerard. ☎ *01-43-54-63-81. Fax: 01-43-25-31-03.* www. hotel-marignan.com. *Métro: Maubert-Mutualité or St-Michel. Rates: 42€–47€ ($48–$54) single with toilet and shower on floor, 49€–58€ ($56–$67) single with toilet in room, shared shower, 65€ ($75) in-room toilet and shower; 55€–63€ ($63–$72) double with shared toilet and shower, 69€–74€ ($79–$85) double with toilet, 78€–88€ ($90–$101) double with toilet and shower; 75€ ($86) triple with toilet and shower on floor, 85€–95€ ($98–$109) triple with toilet, 100€–110€ ($115–$127) triple with shower and toilet; 85€ ($98) quad with shower and toilet on floor, 95€–100€ ($109–$115) quad with toilet, 120€–130€ ($138–$150) quad with toilet and shower;*

105€ ($121) quintuple with shower and toilet on floor, 105€–115€ ($121–$132) quintuple with toilet, 135€–150€ ($155–$173) quintuple with shower and toilet. Continental breakfast included. MC, V.

Hôtel Meurice
$$$$ Louvre (1er)

This palace hotel is positively regal from its mosaic and marble floors to its towering ceilings with chandeliers, gold-leaf walls, hand-painted friezes, and 18th-century furnished grand lobby. (A recent visit featured plush red velvet chairs and loveseats with huge rose-shaped backs and matching cactus-like ottomans by Italian artist Carla Tolomeo.) You'll think you're staying at Versailles, and, indeed, royalty stays here (the hotel's slogan is "The Hotel of Kings"). Each floor corresponds to a particular period of decor. Rooms are spacious, soundproof, air-conditioned, and have ornate molded ceilings. They lack nothing in the way of luxuries, from fresh flowers and antique furnishings to walk-in closets, satellite television, and computer ports. On-site restaurants include the marble-trimmed Meurice, for a true French gastronomic experience, and the lighter-fare Winter Garden with its splendid Art Nouveau glass roof and live piano music. Amenities include an on-site health club and spa with Jacuzzi, Turkish baths, and massage; a laundry and dry cleaners; office and translation services; and round-the-clock maid service. The hotel faces the Jardin des Tuileries and is around the corner from the couture houses of the Faubourg St-Honoré and the elegant place Vendôme. The Louvre is just a few minutes west on rue de Rivoli. Rooms in the upper price categories have Tuileries views.

See map p. 110. 228 rue Rivoli. ☎ 01-44-58-10-06. Fax: 01-44-58-10-19. www.meurice hotel.com. *Métro: Tuileries, but if you're going to stay here, you want to arrive by limo or taxi, at the very least. Rates: 490€–650€ ($564–$478) singles; 650€–800€ ($478–$920) doubles; 800€–2,600€ ($920–$2,990) suites; prices for apartments and royal suite with private terrace available on request. Continental breakfast 32€, ($37) American breakfast 45€ ($52). AE, DC, MC, V.*

Hôtel Minerve
$–$$ Latin Quarter (5e)

Owners of the Familia Hotel (reviewed earlier in this chapter), Eric and Sylvie Gaucheron also own Hotel Minerve next door. More upscale than the Familia, rooms are larger and have wood-beamed ceilings, exposed stone walls, carved mahogany wood furnishings, and expensive wallpapers. Pretty hand-painted sepia frescos can be found in several of the rooms, as well as provincial fabrics. All have modern bathrooms with hair dryers, satellite TV, and Internet broadband access (at 19€/$22 a day). Ten rooms have large balconies with a table and chairs overlooking the street. The Minerve is as welcoming to kids as the Familia. If you're craving an American breakfast, head just a few blocks down to the delicious fare at Breakfast in America at 73 rue des Écoles.

See map p. 114. 13 rue des Écoles. ☎ 01-43-26-26-04. Fax: 01-44-07-01-96. www. hotel-paris-minerve.com. *Métro: Cardinal Lemoine or Jussieu. Rates:*

82€–115€ ($94–$132) single; 96€–112€ ($110–$129) double; 98€ ($113) twin; 148€ ($170) triple; 128€ ($147) large double with balcony, patio, or cathedral ceiling. Breakfast 8€ ($9.20). Parking 20€ ($23). AE, MC, V.

Hôtel Montpensier
$–$$　Louvre (1er)

Supposedly the former residence of Mademoiselle de Montpensier, cousin of Louis XIV, this hotel's high ceilings and windows, the stained-glass ceiling in its lounge, and its grand staircase create a sense of faded grandeur. Many rooms on the first two floors, which date from the 17th century, are either drab or have a faded elegance (depending on your point of view), while rooms on the fifth floor (an elevator is available) have attractive slanted ceilings and good views over the rooftops. Most rooms are comfortably outfitted with easy chairs, ample closet space, and modern bathrooms with hair dryers. Reserve at least a month in advance for July. The prices are terrific for this location, just two blocks from the Jardin du Palais Royal and right down the street from the Louvre and the Jardin des Tuileries.

See map p. 110. 12 rue Richelieu. ☎ *01-42-96-28-50. Fax: 01-42-86-02-70.* www. hotel-paris-montpensier.com. *Métro: Palais-Royal–Musée du Louvre. Rates: 54€–57€ ($62–$65) single with sink, 59€ ($68) single with toilet and sink; 57€ ($65) double with sink, 59€ ($68) double with sink and toilet, 78€ ($90) double with shower and toilet, 92€ ($106) double with full bath; 106€ ($122) triple with full bath; 119€ ($137) quad with full bath. Ask about special promotions when booking or check the Web site. Breakfast 7€ ($8.05). AE, MC, V.*

Hôtel Prince
$–$$　Eiffel Tower (7e)

Just a ten-minute walk from the Eiffel Tower, the Prince is a good value for the location. Rooms are modern, soundproof, and have exposed brick walls, matching curtains and bedspreads, and big bathrooms with fluffy towels. Although they vary in size, all rooms are pleasant, comfortable, and well kept, with double-glazed windows, suitcase racks, TV, mini-fridges, and ample closets; some have hair dryers and safes. If you're too worn out from sightseeing to stagger out the door to the two downstairs cafes (not a part of the hotel), the hotel can arrange for a local restaurant to deliver a meal. A ground-floor room is available with facilities for travelers with disabilities.

See map p. 114. 66 av. Bosquet. ☎ *01-47-05-40-90. Fax: 01-47-53-06-62.* www.hotel-paris-prince.com. *Métro: École-Militaire. Rates: 69€ ($79) single with shower; 83€–107€ ($95–$123) double; 91€–105€ ($105–$121) twin; 115€ ($132) triple. Buffet breakfast 7.50€ ($8.60). AE, MC, V.*

Hôtel Saint-Merry
$$$–$$$$　Le Marais (4e)

If you're passionate about the Gothic, this hotel is for you. Located on a pedestrian-only street in the Marais, the hotel was formerly the

17th-century presbytery of the Church of Saint-Merry next door (and was once a brothel as well), and it retains a medieval atmosphere. Beds have wood screens for headboards, except for Room 9, in which the bed has flying buttresses on either side (easy to trip over in the dark, but original, nonetheless!) that make you feel as if you're sleeping in Notre-Dame. The rooms are dark with beamed ceilings, stone walls, wrought-iron chandeliers, sconces, and candelabras. Fabrics are sumptuous, rugs are Oriental, and bathrooms are pleasantly modern, fully tiled, and equipped with hair dryers. Staff is very helpful and friendly. Higher prices are for larger rooms with views. In keeping with its medieval church-like feeling, the phone in the lobby is in a confessional, and you won't find an elevator in the building. TVs are in suites only. The hotel location is a few short blocks from the Seine and Hôtel de Ville. The Louvre is about a 15-minute walk down nearby rue de Rivoli.

See map p. 110. 78 rue de la Verrerie. ☎ *01-42-78-14-15. Fax: 01-40-29-06-82.* www. hotelmarais.com *(for booking only). Métro: Hôtel-de-Ville or Châtelet. Rates: 160€–230€ ($184–$265) double; 160€–230€ ($184–$265) room with twin beds; 205€–275€ ($236–$316) triple; 335€–407€ ($385–$468) suites. In-room breakfast 11€ ($13). AE, V.*

Hôtel Saints-Pères
$$–$$$ St-Germain-des-Prés (6e)

The poet Edna St. Vincent Millay loved the garden filled with camellias, and travelers have made this romantic hotel one of the Left Bank's most popular. Designed in the 17th century by Louis XIV's architect, the hotel is furnished with antiques, old paintings, tapestries, and gilt mirrors, but its 39 rooms have modern amenities such as air-conditioning, satellite TV and minibars. The most requested room is the *chambre à la fresque* (shamb ah lah *fresk*), which has a 17th-century painted ceiling. Breakfast and cocktails are served in the garden when the weather is good. The hotel is a stone's throw from Brasserie Lipp, Café de Flore, and the Deux Magots.

See map p. 114. 65 rue des St-Pères. ☎ *01-45-44-50-00. Fax: 01-45-44-90-83.* www. esprit-de-france.com *(booking only). Métro: St-Germain-des-Prés or Sèvres-Babylone. Rates: 105€ ($121) single; 120€–260€ ($138–$30) double; 185€–195€ ($213–$224) twin; 290€ ($333) suite and chambre à la fresque. Breakfast 12€ ($14). AE, MC, V.*

Hôtel de Seine
$$–$$$ St-Germain-des-Près (6e)

More like a private mansion than a hotel, the Hôtel de Seine is centrally located on a street full of art galleries in St-Germain-des-Près, between boulevard St-Germain and rue Jacob. It's a few blocks from the Seine and the pedestrian bridge Pont des Arts that leads to the Louvre. Each room is distinctly decorated with either French provincial furniture and flowered wallpaper or Provence-inspired jewel-toned paint and Louis XVI reproductions. Rooms have satellite TV, marble bathrooms, hair dryers. Check the Web site for specials: For all of 2004, proprietor Monsieur

Henneveux offered a 30 percent discount to WWII veterans and 15 percent to their families.

See map p. 114. 52 rue de Seine. ☎ *01-46-34-22-80. Fax: 01-46-34-04-74.* www. paris-hotel-seine-river.com. *Métro: St-Germain-des-Près, Mabillon. Rates: 138€ ($159) single; 155€ ($178) double; 165€ ($190) twin; 200€ ($230) triple. Breakfast 10€ ($12); breakfast served in room 11€ ($13). V.*

Hôtel St-Jacques
$$ Latin Quarter (5e)

This building was designed by Baron Haussmann (architect of modern Paris and its grand boulevards) and has been beautifully preserved. Several of its 35 rooms have restored 19th-century ceiling murals, and most of the high ceilings have elaborate plasterwork, giving the decor an old-Paris feel that is accentuated with traditional furniture and fabric-covered walls. The owners have added their own touches in the hallways, with stenciling on the walls and *trompe l'oeil* painting (a clever technique in which architectural elements are added to a room by painting them in to appear real) around the doors and walls and ceiling murals in the breakfast room and lounge. Modern comforts include generally spacious rooms, an elevator, immaculate tiled bathrooms with hair dryers and toiletries, double-glazed windows, ample closet space, fax and computer outlets, and satellite TV. Although they aren't accessible by elevator (which stops a floor down), the rooms on the top floor are less expensive and have great views. The hotel is in a good location near the Sorbonne, Panthéon, and the Musée de Cluny, and a short walk from boulevard St-Germain, boulevard St-Michel, and rue Mouffetard.

See map p. 114. 35 rue des Écoles (at rue des Carmes). ☎ *01-44-07-45-45. Fax: 01-43-25-65-50. Métro: Maubert-Mutualité. Rates: 49€ ($56) single without shower or toilet, 75€ ($86) single with bathroom; 85€–112€ ($98–$129) double; 135€ ($155) triple. Breakfast 9€ ($10). AE, DC, MC, V.*

Hôtel Tiquetonne
$ Opéra (2e)

If a view is more important than space, ask the owner, Madame Sirvain, to give you one of the top rooms at this no-frills budget hotel. Rooms at the top boast views of the Eiffel Tower or Sacré-Coeur. Some have been renovated with new wallpaper, but most are in need of updating (the furniture is old and the wallpaper faded), though they nevertheless are spotless, with firm beds and adequate storage space. Each has the basics: a bed with a wall-mounted wooden headboard, table, and comfortable chairs. Walls tend to be thin. The Tiquetonne is located just off a busy pedestrian street containing food stores, body piercing establishments, and artsy jewelry shops, and is not too far from the red-light district of rue St-Denis and a five-minute walk to the Marais. Still, it manages to be a haven from the outside world. Ask for rooms facing the quieter rue Tiquetonne.

See map p. 110. 6 rue Tiquetonne. ☎ *01-42-36-94-58. Fax: 01-42-36-02-94. Métro: Etienne Marcel or Réamur-Sébastopol. Rates: 35€ ($40) single with toilet, 40€ ($46) single with shower; 50€ ($58) double with shower or bath. Shower 5€ ($5.75) per person. V only. The hotel is closed during August.*

Hôtel Vivienne
$–$$ Opéra (2e)

Hôtel Vivienne is well located between the Louvre and the Opéra and offers comfortable, if not the most luxurious, rooms at a good price. A gorgeous renovation of the lobby produced sleek cream and dark wood furniture and a curved reception desk. Rooms, some of which have been freshened up with new paint and wallpaper, and bathrooms vary in size from adequate to huge, and all are in good shape with satellite television and modem jacks. Some rooms have adjoining doors, perfect for families, others have small terraces. The newly renovated bathrooms have hair dryers and wall-mounted showers in the tubs, and some rooms have views of the Eiffel Tower. Before venturing from the neighborhood, explore the Galeries Vivienne and Colbert, gorgeous historic covered passageways with pretty shops, intimate restaurants, and art galleries. There's an entrance at 6 rue Vivienne down the street.

See map p. 110. 40 rue Vivienne. ☎ *01-42-33-13-26. Fax : 01-40-41-98-19. E-mail:* paris@hotel-vivienne.com. *Métro: Bourse, Richelieu-Drouot, Grands Boulevards. Rates: 52€ ($59) single with shower, shared toilet; 67€ ($77) double with shower, shared toilet; 79€–82€ ($91–$94) double with toilet and shower or bathtub; 82€–88€ ($83–$101) twin with toilet and shower or bathtub. Breakfast 7€ ($8.05). MC, V.*

Lord Byron Hôtel
$$–$$$ Champs-Elysées (8e)

Located just off the Champs-Elysées on a narrow street lined with town houses, the Lord Byron is one of the best values in the neighborhood. Exuding a sense of luxury and peacefulness, draperies filter the sun in the Lord Byron's lobby, the reception desk is under an arch, and a pleasant little garden makes you feel miles away from the busy Champs-Elysées. Rooms are furnished with antique reproductions, Provençal and classic French fabrics, and framed landscapes. They also feature minibars, satellite TV, hair dryers, and full bathrooms. Near the Arc de Triomphe, this is a good hotel to stay in during the Tour de France or the Bastille Day military parade; you're close enough to walk to the action early yet are on a side street so that crowds won't interfere.

See map p. 110. 5 rue de Chateaubrand. ☎ *01-43-59-89-98. Fax: 42-89-46-04. Métro: George V, then rue Washington for 1 block, turn left. Rates: 140€ ($161) single with bathroom; 175€–190€ ($201–$219) double or twin; 270€ ($311) suite. Breakfast is included.*

Pavillon de la Reine
$$$$ Le Marais (3e)

This hotel right off the Place des Vosges is the epitome of serene elegance from the moment you first set eyes on it. The facade positively drips with ivy, and flowers bloom from its window boxes. Enter through wrought-iron gates to a pretty flowered courtyard and on into the cozy wood-beamed and flagstone-floored lobby. In winter, a welcoming fire burns in the marble fireplace in the antique-filled lounge, just off the lobby. Rooms are simply divine: from the large standard rooms decorated with such country touches as gingham wallpaper and Louis XIII-style furniture, to superior duplex rooms where modern beds (some decorated in purple velvet and taffeta) are located in a loft above a cozy sitting room with comfortable chairs and couches, to suites with four-poster beds and beamed ceilings opening onto the courtyard. Rooms overlook the courtyard or a flowered patio and have all the amenities: air conditioning, cable TV, room service, minibars, and laundry service. Breakfast is served in the vaulted cellar, amidst tapestries; pastries are made at the boulangerie next door.

See map p. 110. 28 place des Vosges. ☎ *01-40-29-19-19. Fax: 01-40-29-19-20.* www. pavillon-de-la-reine.com. *Métro: St-Paul. Rates: 335€–410€ ($385–$472) double; 600€–780€ ($690–$897) suites. Continental breakfast 20€ ($23), buffet breakfast 25€ ($29). AE, DC, MC, V.*

Paris's Runner-Up Hotels

You can also try the following very good hotels — there just isn't enough space to include a full listing!

Atelier Montparnasse
$$ St-Germain-des-Prés (6e)   Here you find Art Deco–inspired elegance within shouting distance of three cafes favored by 1920s artists — Le Dôme, Le Select, and La Coupole. See map p. 114. *49 rue Vavin.* ☎ *01-46-33-60-00. Fax: 01-40-51-04-21.*

Costes
$$$$ Louvre (1er)   This may just be Paris's trendiest, most opulent hotel, where celebrity spotting is the norm in its popular Costes bar and Costes restaurant with swimming in the hotel pool an added treat. See map p. 110. *239 rue St-Honoré.* ☎ *01-42-44-50-00. Fax: 01-42-44-50-01.*

Hilton Arc de Triomphe
$$$$ Champs-Elysées (8e)   This brand new luxury hotel has endless amenities from the latest high technology advances, some rooms with private terraces, beautiful terraced eateries Brasserie Le Safran and the Purple Bar, and the Carita/Decléor Spa. See map p. 110. *51-57, rue de Courcelles.* ☎ *01-58 36 6700. Fax: 01-58 36 6777.* www.hilton.com.

Hôtel Henri IV

$$ Latin Quarter (5e) No, this isn't that super-budget hotel on place Dauphine, but a beautiful and refined lodging with views of St-Severin Church located close to Notre-Dame and the quays of the Seine. See map p. 110. *9-11 rue St-Jacques.* ☎ *01-46-33-20-20. Fax: 01-46-33-90-90.* www.hotel-henri4.com.

La Sanguine

$$ Champs-Elysées (8e) Just steps away from the Madeleine and the rue du Faubourg St-Honoré, this hotel is pleasant and filled with flowers; don't neglect to say *bonjour* to the owner's pet Dachshund, Tokyo. See map p. 110. *6 rue de Surène.* ☎ *01-42-65-71-61. Fax: 01-42-66-96-77.*

Index of Accommodations by Neighborhood

Louvre (1er)

Citadines Les Halles Aparthotel $$–$$$
Citadines Louvre Aparthotel $$$
Costes $
Hôtel Agora $–$$
Hôtel Henri IV $
Hôtel Louvre Forum $
Hôtel Louvre Richelieu $–$$
Hôtel Meurice $$$$
Hôtel Montpensier $–$$

Opéra (2e)

Citadines Paris Opéra-Grands Boulevards Aparthotel $$$–$$$$
Hôtel Tiquetonne $–$$
Hôtel Vivienne $–$$

Le Marais (3e, 4e)

Castex Hôtel $
Hôtel de la Place des Vosges $$–$$$
Hôtel des Deux-Iles $$–$$$
Hôtel du Vieux Saule $–$$
Hôtel Jeanne d'Arc $–$$
Hôtel Saint-Merry $$$–$$$$
Pavillon de la Reine $$$$

Latin Quarter (5e)

Familia Hôtel $–$$
Grand Hôtel de Suez $–$$
Hôtel Claude-Bernard $$–$$$
Hôtel Esmeralda $–$$

Hôtel Henri IV $$
Hôtel Marignan $–$$
Hotel Minerve $–$$
Hôtel St-Jacques $$

St-Germain-des-Prés (6e)

Atelier Montparnasse $$$–$$$$
Grand Hôtel des Balcons $$–$$$
Hôtel de Fleurie $$$–$$$$
Hôtel de l'Abbaye Saint-Germain $$$–$$$$
Hôtel du Lys $$
Hôtel Saints-Pères $$–$$$
Hôtel de Seine $$–$$$

Eiffel Tower (7e)

Grand Hôtel Lévêque $
Hôtel Amélie $
Hôtel du Champ de Mars $–$$
Hôtel le Tourville $$–$$$
Hôtel Lindbergh $$
Hôtel Prince $–$$

Champs-Elysées–Madeleine (8e)

Citadines Préstige Haussmann Aparthotel $$$$
Four Seasons George V $$$$
Hilton Arc de Triomphe $$$$
Hôtel Alison $$
La Sanguine $$
Lord Byron Hôtel $$–$$$
Hôtel le Faubourg Paris, Sofitel Demeure $$$$

Index of Accommodations by Price

$

Familia Hôtel (5e)
Grand Hôtel de Suez (5e)
Grand Hôtel Lévêque (7e)
Hôtel Agora (1er)
Hôtel Amélie (7e)
Hôtel du Champ de Mars (7e)
Hôtel du Vieux Saule (3e)
Hôtel Esmeralda (5e)
Hôtel Henri IV (1er)
Hôtel Jeanne d'Arc (4e)
Hôtel Louvre Forum (1er)
Hôtel Louvre Richelieu (1er)
Hôtel Marignan (5e)
Hôtel Minerve (5e)
Hôtel Montpensier (1er)
Hôtel Prince (7e)
Hôtel Tiquetonne (2e)
Hôtel Vivienne (2e)

$$

Atelier Montparnasse (6e)
Castex Hôtel (3e)
Citadines Les Halles Aparthotel (1er)
Citadines Louvre Aparthotel (1er)
Grand Hôtel des Balcons (6e)
Hôtel Alison (8e)
Hôtel Claude-Bernard (5e)
Hôtel de la Place des Vosges (4e)

Hôtel des Deux-Iles (4e)
Hôtel du Lys (6e)
Hôtel Henri IV
Hôtel le Tourville (7e)
Hôtel Lindbergh (7e)
Hôtel Louvre Richelieu (1er)
Hôtel Saints-Pères (6e)
Hôtel de Seine (6e)
Hôtel St-Jacques (5e)
La Sanguine (8e)
Lord Byron Hôtel (8e)

$$$

Citadines Paris Opéra-Grands
Boulevards Aparthotel (2e)
Hôtel de Fleurie (6e)
Hôtel de l'Abbaye Saint-Germain (6e)
Hôtel Saint-Merry (4e)

$$$$

Citadines Préstige Haussmann
Aparthotel (8e)
Costes (1er)
Four Seasons Georges V (8e)
Hilton Arc de Triomphe (8e)
Hôtel le Faubourg Paris, Sofitel
Demeure (8e)
Hôtel Meurice (1er)
Pavillon de la Reine (3e)

Chapter 10

Dining and Snacking in Paris

In This Chapter

▶ Getting the inside scoop on Paris's dining scene
▶ Eating well without breaking the bank
▶ Revealing Paris's best dining establishments
▶ Grabbing something on the go
▶ Discovering the best bakeries, cafes, wine bars, and tea salons
▶ Finding a restaurant by location, cuisine, and price

*P*aris is restaurant heaven, and one of the best things about visiting Paris is finding out for yourself what a high-quality meal *à la française* can be. If you want to experience a true French meal that stretches blissfully over several courses, you can do just that at the establishments listed in this chapter. Each has all the ingredients of an excellent dining spot — fantastic cooking, reasonable prices, and great atmosphere — and creates the kind of experience that lingers on in your memory after the last dish is cleared away. Then, when you just can't sit down to another multiple-course meal, you can choose from street food and sandwiches to cafeterias and tea salons to cafes listed later in the chapter.

This chapter is designed to make you feel comfortable about dining in Parisian restaurants, so that your experiences are pleasant and memorable, as well as delicious because, let's face it, unless you grew up in France, it can be quite intimidating to translate a menu and figure out what to eat. Here, you'll find the differences between bistros and brasseries, cafes and restaurants, in addition to money-saving tips and suggestions on what to wear.

For detailed culinary information see Chapter 2, where I give a little history of French cuisine, a useful glossary of French culinary terms, and a user's guide to typical French dishes.

Getting the Dish on the Local Scene

In France, as anywhere, you should never underestimate the importance of good manners. Your meal will be much smoother if you remember essential but basic phrases such as *"Bonjour, monsieur"* (hello, sir) and *"Merci, madame"* (thank you, madam). Keep in mind, too, that French table manners require that all food, even fruit, be eaten with a knife and fork.

Contrary to what you may have seen in the movies, *never, ever* refer to the waiter as *"garçon,"* (boy) and don't snap your fingers at him or her. Instead, say, *"Monsieur, s'il vous plaît!"* or *"Madame/Mademoiselle, s'il vous plaît!"* (Sir/Madam/Miss, if you please!).

Most French restaurants are small enough that you may feel as if all eyes are upon you. To feel more comfortable, follow the advice set out in this section, and you can dine in Paris like a local.

Making reservations for dinner

The vast majority of French restaurants are very small establishments with limited seating, and tables are scrupulously saved for folks who book. Always try to make at least a same-day reservation, even for a modest neighborhood bistro. Some top restaurants require several weeks' notice. Remember to call if you're going to be more than 20 minutes late. Showing up late is considered bad form.

If you're staying at a hotel with a staff concierge, phone or fax ahead and ask the concierge to make a reservation if you'd like to eat at a sought-after restaurant. Make the call as early as possible, specifying your preferred date with a back-up date or two. Don't forget to tip the concierge (slip 10€/$12 discreetly into an envelope and present it when checking out).

Dressing to dine

Only the most expensive restaurants enforce dress codes (suit and tie), and in theory, you can dress up or down as you like. Realize, however, that Parisians are a pretty stylish lot, even when dressing informally in jeans. Relaxed dressing doesn't mean sloppy jeans and sneakers — *especially* sneakers. The look to aim for is casual Fridays at work. You can't go wrong if you dress in neutral colors — think black, beige, cream, navy, and chocolate. If you wear jeans, pair them with a nice jacket, sweater, or shirt and good shoes. Go a notch dressier than what you'd wear at home.

Knowing the difference between a cafe and a bistro

Eateries go by various names in France, and in theory at least, these labels give you some clue to how much a meal costs. From most expensive to least expensive, the lineup generally goes like this: restaurant, bistro, brasserie, cafe. The key word is *generally.* Never rely on the name of an establishment as the sole price indicator; Some of the city's most expensive eateries call themselves cafes. Furthermore, the awnings above quintessential cafes often claim the labels of restaurant, cafe, brasserie, or some other combination. The only way to be sure of the price is to read the menu, which by law is posted outside.

✔ **Restaurants** are where you go to savor French cuisine in all its glory. At their best, classic dishes are excellent, and new dishes are inventive. Dining is usually more formal than in bistros or brasseries, and service is slower. You may also have more than one server. Generally, restaurants serve lunch between noon and 2:30 p.m. and dinner between 7:00 and 10:00 p.m. You must be seated for lunch no later than 2 p.m. If you want a full meal.

Between 3 and 7 p.m., you may find it nearly impossible to have a sit-down meal in a Paris restaurant or bistro. During this swing shift, your best bet is to head to a cafe, tearoom, or wine bar. Dining at 7 p.m. is considered very early for dinner in Paris; most Parisians wouldn't think about sitting down before 8 p.m. But starting too late — 10 p.m. is getting dangerous — can also leave you without many options.

Restaurant critics are divided about the *ménu dégustation* (sampler, or tasting, menu; meh-*noo* day-goo-*stah*-see-oh), featured in many of the city's top restaurants. Made up of small portions of the chef's signature dishes, it offers tremendous value because you have the opportunity to try more dishes. But some say there are too many portions for a customer to get a sense of the chef's artistry, and the mixture of so many flavors just confuses, instead of enriches, the palate.

✔ The typical **bistro** used to be a mom-and-pop operation with a menu confined to Parisian standbys such as *boeuf bourguignon* (braised beef in red wine sauce), and *tarte Tatin* (caramelized upside-down apple pie). Today, many bistros have expanded upon the old classics but retain the tradition of offering hearty, relatively low-priced dishes in a convivial, intimate atmosphere. Think crush of elbows and the sounds of corks popping, glasses clinking, and people having a good time. Bistros are where Parisians come to dine most often.

✔ Literally, the word **brasserie** means "brewery" and refers to the Alsatian menu specialties that include staples such as beer, Riesling wine, and *choucroute* (a sauerkraut-based dish, usually topped by cuts of ham). Most brasseries are large, cheerful, brightly lit places that open early and close late (some are open 24 hours a day), and have an immense selection of dishes on the menu, although many no longer specialize in Alsatian fare. At brasseries, you can usually get a meal at any time of day, even in hours when restaurants and bistros are closed, and the food is relatively inexpensive.

Sadly, brasseries began to fall to corporate acquisition in the 1970s, and today most are part of one all-encompassing chain. Although this fact shouldn't stop you from visiting some of Paris's legendary eateries, look out for places that list mundane and repetitive food on their menus — they're more numerous than you think. Your best bet is to get a look at the menus of brasseries that interest you and compare costs, as well as listings. If *poulet rôti* (rotisserie chicken), *steak frites* (steak and fries), and omelets seem to be highlights, you may want to try eating somewhere else.

✔ **Cafes** are typically open from about 8 a.m. to 1 a.m. They serve drinks and food all day from a short menu that often includes salads, sandwiches, mussels, and french fries. Prime locations or famous literary cafes carry higher price tags. Most cafes offer reasonably priced omelets, sandwiches, soups, or salads. Omelets come plain with just a sprinkling of herbs or filled with cheese, ham, or other hearty additions. Onion soup (*soupe à l'oignon*) is a traditional Parisian dish, and you may see *soupe de poisson* (fish soup) on the menu. Another cafe favorite is *croque monsieur*, a grilled ham sandwich covered with melted cheese, or a *croque madame*, the same dish topped with an egg. Or try a *salade Niçoise*, a huge bowl filled with lettuce, boiled potatoes, tuna, hard-boiled eggs, capers, tomatoes, olives, and anchovies or a *salade de chèvre chaude*, fresh greens topped with warm goat cheese on croutons. These dishes make a light, pleasant meal for 6€ to 12€ ($7–14).

Parisians use cafes the way the British use pubs — as extensions of their living rooms. They're places where you meet friends before heading to the movies or a party, read your newspaper, write in your journal, or just hang out and people watch. Regardless of whether you order a cup of coffee or the most expensive cognac in the house, no one will ask you to leave. Coffee, of course, is the chief drink. It comes black in a small cup, often with a thin wrapped square of chocolate, unless you order a *café crème* or *café au lait* (coffee with steamed milk, which Parisians usually have at breakfast). *Thé* (tay; tea) is also fairly popular but generally isn't high quality. *Chocolat chaud* (shock-o-*lah*-shoh; hot chocolate), on the other hand, is absolutely superb and made from real ground chocolate.

✔ **Tearooms,** or *salons de thé,* usually open mid-morning and close by early evening. Some serve light lunches, but most are at their best in the afternoon for desserts with coffee or tea.

✔ **Wine bars** operate from mid-morning to late evening when you can order wine by the glass and munch on snacks such as *tartines* (open-face sandwiches), olives, and cheese. Some offer simple lunch menus, but like cafes and tearooms, they're generally better for light bites.

Understanding the order of a meal

A proper meal consists of three, or sometimes four, courses, so portions are usually moderate. Be aware of the traditional way French restaurants serve food:

✔ An *apéritif* is a light drink that precedes the meal. The French don't like to start a meal by numbing the palate with strong liquor. They usually stick to such offerings as a *kir*, a mixture of white wine and *crème de cassis* (black currant liqueur), which is light and the most common pre-meal drink.

✔ You're always served bread with your meal, but you must request butter.

✔ Water isn't placed on the table automatically — you must ask for it. To get regular tap water (which is perfectly fine to drink), as opposed to the pricey equivalent in a bottle, simply ask for *une carafe d'eau* (oon kar-*aff* doh).

✔ Cheese comes after the main course and is usually accompanied by a red wine.

✔ Dessert comes after the cheese course, but dessert and cheese can be served at the same time at your request.

✔ Diners traditionally don't drink coffee during the meal. Black coffee is served after dessert in a demitasse cup with sugar cubes on the side. If you want milk with your coffee, you must ask for a *café au lait* (ka-*fay* oh lay) or *café crème* (ka-*fay* krem).

✔ If you have food left on your plate, don't ask for a doggie bag. Restaurants are not accustomed to handling these type of requests.

The *menu du jour* at many establishments includes red or white wine. The standard measure is *un quart* (a quarter-liter carafe), sometimes served in *un pot* or *un pichet* (a pitcher). If wine isn't included, you can order *vin ordinaire* (house wine) or a Beaujolais (a light, fruity red wine), a Côtes du Rhône (a dry red wine), or a Chardonnay (a light white wine), which are very reasonably priced. And you can always opt for soda, juice, or water instead (*l'eau plat* is still water; *l'eau gazeuse* is carbonated water). Cocktails are available but discouraged because they're thought to numb the palate.

To tip or not to tip

In France, waiting tables is an esteemed profession with benefits and retirement security, and the French treat waiters with respect. When it comes to tipping them, you may have heard not to leave anything since a gratuity is already included in the bill. It's true that a 15 percent service charge, which appears on the bill as *service compris,* is added. But waiters never get the full 15%. Thus it's customary to leave a few euro, or about 5% of the bill after a meal, unless the service was truly terrible.

Trimming the Fat from Your Budget

If you're watching your pocketbook when it comes to dining out, following a few of these simple tips can go a long way toward making the bill as appealing as the food.

- ✔ **Order prix-fixe (set-price) meals.** These set-price meals are up to 30% cheaper than ordering the same dishes a la carte. What's the trade-off? Your options are more limited than if you order from the main menu. Review the prix-fixe option carefully to determine what you're getting at that price. Does the meal come with wine, and if so, how much — a glass or a half-bottle? Is dessert or coffee included?

- ✔ **Make lunch your main meal.** Many restaurants offer great deals on a fixed-price lunch. You probably won't be hungry for a full meal at dinnertime after two or three courses at lunch.

- ✔ **Try the crêperies.** Crêperies (many are off the boulevard du Montparnasse around the Square Délambre) offer a great value. Try savory meat- or vegetable-filled crêpes called *galettes* with a bowl of cider for your main meal and honey, jam, *chantilly* (whipped cream), chocolate, or fruit-filled crêpes for dessert. Surroundings are usually Brittany-inspired with red-checked tablecloths, wooden beams, maritime souvenirs, and pictures of Bretagnons in native dress.

- ✔ **Try chain restaurants or sandwich shops.** Batifol, Hippopotamus, Léon de Bruxelles, and l'Écluse offer some good-value, though not inspired, meals. Pomme de Pain, Cosi, and Lina's have fresh and tasty sandwiches.

- ✔ **Pay attention to the menu's details.** On most menus, the cheaper dishes are made of cheaper cuts of meat or the organs of animals, such as brains, tripe, and the like.

- ✔ **Don't eat breakfast at your hotel.** Doing so adds at least $5 more per person to your hotel bill. Grab a croissant or a *pain au chocolat* (chocolate-filled pastry) from a *boulangerie* (bakery).

- ✔ **Know the tipping rules.** Service is usually included at restaurants but it's customary to leave about 5% for your server.

Paris's Best Restaurants

Restaurants are listed alphabetically for easy reference, followed by the price range, neighborhood, and type of cuisine for each. Price ranges reflect the cost of a three-course meal for one person ordered à la carte, featuring an appetizer, main dish, dessert, and coffee — note that alcohol is not included.

The number of dollar signs used to describe each restaurant gives you a general idea of how much a meal costs at dinner, but don't make price your only criteria for choosing a restaurant. Most establishments offer fixed-price menus (also called *formules* or *prix fixe*) that can bring the cost down one whole price category. Likewise, if you're dying to try a place that's above your budget, visit it at lunch when meals are cheaper. See Table 10-1 for a key to the restaurant prices.

Table 10-1	Key to Restaurant Prices
Dollar Sign(s)	*Price Range*
$	Less than 20€ ($23)
$$	21€–50€ ($24–$58)
$$$	51€–100€ ($59–$115)
$$$$	Over 101€ ($116)

The restaurants listed here range from moderately-priced establishments to homey neighborhood favorites to chic "in" spots. Also included are some bargain eateries and a few of the city's most sumptuous restaurants where haute cuisine is an art form.

See the "Restaurants on the Right Bank" and "Restaurants on the Left Bank" maps for locations of restaurants in this section.

Au Bascou
$$ Le Marais (3e)   BASQUE/SOUTHWEST

Specializing in dishes from the Basque country, the corner of southwestern France resting along the Spanish border, Au Bascou offers excellent meals and fills up fast. Start with *piperade basquaise,* a delicious concoction of sautéed peppers and onions served on salad leaves and topped with ham; then try superb seasonal fish such as tuna poached in a puff pastry with legumes, or *agneau de lait des Pyrénées rôti* (roasted milk-fed lamb). Finish up with a plate of local cheese served with a cherry jam or a duo of two Basque cakes. A bottle of Irrouleguy, a smooth red Basque wine, makes a nice accompaniment to meals, and the service is friendly without being condescending.

See map p. 142. 38 rue Réaumur. ☎ *01-42-72-69-25. Métro: Arts et Métiers. (Exit the station at rue de Turbigo and cross over it to rue Réamur. Head east 1 block; the restaurant is on the corner of rue Réamur and rue Volta.) Main courses: 15€ ($17). AE, V. Open: Mon–Fri noon–2 p.m. and 8–10:30 p.m.*

Restaurants on the Right Bank

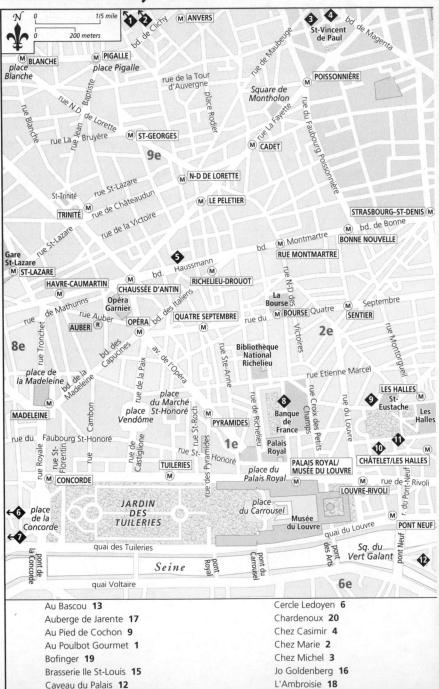

Au Bascou **13**
Auberge de Jarente **17**
Au Pied de Cochon **9**
Au Poulbot Gourmet **1**
Bofinger **19**
Brasserie Ile St-Louis **15**
Caveau du Palais **12**

Cercle Ledoyen **6**
Chardenoux **20**
Chez Casimir **4**
Chez Marie **2**
Chez Michel **3**
Jo Goldenberg **16**
L'Ambroisie **18**

La Poule au Pot **16**
La Tour de Montlhéry Chez Denise **11**
L'Ébauchoir **21**
Le Cinq **7**
Restaurant du Palais-Royal **8**
16 Haussmann **5**
Zimmer **14**

Restaurants on the Left Bank

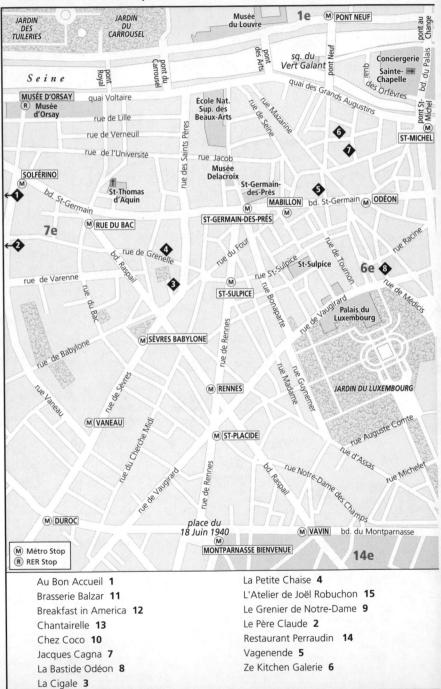

Au Bon Accueil **1**
Brasserie Balzar **11**
Breakfast in America **12**
Chantairelle **13**
Chez Coco **10**
Jacques Cagna **7**
La Bastide Odéon **8**
La Cigale **3**

La Petite Chaise **4**
L'Atelier de Joël Robuchon **15**
Le Grenier de Notre-Dame **9**
Le Père Claude **2**
Restaurant Perraudin **14**
Vagenende **5**
Ze Kitchen Galerie **6**

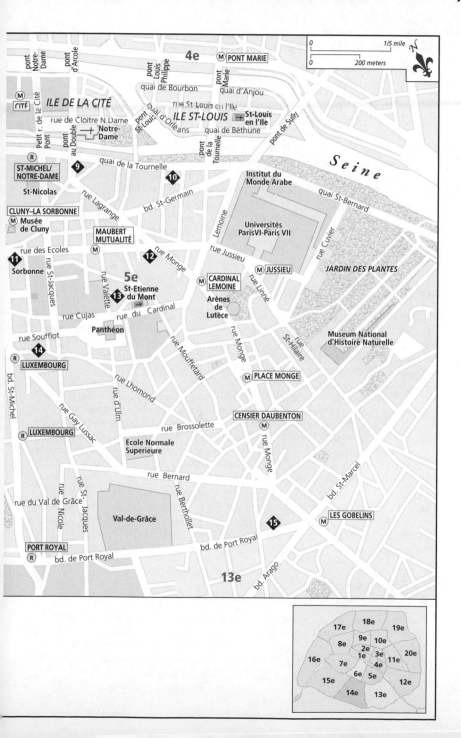

Auberge de Jarente
$$ Le Marais (4e) BASQUE

When you've had enough of cream sauces, come here for the taste of southwest France. Since 1964, cooks here have been using olive oil, tomatoes, and all kinds of peppers to create mouth-watering fare. The 29€ ($33) prix-fixe menu may include starters of *timbale de calamars and chorizo* (calamari and chorizo cooked in a molded pan) or *l'escalope de saumon au piment d'espelette* (salmon cutlet spiced with a type of Basque hot pepper), and for a main course, such Basque-influenced dishes as cassoulet, or duck breast with oyster mushrooms and sautéed apples. Choose from smooth Basque wines like Irrouleguy, tursan, and madiran. The rustic decor includes a cave-like, cozy downstairs, and service is friendly.

See map p. 142. 7 rue de Jarente (between rue de Sevigné and rue de Turenne, just west of place des Vosges). ☎ *01-42-77-49-35. Métro: Bastille or St-Paul. (Take rue de Turenne and follow it 1 block to rue de Jarente.) 29€ ($33) prix fixe. AE, V. Open: Tues–Sat noon–2:30 p.m. and 7:30–10:30 p.m. Closed three weeks in Aug.*

Au Bon Accueil
$$ Eiffel Tower (7e) MODERN BISTRO

Almost as much ingenuity goes into the menu at vibrant and fun-filled Au Bon Accueil as it did into designing the Eiffel Tower, of which you have a spectacular view from one of the outside tables. And a renovation in 2003 has only made the place better (a new ventilation system clears cigarette smoke from the room, so everyone is *très content!*). The ingredient-based menu here is simply amazing. It changes daily according to what owner Jacques Lacipière finds in the markets. If you're ordering from the prix-fixe menu, you may start with cold cucumber soup followed by *steack de thon poélé et son caviar d'aubergine aux olives* (seared tuna steak with eggplant, caviar, and olives). Main dishes are divine and can include scallops with asparagus or whole lobster from Brittany roasted in herbs and tomatoes. Fantastic desserts include fig tart and crème brûlée made with walnuts. The dining room only seats 25, so reserve in advance.

See map p. 144. 14 rue de Monttessuy. ☎ *01-47-05-46-11. Métro: Alma Marceau. (Exit the station, cross the Pont l'Alma and the quai Branly, and turn onto av. Rapp; follow av. Rapp 2 blocks to rue de Monttessuy and turn right.) Reservations strongly recommended. Main courses: 11€–54€ ($13–$62); three-course prix fixe 29€ ($33). MC, V. Open: Mon–Fri noon–2:30 p.m. and 7:30–10:30 p.m.*

Au Pied de Cochon
$$ Les Halles (1er) CLASSIC FRENCH

The welcoming gardenia-bedecked restaurant on a side street in Les Halles opened in 1946 and has played a vibrant part of the history of this old market neighborhood. With marble, murals, elaborate sconces, chandeliers, and plenty of tourists, the restaurant provides great fun at manageable prices. You can have a plate of a half-dozen oysters or onion soup to start. Follow with grilled salmon or an *entrecôte maître d'hôtel* (rib steak in a rich red wine sauce) or their specialty and namesake, pied de cochon (pigs' feet). Or, if you're daring — and hungry — have the plateau rouge: half a Canadian lobster, crayfish, shrimp, crabs, and other red fish served on a towering pile of shaved ice. Finish with mouth-watering *profiteroles* (cream puffs).

See map p. 142. 6 rue Coquillière (between rue du Jour and rue Jean-Jacques Rousseau on the northwest side of the garden of the Forum des Halles shopping center). ☎ **01-40-13-77-00.** *Métro: Châtelet–Les Halles. Main courses: 15€–28€ ($17–$32). AE, DC, V. Open: Daily 24 hours.*

Au Poulbot Gourmet
$-$$ Montmartre (18e)   CLASSIC FRENCH

Photos of old Montmartre and original drawings by illustrator Francisque Poulbot adorn the walls, and chic burgundy leather banquettes are usually filled with a local crowd savoring moderately priced classic cuisine. Chef Jean-Paul Langevin brings tremendous finesse to the preparation and presentation of dishes such as *noisette d'agneau* (lamb slices) served with delicate splashes of mashed potatoes and spinach, and *la douceur de saumon mariné a l'aneth* (salmon marinated in dill). As an appetizer, try the *mosaique de chevre frais et ratatouille sur paillason de radis* (fresh goat cheese and a stew of eggplant, tomatoes, zucchini, peppers, and onions, seasoned with herbs and garlic and served with radishes). For dessert, try the *le blancmange au lait d'amandes* (pudding flavored with almond milk) or the *coulis de fruits rouges* (red fruit purée).

See map p. 142. 39 rue Lamarck. ☎ **01-46-06-86-00.** *Métro: Lamarck-Caulincourt. (Follow rue Lamarck from Sacré-Coeur; the restaurant is about a third of the way down the hill.) Three-course lunch (Mon–Fri) 18€ ($21); three-course dinner 35€ ($40). MC, V. Open: Mon–Sat noon –1:30 p.m. and 7:30–10 p.m.; lunch served Sundays between Oct–May Sun noon–1:30 p.m.*

Finding ethnic eateries

Even the French need a break from French food every once in a while, and you may find your taste buds craving something different and perhaps highly spiced. If you're in the mood for ethnic cuisine, take advantage of the Chinese, Thai, Vietnamese, Indian, Tex-Mex, and Russian restaurants popular with residents, although they're not necessarily cheaper (or tastier) than French restaurants.

Try the 10e or 18e for North African, Turkish, Vietnamese, and Thai. Probably the most popular ethnic dish in France is couscous from North Africa — steamed semolina garnished with broth, stewed vegetables, and meat. You can find at least one restaurant or *couscouserie* on nearly every street in the capital.

Bofinger
$$ Le Marais (4e)   ALSATIAN/BRASSERIE

Bofinger is one of Paris's best-loved restaurants with its dark wood, gleaming brass, bright lights, curved and painted glass ceiling, and waiters with long white aprons delivering good food. It's owned by the Flo brasserie chain, which means that you'll see similar menus in the chain's other restaurants, which include Julien and Brasserie Flo. The downstairs dining room is ornately decorated with Art Nouveau flourishes and a glass-domed ceiling. Upstairs is cozier with wood paneling and separate rooms for smokers. The 22€ ($25) lunch menu may feature Brittany oysters to start, a thick poached pollack served with a légume risotto, and *floating island* (soft custard with mounds of beaten egg whites or whipped cream floating on its surface) for dessert. The 32€ ($37) Ménu Bofinger may start with homemade duck foie gras, breast of chicken served Suprème style (in a white gravy with cream) and a cherry *clafoutis* (a baked pancake with cherries). The restaurant is renowned for its oysters and foie gras. Best of all: The prices are actually quite moderate for Paris. Children under 12 can get the prix fixe for 14€ ($16). The more intimate Le Petit Bofinger is directly across the street; prices and fare are similar.

See map p. 142. 5–7 rue de la Bastille. ☎ *01-42-72-87-82. Métro: Bastille. (Exit the station at bd. Beaumarchais and turn left at rue de la Bastille.) Main courses: 15€–35€ ($17–$40); lunch and dinner prix fixe including a half-bottle of wine 22€ ($25) and 32€ ($37), respectively. AE, MC, V. Open: Mon–Fri noon–3 p.m. and 6:30 p.m.–1:00 a.m.; Sat–Sun noon–1 a.m.*

Brasserie Balzar
$$ Latin Quarter (5e)   ALSATIAN/BRASSERIE

Since its opening in 1898, Brasserie Balzar has played host to some of France's most famous intellectuals, including Jean-Paul Sartre. It's always full of rich yuppies, even during off hours. The brasserie was the center of a controversy a few years ago when a group of regulars, including Adam Gopnik of the *New Yorker,* fought but ultimately failed to keep the Flo chain from buying it (see Mr. Gopnik's account in *Paris to the Moon,* Random House). Nothing obvious has changed, however. People still stop here for coffee and pastries between lunch and dinner and drop in for drinks in the evening. Regulars go for such hearty French classics as *poulet rôti avec frites* (roast chicken with french fries) or *choucroute garni* (sauerkraut garnished with cuts of meat, usually ham)but you can also get a good veal liver (*foie de veau*), *steak au poivre* (steak with crushed peppercorns), and a few fresh fish dishes. Portions are copious.

See map p. 144. 49 rue des Écoles (on the corner of rue de la Sorbonne and rue des Écoles, 1 block south of the Musée de Cluny). ☎ *01-43-54-13-67. Métro: Cluny-Sorbonne. Main courses: 15€–20€ ($17–$23). AE, MC, V. Open: Daily noon–midnight. Closed Aug.*

Brasserie Ile St-Louis
$$ Ile St-Louis (4e) ALSATIAN/BRASSERIE

Brasserie Ile St-Louis is loud and bustling. Though the tastiness of its comfort food has been inconsistent recently, I still include it in the hopes that this is temporary, and because it's so ideally situated: directly off the footbridge from Ile de la Cité to Ile St-Louis with an unparalleled view of the eastern tip of Ile de la Cité (including the back of Notre-Dame). The food is quintessentially Alsatian — choucroute(heaps of tender, biting sauerkraut and meaty slices of ham); the hearty cassoulet, laden with rich beans and tender pieces of lamb and pork; and ham shank atop a bed of lentils.

See map p. 142. 55 quai de Bourbon. ☎ 01-43-54-02-59. Métro: Pont Marie. Main courses: 15€–26€ ($17–$30) lunch and dinner. V. Open: Fri–Tues noon–1 a.m.; Thurs 6 p.m.–1 a.m.

Breakfast in America
$ Ile de la Cité (5e) AMERICAN

When the charm of spending 15€ ($17) on a Continental breakfast wears off, or when your longing for a hamburger becomes so powerful that McDonald's is actually tempting, get thee to Breakfast in America. Connecticut-born filmmaker Craig Carlson opened this diner in 2003 after years of craving American-style big breakfasts. The food here is even better than what you get in the roadside spots back home. American travelers and expats in need of a fix are often outnumbered by Parisians who've discovered the joys of a rib-sticking breakfast; they pack out the place for fluffy pancakes, crispy bacon, omelets, and a 2€ ($2.30) "bottomless mug o' joe." Breakfast is served all day every day, but the menu also includes burgers, nachos, chicken wings, and sandwiches. Sunday brunch is, of course, particularly busy, and Friday night is *Student Night* (happy hour) featuring 4€ ($4.60) cocktails from the full bar. Service is efficient and friendly; you may even be seated by Craig himself. *Note:* Tip is *not* included in the final tab here.

See map p. 144. 17 rue des Ecoles, 5e. ☎ 01-43-54-50-28. www.breakfast-in-america.com; *Métro: Cardinal Lemoine or Jussieu. Main courses: 5.95€–8.95€ ($6.85–$10). MC, V. Open Mon–Thurs 8:30 a.m.–10 p.m.; Fri–Sat 8:30 a.m.–10:30 p.m.; Sun 9 a.m.–9 p.m. (bar open till 2 a.m. Thurs–Sat).*

Caveau du Palais
$$ Ile de la Cité (4e) CLASSIC FRENCH

The artist André Renoux painted the interior *(Interior Restaurant Caveau du Palais)* of this cozy wood-beamed restaurant (a well-kept Parisian secret) which is a lunch favorite of lawyers from the nearby Palais de Justice and locals (who once included Yves Montand and Simone Signoret). It's located in the heart of the serene, tree-lined place Dauphine, a secluded little park nestled off Pont Neuf near the tip of Isle de la Cité. Try the house's special *côte de boeuf,* grilled giant ribs, which are prepared for two. The *confit de canard et pommes Sarladaise,* duck served with crispy potato bits sautéed in goose liver drippings, is another must. The owners display the work of up-and-coming artists.

See map p. 142. 19 place Dauphine. ☎ *01-43-26-04-28. Métro: Pont Neuf. Main courses: 18€–25€ ($21–$29). AE, DC, MC, V. Open: Mon–Sat 12:15–2:30 p.m. and 7:15–10:30 p.m.*

Cercle Ledoyen
$$$$ Champs-Elysées (8e)   CLASSIC FRENCH

The less expensive sister of multi-starred Ledoyen, with which it shares the building and a kitchen, Cercle Ledoyen is a haven of greenery and gourmet pleasures off the noisy Champs-Elysées. It's also pricey (one of the house specialties, sweetbreads, is 71€/$82, and desserts start at 24€/$28), but oh, is it worth it! Former chef Ghislaine Arabian has gone on to greener pastures, but the kitchen is skillfully run by her successor, Christian Le Squer, who brings his own touch to Arabian's light classic French and Flemish dishes. The menu varies but may include appetizers of *araignée de mer décortiquée à l'écume de jus de carapace* (shelled spider crab served with a mousse shell) or *mousserons des prés en ravioli dans leur sucs truffés* (wild mushroom ravioli served in juices with truffle flavoring). Main dishes may include *sole côtière au caviar, crémeux de chou fleur* (coastal sole served with caviar and creamy cauliflower), or *pigeon au pain d'épices, jus de carottes à la coriandre* (pigeon with spicy honey gingerbread served in a juice of carrots and coriander). Desserts, such as a fondant of warm chocolate and raspberries, are divine, too. Although a meal for two here with wine runs around 200€ ($230), this place is well worth the splurge. The restaurant may look familiar to you if you've seen Robert Altman's film *Ready to Wear.*

See map p. 142. 1 av. Dutuit. ☎ *01-53-05-10-02. Métro: Franklin D. Roosevelt. Main courses: 58€–88€ ($67–$101). AE, DC, MC, V. Open: Mon–Sat noon–2:30 p.m. and 7:30–10:30 p.m.*

Beware the barkers

The 5e arrondissement's **rue de la Huchette** and **rue de la Harpe** are quaint and scenic, and the barkers shouting about the good food are unusual, to say the least. But beware of dining in these establishments: The bill is padded with all kinds of extras, from overpriced drinks to extra bread. For another scenic street in the 5e with much better food minus the bill padding, try **rue Mouffetard** behind the Panthéon (Métro: Cardinal Lemoine or Maubert Mutualité).

Chantairelle
$$ Latin Quarter (5e)   AUVERGNE

The door here "moos" for arriving and departing customers. There's a backyard garden that children will love, and parents can appreciate an atmosphere that literally reeks of the Auvergne, the rugged south-central region of France. (The area by the cash register sells products from the region including tiny bottles of essential oils made from native plants and wines.) An old church door and a tiny fountain are incorporated into the decor, and a sound system plays bird songs, rainstorms, and church bells. The delicious peasant food is presented in good-sized portions, and appetizers may include a *jambon du pays avec melon* (country ham with cantaloupe) or *feuilleté à la fourme d'Abert* (pastry stuffed with regional cheese). Main courses include a tender *confit de canard* (duck leg cooked and preserved in its own fat) and a substantial *potée* (a tureen filled with pork, cabbage, potatoes, turnips, and leeks in broth). Although most dishes use ham or pork, vegetarians enjoy the delicious *croustade forestière* of assorted mushrooms and eggs poached with Fourme d'Ambert cheese. The best Auvergne wine is the Chateaugay, a fine fruity red. The restaurant is a block from the Panthéon.

See map p. 144. 17 rue Laplace. ☎ *01-46-33-18-59. Métro: Maubert-Mutualité. (Take the street behind the Panthéon, rue Valette, and turn right onto rue Laplace.) Main courses: 13€–21€ ($15–$24); three-course prix fixe: 28€ ($32). MC, V. Open: Mon–Fri noon–2 p.m.; Mon–Sat 7:00–10:30 p.m. Closed Saturday lunch and Sunday.*

Chardenoux
$$ Bastille (11e)   CLASSIC BISTRO

From the etched plate-glass windows to the swirling stucco decorations on the walls and ceiling and the lacy curtains in the windows, this restaurant's turn-of-the-20th-century decor is the very essence of old Paris (it has been appointed a Monument Historique), though the management has changed and is experimenting with the classic French food. Service is friendly and English-speaking. A variety of French regional dishes appears on the menu — appetizers may include *jambon persille de Bourgogne* (parslied ham from Burgundy), or *oeufs en Meurette* (poached eggs in a sauce of red wine and bacon, also from Burgundy). Main courses may include *andouillette* (small chitterling sausages) in a mustard sauce or *homard Bréton a l'Amèricaine* (Brittany lobster with butter). Desserts are pure comfort food, especially the fruit tarts and the nougat in raspberry sauce.

See map p. 142. 1 rue Jules-Valles. ☎ *01-43-71-49-52. Métro: Charonne. (Exit the station on rue Charonne and walk 1 block to rue Jules-Valles. Turn left and walk to the end of the street. The restaurant is on the corner of rue Jules-Valles and rue Chanzy.) Main courses: 7€–22€ ($8–$25); prix-fixe lunch: 23€ ($26). AE, MC, V. Open: daily noon–2 p.m.; 7–10:30 p.m.*

Chez Casimir
$$ Gare du Nord (10e)   CLASSIC FRENCH

Book well in advance for this restaurant far from the more touristy sides of Paris, which packs in loyal customers. It's on the same street as another restaurant well worth the trip, Chez Michel (reviewed later in this list). Chef Philippe Tredgeu works magic in his kitchen, cooking with ingredients he finds at the market that morning or the night before. Start with the refreshing *gaspacho de tomates* (gazpacho), a cold refreshing tomato soup spiced with garlic that will whet your appetite for your main course, then have *saucisson Lyonnais avec beurre a l'échalotte et pommes vapeur* (Lyonnais sausage cooked in shallot butter with steamed potatoes), or leg of lamb cooked on the bone with aromatic juices and fresh peas. For dessert, indulge in *clafoutis aux prunes rouges* (baked pancake with red plums). The wine list is highly affordable with prices starting at 7.50€ ($8.60) for half a bottle.

See map p. 142. 6 rue Belzunce. ☎ *01-48-78-28-80. Métro: Gare du Nord. (Exit the station on rue de Dunkerque and look for rue de Compiegne. Follow rue de Compiegne across bd. Magenta, turn left on Magenta and walk a few steps to the corner. This is rue Belzunce. Make a right here, and walk a block to the top of the street. The restaurant is on your right.) Reservations recommended for dinner. Main courses: 14€–15€ ($16–$17). No credit cards. Open: Mon–Fri noon–2 p.m. and 7–11:30 p.m.; Sat 7–11:30 p.m.*

Chez Coco
$$ Latin Quarter (5e)   CORSICAN

This used to be Vivario, and is still run by one of the original owners. It's also still an excellent spot to sample the hearty flavors of Corsica, Napoléon's birthplace. The products used in Vivario's dishes come straight from sunny Corsica to the dim, cave-like restaurant, with ceiling beams and stone walls. To start, opt for the rich traditional Corsican soup, teeming with beans, vegetables, and generous pieces of dried prosciutto. Or try the onion tart with country ham. Follow with a delicious tender lamb shank flavored with mint or the Corsican veal cutlet. The meal may end with a selection of Corsican cheeses or the Corsican dessert *fiadone*, a cheesecake made with mild *bruccio*, the island's famous, pungent cheese.

See map p. 144. 6 rue Cochin. ☎ *01-43-25-08-19. Métro: Maubert-Mutualité. (From Notre Dame, cross the pont de l'Archeveque [behind the cathedral] and turn left onto the quai de la Tournelle. Make a right onto rue de Pontoise and the first left onto rue Cochin. The restaurant is about 100 feet away.) Main courses: 15€ ($17). AE, MC, V. Open: Tues–Fri noon–2 p.m.; Mon–Sat 7:30–10 p.m.*

Chez Marie
$$ Montmartre (18e)   CLASSIC FRENCH

At the base of the steps heading to the place de Tertre, you can find some of the cheapest eats in this neighborhood, which isn't exactly known for bargain dining. Food is hearty, the owners are charming and friendly, and they welcome children in their humbly decorated, cozy dining room with wood benches, red-and-white picnic tablecloths, and a collage of Toulouse-Lautrec period posters and Lautrec-style paintings of cats dining. Stick to the basics like cassoulet or *cuisse de canard avec pommes de terre* (leg of duck with potatoes) and you're guaranteed to leave full and content and still have money in your wallet.

See map p. 142. 27 rue Gabrielle. ☎ 01-42-62-06-26. Métro: Abbesses. Three-course menus (including apéritif) 15€ ($17), 19€ ($22), 9.50€ ($11) for kids. AE, DC, MC, V. Open: Daily noon–3:30 p.m. and 6 p.m.–1:30 a.m. Closed Jan.

Chez Michel
$$ Gare du Nord (10e) BRETON

Crowds of Parisians come here for excellent, unusual food at very fair prices. Chef Thierry Breton, the chef at the Presidential Palace during François Mitterand's tenure, puts old-fashioned Breton dishes on his menu. Look for succulent scallops, hand picked by scuba divers, served with truffles in the winter. The menu may include *crème d'homard Bréton* (cream of lobster soup topped with shaved Parmesan cheese) or beef cheeks served atop a *ficelle* (small thin baguette) with fresh young vegetables. A nougat ice cream with spiced honey and thin almond cookies makes a satisfying dessert. You can choose to sit in the more casual cellar at wooden tables and eat all the shellfish, patés, and salads you can fit into your stomach — which is stretched by the end of the night. Choose from more than 100 different wines at retail cost, a truly dizzying experience.

See map p. 142. 10 rue Belzunce. ☎ 01-44-53-06-20. Métro: Gare du Nord. (Exit the station on rue de Dunkerque and look for rue de Compiegne. Follow rue de Compiegne across bd. Magenta, turn left on Magenta and walk a few steps to the corner. This is rue Belzunce. Make a right onto Belzunce, walk a block to the top of the street. Make another right, passing restaurant Chez Casimir, and walk to the corner of rue Belzunce and rue St-Vincent de Paul. Chez Michel is here.) Three-course prix-fixe 30€ ($35). MC, V. Open: Tues–Fri noon–2 p.m. and Mon–Fri 7 p.m. to midnight. Closed last week of July and first three weeks of Aug.

Jacques Cagna
$$$ St-Germain-des-Prés (6e) HAUTE CUISINE

This Michelin-starred restaurant has been overshadowed by more recent openings by celebrity chefs, but it should not be overlooked. It's housed on the second floor of a 16th-century townhouse with wood beams and Flemish paintings, where chef Jacques Cagna creates delectable dishes served by a solicitous but not overbearing staff that make dining here a first-class experience. Starters may include a lightly-spiced *homard breton en salade, roquette, mousse de chou-fleur et sauce gaspacho* (Brittany lobster with rocket lettuce, cauliflower mousse, and gazpacho sauce) or *le pomme de terre et le caviar* (warm mashed potatoes with caviar), while main courses can include a delicious *noix de veau en crôute de sel avec romarin, champignons des bois et épinards* (veal sweetbreads in salted pastry flavored with rosemary and served with wood mushrooms and spinach) or *le turbo rôti avec sauce au vermouth acidulé et purée de pommes Granny-Smith,* (roasted turbot with vermouth sauce and a side of Granny Smith apple sauce). Desserts include *le chocolat Guanaja Moelleux à la pistache, glace à la confiture de lait* (soft chocolate cake with pistachio cream and a milk and caramel topping) or *fraises et les framboises au poivre de Setchouan, glace à l'avocat* (strawberries and raspberries with Szechwan pepper served with avocado ice cream). This is a truly special dining experience.

See map p. 144. 14 rue des Grands Augustins. ☎ *01-43-26-49-39. Métro: St-Michel, Odéon. Reservations required. Main courses: 32€–70€ ($37–$81); prix-fixe lunch: 39€ ($45); Le Menu Jacques Cagna (chef's choice tasting menu): 85€ ($98). MC, V, DC. Open: Tues–Sat noon–2 p.m.; Tues–Thurs 7:30–11 p.m.; Fri–Sat 7:30–11:30 p.m. July 31–Aug 25 closed for lunch on Mon and Sat and all day Sun.*

Jo Goldenberg
$-$$ Le Marais (4e) CENTRAL EUROPEAN

Jo Goldenberg is a nearly 100-year-old institution that is the closest thing to a New York deli you'll find in Paris. Plump sausages dangle from the ceiling and baklava beckons from a glass case in the front. The atmosphere in the restaurant is convivial amid long red banquettes surrounded by photographs of famous patrons, including former French President Mitterand, and original paintings of up-and-coming artists. Eastern specialties abound, such as chicken paprika, goulash, bagels, and Wienerschnitzel, along with typical deli offerings such as pastrami and corned beef — allegedly invented right here by Goldenberg senior in the 1920s. The food can be bland, however, so keep that in mind when making your decision to dine here. Musicians begin playing around 9 p.m. most evenings.

See map p. 142. 7 rue des Rosiers. ☎ *01-48-87-20-16. Métro: St-Paul. (Exit the station and cross over rue de Rivoli to rue Pavée. Follow rue Pavée to rue des Rosiers, about 800 feet. Turn left onto rue des Rosiers and walk about 350 feet.) Main courses: 11€–16€ ($13–$18). AE, DC, MC, V. Open: Daily 8 a.m. to 1 a.m.*

L'Ambroisie
$$$$ Le Marais (4e) HAUTE CUISINE

This gorgeous, three Michelin-starred, spare-no-expense restaurant located in a 17th-century townhouse is one of the best in France. It counts among its diners former U. S. President Bill Clinton, who ate here as a guest of Jacques Chirac. Chef Bernard Pacaud creates exquisite food with an emphasis on perfection. Served in two mirrored and frescoed high-ceilinged dining rooms and a cozy back room (in summer there is an outdoor terrace), the seasonal specialties may include Bresse chicken roasted with herbs and butter, or a beef filet pan-fried in its own marrow with crushed pepper and shallots. For dessert, try Pacaud's *tarte fine,* which has won awards: it's a chocolate pie served with bitter chocolate and mocha ice cream. If you can afford it, this restaurant just begs to be the setting for marriage proposals, anniversaries, and other special and romantic events.

See map p. 142. 9 place des Vosges. ☎ *01-42-78-51-45. Métro: St. Paul. (Exit the station on rue St-Antoine and head east to rue de Birague, which leads into the place des Vosges. Turn left at the place des Vosges and follow the arcade around the corner to the restaurant.) Reserve at least four weeks ahead. Jacket and tie advised. Main courses: 80€–170€ ($92–$196). AE, MC, V. Open: Tues–Sat noon–1:30 p.m. and 8–9:30 p.m. Closed two weeks in Feb and three weeks in Aug.*

La Bastide Odéon
$$ St-Germain-des-Prés (6e)   PROVENÇAL

Located on a narrow stretch of sidewalk next to the Théâtre de l'Odéon and a short walk from the Jardins du Luxembourg's place Edmond Rostand/boulevard St-Michel entrance, delicious Provençal cooking has been served here since 1994 in a lovely cream-colored dining room accented with weathered wood and Provençal fabrics in shades of red. The menu changes regularly, but Chef Gilles Ajuelos's dynamic creations may include starters of salmon tartare in an anchovy sauce served with potato salad or warm grilled eggplant layered with tomato and ricotta cheese. Main dishes may include Hereford tenderloin with chive mashed potatoes or a grilled tuna steak served with orechiette pasta sautéed with anchovies, mushrooms, and tomatoes. For dessert, try lemon-and-saffron flavored roasted pears with gingerbread and cottage cheese ice cream.

See map p. 144. 7 rue Corneille. ☎ *01-43-26-03-65. Métro: Odéon. (Exit the station and take rue de l'Odéon south to pl. de l'Odéon, where the Théâtre de l'Odéon is located. To the left of the theater is rue Corneille; take this about 150 feet to the restaurant.) Main courses: 19€ ($22). AE, MC, V. Open: Tues–Sat 12:30– 2 p.m. and 7:30–10:30 p.m. Closed first three weeks in Aug and Dec 25–Jan 1.*

La Cigale
$$ Eiffel Tower (7e)   CLASSIC BISTRO

La Cigale has moved from its intimate space on rue Chomel to a quiet garden location on square Chaise Récamier and now has room for elegant outdoor dining. Still serving its delicious soufflés (among other specialties) to a sophisticated clientele, the food is simply some of the best you can get in Paris for these prices. The delicate soufflés are beaten high and brim with Camembert, sautéed spinach, or tarragon cream. Try the Henri IV with regional cheese and a sauce *volaille* (chicken gravy) or one made with *farine de sarrasin* (buckwheat flour) and tomatoes and mozzarella. If you're not in the mood for a soufflé, other tempting entrées include steak au poivre (steak with coarsely ground peppercorns) or *filet de dorade* (filet of sea bream). For dessert try — you got it! — a soufflé made with, among other things, pistachios or melt-in-your-mouth chocolate or Grand Marnier or almonds with rhubarb marmalade.

See map p. 144. 4 rue Récamier. ☎ *01-45-48-86-58. Métro: Sèvres-Babylone. (Exit the station at rue de Sèvres and cross over bd. Raspail to the Hôtel Lutétia. Rue Récamier is the street just behind the hotel. The restaurant is about 80 feet down.) Reservations recommended. Main dishes: 15€–18€ ($17–$21). MC, DC, V. Open: Mon–Fri noon–2 p.m.; Mon–Sat 7:30–11 p.m.*

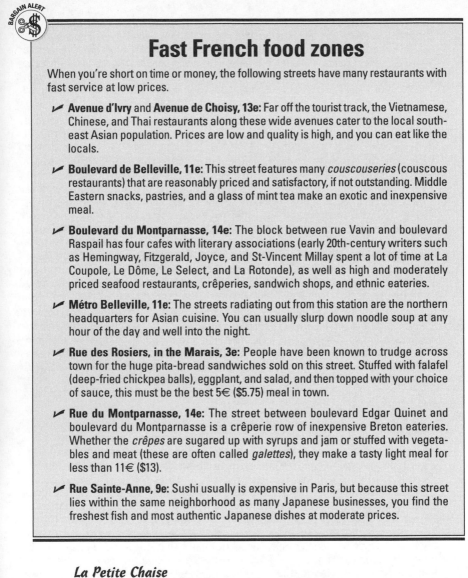

Fast French food zones

When you're short on time or money, the following streets have many restaurants with fast service at low prices.

✔ **Avenue d'Ivry** and **Avenue de Choisy, 13e:** Far off the tourist track, the Vietnamese, Chinese, and Thai restaurants along these wide avenues cater to the local southeast Asian population. Prices are low and quality is high, and you can eat like the locals.

✔ **Boulevard de Belleville, 11e:** This street features many *couscouseries* (couscous restaurants) that are reasonably priced and satisfactory, if not outstanding. Middle Eastern snacks, pastries, and a glass of mint tea make an exotic and inexpensive meal.

✔ **Boulevard du Montparnasse, 14e:** The block between rue Vavin and boulevard Raspail has four cafes with literary associations (early 20th-century writers such as Hemingway, Fitzgerald, Joyce, and St-Vincent Millay spent a lot of time at La Coupole, Le Dôme, Le Select, and La Rotonde), as well as high and moderately priced seafood restaurants, crêperies, sandwich shops, and ethnic eateries.

✔ **Métro Belleville, 11e:** The streets radiating out from this station are the northern headquarters for Asian cuisine. You can usually slurp down noodle soup at any hour of the day and well into the night.

✔ **Rue des Rosiers, in the Marais, 3e:** People have been known to trudge across town for the huge pita-bread sandwiches sold on this street. Stuffed with falafel (deep-fried chickpea balls), eggplant, and salad, and then topped with your choice of sauce, this must be the best 5€ ($5.75) meal in town.

✔ **Rue du Montparnasse, 14e:** The street between boulevard Edgar Quinet and boulevard du Montparnasse is a crêperie row of inexpensive Breton eateries. Whether the *crêpes* are sugared up with syrups and jam or stuffed with vegetables and meat (these are often called *galettes*), they make a tasty light meal for less than 11€ ($13).

✔ **Rue Sainte-Anne, 9e:** Sushi usually is expensive in Paris, but because this street lies within the same neighborhood as many Japanese businesses, you find the freshest fish and most authentic Japanese dishes at moderate prices.

La Petite Chaise
$$ **St-Germain-des-Prés (7e)** CLASSIC FRENCH

If shopping le Bon Marché department store makes you ravenous for classic French fare, come to this restaurant, which is a favorite of the "ladies who lunch" crowd. Founded in 1680, this small gem is alleged to be the oldest restaurant in Paris. The entry way, adorned with a smoky antique mirror from the early 18th century, leads to a softly illuminated, cozy dining room reminiscent of an old country inn, which it once was. Start with *saumon mariné à l'aneth* (smoked salmon marinated in dill) or the homemade *foie gras de canard* (duck liver pâté). Main courses may include a *filet de cabillaud avec l'estragon* (cod fillet cooked in tarragon) or leg of lamb cooked in its own juices. The house special dessert is *gateau au chocolat* — a rich chocolate cake topped with English cream.

See map p. 144. 36 rue de Grenelle. ☎ 01-42-22-13-35. Métro: Sèvres-Babylone. (Exit the station on bd. Raspail and walk 1 block north to rue de la Chaise. Follow the street to the end, where it intersects rue de Grenelle.) Prix fixe (main course with appetizer or dessert): 24€ ($28), or 29€ ($33) for three courses. AE, MC, V. Open: Daily noon–2 p.m. and 7–10:45 p.m.

L'Atelier de Joël Robuchon
$$-$$$ Eiffel Tower (7e)   **Modern Bistro**

This is one of Paris's hottest restaurants at the moment. Joel Robuchon, arguably the most famous chef in France when he retired in the 1990s, has come out of retirement to open this chic red-and-black lacquered, sushi bar-type restaurant that serves simple French and Asian fusion food in which the ingredients are the real stars. Seating is at a 40-person sushi bar that wraps around the open kitchen. The idea is to give diners a "behind the line" experience, so you may see Robuchon giving orders, sous-chefs saucing main dishes, or a pig being roasted on a spit. The menu continually changes. Instead of starters, Robuchon offers 22 small tasting plates that diners are encouraged to share. Main dishes can include sushi (served with delicious sourdough bread), steak tartare in a creamy morel sauce and hand-cut fries. Robuchon has a no-reservations policy so get here early.

See map p. 144. In the Hôtel Pont-Royal, 5-7 rue de Montalembert, 7e. ☎ 01-42-22-56-56. Métro: Rue du Bac. Reservations not accepted. Main courses: 15€–50€ ($17–$58); prix fixe 80€ ($92). AE, DC, MC, V. Open daily 11 a.m.– 2 a.m.

La Poule au Pot
$$-$$$ Les Halles (1er)   **CLASSIC BISTRO**

Poule au pot, an old French recipe of chicken stewed with broth and vegetables, has been served here since 1935 with much success if the *livre d'or* (a gold book filled with the names of visiting celebrities) means anything. When Les Halles still was Paris's marketplace, its workers came to La Poule au Pot to share this signature dish. After the market's demise, visits from such celebrities as Maurice Chevalier, Miou Miou, the Rolling Stones, and Prince kept this Parisian bistro on the map. The atmosphere created by the long zinc bar, *pots* of wine, red leather banquettes, wood paneling, and waiters in long aprons transports you to another era. How can the menu serve anything other than traditional French fare? Begin with *foie gras maison* (house goose liver pâté) or *oeufs cocotte à la crème* (eggs baked with cream), then try the *rognons de veau à la graine de moutarde* (veal kidneys cooked with mustard grains), or the succulent house *poule au pot* (28€/$32) with a tureen of the broth on the side. Finish with a velvety crème brûlée.

See map p. 142. 9 rue Vauvilliers. ☎ *01-42-36-32-96. Métro: Louvre-Rivoli. (Exit the station on rue de Rivoli and cross the street to rue du Louvre. Walk 2 blocks to rue St-Honoré and make a right. Proceed 2 blocks to rue Vauvilliers. The restaurant is near the end of the street, close to the gardens of the Forum des Halles.) Main courses: 21€–40€ ($24–$46); 30€ ($35) prix-fixe. MC, V. Open: Mon–Sat 7 p.m.–5 a.m.*

La Tour de Montlhéry Chez Denise
$$-$$$ **Les Halles (1er) CLASSIC FRENCH**

This is a meat lover's paradise as evidenced by the hams and sausages dangling from the wood beams of this true Parisian restaurant that features a zinc bar with barrels of wine and a homey dining room. The less expensive items on the menu tend to be dishes like tripe Calvados and stuffed cabbage and kidneys, though the proprietors do pay a nod to fish lovers with a tasty seafood terrine and haddock in a *beurre blanc* (white butter) sauce. Other typical dishes are grilled lamb chops and, for those who want to try truly authentic, reputably delicious French fare, *cervelles d'agneau* (sautéed lamb's brain). *Bon courage!*

See map p. 142. 5 rue des Prouvaires. ☎ *01-42-36-21-82. Métro: Louvre-Rivoli. (Exit the station on rue de Rivoli and head east to rue du Roule. Follow rue du Roule to rue St-Honoré, where Roule becomes rue des Prouvaires. The restaurant is near the corner of Prouvaires and St-Honoré.) Reservations required. Main courses: 16€–52€ ($18–$60). V. Open: Mon–Fri 24 hours. Closed the middle of July to the middle of Aug.*

L'Ébauchoir
$$ **Bastille (12e) CLASSIC BISTRO**

Tucked into a part of the Bastille often overlooked by tourists, this restaurant is well worth the visit. A mural pays homage to the working-class roots of the neighborhood, and the space is just large enough to render dining here a bit noisy. Friendly but rushed waiters show diners seated at the first-come, first-served tables the day's offerings written on a tall chalkboard. Once you sample lunch or dinner, you find the superb food more than makes up for the decibel level. Diners may be offered appetizers of gazpacho, tuna tartare, or a homemade terrine followed by a mouthwatering, top-quality filet of bass with a saffron cream or steak in a red wine Bordelaise sauce. For dessert, try the apple crumble or the *pot-de-crème* (homemade custard).

See map p. 142. 45 rue de Citeaux. ☎ *01-43-42-49-31. Métro: Faidherbe-Chaligny. (Exit the station on rue du Faubourg St-Antoine. Walk 1 block to rue de Citeaux and turn left. The restaurant is next to a small alley called the Impasse Druinot.) Reservations not accepted. Main courses: Two-course lunch with apéritif 13€ ($15); three-course dinner, no apéritif 23€ ($26). MC, V. Open: Mon–Thurs noon–2:30 p.m. and 8–10:30 p.m. (Fri–Sat till 11 p.m.).*

Le Cinq
$$$$ Champs-Elysées (8e)   HAUTE CUISINE

Dining in this five-year-old bastion of elegance is a heavenly experience. Chef Phillippe Legendre has earned three Michelin stars for Le Cinq, where every element is in place, from the stately yet serene dining room with its high ceilings and overstuffed chairs to the Limoges porcelain and Riedel stemware created for the restaurant to the perfect waitstaff. The sumptuous and inventive cuisine may start with *tarte d'artichaut et de truffe noire du Périgord* (savory tart of artichokes and black truffles from Périgord) or *langoustines bretonne en carpaccio au Cédrat et au caviar Osciètre* (carpaccio of Brittany prawns with lemon and Osetra caviar), and continue with *ris de veau fermier poêlé aux asperges et aux morilles, à l'huile de noix* (pan-seared, farm-raised veal sweetbreads with asparagus and morel mushrooms in hazelnut oil) or the 210€/$242 (for two) *poulette de Bresse et homard George V en cocotte lutée* (young Bresse chicken and lobster cooked George V style). For dessert, you may choose from *croquant de framboises aux saveurs d'hibiscus et crème glacée à la rose* (raspberry in meringue flavored with hibiscus scent with rose ice cream) or *ananas Victoria rôti, coeur glacé au gingembre* (roasted Victoria pineapple with ginger ice cream) or the chef's choice of assorted chocolate desserts. The wine list here is magnificent; Make sure to consult the sommelier, Enrico Bernardo, who, in 2002, won the prestigious Ruinart Trophy declaring him Best Sommelier in Europe.

See map p. 142. 31 av. George V (in the Four Seasons George V Hotel). ☎ *01-49-52-71-54. Métro: George V. Reservations required. Light tasting menu: 120€ ($138), gourmet tasting menu (without beverage): 230€ ($265); main courses: 45€–210€ ($52–$242). AE, MC, V. Open: Daily noon–2:30 and 6:30–11 p.m.*

Le Grenier de Notre-Dame
$-$$ Latin Quarter (5e)   VEGETARIAN

Yes, a vegetarian can eat heartily and well in Paris, and Le Grenier has been proving that since 1978. The cozy two-level restaurant near Notre-Dame blooms with live plants hanging from the ceiling and decorating the spiral staircase. The food is good, filling, and nearly all vegetarian (but not vegan as eggs and cheese are used here. There is also a fish soup on the menu.). Especially recommended is the vegetable paté served with warm toast, *les lasagnes végétarienne,* with eggplant, onions, tomatoes, cheese, tofu, and mushrooms, and the enormous portions of lentil moussaka made with lentils, white cheese, egg, tomatoes, and eggplant. Le Grenier has a well-deserved reputation for desserts, such as the hot apple tart with caramel and vanilla ice cream and the homemade chocolate cake with orange sauce. The wine list includes a variety of organic offerings.

See map p. 144. 18 rue de la Bûcherie. ☎ *01-43-29-98-29. RER: St-Michel/Notre-Dame. (Exit onto quai de Montebello; turn right onto rue d'Arcole, then left onto rue de la Bûcherie.) Three courses at lunch: 13€ ($15), at dinner: 15€ ($17); main courses: 12€–14€ ($14–$16). MC, V. Open: Mon–Thurs 12:30–2:30 p.m. and 7:30–11 p.m.; Fri–Sat noon–2:30 p.m. and 7:30–11:30 p.m.; Sun noon–3 p.m.*

Le Père Claude
$$ Eiffel Tower (5e)   CLASSIC BISTRO

Le Père Claude is known for its enormous portions of red meat dishes. Starters include warm sausage with pistachios and apples, *terrine de gibier et foie gras de canard* (game terrine with duck liver) and yes, frogs' legs. The *panaché de viandes* is an assortment of perfectly roasted meats served with a comforting heap of mashed potatoes. Make sure you specify how you want the beef cooked, or it will be served the way the French like it — *bleue,* which means very, very rare. Seafood lovers won't be disappointed in the mussel soup with saffron or the *assiette de pecheur aux pates fraiches* (fisherman's plate with fresh terrine). President Jacques Chirac and Don King have been spotted (separately) chowing down here, but it's usually home to families and, to a lesser extent, tourists with big appetites. After dinner, you can stroll up the avenue de La Motte-Picquet and take in a view of the spectacular illuminated Eiffel Tower.

See map p. 144. 51 av. de La Motte-Picquet. ☎ *01-47-34-03-05. Métro: La-Motte-Picquet–Grenelle. (Exit the station on av. de La Motte-Picquet and head northeast about ¼-mile, toward the Champ de Mars.) Main courses: 15€–24€ ($17–$28). AE, MC, V. Open: Daily 11:30am–2:30 p.m. and 7 p.m.–midnight.*

Restaurant du Palais-Royal
$$-$$$ Louvre (1er)   CLASSIC FRENCH

The elegant arcade that encircles the gardens inside the Palais-Royal also surrounds this restaurant, making it one of the most romantic locations in Paris. Sit at the terrace on warm, sun-filled days and begin your meal with starters such as escargot with chives or duck liver terrine with red onion. Main dishes vary with the season but may include lamb roasted with rosemary and a side of creamy polenta or semi-salted sole. Try the good house red wine, served Lyonnaise-style in thick-bottomed bottles. The desserts are delicious; the pistachio and chocolate *mille-feuille* (puff pastry) are divine. Whenever dining outside just isn't an option, enjoy the recently renovated dining room that shines in tones of gold, silver, and warm red.

See map p. 142. 43 rue Valois (on the northeast side of the Palais-Royal arcade). ☎ *01-40-20-00-27. Métro: Palais-Royal-Musée du Louvre. Main courses: 20€–35€ ($23–$40). AE, DC, MC, V. Open: Mon–Fri 12:15–2:15 p.m. and Mon–Sat 7:15–9:30 p.m. Closed from the end of Dec to the end of Jan.*

Restaurant Perraudin
$$ Latin Quarter (5e)   CLASSIC BISTRO

The delicious home cooking and low prices draw a big clientele made up of students attending the nearby universities — and their professors. At this historic bistro, with its red-checked tablecloths and lace lampshades, jolly atmosphere, and staff that welcomes kids, you can get a bargain three-course lunch that may start with *oeufs cocotte* (eggs baked with cream), or *flammekueche* (square, thin-crusted pizza topped with cream, herbs, or cheese), followed by the house specialty, *chateaubriand* (porterhouse steak) served in a variety of ways including with foie gras, or in the style of the Vallée d'Auge with mushrooms, cream, and Calvados (apple brandy). Classic dishes such as duck confit and *gigot d'agneau* (leg of lamb) with *gratin Dauphinois* (cheese-topped potatoes) are on the à la carte menu. For dessert, the *tarte Tatin* (caramelized upside-down apple pie) is heavenly. Arrive early for a table because reservations aren't accepted here.

See map p. 144. 157 rue St-Jacques (on the west side of the Panthéon, take rue Soufflot to rue St-Jacques and turn left). ☎ *01-46-33-15-75. RER: Luxembourg. Reservations not accepted. Main courses: around 15€–25€ ($17–$29); three-course lunch menu: 18€ ($21), three-course dinner menu: 28€ ($32). No credit cards. Open: Tues–Fri noon–2:30 p.m.; Mon–Sat 7:30–10 p.m.*

16 Haussmann
$$ Opéra (9e) CLASSIC FRENCH

Located in the Hotel Ambassador just five minutes from Opéra Garnier, Galeries Lafayette, and Printemps, the Phillipe Starck furniture and bold color scheme — royal blue, bright yellow, and mahogany — reflects the bold — and delicious — concoctions that are the hallmarks of Chef Michel Hache. Starters may include a summer vegetable terrine or *oeufs coques à la crème d'épices et caramel de xérés* (soft-boiled eggs in sherry cream sauce with caramel and spices), while choices for main courses could be veal filet with asparagus and mushrooms or filet of duckling marinated in fenugreek with turnips. The two-course menu may not satisfy a large appetite, so plan on sampling such luscious desserts as roasted apples with rosemary and verbena tea ice cream or velvety Caribbean chocolate cake and bitter cocoa. A good selection of wines is available by the glass, and the plant and teak-furnished outdoor terrace, open in summer, is the perfect place to relax after a day of shopping the nearby department stores.

See map p. 142. In the Hôtel Ambassador, 16 bd. Haussmann. ☎ *01-48-00-06-38. Métro: Chausée d'Antin or Richelieu-Drouot. Two-course menu 26€ ($30); three-course menu 30€ ($35); three-course menu with glass of wine or bottle of water 37€ ($42). AE, DC, MC, V. Open: Mon–Fri noon–2:30 p.m. and 7–10:30 p.m.*

Vagenende
$ St-Germain-des-Prés (6e) ALSATIAN/BRASSERIE

This is one of the few remaining independent brasseries in Paris. Founded in 1904 as a *bouillon* (a workers' canteen or soup kitchen), the restaurant evolved into a brasserie that is now classified as a Monument Historique. The Art Nouveau decor is authentic — mirrors, frescoes, and swirling floral patterns abound within walls of dark wood. Lace curtains, globe lights, and spacious booths enhance the classic atmosphere. The dishes are equally classic: You may start out with a half-dozen Fine des Claires oysters or chilled cucumber soup. Main courses include *fricassé de poulet de ferme "Grandmère," pommes fondantes* (farm-raised chicken stew with mashed potatoes) or sauteéd veal with spring vegetables. A "minestrone" of seasonal fruit marinated in wine from the Pays d'Oc region of France makes a refreshing dessert. If it's not too busy, maybe your waiter will crank up the old mechanical piano for a little taste of times past.

See map p. 144. 142 bd. St-Germain. ☎ 01-43-26-68-18. Métro: Odéon. Main courses: 11€–31€ ($13–$15); prix fixe (two courses, drinks not included served noon–6 p.m.) 19€ ($22); dinner prix fixe (three courses, drinks not included) 23€ ($26). AE, MC, V. Open: Daily noon–1 a.m.

Ze Kitchen Galerie
$$ St-Germain-des-Prés (6e)   MODERN BISTRO

William Ledeuil became a popular chef at the trendy Les Bookinistes and in 2002 opened this hip and sophisticated place nearby (Laura Bush paid it a visit in 2003). It is indeed an art gallery and kitchen: the walls of the spacious and spare dining room feature as their only decoration art work that changes every three months. The innovative, Asian-inspired menu, created from a tiny windowed kitchen at the far side of the room, changes every five weeks. The menu is broken down into four parts: soup, raw (usually fish), pasta, and grilled (*à la plancha*). Starters may include a cold artichoke soup with lemongrass or raw tuna sashimi style. Mains may be sole on the bone flavored with mango or veal topped with sweet red peppers flavored with tamarind. Since portions are on the small side, you'll more than likely have room for dessert, which may include tasty roasted pineapple served with a tiny vanilla milk shake with creamy vanilla ice cream. Reservations are recommended because this restaurant fills up fast.

See map p. 144. 4 rue des Grands Augustins. ☎ 01-44-32-00-32. Métro: St-Michel. Reservations recommended. Main courses: 19€–26€ ($22–$30). AE, DC, MC, V. Open: Mon–Fri noon–2:30 p.m. and Mon–Sat 7–11 p.m.

Zimmer
$$ Louvre (1er)   BRASSERIE

Founded by the Alsatian Zimmer family after the Franco-Prussian war of 1870, this beautiful, centrally-located brasserie was restored in 2000 by the Costes brothers, who also own the hotel by the same name and 10 other restaurants in Paris. Diners can now relax in plush surroundings of blue and rose velvet beneath a gorgeous gold molded ceiling and doorways framed by rose velvet draperies. Separated by a door from the Théâtre du Châtelet, it has counted among its patrons actors such as Sarah Bernhardt and such artists as Toulouse-Lautrec and Picasso. One of its three basements, now sealed, was used by the Résistance during World War II as a meeting place, an arsenal, and a hiding place for Jews. The food here is simple and delicious. You may start with a dish from the south of France like thin slices of beef marinated in olive oil and basil and sprinkled with Parmesan cheese or homemade duck liver pâté. Main courses include traditional *choucroute* (sauerkraut made with seafood or Frankfurt, Montbéliard, and Nuremberg sausages, cured bacon, and short ribs) or a Gascony smoked filet of duck breast sautéed in Armagnac. Desserts change daily, but may include a crème brulée or homemade ice cream.

See map p. 142. 1 place du Châtelet. ☎ 01-42-36-74-03. Métro: Châtelet. Main courses: 14€–24€ ($16–$28); two-course menu 19€ ($22). AE, DC, MC, V. Open: Daily 8 a.m.–1:30 a.m.

Dining and Snacking on the Go

Face it: Who can sit down to multiple-course meals every day — even if they are cooked by legendary chefs? Fortunately, many alternatives to a full meal are available. You can choose from street food and sandwiches to cafeterias and tea salons. And of course, there's the Parisian institution, the cafe. Listed here are some of Paris's best cafes and their more sophisticated sisters, the wine bars where you, too, can join in the great French art of people watching!

See the "Light Meals in the Heart of the Right Bank" and "Light Meals in the Heart of the Left Bank" maps for locations of establishments in this section.

Partaking of Paris street food

Some street vendors sell Belgian waffles, called *gaufres,* served warm with powdered sugar or chocolate sauce, but the Parisian street food you see the most is the *crêpe* — a thin wheat pancake stuffed with a filling that's either salty or sweet. When served with savory fillings, such as cheese or mushrooms, the crêpe becomes a *galette.* Sweet crêpe fillings include plain powdered sugar, chocolate-hazelnut spread, ice cream, or jam (called *compote*). Talk about a sugar rush!

You can find stalls or carts selling crêpes near most of the major attractions, in the parks and bigger gardens, and along the rue de Rivoli between the Marais and the place de la Concorde. When you buy a crêpe from a street vendor, you won't have much of a choice of sweet fillings; for a more extensive menu visit a crêperie.

Make a meal of crêpes at one of the many good establishments on rue du Montparnasse, where you can settle down in a peaceful atmosphere with a bowl of cider (a Breton specialty), a galette for a main course, and a crêpe for dessert — usually under 12€ ($14) a person (Métro: Edgar Quinet or Montparnasse-Bienvenüe).

The other typical Parisian street food, *panini,* is also sold just about anywhere. Named for the Italian-style bread they're made with, panini can be almost any filling stuck between two slices of bread, then flattened and grilled between two hot plates. The most common fillings are mozzarella, basil, and sun-dried tomatoes (a pizza sandwich, if you will). Panini are cheap, tasty, and easy to eat on the run.

Light Meals in the Heart of the Right Bank

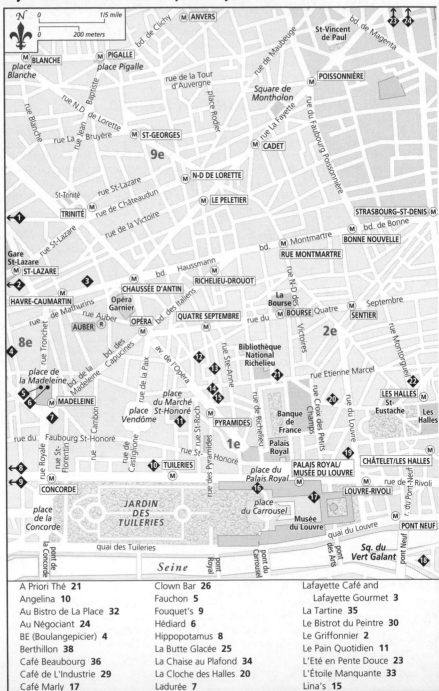

A Priori Thé **21**
Angelina **10**
Au Bistro de La Place **32**
Au Négociant **24**
BE (Boulangepicier) **4**
Berthillon **38**
Café Beaubourg **36**
Café de L'Industrie **29**
Café Marly **17**

Clown Bar **26**
Fauchon **5**
Fouquet's **9**
Hédiard **6**
Hippopotamus **8**
La Butte Glacée **25**
La Chaise au Plafond **34**
La Cloche des Halles **20**
Ladurée **7**

Lafayette Café and
    Lafayette Gourmet **3**
La Tartine **35**
Le Bistrot du Peintre **30**
Le Griffonnier **2**
Le Pain Quotidien **11**
L'Eté en Pente Douce **23**
L'Étoile Manquante **33**
Lina's **15**

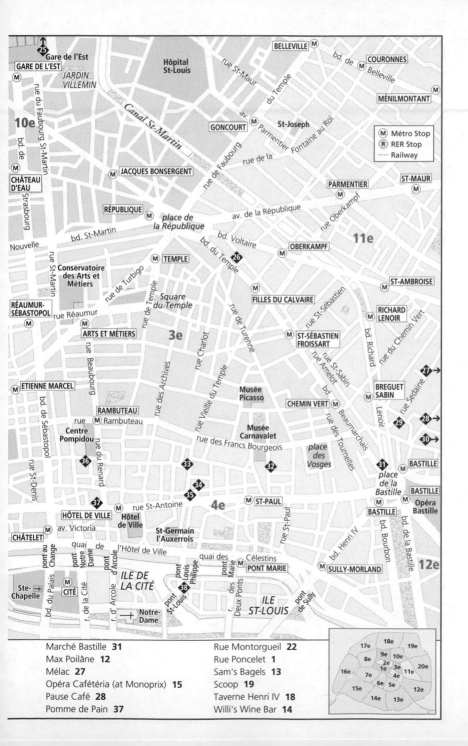

Marché Bastille **31**
Max Poilâne **12**
Mélac **27**
Opéra Cafétéria (at Monoprix) **15**
Pause Café **28**
Pomme de Pain **37**

Rue Montorgueil **22**
Rue Poncelet **1**
Sam's Bagels **13**
Scoop **19**
Taverne Henri IV **18**
Willi's Wine Bar **14**

Light Meals in the Heart of the Left Bank

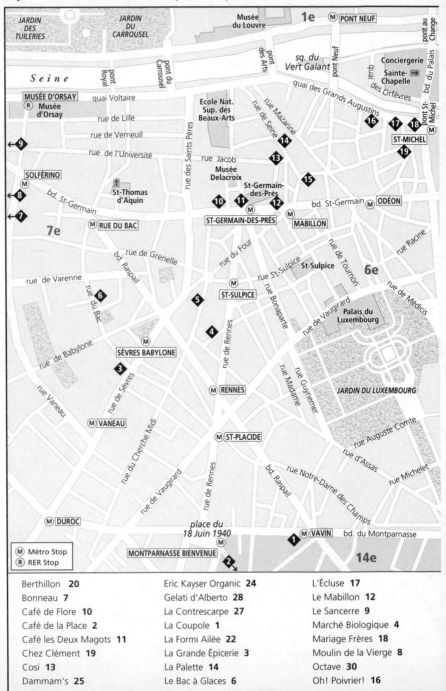

Berthillon **20**	Eric Kayser Organic **24**	L'Écluse **17**
Bonneau **7**	Gelati d'Alberto **28**	Le Mabillon **12**
Café de Flore **10**	La Contrescarpe **27**	Le Sancerre **9**
Café de la Place **2**	La Coupole **1**	Marché Biologique **4**
Café les Deux Magots **11**	La Formi Ailée **22**	Mariage Frères **18**
Chez Clément **19**	La Grande Épicerie **3**	Moulin de la Vierge **8**
Cosi **13**	La Palette **14**	Octave **30**
Dammam's **25**	Le Bac à Glaces **6**	Oh! Poivrier! **16**

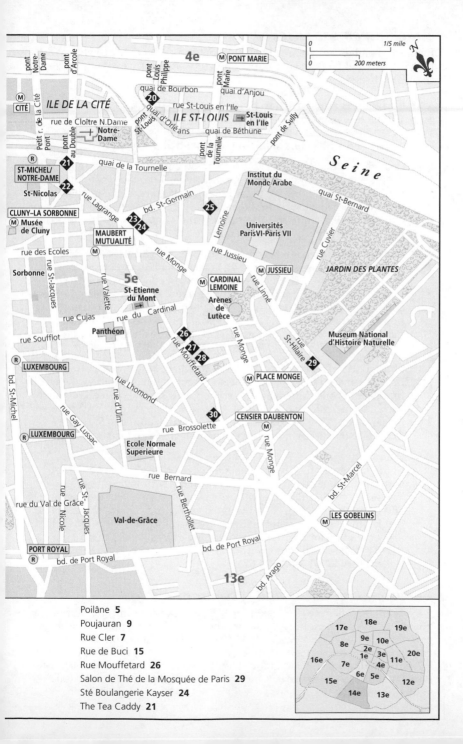

0   1/5 mile

0   200 meters

pont Notre-Dame
pont d'Arcole
4e   Ⓜ PONT MARIE
pont Louis Philippe
quai de Bourbon   pont Marie   quai d'Anjou
Ⓜ CITÉ   ILE DE LA CITÉ   **20**
quai d'Orléans   rue St-Louis en l'Île   St-Louis en l'Île
rue de Cloître N.Dame   ILE ST-LOUIS
pont St-Louis
Notre-Dame   quai de Béthune
pont de Sully
Petit r. de la Cité
Pont au Double
pont de la Tournelle
Ⓡ **21**   quai de la Tournelle   *S e i n e*
ST-MICHEL/ NOTRE-DAME   **22**
St-Nicolas   rue Lagrange   Institut du Monde Arabe   quai St-Bernard
CLUNY–LA SORBONNE   bd. St-Germain   **25**
Ⓜ Musée de Cluny   **23**   Lemoine
24   Universités ParisVI-Paris VII   rue Cuvier
MAUBERT MUTUALITÉ   Ⓜ
rue des Ecoles   rue Monge   rue Jussieu   JARDIN DES PLANTES
Sorbonne   rue St-Jacques   Ⓜ JUSSIEU
5e   Ⓜ CARDINAL LEMOINE   rue Linné
St-Etienne du Mont   Arènes de Lutèce   rue St-Hilaire   Museum National d'Histoire Naturelle
rue Valette
rue Cujas   rue du Cardinal
Panthéon   **26**   rue Monge   **29**
rue Soufflot   **27**
Ⓡ LUXEMBOURG   **28**   Ⓜ PLACE MONGE
rue Lhomond
bd. St-Michel   rue Gay Lussac   rue d'Ulm
30   CENSIER DAUBENTON
Ⓡ LUXEMBOURG   rue Brossolette   Ⓜ
Ecole Normale Superieure   rue Monge
rue Bernard   bd. St-Marcel
rue St-Jacques
rue Nicole   rue Berthollet
rue du Val de Grâce   Val-de-Grâce   LES GOBELINS
Ⓜ
PORT ROYAL   bd. de Port Royal
Ⓡ bd. de Port Royal
13e   bd. Arago

17e   18e   19e
8e   9e   10e
16e   2e   3e   11e   20e
1e   4e
7e   6e   5e   12e
15e   14e   13e

Snacking on sandwiches

Even sandwiches are yummy in France. Sandwich (and more) shops Lina's, Cosi, and Le Pain Quotidien, open until the early evening, make their own breads.

✔ If baguettes are starting to bore you, then **Sam's Bagels** (formerly The Bagel Place)**,** 51 pass Choiseul, 2e (☎ **01-42-86-07-36;** Métro: Pyramides; see map p. 164), is for you. It offers New York-style bagels and a blackboard full of bagel sandwich specials.

✔ **Cosi,** 54 rue de Seine, 6e (☎ **01-46-33-35-36;** Métro: St-Germain-des-Prés; see map p. 166), serves its sandwiches on delicious homemade flat bread, and fillings are plentiful and delicious. You can choose from an assortment of specialties, including mozzarella and Parmesan cheeses, Italian ham, roast tomatoes, and *tapenade* (olive spread). Another branch is at 95 rue Réamur, 2e (☎ **01-40-26-13-30**).

✔ **Le Pain Quotidien,** 18 Marché-St-Honoré, 1er (☎ **01-42-96-31-70;** Métro: Tuileries; see map p. 164), is part of a Belgian chain serving mouth-watering tartines (open-faced sandwiches) made with combinations such as country ham and Gruyère cheese, a goat-cheese-and-honey duo; or a beef, basil, and Parmesan recipe. Locations are popping up all over; one is in the Marais at 18 rue des Archives, 4e (☎ **01-44-54-03-07**) and another is in the Latin Quarter, not far from the Panthéon at 136 rue Mouffetard, 5e (☎ **01-55-43-91-99**).

✔ **Lina's,** 22 rue St-Pères, 6e (☎ **01-40-20-42-78;** Métro: St-Germain-des-Près; see map p. 164), packs an assortment of fillings onto whole-meal breads and rolls, American deli-style. Add a soup or salad and finish with a brownie for a quick meal. Other locations are at 7 av. de l'Opéra, 1er (☎ **01-47-03-30-29**), and 105 rue Faubourg St-Honoré, 8e (☎ **01-42-89-93-00**), not far from the designer boutiques.

✔ **Pomme de Pain,** 76 rue de Rivoli, 4e (☎ **01-42-78-57-29;** Métro: Châtelet; see map p. 164), boasts a fast-food–style counter where staff slice baguettes in half and layer on the toppings of your choice. You can try the Lyonnaise, with slices of *saucisson sec* (dry sausage) and cornichon pickles, or a hot mozzarella and tomato special. The drink and sandwich combinations are usually good buys. Branches are located all across the city, including one at 2 bd. Haussmann, 9e (☎ **01-48-24-20-60**) and another at 1 rue Pierre Lescot, Forum des Halles, 1er (☎ **01-40-39-94-63**).

Choosing cafeterias and restaurant chains

You can fill up cheaply (for less than 15€) at cafeterias and restaurant chains, which are generally open for lunch and dinner, and the offerings can be quite tasty. They're also kid-friendly. My personal favorite is the cafeteria at the department store Galeries Lafayette — the food is fresh, the surroundings sleek and modern, and the views over the rooftops of Paris are superb — the perfect pick-me-up after a morning spent souvenir shopping.

✔ **Opéra Cafétéria (at Monoprix),** 23 av. Opéra, 1er; ☎ **01-42-96-34-96;** Métro: Palais Royal-Musée du Louvre; see map p. 164. Not as glamorous as the sleek Galerie Lafayette cafeteria (see later in this list), you still find tasty grilled entrees, prepared foods and a salad bar at prices that fit the tightest budget.

✔ **Chez Clément,** 9 place St-Andre des Arts, 6e; ☎ **01-56-81-32-00;** Métro: St-Michel; see map p. 166.; or 123 av. du Champs-Elysées, 8c (☎ **01-43-73-87-09**) Métro: Charles-de-Gaulle–Étoile. Specialties in this restaurant, with a decor heavy on the copper pots, include spit-roasted meats.

✔ **Hippopotamus,** 1 bd. Beaumarchais, 4e; ☎ **01-44-61-90-40;** Métro: Bastille; see map p. 164. Their red awnings are all across town. You, and your very welcome child, can get a hot meal here when most other places are closed.

✔ **Lafayette Café,** (6th floor, Galeries Lafayette), 40 bd. Haussmann, 9e; ☎ **01-42-82-34-56** (information desk); Métro: Havre-Caumartin; see map p. 164. This self-service cafeteria on the sixth floor of Galeries Lafayette's main building has plenty of seating (some tables have terrific views over the rooftops of Paris) and fresh food (the salad bar is particularly recommended).

✔ **Oh! Poivrier!,** 25 quai des Grands Augustins; 6e ☎ **01-43-29-41-77;** Métro: St-Michel; see map p. 166. Light fare, the specialty is open-faced sandwiches at moderate prices. Long hours. This particular branch is on a quay of the Seine.

Assembling a picnic, Parisian style

Grab a crusty baguette or two, some dried sausage, a wedge of cheese, and a few pieces of fruit and head to the nearest park or to a garden that strikes your fancy. Picnicking in Paris can be as fun and as unforgettable as a meal in a 3-star restaurant at just a fraction of the cost. In this section, discover where to stock up on provisions. (*Note:* You can also assemble picnic fixings cheaply at Parisian supermarkets all across the city.)

The traiteurs (Gourmet food shops)

Look for the word *traiteur,* which designates a food shop that sells ready-made meat, pasta, and salad dishes. The two most famous, **Fauchon** and **Hédiard,** have main stores at place de la Madeleine, 8e (Métro: Madeleine), and branches all across Paris. Every neighborhood has several good *traiteurs,* so be on the lookout and don't hesitate to ask your hotel staff for recommendations.

✔ **Fauchon,** 42 place du Marché-St-Honoré, 1er (☎ **01-42-61-45-46;** Métro: Pyramides; see map p. 164), was founded in 1886. It is THE high-end food shop with everything from foie gras and Norwegian smoked salmon to caviar to fancy breads and cheeses. There are branches around the city. Open Monday to Saturday 9:30 a.m. to 7:00 p.m.

✔ **Hédiard,** 21 place de la Madeleine, 8e (☎ 01-43-12-88-77; Métro: Madeleine; see map p. 164), is a gourmet food shop that sells upscale products, wine, and readymade food to go. Open daily from 9 a.m. to 11 p.m.

✔ **La Grande Épicerie,** Bon Marché, 38 rue de Sèvres, 6e (☎ 01-44-39-81-00; Métro: Sèvres-Babylone; see map p. 166), may be the best grocery store on the Left Bank. It has large *traiteur* and wine departments and sells everything from cleaning supplies to gourmet chocolate to fresh fish. Open Monday to Saturday from 8:30 a.m. to 9:00 p.m.

✔ **Lafayette Gourmet,** 48 bd. Haussmann, 9e (☎ 01-42-82-34-56; Métro: Havre-Caumartin; see map p. 164), is another wonderful grocery store that has everything you need for a picnic. It's located smack in the middle of the Galeries Lafayette complex (in the men's store). Open Monday to Saturday from 9:30 a.m. to 8:30 p.m.; open Thursday until 9:00 p.m.

The street markets

Every neighborhood in Paris has its street market, and it's probably the best place to find the freshest produce, cheeses of excellent quality, and other picnic supplies. Even when you don't buy anything, visiting one or two is worth the authentic reflection of Parisian society you encounter. Markets are generally open from Tuesday through Saturday, from around 7 a.m. to 1 p.m., and of course, the pickings are better the earlier you go. The ones open on Sunday are indicated. Some of the more well known include:

✔ **Marché Bastille,** 11e (Métro: Bastille; see map p. 164): This huge market sells everything from game, cheese, and vegetables to fish and condiments. Open Thursday from 7:00 a.m. to 2:30 p.m. and Sunday 7:00 a.m. to 3:00 p.m.

✔ **Marché Biologique,** boulevard Raspail between rue du Cherche-Midi and rue de Rennes, 6e (Métro: Rennes; see map p. 166): This all-organic market features greengrocers, winemakers, butchers, and bakers. Open Sunday 8:30 a.m. to 1:30 p.m. An "unorganic" market takes place here Tuesday and Friday mornings.

✔ **Rue Cler,** 7e (Métro: Ecole-Militaire; see map p. 166): See how diplomats shop for their dinner in this chic market. Open Tuesday through Sunday mornings between 7:30 a.m. and noon.

✔ **Rue de Buci,** 6e (Métro: Odéon; see map p. 166): This lively market is close to all the Latin Quarter action. Open Tuesday to Sunday mornings between 7:30 a.m. and noon.

✔ **Rue Montorgueil,** 1er (Métro: Les Halles/Châtelet; see map p. 164): Have breakfast at one of the many sidewalk cafes before choosing your produce. Open Tuesday through Saturday from 8 a.m. to 1 p.m. and 4 p.m. to 7 p.m.

✔ **Rue Mouffetard,** 5e (Métro: Monge; see map p. 166): One of the oldest markets in Paris on one of the city's more interesting streets. Sing along with accordion players on Sunday mornings. Open Tuesday through Sunday mornings between 7:30 a.m. and noon.

✔ **Rue Poncelet,** 17e (Métro: Ternes; see map p. 164): The Poncelet market is especially renowned for its fresh fruit stalls. Open Tuesday through Saturday mornings between 7:30 a.m. and noon.

The best bakeries

You want a fresh baguette for your picnic, and you can find bakeries (*boulangeries*) on nearly every corner in residential neighborhoods. Keep in mind that quality of the breads varies considerably.

Long lines of locals on weekend mornings or evenings before dinner give away the best bakeries. You can get a sandwich or a quiche to go, but be warned that most bakeries make very plain sandwiches — often just a slice of bread or cheese on a baguette with no condiment or other accoutrement. Some of the best bakeries are

✔ **BE (Boulangepicier),** 73 bd. de Courcelles, 8e; ☎ 01-46-22-20-20. Open Monday to Saturday from 7 a.m. to 8 p.m. Métro: Courcelles or Ternes; see map p. 164.

✔ **Bonneau,** 75 rue d'Auteuil, 16e; ☎ 01-46-51-12-25. Open Tuesday through Sunday from 6:30 a.m. to 8:30 p.m. Métro: Michel–Ange–Auteuil; see map p. 166.

✔ **Eric Kayser Organic,** 14 rue Monge, 5e; ☎ 01-44-07-17-81. Open Tuesday through Sunday 8 a.m. to 8 p.m. Métro: Maubert Mutualité; see map p. 166.

✔ **Max Poilâne,** 42 place Marché St-Honoré, 1er. Open Monday to Saturday from 7:30 a.m. to 8:00 p.m. Métro: Pyramides; see map p. 164.

✔ **Moulin de la Vierge,** 166 av. de Suffren, 15e; ☎ 01-47-83-45-55. Open Monday to Saturday from 7 a.m. to 8 p.m. Métro: Sèvres-Lecourbe; see map p. 166.

✔ **Poilâne,** 8 rue du Cherche-midi, 6e; ☎ 01-45-48-42-59. Open Monday to Saturday from 7:15 a.m. to 8:15 p.m. Métro: St-Sulpice or Sèvres Babylone; see map p. 166.

✔ **Poujauran,** 20 rue Jean Nicot, 7e; ☎ 01-43-17-35-20. Open Monday to Saturday from 8:00 a.m. to 8:30 p.m. Métro: Latour Maubourg; see map p. 166.

✔ **Sté Boulangerie Kayser,** 8 rue Monge, 5e; ☎ ☎ 01-44-07-01-42. Open Wednesday through Monday from 6:30 a.m. to 8:30 p.m. Métro: Maubert Mutualité; see map p. 166.

Watching the world go by at a cafe

There are just too many good cafes in Paris — after all, the French have been perfecting these institutions for centuries — and to list them all here would be *am-poh-seebl,* as they say in French. Instead, I've compiled some of my favorites — places where you'll be comfortable reading the paper, writing postcards, watching people, and soaking up the city's atmosphere while relaxing with a cup of coffee, a glass of wine or beer, or a sandwich, salad, or traditional French specialty like *pot-au-feu* (beef boiled with vegetables). Cafes are generally open from about 8 a.m. until 1 a.m., and most take MasterCard and Visa.

Au Bistro de La Place

This square on the place du Marché Sainte-Catherine is a pedestrian zone on the site of an 18th-century market, and this is the prettiest of all the bistros on the outdoor terrace here. The food is also the best; you may find fresh vegetable soup served hot or cold or fresh goat cheese marinated in olive oil with salad. Even if you don't come here for a meal, visit after the lunch hour (noon–2:30 p.m.) to enjoy a leisurely drink or pastry on the terrace.

See map p. 164. 2 place du Marché Sainte-Catherine (between rue de Turenne and rue de Sevigné), 4e. ☎ 01-42-78-21-32. Métro: St-Paul.

Café Beaubourg

This is the hip cafe overlooking the Centre Pompidou; The backs of its white terrace chairs (nearly always full with a good mix of tourists and locals) resemble the lips in the Stravinsky Fountain just around the corner. The dark bi-level interior has large circular columns that soar to an illuminated ceiling. The walls are filled with books, and a small wooden bridge spans the upper part of the cafe and leads to quieter, artistically designed tables. Even the bathrooms are attractions in themselves; they have the serenity of Zen gardens. Simple food may include a smooth gazpacho, salmon club sandwich, or goat cheese salad. You'll become a main attraction yourself as passersby cast curious glances at the people chic enough to eat here.

See map p. 164. 43 rue St-Merri, 4e. ☎ 01-48-87-63-96. Métro: Rambuteau or Hôtel-de-Ville.

Café de Flore

In the heart of St-Germain-des-Prés, this cafe is still going strong, even though the famous writers have moved on, and you now pay high prices. Sartre is said to have written *Les Chemins de la Liberté* (*The Roads to Freedom*) at his table here, and he and Simone de Beauvoir saw people by appointment here. Other regulars included André Malraux and Guillaume Apollinaire. Paris's leading intellectual bookstore, La Hune, is right next door.

See map p. 166. 172 bd. St-Germain, 6e. ☎ 01-45-48-55-26. Métro: St-Germain-des-Prés.

Café de la Place

This old-fashioned cafe overlooking small, tree-lined place Edgar Quinet, is a popular spot for young neighborhood residents. Browse the menu of inexpensive bistro specialties, or opt for a simple sandwich and a glass of wine. If you're lucky, there will be a *brocante* (flea market) or art fair in the square across the street. This is a great place to fill up before any trips outside Paris from the Gare du Montparnasse railroad station, which is around the corner and just down the street.

See map p. 166. 23 rue d'Odessa, 14e. ☎ *01-42-18-01-55. Métro: Edgar-Quinet.*

Café de L'Industrie

This cafe is young, friendly, casual, and extremely popular; At night, a capacity crowd flows to a former Moroccan restaurant across the street. Mod meets retro meets country in spacious rooms that also have a vaguely colonial flavor. Hip Bastille denizens drift in and out all day. Bartenders specialize in rum drinks. An 18€ ($21) brunch is served on weekends.

See map p. 164. 16 rue St-Sabin (the corner of rue Sedaine and rue St-Sabin), 11e. ☎ *01-47-00-13-53. Métro: Breguet-Sabin.*

Café les Deux Magots

Like its neighbor, Café de Flore, Café les Deux Magots was a hangout for Sartre and Simone de Beauvoir. The intellectuals met here in the 1950s, and Sartre wrote at his table every morning. With prices that start at 4€ ($4.60) for coffee, the cafe is an expensive place for literary-intellectual pilgrims, but a great spot to watch the nightly promenade on the boulevard St-Germain.

See map p. 166. 6 place St-Germain-des-Prés, 6e. ☎ *01-45-48-55-25. Métro: St-Germain-des-Prés.*

Café Marly

Sinking into one of the plush red chairs here amid high ceilings, warmly painted pastel walls, and luxurious sofa chairs with a drink or cup of tea is the best antidote to Louvre fatigue! This stunning cafe has a gorgeous view of the glass pyramid that is the museum's main entrance. You almost forget food is served here, but that would be a mistake — it's very good, if not abundant. There is outdoor balcony seating where you can enjoy the exquisite lighting on the pyramid and surrounding 18th-century facades. After 8 p.m., seating is for dinner only.

See map p. 164. 93 rue de Rivoli, cour Napoléon du Louvre, 1er. ☎ *01-49-26-06-60. Métro: Palais-Royal–Musée du Louvre.*

Fouquet's

This is the place with the red umbrellas on the Champs-Elysées, not far from the Arc de Triomphe, a 20th-century Parisian institution. The restaurant has undergone a renovation that restored the red plush and wood splendor of the days when it hosted such guests as James Joyce, Charlie Chaplin, Marlene Dietrich, Winston Churchill, Franklin D. Roosevelt, François Truffaut, Claude Chabrol, and Jean-Luc Godard. Opened in 1899, it is now registered as a historic monument. Expensive.

See map p. 164. 99 av. des Champs-Elysées, 8e. ☎ *01-47-23-50-00. Métro: George V.*

La Chaise au Plafond

This friendly, stylish place tucked away on a pedestrian-only side street in the heart of the Marais is always packed. Maybe that's because it's the perfect spot to refuel after visiting the Musée Picasso. It serves enormous salads, imaginative sandwiches, and thick tartes to a local crowd sprinkled with tourists in the know.

See map p. 164. 10 rue Trésor, 4e. ☎ *01-42-76-03-22. Métro: Hôtel-de-Ville.*

La Contrescarpe

After the demise of La Chope, patrons gravitated to this cafe just across the pretty place de la Contrescarpe centering on four lilac trees and a fountain. This is a good place to take a break after marketing on rue Mouffetard or visiting the nearby Panthéon. The 14€ ($16) menu is a good deal.

See map p. 166. 57 rue Lacépède, 5e. ☎ *01-43-36-82-88. Métro: Cardinal Lemoine.*

La Coupole

La Coupole has been packing them in since Henry Miller came here for his morning porridge. The cavernous interior is always jammed and bristling with energy. Japanese business people, French yuppies, models, tourists, and neighborhood regulars keep the frenzied waiters running until 2 a.m. You won't know which is more interesting, the scene on the street, or the parade that passes through the revolving doors. The food is good, too, though prices are high.

See map p. 166. 102 bd. Montparnasse, 14e. ☎ *01-43-20-14-20. Métro: Vavin.*

La Palette

Students from the nearby Ecole des Beaux-Arts, artists, and gallery owners linger and watch the life of the Left Bank flow by from tables here. The interior is decorated with colorful murals, and a palette hangs above the bar. The fare is open-faced sandwiches and salads at reasonable prices. Waitstaff can be snippy.

See map p. 166. 43 rue de Seine, 6e. ☎ *01-43-26-68-15. Métro: Mabillon.*

L'Eté en Pente Douce

Escape the shoulder-to-shoulder tourists on Montmartre's place du Tertre at this cute cafe. To find it, turn right after exiting the *funiculaire*, and take the first set of steps leading down. You find yourself on a leafy square facing a small park. The terrace looks out on the stairs and iron lamps that

Utrillo did a painting of, and someone always is performing for the captive audience. The interior is brightly decorated with painted borders of leaves and plants, mosaics, unusual *objets d'art,* and a painted ceiling. Between lunch and dinner, the restaurant serves tea, pastries, and sandwiches. *See map p. 164. 23 rue Muller, 18e.* ☎ *01-42-64-02-67. Métro: Chateau-Rouge.*

L'Étoile Manquante

Translated as "the missing star," this is a modern, tasteful, and above all, fun cafe that plays host to all kinds of locals, artists, and writers who enjoy reasonably priced, somewhat inventive food in an atmosphere that whispers rather than shouts "cool." Little stars in the floor tiles twinkle in the dim light from recessed round ceiling lights outlined in brown circles and from baguette-shaped sconces with artfully placed tiny holes to let the light through. The vibrant scene is reflected in the wall of rectangular mirrors in the back of the restaurant. A visit to the very dark bathrooms lit from above by "starlight" is a must. A camera is hidden behind the mirror of the trough-like sink, turn around and see yourself on the TV screen. *See map p. 164. 34 rue e Vieille du Temple, 4e.* ☎ *01-43-26-68-15. Métro: Hôtel de Ville or St-Paul.*

Le Mabillon

If you only have one night in Paris, make the most of it and welcome the dawn at Café Mabillon, which stays open all night. During the day, contemporary rock music draws a young, hip crowd to relax on the outdoor terrace or in the ultramodern interior. At night the music changes to techno, and the bordello-red banquettes fill with a wide assortment of night owls. As dawn approaches, the sound drops to a level just loud enough to keep you from dozing off in your seat. *See map p. 166. 164 bd. St-Germain, 6e.* ☎ *01-43-26-62-93. Métro: Mabillon.*

Pause Café

Featured in the French film *Chacun Cherche Son Chat* (released in the United States as *When the Cat's Away*), this cafe has proved so popular that it underwent a recent expansion. Its hip clientele are denizens of the club scene (flyers inside give dates for upcoming events) or cool residents of the neighborhood. A groovy distressed interior features found art, while outdoors is made tropical with cloth and bamboo umbrellas and potted palms. The food is fresh and tasty. *See map p. 164. 41 rue de Charonne, 11e.* ☎ *01-48-06-80-33. Métro: Lédru-Rollin.*

Steeping and sipping at a tea salon (Salons de thé)

Sitting down to tea in Paris can be an elegant and refined undertaking, or a relaxing break between bouts of *musée*-hopping. The tea salons have a wide range of blends, steeped to perfection, and the pastry selections are usually excellent (Ladurée's macaroons are world-famous). Save your full meals, however, for a restaurant because tea salons tend to be expensive.

✔ **Angelina,** 226 rue de Rivoli, 1er; ☎ **01-42-60-82-00.** Open daily from 9:00 a.m. to 5:45 p.m. Lunch is served from 11:45 a.m. to 3:00 p.m. Métro: Concorde or Tuileries; see map p. 164.

✔ **A Priori Thé,** 35–37 Galerie Vivienne (enter at 6 rue Vivienne, 4 rue des Petits-Champs, or 5 rue de la Banque), 2e; ☎ **01-42-97-48-75.** Open Monday to Friday 9 a.m. to 6 p.m.; Saturday from 9 a.m. to 6:30 p.m., and Sunday from 12:30 to 6:30 p.m. Métro: Bourse, Palais-Royal–Musée du Louvre, or Pyramides; see map p. 164.

✔ **Ladurée,** 16 rue Royale, 8e; ☎ **01-42-60-21-79.** Open Monday through Saturday from 8:30 a.m. to 7:30 p.m. Métro: Concorde; see map p. 164. Also on Champs-Elysées at number 75. ☎ **01-40-75-08-75.** Métro: Franklin-D-Roosevelt.

✔ **La Formi Ailée,** 8 rue du Fouarre, 5e; ☎ **01-43-29-40-99.** Open daily from noon to 1 a.m. Métro: Maubert-Mutualité; see map p. 166.

✔ **Mariage Frères,** 13 rue Grands Augustins, 6e; ☎ **01-40-51-82-50.** This location is open daily from noon to 7 p.m. Métro: St-Michel.; see map p. 166.

✔ **Salon de Thé de la Mosquée de Paris,** 39 rue Geoffroy-St-Hilaire, 5e; ☎ **01-43-31-18-14.** Open daily from 10 a.m. to 10 p.m. Métro: Monge; see map p. 166.

✔ **The Tea Caddy,** 14 rue St-Julien-le-Pauvre, 5e; ☎ **01-43-54-15-56.** Open daily from noon to 7 p.m. Métro: St-Michel; see map p. 166.

A heady mix of wine bars

With good selections of wines by the glass, and tasty light meals served all day in pleasant surroundings, the Paris wine bar is often a cozy and sophisticated alternative to the cafe.

Au Négociant

The photographer Robert Doisneau came here often (his picture is on the wall), but today a discerning crowd of regulars keep this tiny, hole-in-the-wall wine bar near Montmartre humming. The excellent pâtés and terrines are homemade and served with fresh, chewy bread.

See map p. 164. 27 rue Lambert, 18e. ☎ *01-46-06-15-11. Mon–Fri noon–3 p.m.; Tues–Thurs 6:30–10:30 p.m. Métro: Château-Rouge or Lamarck-Caulincourt.*

Clown Bar

It's hard to say what gets more attention here, the wine or the clowns from the nearby Cirque d'Hiver, who frequent this place. The bar is decorated with a mélange of circus posters and circus-themed ceramic tiles. The wine list features an extensive selection of French offerings.

See map p. 164. 114 rue Amelot, 11e. ☎ *01-43-55-87-35. Mon–Sat noon–2:30 p.m. and 7 p.m.–1 a.m. Métro: Filles du Calvaire.*

La Cloche des Halles

This tiny bar and cafe is crowded at lunchtime with people dining on plates of ham or quiche accompanied by a bottle of wine. It's convivial and fun, but very noisy and crowded. If you can't find a seat, you can usually stand at the bar and eat. Look closely at the exterior for the bell that once tolled the opening and closing of the vast food market for which this neighborhood was named.

See map p. 164. 28 rue Coquillière, 1er. ☎ *01-42-36-93-89. Mon–Fri 8 a.m.–10 p.m.; Sat 10 a.m.–5 p.m. Métro: Les Halles or Palais-Royal–Musée du Louvre.*

La Tartine

This used to be the wine bar that time forgot with nicotine-browned walls and worn wood furniture. But no more. A renovation in September 2003 spruced up the place that now sports pistachio and burgundy–trimmed walls, new furniture, and updated bathrooms. The same mix of working class and well heeled frequent La Tartine, and it's still a great place to get a light lunch or pick-me-up of tartine (open faced sandwich), cheese, or *charcuterie* (assorted sliced meats) plate and a glass of wine.

See map p. 164. 24 rue de Rivoli, 4e. ☎ *01-42-72-76-85. Wed–Mon noon–10 p.m. Métro: St-Paul. Closed Tues.*

Le Bistrot du Peintre

Painters, actors, and night crawlers hang out here nightly. The delicious and reasonably priced food, zinc bar, wood paneling, large terrace, and superb Belle Époque style would make this wine bar a highlight even if the wine selection wasn't as reasonably priced as it is.

See map p. 164. 116 av. Ledru-Rollin, 11e. ☎ *01-47-00-34-39. Daily 7 a.m. to midnight. Métro: Ledru-Rollin.*

L'Écluse

This location originally was home to a small chain of wine bars. L'Écluse is casually chic and authentic. Have one of its 20 wines by the glass and a light bites such as *carpaccio,* salad, or soup.

See map p. 166. 15 quai des Grands-Augustins, 6e. ☎ *01-46-33-58-74. Daily 11:30 a.m.–1:30 a.m. Métro: St-Michel.*

Le Griffonnier

The kitchen staff at Le Griffonnier deliver first-rate cuisine, and the wine cellar is superb. Sample bistro specialties such as *confit de canard maison* (duck preserved and cooked in its own fat until it's so tender that it falls off the bone), or try a hearty plate of *charcuterie* (regional sliced meats), terrines, and cheese, usually from the Auvergne region of central France, and ask your waiter to recommend the wine. Hot meals are served only at lunchtime and on Thursday evenings.

See map p. 164. 8 rue des Saussaies, 8e. ☎ 01-42-65-17-17. Mon–Fri 7:30 a.m.–9 p.m. Métro: Champs-Elysées–Clemenceau.

Le Sancerre

Le Sancerre is a quiet place to relax for a light meal or glass of wine after visiting the Eiffel Tower. Loire wines are the specialty here, including, of course, Sancerre. La Sancerre serves typically French items, such as omelets of all varieties with a side of fried potatoes, and duck liver terrine. The more adventurous can sample the ubiquitous *andouillette,* the sausage that is decidedly an acquired taste.

See map p. 166. 22 av. Rapp, 7e. ☎ 01-45-51-75-91. Mon–Fri 8 a.m.–10 p.m.; Sat 8 a.m.–4 p.m. Métro: Alma Marceau.

Mélac

Owner Jacques Mélac has an excellent selection of wine from nearly all the regions of France, which he dispenses to a lively crowd of regulars. He's happy to give you recommendations. Usually a hot *plat du jour* is available for lunch, but you can feast on a selection of first-rate pâtés, terrines, *charcuterie* (regional sliced meats), and cheeses all day.

See map p. 164. 42 rue Léon Frot, 11e. ☎ 01-43-70-59-27. Mon 9 a.m.–2 p.m.; Tues–Sat 9 a.m.–10:30 p.m. Métro: Charonne.

Taverne Henri IV

Although on the expensive side, the wine and food are excellent at this authentic, old-fashioned bar, where regulars, mostly male, read newspapers, discuss the news of the day, and smoke nonstop. The variety of wines by the glass can accompany open-faced sandwiches, pâtés, and such cheeses as Cantal and Auvergne blue.

See map p. 164. 13 place du Pont Neuf, 1er. ☎ 01-43-54-27-90. Mon–Fri noon–10 p.m.; Sat noon–4 p.m. Métro: Pont-Neuf.

Willi's Wine Bar

Since 1980, an upscale crowd of professionals and tourists have sampled more than 250 different varieties of wine while seated at the polished oak bar or have dined in the high-ceilinged oak-beamed dining room from a full menu of main courses that these days cost just 15€ ($17). Each year the owners commission an image relating to wine from an artist, and the colorful paintings are available for sale as prints for between 49€ and 400€ ($56–$460).

See map p. 164. 13 rue des Petits-Champs, 1er. ☎ 01-42-61-05-09. Mon–Sat noon–2:30 p.m., and 7–11 p.m.; bar open Mon–Sat noon–midnight.

Getting the scoop on Paris ice cream

Rhubarb, plum, cassis, honey nut. . . . If Paris doesn't have the best ice cream in the world, it must run a close second. Such flavors, such creaminess! Ask for a *cornet seule* (kor-*nay* sul; single-scoop cone) or *cornet double* (kor-*nay* doobl; double scoop) — even the cone is yummy. Prices range from 3€ ($3.45) for a single to 5€ ($5.75) for a double-scoop cone. Most places open daily around 10:30 a.m. and close around 8:00 p.m. *Note:* Sitting down when ordering ice cream is always more expensive — sometimes twice as much as ordering your cone to go. Parisians cite **Berthillon,** 31 rue St-Louis-en-l'Ile, 4e (☎ 01-43-54-31-61; Métro: Cité; see map p. 164) as the best in the city, but the following establishments also put soft-serve to shame. Although Berthillon closes from July 15 through the first week in September, a note on the door directs customers to other nearby shops that sell its ice cream.

- ✔ **Dammam's,** 20 rue Cardinal Lemoine, 5e; ☎ **01-46-33-61-30;** Métro: Cardinal Lemoine; see map p. 166.

- ✔ **Gelati d'Alberto,** 45 rue Mouffetard, 5e; ☎ **01-43-37-88-07;** Métro: Monge; see map p. 166.

- ✔ **La Butte Glacée,** 14 rue Norvins, 18e; ☎ **01-42-23-91-58;** Métro: Abbesses; see map p. 164.

- ✔ **Le Bac à Glaces,** 109 rue du Bac, 7e; ☎ **01-45-48-87-65;** Métro: Rue du Bac; see map p. 166.

- ✔ **Octave,** 138 rue Mouffetard, 5e; ☎ **01-45-35-20-56;** Métro: Monge; see map p. 166.

- ✔ **Scoop,** 154 rue St-Honoré, 1er (behind the Louvre des Antiquaires); ☎ **01-42-60-31-84;** Métro: Louvre-Rivoli; see map p. 164.

Index of Establishments by Neighborhood

Louvre, Les Halles (1er)

Angelina $
Au Pied de Cochon $$
Café Marly $
Fauchon $
La Cloche des Halles $
La Pain Quotidien $
La Poule au Pot $$-$$$
La Tour de Montlhéry Chez Denise $$-$$$

Max Poilâne $
Restaurant du Palais-Royal $$-$$$
Scoop $
Taverne Henri IV $
Willi's Wine Bar $
Zimmer $$

Sentier (2e)

A Priori Thé $
Sam's Bagels $

Le Marais, Ile St-Louis/Ile de la Cité (3e, 4e)

Au Bascou $$
Auberge de Jarente $$
Au Bistro de la Place $
Bofinger $$
Brasserie Ile St-Louis $$
Café Beaubourg $
Caveau du Palais $$
Hippopotamus $
Jo Goldenberg $-$$
L'Ambroisie $$$$
La Chaise au Plafond $
La Tartine $
L'Étoile Manquante $
Pomme de Pain $

Latin Quarter (5e)

Brasserie Balzar $$
Breakfast in America $
Chantairelle $$
Chez Coco $$
Dammam's $
Eric Kayser Organic $
Gelati d'Alberto $
Hédiard $
La Contrescarpe $
La Formi Ailée $
La Pain Quotidien $
Le Grenier de Notre-Dame $-$$
Octave $
Restaurant Perraudin $$
Salon de Thé de la Mosquée de Paris $
Sté Boulangerie Kayser $
The Tea Caddy $

St-Germain-des-Près (6e)

Café de Flore $
Café les Deux Magots $
Chez Clément $$
Cosi $
Jacques Cagna $$$
La Bastide Odéon $$
La Grande Épicerie $
La Palette $
La Petite Chaise $$

L'Écluse $
Le Mabillon $
Lina's $
Oh! Poivrier! $
Poilâne $
Vagenende $
Ze Kitchen Galerie $$

Eiffel Tower and Invalides (7e, 15e)

Au Bon Accueil $$
La Cigale $$
L'Atelier Joël Robuchon $$-$$$
Le Bac à Glaces $
Le Père Claude $$
Le Sancerre $
Moulin de la Vierge $
Poujauran $

Champs-Elysées (8e)

BE (Boulangepicier) $
Cercle Ledoyen $$$$
Fouquet's $
Ladurée $
Le Cinq $$$$
Le Griffonier $
Mariage Frères $

Opéra/Gare du Nord (9e, 10e)

Chez Casimir $$
Chez Michel $$
Opéra Cafétéria at Monoprix $
Lafayette Café $
Lafayette Gourmet $
16 Haussmann $$

Bastille/Oberkampf (11e, 12e)

Café de l'Industrie $
Chardenoux $$
Clown Bar $
L'Ébauchoir $$
Le Bistrot du Peintre $
Mélac $
Pause Café $

Montparnasse (14e)
Café de la Place $
La Coupole $

Trocadèro (16e)
Bonneau $

Montmartre (18e)
Au Négociant $
Au Poulbot Gourmet $-$$
Chez Marie $$
La Butte Glacée $
L'Été en Pente Douce $

Index of Establishments by Cuisine

Alsatian/Brasserie
Bofinger ($$, Le Marais)
Brasserie Balzar ($$, Latin Quarter)
Brasserie Ile-Louis ($$, Ile St-Louis)
Vagenende ($, St-Germain-des-Prés)
Zimmer ($$, Louvre, Les Halles)

American
Breakfast in America ($, Latin Quarter)
Sam's Bagels ($, Sentier)

Auvergne
Chantairelle ($$, Latin Quarter)

Basque/Southwest
Au Bascou ($$, Le Marais)
Auberge de Jarente ($$, Le Marais)

Boulangeries
BE (Boulangepicier) ($, Champs-Elysées)
Bonneau ($, Trocadèro)
Eric Kayser Organic ($, Latin Quarter)
Max Poilâne ($, Louvre)
Poilâne ($, St-Germain-des-Prés)
Poujauran ($, Eiffel Tower)
Moulin de la Vierge ($, Eiffel Tower)
Sté Boulangerie Kayser ($, Latin Quarter)

Breton
Chez Michel ($$, Gare du Nord)

Cafes
Au Bistro de la Place ($, Le Marais)
Café Beaubourg ($, Le Marais)

Café de Flore ($, St-Germain-des-Près)
Café de la Place ($, Montparnasse)
Café de l'Industrie ($, Bastille-Oberkampf)
Café les Deux Magots ($, St-Germain-des-Près)
Café Marly ($, Louvre)
Fouquet's ($, Champs-Elysées)
La Chaise au Plafond ($, Le Marais)
La Contrescarpe ($, Latin Quarter)
La Coupole ($, Montparnasse)
La Palette ($, St-Germain-des-Près)
Le Mabillon ($, St-Germain-des-Près)
L'Eté en Pente Douce ($, Montmartre)
L'Étoile Manquante ($, Le Marais)
Pause Café ($, Bastille)

Cafeterias and Chains
Chez Clément ($, St-Germain-des-Près)
Hippopotamus ($, Le Marais)
Lafayette Café ($, Opéra, Grands-Boulevards)
Oh! Poivrier ! ($, St-Germain-des-Près)
Opéra Cafétéria at Monoprix ($,Opéra, Grands-Boulevards)

Central European
Jo Goldenberg ($-$$, Le Marais)

Classic Bistro
Chardenoux ($$, Bastille)
La Cigale ($$, Eiffel Tower)
La Poule au Pot ($$-$$$, Les Halles)
L'Ébauchoir ($$, Bastille)
Le Père Claude ($$, Eiffel Tower)
Restaurant Perraudin ($$, Latin Quarter)

Classic French
Au Pied de Cochon ($$, Les Halles)
Au Poulbot Gourmet ($-$$, Montmartre)
Caveau du Palais ($$, Ile de la Cité)
Cercle Ledoyen ($$$$, Champs-Elysées)
Chez Casimir ($$, Gare du Nord)
Chez Marie ($$, Montmartre)
La Petite Chaise ($$, St-Germain-des-Prés)
La Tour de Montlhéry ($$-$$$, Les Halles)
Restaurant du Palais-Royal ($$-$$$, Louvre)
16 Haussmann ($$, Opéra)

Corsican
Chez Coco ($$, Latin Quarter)

Haute Cuisine
Jacques Cagna ($$$, St-Germain-des-Près)
L'Ambroisie ($$$$, Le Marais)
Le Cinq ($$$$, Champs-Elysées)

Ice Cream
Berthillon ($, Ile de la Cité)
Dammam's ($, Latin Quarter)
Gelati d'Alberto ($, Latin Quarter)
La Butte Glacée ($, Montmartre)
Le Bac à Glaces ($, Eiffel Tower)
Octave ($, Latin Quarter)
Scoop ($, Louvre)

Modern Bistro
Au Bon Accueil ($$, Eiffel Tower)
L'Atelier Joël Robuchon ($$-$$$, Eiffel Tower)
Ze Kitchen Galerie ($$$, St-Germain-des-Près)

Provençal
La Bastide Odéon ($$, St-Germain-des-Prés)

Sandwiches
Cosi ($, St-Germain-des-Près)
Le Pain Quotidien ($, Latin Quarter)
Lina's ($, St-Germain-des-Près)
Pomme de Pain ($, Le Marais)

Tea Salons
Angelina ($, Louvre)
A Priori Thé ($, Sentier)
Ladurée ($, Champs-Elysées)
La Formi Ailée ($, Latin Quarter)
Mariage Frères ($, Madeleine, 8e)
Salon de Thé à la Mosquée de Paris ($, Latin Quarter)
The Tea Caddy ($, Latin Quarter)

Traiteurs
Fauchon ($, Louvre)
Hédiard ($, Latin Quarter)
La Grande Épicerie ($, St-Germain-des-Près)
Lafayette Gourmet ($, Opèra)

Vegetarian
Le Grenier de Notre-Dame ($-$$, Latin Quarter)

Wine Bars
Au Négociant ($, Montmartre)
Clown Bar ($, Bastille)
La Bistrot du Peintre ($, Bastille)
La Cloche des Halles ($, Louvre/Les Halles)
La Tartine ($, Le Marais)
L'Écluse ($, St-Germain-des-Près)
Le Griffonier ($, Champs-Elysées)
Le Sancerre ($, Eiffel Tower)
Mélac ($, Bastille)
Taverne Henri IV ($, Louvre)
Willi's Wine Bar ($, Louvre)

Index of Establishments by Price

$

Angelina (Louvre)
A Priori Thé (Sentier)
Au Bistro de la Place (Le Marais)
Au Négociant (Montmartre)
Au Poulbot Gourmet (Montmartre)
BE (boulangepicier) (Champs-Elysées)
Berthillon (Ile de la Cité)
Bonneau (Trocadèro)
Breakfast in America (Latin Quarter)
Café Beaubourg (Le Marais)
Café de Flore (St-Germain-des-Près)
Café de la Place (Montparnasse)
Café de l'Industrie (Bastille-Oberkampf)
Café les Deux Magots (St-Germain-des-Près)
Café Marly (Louvre)
Chez Clément (St-Germain-des-Prés)
Clown Bar (Bastille/Oberkampf)
Cosi (St-Germain-des-Près)
Dammam's (Latin Quarter)
Eric Kayser Organic (Latin Quarter)
Fauchon (Louvre)
Fouquet's (Champs-Elysées)
Gelati d'Alberto (Latin Quarter)
Hédiard (Latin Quarter)
Hippopotamus (Le Marais)
Jo Goldenberg (Le Marais)
La Butte Glacée (Montmartre)
La Chaise au Plafond (Le Marais)
La Cloche des Halles (Louvre/Les Halles)
La Contrescarpe (Latin Quarter)
La Coupole (Montparnasse)
Ladurée (Champs-Elysées)
Lafayette Gourmet (Opèra)
La Fourmi Ailée (Latin Quarter)
Lafayette Café (Opèra)
La Grande Épicerie (St-Germain-des-Près)
La Palette (St-Germain-des-Près)
La Tartine (Le Marais)
Le Bac à Glaces (Eiffel Tower)
Le Bistrot du Peintre (Bastille/Oberkampf)
L'Écluse (St-Germain-des-Près)
Le Grenier de Notre-Dame (Latin Quarter)

Le Griffonier (Champs-Elysées)
Le Mabillon (St-Germain-des-Près)
Le Pain Quotidien (Latin Quarter)
Le Sancerre (Eiffel Tower)
L'Été en Pente Douce (Montmartre)
L'Étoile Manquante (Le Marais)
Lina's (St-Germain-des-Près)
Mariage Frères (Champs-Elysées)
Max Poilâne (Louvre)
Mélac (Bastille/Oberkampf)
Moulin de la Vierge (Eiffel Tower)
Octave (Latin Quarter)
Oh! Poivrier! (St-Germain-des-Près)
Opéra Cafétéria (Opéra)
Pause Café (Bastille-Oberkampf)
Poilâne (St-Germin-des-Près)
Pomme de Pain (Le Marais)
Poujauran (Eiffel Tower)
Salon de thé de la Mosquée de Paris (Latin Quarter)
Sam's Bagels (Sentier)
Scoop (Louvre)
Sté Boulangerie Kayser (Latin Quarter)
Taverne Henri IV (Louvre)
The Tea Caddy (Latin Quarter)
Vagenende (St-Germain-des-Prés)
Willi's Wine Bar (Louvre)

$$

Au Bascou (Le Marais)
Auberge de Jarente (Le Marais)
Au Bon Accueil (Eiffel Tower)
Au Pied de Cochon (Les Halles)
Au Poulbot Gourmet (Montmartre)
Bofinger (Le Marais)
Brasserie Balzar (Latin Quarter)
Brasserie Ile St-Louis (Ile-St-Louis)
Caveau du Palais (Ile de la Cité)
Chantairelle (Latin Quarter)
Chardenoux (Bastille)
Chez Casimir (Gare du Nord)
Chez Coco (Latin Quarter)
Chez Marie (Montmartre)
Chez Michel (Gare du Nord)
Jo Goldenberg (Le Marais)
La Bastide Odéon (St-Germain-des-Prés)
La Cigale (Eiffel Tower)

La Petite Chaise (St-Germain-des-Prés)
La Poule au Pot (Les Halles)
L'Atelier Joël Robuchon (Eiffel Tower)
La Tour de Montlhéry (Les Halles)
L'Ébauchoir (Bastille)
Le Grenier de Notre-Dame (Latin Quarter)
Le Père Claude (Eiffel Tower)
Restaurant du Palais-Royal (Louvre)
Restaurant Perraudin (Latin Quarter)
16 Haussmann (Opéra)
Ze Kitchen Galerie (St-Germain-des-Près)
Zimmer (Louvre, Les Halles)

$$$
Jacques Cagna (St-Germain-des-Près)
La Poule au Pot (Les Halles)
L'Atelier Joël Robuchon (Eiffel Tower)
La Tour de Montlhéry (Les Halles)
Restaurant du Palais-Royal (Louvre)

$$$$
Cercle Ledoyen (Champs-Elysées)
L'Ambroisie (Le Marais)
Le Cinq (Champs-Elysées)

Part IV
Exploring Paris

The 5th Wave

By Rich Tennant

"Now THAT was a great meal! Beautiful presentation, an imaginative use of ingredients, and a sauce with nuance and depth. The French really know how to make a 'Happy Meal'."

In this part . . .

So many things to see in Paris . . . what do you do first . . . and how long will it take? Chapter 11 tells you a bit about what's worth seeing, lists some more cool things to see and do for kids, teens, history buffs, and art and literature lovers, and suggests gardens and parks to relax in after visiting all those museums. You also find here guided tour options, from buses to bicycles! Chapter 12 describes today's shopping scene in Paris, previews four great shopping neighborhoods, covers the outdoor markets, and provides reviews of local shops of interest. In Chapter 13, you have the chance to discover Paris in four itineraries and on a walking tour. And just when you're getting used to Paris, Chapter 14 sends you away on one of five popular day-trips in the Ile-de-France region.

Chapter 11

Discovering Paris's Best Attractions

· ·

In This Chapter

▶ Exploring Paris's top attractions

▶ Finding sights and activities for all types of interests

▶ Considering a guided tour

· ·

*O*ne of the major reasons you go to Paris is to see its sights, and this chapter starts you off with a succinct review of 20 of Paris's top sights, giving you the lowdown on when to go, how to get there, and why to visit it in the first place. A word of advice: Figure out which sights you would be heartbroken to miss, and plan to do those first. After that, if you have the flexibility, improvise! There's so much to see that you'll reorder your itinerary daily.

Before you leave, log onto www.weather.com and print out the extended forecast for Paris. Or when you arrive, pick up a copy of the *International Herald Tribune* or *USA Today*'s international edition for extended weather forecasts and save museum visits for rainy days (But keep in mind that most museums close on Mondays or Tuesdays and admission is free the first Sunday of the month at national museums). For a list of suggestions of what else to do on rainy days in Paris, see Chapter 17 in the Part of Tens.

Paris's Top Sights

In Paris, you're never at a loss for something to see. In this section, I list the cream of the crop.

Paris's Top Attractions

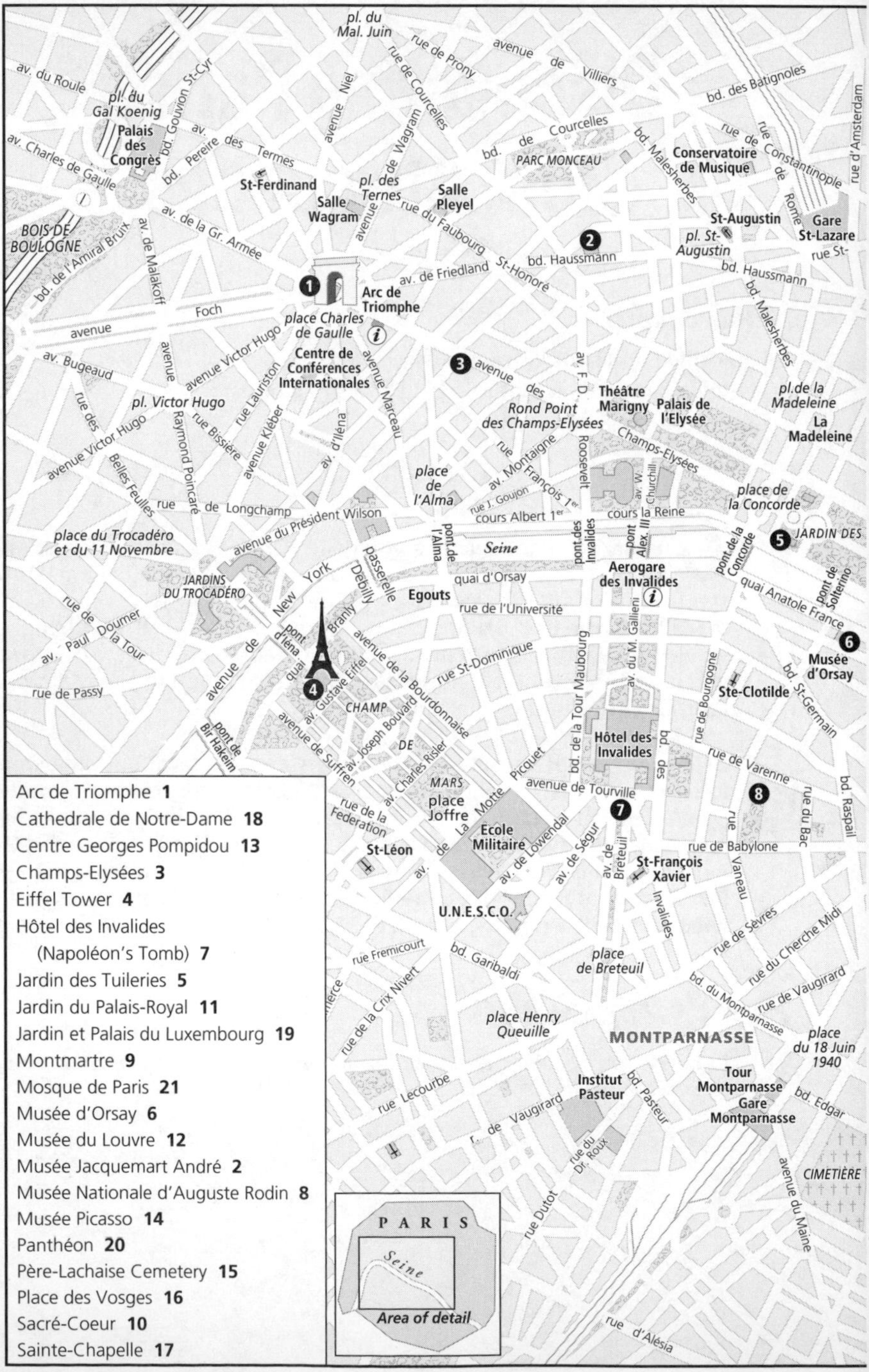

Map labels (selection):

pl. du Mal. Juin · rue de Prony · avenue de Villiers · bd. des Batignoles · av. du Roule · rue Niel · rue de Courcelles · pl. du Gal Koenig · St-Cyr · bd. Gouvion · av. Pereire · des Termes · avenue de Wagram · de Courcelles · bd. Malesherbes · Conservatoire de Musique · rue d'Amsterdam · av. Charles de Gaulle · Palais des Congrès · St-Ferdinand · pl. des Ternes · Salle Wagram · Salle Pleyel · av. du Faubourg · PARC MONCEAU · rue de Rome · rue de Constantinople · St-Augustin · Gare St-Lazare · BOIS DE BOULOGNE · av. de la Gr. Armée · pl. St-Augustin · rue St- · av. de l'Amiral Bruix · av. de Malakoff · **①** · Arc de Triomphe · av. de Friedland · St-Honoré · bd. Haussmann · **②** · Foch · place Charles de Gaulle · **③** · avenue des · Théâtre Marigny · Palais de l'Elysée · pl. de la Madeleine · av. Bugeaud · avenue Victor Hugo · Centre de Conférences Internationales · avenue Marceau · Rond Point des Champs-Elysées · La Madeleine · pl. Victor Hugo · rue Lauriston · rue Kléber · av. d'Iéna · place de l'Alma · av. Montaigne · cours la Reine · place de la Concorde · avenue Victor Hugo · Belles Feuilles · Raymond Poincaré · rue de Longchamp · avenue du Président Wilson · cours Albert 1er · **⑤** · JARDIN DES · place du Trocadéro et du 11 Novembre · JARDINS DU TROCADÉRO · New York · Debilly · passerelle · Seine · pont de l'Alma · Aerogare des Invalides · quai Anatole France · **⑥** · rue de Dourner · av. Paul Dola Tour · pont d'Iéna · quai Branly · quai d'Orsay · Egouts · rue de l'Université · Musée d'Orsay · rue de Passy · avenue de · avenue Gustave Eiffel · av. de la Bourdonnais · rue St-Dominique · Ste-Clotilde · rue de Varenne · **④** · CHAMP · av. Joseph Bouvard · DE · Hôtel des Invalides · **⑧** · pont de Bir Hakeim · avenue de Suffren · rue de la Fédération · MARS · place Joffre · rue Charles Risler · av. de la Motte Picquet · avenue de Tourville · **⑦** · bd. du Raspail · Arc de Triomphe **1** · Ecole Militaire · St-Léon · St-François Xavier · rue de Babylone · rue Fremicourt · U.N.E.S.C.O. · bd. Garibaldi · place de Breteuil · rue de Sèvres · rue du Cherche Midi · place Henry Queuille · MONTPARNASSE · place du 18 Juin 1940 · rue Lecourbe · Institut Pasteur · Tour Montparnasse · Gare Montparnasse · bd. Edgar · rue de Vaugirard · CIMETIÈRE · avenue du Maine · PARIS · Seine · Area of detail · rue d'Alésia

Saving on seeing the sights

One of the best bargains for tourists visiting Paris is the *Carte Musées et Monuments*, which offers free and unlimited admission to 70 of the top sights of Paris and the Ile-de-France. The card also promises no waiting in admission lines, but you still have to stand in line for security checkpoints at the museums that have them. *Note:* The pass is *not* accepted at the Eiffel Tower.

A one-day pass is 18€ ($21), a three-consecutive-day pass costs 36€ ($41), and a five-consecutive-day pass is 54€ ($62). Your best bet is to jot down a list of all the museums and monuments you want to see and use this book to add up their costs. For example, say that you decide to visit attractions in the 7e on a designated day. It would cost 19€ ($22) to see the Musée d'Orsay (7€/$8.05), Invalides (7€/$8.05) and the Musée Rodin (5€/$5.75). Using the one-day *Carte Musées et Monuments* (18€/$21) saves you 1€ ($1.15). You're better off, however, buying a three-day pass, so you aren't rushing to fit all those attractions into one day.

You can buy the pass at one of the branches of the Office de Tourisme de Paris (try the branch right near the Louvre in the Carrousel du Louvre, beneath the Pyramides, 99, rue de Rivoli, 1er, open daily 10 a.m. to 7 p.m. (Métro: Palais Royal/Musée du Louvre), in principal Métro stations, at the 70 museums and monuments that accept it, and at Fnac- ticket branches.

Arc de Triomphe
Champs-Elysées (8e)

To the French, General Charles De Gaulle's stride through the Arc de Triomphe to symbolize Paris's liberation in 1944 is one of the country's most cherished memories. It was to the Arc that joyous soccer fans crowded when France won the World Cup in 1998 and the Euro Cup in 2000. Every year, the last day of the Tour de France sees the racers riding up the Champs and around the Arc in a series of laps before the victor is declared. The Arc de Triomphe represents victory to the French, although it has also witnessed the agony of defeat, as in 1871 when Paris was seized by the Prussians during the Franco-Prussian War, and in 1940 when Nazi armies marched victoriously through the arch and down the Champs-Elysées. The largest triumphal arch in the world, the Arc was commissioned by Napoléon to honor his army and its 128 victorious battles. Today it houses the Tomb of the Unknown Soldier, which was dedicated in 1921 to honor the 1,500,000 French soldiers who died during World War 1. An eternal flame beneath the Arc pays tribute to the lost soldiers and is symbolically re-lit every evening at 6:30. The panoramic view, however, is the real attraction for visitors. From the top, 162 feet up, you can see in a straight line the Champs-Elysées, the obelisk in the place de la Concorde, and the Louvre. That big cube at the far end is the Grande Arche de la Défense in St-Denis, built to be the modern equivalent to this arch. Allow an hour to visit, an hour and a half in high summer.

Please don't try to cross to the Arc de Triomphe on surface streets! Attempting to dodge the warp-speed traffic zooming around the Arc will likely get you seriously hurt. Instead, use one of the clearly marked entrances to the underpass beneath the Arc, which you find on surrounding streets.

You buy your ticket at the end of the underpass from a clerk in a small booth, then climb the stairs to find yourself standing at the base of the Arc near the Tomb of the Unknown Soldier. You have two choices to reach the top: by a set of more than 250 winding steps or by an elevator. The line for the stairs is always shorter. Both stairs and elevator lead to the small interior museum and store on the Arc's top floor. To get to the outdoor viewing platform you need to climb another flight of narrow steps; the viewing platform is *not* wheelchair accessible.

 Keep in mind that on busy days, there will be a line of people in the underpass waiting to buy tickets. Go early if you're visiting during the height of tourist season.

Place Charles-de-Gaulle. ☎ *01-55-37-73-78. Métro: Charles-de-Gaulle–Étoile. Bus: 22, 30, 31, 52, 73, 92. Admission: 7€ ($8.05) adults, 4.50€ ($5.20) ages 12–25, free for children younger than 12. Open: April–Sept 10 a.m.–11 p.m.; Oct–March 10 a.m.– 10:30 p.m. Closed major holidays.*

 ### *Cathédral de Notre-Dame*
Ile de la Cité (4e)

This Gothic church dominates the Seine and the Ile de la Cité, as well as the history of Paris. A circular bronze plaque in the cathedral marks Kilomètre Zéro, from which all distances in France have been measured since 1768. And in many ways, Notre-Dame *is* the center of France. Crusaders prayed here before leaving for the holy wars. Napoléon crowned himself emperor here, and then crowned his wife Josephine empress. When Paris was liberated during World War II, General de Gaulle rushed to this cathedral to give thanks.

Construction of Notre-Dame (see the nearby "Notre-Dame de Paris" map) started in 1163 when Pope Alexander III laid the cornerstone and was completed in the 14th century. Built in an age of illiteracy, the cathedral windows tell the stories of the Bible in its portals, paintings, and stained glass. Angry citizens pillaged Notre-Dame during the French Revolution, mistaking religious statues above the portals on the west front for representations of kings and beheading them.

Nearly 100 years later, after Notre-Dame had been turned into a barn, writer Victor Hugo and other artists called attention to its dangerous state of disrepair and architect Viollet-le-Duc began the much-needed restoration. He designed Notre-Dame's spire, a new feature, and Baron Haussmann (Napoléon III's urban planner) evicted the residents of the houses that cluttered the cathedral's vicinity and tore down the houses for better views of the cathedral.

Notre-Dame de Paris

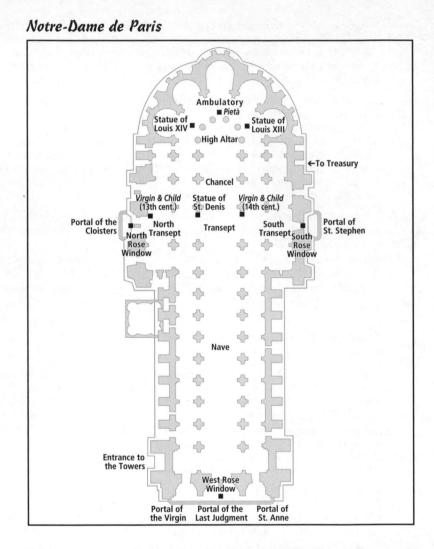

Before entering, walk around to the east end of the church to appreciate the spectacular flying buttresses. Visit on a sunny morning to catch the giant rose windows — which retain some of their 13th-century stained glass — in all their glory. The highlight for kids will undoubtedly be climbing the 387 narrow and winding steps to the top of one of the towers for a fabulously Quasimodo view of the gargoyles and of Paris. My advice: If you plan to visit the tower, go early in the morning! Lines stretch down the square in front of the cathedral during the summer. Of interest to history buffs will be the Cathedral's Treasury (on the Seine side of the building) which houses such valuable items as gold and jeweled chalices and other items from Notre-Dame's long history.

6 Parvis Notre-Dame. ☎ *01-42-34-56-10. Métro: Cité or St-Michel. RER: St-Michel. Bus: 21, 38, 85, 96. Admission: Church free; tower 6.10€ ($7) adults, 4.10€ ($4.70) ages 18–26 and seniors, free for youth younger than 18. Open: Cathedral and tower daily 9 a.m.–7:30 p.m. Treasury Mon–Sat 9:30 a.m.–5:30 p.m. Six masses celebrated on Sun, four on weekdays, one on Sat. Free guided visits in English Wed and Thurs at noon.*

Centre Georges Pompidou
Le Marais (4e)

Brightly colored escalators, elevators, air conditioning, and tubular passages resembling a giant gerbil habitat run along this building's facade, but the inside is a wonderfully spacious haven in which to view, touch, or listen to modern art and artists. British architect Richard Rogers and Italian architect Renzo Piano designed this building in the late 1960s as part of a redevelopment plan for the neighborhood, and since its opening in 1966, the Centre National d'Art et de Culture Georges Pompidou has been a surprisingly popular attraction. So popular that the wear and tear of about 160 million visitors caused the building to begin crumbling. In 1997, it closed for three years, undergoing a renovation that cost more than $100 million. It reopened with a celebration that also kicked off the new millennium on January 1, 2000. The newer of Paris's two modern art museums, the Centre Georges Pompidou includes two floors of work from the Musée National d'Art Moderne, France's national collection of modern art. The Centre Pompidou also houses a cinema, a huge public library, spaces for modern dance and music, temporary exhibits that often include video and computer works, and nearly 150 drawings, paintings, and other works by Romanian sculptor Constantin Brancusi in the Brancusi Atelier, a small building near the Pompidou's entrance. Dedicate at least two hours to viewing the works.

Sadly, taking a free escalator ride to the top for the breathtaking panoramic view of Paris is no more; You must purchase admission to the museum. However, if all you're interested in is the view, consider stopping at the Pompidou's ultra-hip top-floor restaurant Georges. For the same price as an adult's full-package admission to the museum (10€/$12), you can relax with a glass of wine and enjoy the view from indoors.

As a bonus, visit the nearby Igor Stravinsky fountain, which is free. Its fun sculptures by Jean Tinguely and Niki de Saint Phalle include red lips spitting water, a mermaid squirting water from strategic body parts, and a twirling grinning skull, all representations of Stravinsky's compositions.

Place Georges-Pompidou. ☎ *01-44-78-12-33.* www.centrepompidou.fr. *Métro: Rambuteau, Hôtel-de-Ville, Châtelet. Bus: 21, 29, 38, 47, 58, 69, 70, 72, 74, 75, 76, 81, 85, 86. Admission: A one-day package to all exhibits, the Brancusi Atelier, and the National Museum of Modern Art costs 10€ ($12) adults, 8€ ($9.20) ages 13–25, free for children younger than 13; admission to only exhibits is 9€ ($10.35) adults, 7€ ($8.05) ages13–25, free for children younger than 13; admission to National Museum of Modern Art and Brancusi Atelier is 7€ ($8.05) adults, 5€ ($5.75) ages 13–25. Free the first Sun of the month. Museum and exhibitions open: Wed–Mon 11 a.m.–9 p.m.; ticket counters close at 8 p.m.*

Champs-Elysées
Champs-Elysées (8e)

When Lance Armstrong became the first cyclist to win a sixth Tour de France in July 2004, he was crowned on a podium on the Champs-Elysées, France's most famous avenue, and the one where French citizens flock to celebrate victory. If you were in Paris when the French won the World and Euro Cup soccer championships (1998 and 2000, respectively), you understand what the Champs-Elysées means to the French. When close to a million singing, flag-waving Parisians spilled into the avenue, it was said that the country hadn't experienced such group euphoria since the days following the Liberation of Paris by the Allies in 1944. The Champs also overlooked the city's biggest New Year's party; in 2000, crowds of people gathered here to watch astonishing fireworks and cheer in the new century. The Champs is the avenue where the military march on Bastille Day. The scene on France's most famous street is liveliest at night, with people lining up for the numerous cinemas (see English-language films here by looking for *v.o.* for *version originale* on schedules and movie posters), and floodlights illuminating the Arc de Triomphe and place de la Concorde. Restaurants consist mainly of standard chain cafes (Chez Clément, Hippo) and American-style fast food (McDonald's, Planet Hollywood, Chi-Chi's), although good restaurants abound on the streets surrounding the avenue (see Chapter 10). You can shop at reasonably priced stores, such as Zara, get good deals on T-shirts at Petit Bateau, pick up what all of Europe is listening to at Fnac or Virgin, wander the very luxe (Louis Vuitton), and pass chain stores that you'd see in any American mall (the Disney Store, Quiksilver). Some of the stores are open on Sunday. Allow an hour to walk from top to bottom, longer if you want to shop, eat, or dawdle.

Métro: Concorde, Champs-Elysées Clémenceau, Franklin-D-Roosevelt, George V, Charles-de-Gaulle–Étoile. Bus: Many lines cross it, but only the 73 travels its entire length.

Eiffel Tower (La Tour Eiffel)
Eiffel Tower/Les Invalides (7e)

Did you know that the Eiffel Tower has its own post office? Whenever you mail anything from the town, it is postmarked with an Eiffel Tower stamp. Gustave Eiffel beat out 699 others in a contest to design what was supposed to be a temporary monument for the 1889 Exposition Universelle (World's Fair). His designs for the tower spanned 6,000 square yards of paper. Praised by some and criticized by others, the tower created as much controversy in its time as did I.M. Pei's pyramid at the Louvre 100 years later. Upon completion, the Eiffel Tower was the tallest human-built structure in the world, and the Prince of Wales (later Edward VII) and his family were invited to ascend it first. People have climbed it, bungee-jumped from it, and cycled down the tower's steps. In 1989, the tower's centennial was celebrated with 89 minutes of music and fireworks, and in the 1990s it counted down the days and then the minutes until the start of the new millennium. Since 2003, 20,000 lights sparkle for ten minutes an hour each evening until 2 a.m. in summer and 1 a.m. in winter.

You can fill an entire page with trivia about Paris's most famous symbol, which weighs 7,000 tons, soars 1,056 feet, and is held together with 2.5 million rivets. But what you really want to know are the practicalities: *Do I have to climb stairs? Do elevators go to the top? Are there bathrooms? Do they have snacks? Can I ascend in a wheelchair?* The answers: The Tower has three levels that are accessible by elevator. No elevator goes directly from ground level to the top; you must change elevators at the second level. Although you can take stairs from the ground to the first and second levels, you can't take stairs from the second level to the top. Most likely you'll wait for elevators on the first and second levels in specially roped-off lines. In high season, the wait sometimes is as long an hour — for each line. Restrooms are located on each level, and snack bars and souvenir stands are on the first and second levels. The tower is wheelchair accessible to the second level but not to the top.

Some advice: Six million people visit the Eiffel Tower each year. To avoid loonnnggg lines, go early in the morning or in the off-season. If this isn't possible, allow at least three hours for your visit: one hour to line up for tickets and another two just to access the elevators on levels one and two.

Food is available at the Altitude 95 restaurant on the first floor, which is simply gorgeous, but overpriced for the quality of its meals. A first-floor snack bar and second-floor cafeteria are open, but again they're not the best values. The best food at the Eiffel Tower is also its most expensive, without a doubt: The Michelin-starred Jules Verne, one of Paris's most celebrated restaurants, is on the Eiffel Tower's second level. (One of the pluses of dining here is that you get your own private elevator to the restaurant.)

If you have the patience to wait until sunset, the Eiffel Tower at night is recommended! Its lights frame the lacy steelwork beneath you in a way that daylight doesn't, and the Seine reflects it all.

Parc du Champ de Mars. ☎ *01-44-11-23-23.* www.tour-eiffel.fr. *Métro: Trocadéro, Bir-Hakeim, École-Militaire. RER: Champs-de-Mars. Bus: 42, 69, 82, 87. Admission to highest level: 10€ ($12), adults, 5.70€ ($6.55) ages 3–11; to second level: 7.30€ ($8.40) adults, 5.70€ ($6.55) ages 3–11; to 1st level: 4€ ($4.60) adults, 2.20€ ($2.50) ages 3–11; for stairs to first and second levels: 3.50€ ($4). Children younger than 3 are free. Open: Aug 30–June 18 daily 9:30 a.m.–11 p.m., stairs close at 6:30 p.m.; June 19–Aug 29 daily 9:30 a.m. to midnight, stairs close at midnight. Closed major holidays.*

Hôtel des Invalides (Napoléon's Tomb)
Eiffel Tower/Les Invalides (7e)

Louis XIV, who liked war and waged many, built Invalides as a hospital and home for all veteran officers and soldiers "whether maimed or old or frail." It still has offices for departments of the French armed forces, and part of it is still a hospital. The value of the Invalides goes far beyond its symbolic significance for the French military, however. The building is one of Europe's architectural masterpieces. The best way to get the sense of the awe that the Hôtel des Invalides inspires is to walk to it by crossing the Alexander III bridge. The dome of the **Église du Dôme** (gilded with 12 kilograms of real gold), is one of the high points of classical art, with a skylight rising 107 meters from the ground. Sixteen green copper cannons point outward in a powerful display.

Enemy flags captured during the military campaigns of the 19th and 20th centuries hang from the rafters in two impressive rows at the **Église de St-Louis,** known as the Church of the Soldiers, but most visitors come to see the **Tomb of Napoléon,** where the emperor is buried in six coffins, one inside the other, under the great dome. The first coffin is iron, the second mahogany, the third and fourth lead, the fifth ebony, and the outermost oak. The emperor's remains were transferred here 20 years after his death in 1820 on the island of St. Helena, where he was exiled following his defeat at Waterloo.

A must-see is the **Musée de l'Armée,** one of the world's greatest military museums; admission is included when you buy your ticket for Napoléon's tomb. It features thousands of weapons from prehistory to World War II including spearheads, arrowheads, maces, cannons, and guns in addition to battle flags, booty, suits of armor, and uniforms from around the world. The DeGaulle wing opened in 2000 with the goal of telling the story of World War II on touch screens with videos, a decoding machine, and other artifacts. Set aside two hours for a complete visit or a half-hour to see only the tomb.

Place des Invalides. ☎ *01-44-42-37-65. Métro: Latour-Maubourg, Invalides, or Varenne. Bus: 63, 83, 93. Admission 7€ ($8.05) adults; 5€ ($5.75) seniors and students 18–26; free for children younger than 18. Open: Oct–March daily 10 a.m.–5 p.m.; April–Sept daily 10 a.m.–6 p.m. Tomb of Napoléon open until 7 p.m. June 15–Sept 15. Closed major holidays.*

Keeping an eye on your wallet while eyeing the goods

You won't be able to avoid pesky (and illegal) vendors trying to cajole you into buying everything from Eiffel Tower key chains to postcards to mechanical butterflies; they constantly approach tourists standing in line for Eiffel Tower admission tickets. Be very attentive — some of these vendors work in tandem with pickpockets who will rip you off while you're busy looking at the displays. As for the quality of the merchandise — it's pretty bad. Buy your souvenirs from shops and licensed vendors. (See Chapter 4 for advice on what to do if you get pickpocketed.)

Jardin des Tuileries
Louvre (1er)

Come for a stroll here either before or after visiting the Louvre. Once a fashionable carriageway, today the Tuileries is Paris's most visited park and a great place to rest your feet and catch some rays on conveniently placed wrought-iron chairs surrounding the garden's fountains. The Orangerie and the Jeu de Paume are at the garden's western edge, and to the east you'll find 40 extraordinarily beautiful Maillol bronzes scattered among the trees, as well as four sculptures by Rodin, and works by Jean Dubuffet, Alberto Giacometti, David Smith, Max Ernst, Henry Moore, and Henri Laurens. In keeping with the French style of parks, trees are planted according to an orderly design and the sandy paths are arrow straight. Spread out across 63 acres, the gardens were originally laid out in the 1560s for Queen Mother Catherine de Medici in front of the Tuileries Palace which was burned down during the 1871 Paris Commune. You can get a light snack at one of the outdoor cafés. During the summer, a carnival features an enormous Ferris wheel (with great views of the city), a log flume, fun house, arcade-style games, snacks, and machine-made soft ice cream (but I find the best is the homemade ice cream sold from a stand right beyond the Arc de Triomphe du Carrousel at the entrance to the Tuileries).

Quai des Tuileries. Entrances on rue de Rivoli and place de la Concorde, 1er. Métro: Concorde or Tuileries. Bus: 42, 69, 72, 73, 94. Admission: Free. Free guided visits of the gardens (in French) Sun, Wed, Fri 3 p.m. Open: Daily 7:30 a.m. to dusk.

 ## *Jardin du Palais-Royal*
Louvre (1er)

In past centuries, gamblers and those seeking more lascivious pleasures flocked to this garden where Cardinal Richelieu ordered the Royal Palace built in 1630 as his personal residence, complete with grounds landscaped by the royal gardener. Today the palace is no longer open to the public, but its statue-filled gardens, including Daniel Buren's wonderful prison-striped columns built in 1986 (which make a great photo op), remain one of the most restful places in the city. The square is also ringed by restaurants, art galleries, and specialty boutiques, and it's home to the Comédie-Française.

Entrances on rue de Rivoli and place de la Concorde. Métro: Concorde or Tuileries. Bus: 42, 69, 72, 73, 94. Admission: Free. Open: Daily 7:30 a.m. to dusk.

Jardin et Palais du Luxembourg
St-Germain-des-Prés (6e)

Not far from the Sorbonne and just south of the Latin Quarter is the 6e arrondissement's **Jardin du Luxembourg,** one of Paris's most beloved parks. Children love it for its playground, pony rides, puppet theater, and the Fontaine de Médicis (the central Médici Fountain) where they can sail toy boats and watch the ducks. Besides pools, fountains, and statues of queens and poets, there are tennis and *boules* courts (*boule* means ball; in this game, players compete to see who can roll their small steel ball closest to a larger steel ball that lies farther down the court). In recent years, art has been exhibited on the wrought iron fence at the garden's northwestern entrance near boulevard St-Michel and rue de Médicis.

The park was commissioned by King Henri IV's queen, Marie de Medici, who also had the **Palais du Luxembourg** built at the northern edge of the park. The Palais resembles the Palazzo Pitti in Florence, where Marie spent her childhood and for which she was homesick. When the queen was banished in 1630, the palace was abandoned until the Revolution in 1789, when it was used as a prison. Now the seat of the French Senate, it is not open to the public.

Orchards in the park's southwest corner contain 360 varieties of apples, 270 kinds of pears, and various grapevines. Members of the French Senate get to eat the fruit, but leftovers go to a soup kitchen. Walk north and you come across a bevy of beehives behind a low fence. A beekeeping course is taught here on weekends. See whether you can find the Statue of Liberty tucked away nearby.

Main entrance at the corner of bd. St-Michel and rue des Médicis. ☎ *01-43-29-12-78. Métro: Odéon. RER: Luxembourg, Port-Royal. Bus: 38, 82, 84, 85, 89. Admission: Free. Open: Daily dawn to dusk.*

Montmartre
On the Right Bank

This neighborhood is for anyone who admires the work of Toulouse-Lautrec, is interested in one of Picasso's earliest studios, or loved the films *Le Destin Fabuleux d'Amélie Poulain* or *Moulin Rouge*. *Amélie's* Amélie Poulain lived here and worked in an actual Montmartre bar, Les Deux Moulins, located at 15 rue Lépic. You can get to Montmartre by taking the Métro to the Anvers or Abbesses stop, the entrance of which is graced by a fabulous Art Nouveau Métro sign. You can either walk to the top of the *butte* (hill) or take the *funiculaire* (outdoor small railway) up. (To take the *funiculaire,* walk from the Anvers Métro station the short distance from rue Steinkerque and turn left onto rue Tardieu, where, for a Métro ticket, the *funiculaire* whisks you from the base of the Montmartre butte to the road right beneath Sacré-Coeur.) After visiting Sacré-Coeur and the touristy but fun place du Tertre, a square with overpriced restaurants and artists clamoring to sketch your portrait, wander down the hill where you eventually stumble across Paris from another era — surprisingly unspoiled lanes, quiet squares, ivy-clad shuttered houses with gardens, and even Paris's only vineyard. Altogether, it creates a sense of the rustic village it once was.

KID FRIENDLY

Paris's top attraction: The Seine river cruise

One of the most romantic and beautiful ways to see Paris is to take a sightseeing cruise up and down the Seine. Don't, however, take one of the overpriced dinner or lunch cruises — they can cost upward of 125€ ($144) per person. Instead, opt for an evening cruise. With its dramatically lit monuments and romantic bridges, Paris is truly breathtaking at night.

Three companies offer the tours, which are all similar and cost about the same price. Perhaps the most well known are the **Bateaux-Mouches** that sail from the pont de l'Alma on the Right Bank and have huge floodlit boats. They offer recorded commentary in up to six languages. You can't miss the huge neon sign at night.

Bateaux-Parisiens sail from the port de la Bourdonnais on the Left Bank, while **Vedettes Pont Neuf** sail from the riverside where the Pont Neuf crosses the Ile de la Cité. Vedettes boats are smaller, more intimate, and not all of them are covered. Live commentary on both.

For a boat ride without commentary, take one of the **Bat-o-bus** shuttles that stop every 25 minutes between 10 a.m. and 9 p.m. at Tour Eiffel, Champs-Elysées, St-Germain-des-Près, Jardin des Plantes, Musée d'Orsay, Louvre, Notre-Dame, and Hôtel de Ville. Cost is 2.50€ ($2.90) for one stop and 2.50€ ($2.90) for each subsequent stop, a one-day ticket costs 11€ ($13) adults, 9€ ($10) for children under 12, and you can jump off and on when you want.

Bateaux-Mouches, pont de l'Alma, Right Bank, 8e. ☎ 01-42-25-96-10; www. bateaux-mouches.fr. Métro: Alma Marceau. Departures: In summer high season (approx April–Oct) every 30 minutes from 10 a.m. to 8 p.m., every 20 minutes from 8:p.m. to 11 p.m.; in winter (approximately November to March) departures are at 11 a.m., 2:30 p.m., 4 p.m., 6 p.m., and 9 p.m. Rates: 7€ ($8.05) for adults, 4€ ($4.60) for children 4 to 12 and adults older than 65; children younger than 4 ride free.

Bateaux-Parisiens Tour Eiffel, port de la Bourdonnais, Left Bank, 7e. ☎ 01-44-11-33-44. Métro: Bir-Hakeim. Departures: From April through November every half-hour from 10 a.m. to 10:30 p.m.; From November through April every hour from 10 a.m. to 10 p.m. No tours at 1:30 p.m. or 7:30 p.m. Rates: 9.50€ ($11) adults; 4.50€ ($5.20) children under 12. Free under age 3.

Bateaux les Vedettes du Pont Neuf, square du Vert-Galant, 1er. ☎ 01-46-33-98-38. Métro: Pont-Neuf, sail from the riverside where the Pont Neuf crosses the Ile de la Cité. Departures: March to October every half-hour from 10 a.m. to 10:30 p.m.; November to February every 45 minutes Monday through Friday from 10:30 a.m. to noon and 2:00 to 6:30 p.m., and at 8 p.m. and 10 p.m. Saturday and Sunday tours leave every 45 min from 10:30 a.m. to noon, every half hour from 2:00 p.m. to 6:30 p.m., and at 8 p.m., and every half hour from 9 p.m. to 10:30 p.m. Rates: 10€ ($12) adults, 5€ ($5.75) children under 12.

Musée d'Orsay
Eiffel Tower/Les Invalides (7e)

In 1986, this brilliantly renovated train station opened to the public, giving the world one of its greatest museums of 19th century art with an unsurpassed collection of Impressionist masterpieces. There are three floors of exhibits. On the ground floor are Ingres's *La Source,* Millet's *L'Angelus,* the Barbizon school, Manet's *Olympia,* and other works of early impressionism. Impressionism continues on the top level, with Renoir's *Le Moulin de la Galette,* Manet's *Déjeuner sur l'Herbe,* Degas's *Racing at Longchamps,* Monet's cathedrals, van Gogh's *Self-Portrait,* and Whistler's *Portrait of the Artist's Mother.* Works by Gauguin and the Pont-Aven school, Toulouse-Lautrec, Pissarro, Cézanne, and Seurat also are exhibited. Symbolism, naturalism, and Art Nouveau are represented on the middle level; the international Art Nouveau exhibit includes wonderful furniture and *objets d'art* as well as Koloman Moser's *Paradise,* a beautiful design for stained glass. Give yourself three hours, including a lunch break in the museum's gorgeous, turn-of-the-20th-century Musée d'Orsay restaurant on the middle level. For less expensive and quicker light bites, the Café des Hauteurs is on the fifth floor (it has a great view of the Seine through its clock window) and a snack bar is on the mezzanine.

62 rue de Lille/1 rue Bellechasse. ☎ *01-40-49-48-14, or 01-40-49-48-48 for information desk.* www.musee-orsay.fr. *Métro: Solférino. RER: Musée-d'Orsay. Bus: 24, 63, 68, 69, 73, 83, 94, 94. Admission (may cost more to include major temporary exhibits): 7€ ($8.05) adults; 5€ ($5.75) ages 18–24 and seniors and on Sun; free for children younger than 18. Free the first Sun of every month. Open: Tues–Wed and Fri–Sat 10 a.m.–6 p.m.; Thurs 10 a.m.–9:45 p.m.; Sun 9 a.m.–6 p.m. From mid-June through the end of Sept, the museum opens at 9 a.m.*

Musée du Louvre
Louvre (1er)

The three steps to an enjoyable Louvre experience are:

✔ Buy your tickets in advance. Visitors from the United States and Canada can purchase tickets online from www.ticketweb.com and have them delivered to their homes before departure. Visitors from other countries can use www.fnac.com or www.ticketnet.com.

✔ Grab a free map of the Louvre at the Information Desk under the Pyramid or get a free guide. The Louvre bookstore in the Carrousel du Louvre sells many comprehensive guides and maps in English; you can also grab brochures for "Visitors in a Hurry," or a guidebook, *The Louvre, First Visit.*

✔ Take a guided tour. You can try a 90-minute tour by a museum guide (☎ 01-43-20-53-17) that covers the most popular works and gives you a quick orientation to the museum's layout. Times and prices vary. If you prefer to set your own pace, a four-hour audiotour (5€/$5.75)) can be rented at the entrance to any of the wings.

The Louvre

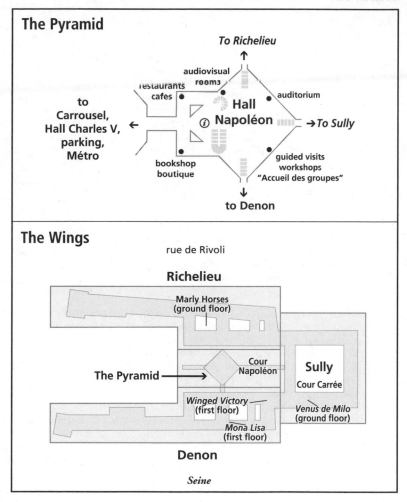

I.M. Pei's glass pyramid is the main entrance to the museum; pregnant women, visitors with children in strollers and the disabled have priority. Avoid this entrance and its long lines by using the **99 rue de Rivoli/Carrousel du Louvre** entrance, or take the stairs at the **Porte des Lions** near the Arc du Triomphe du Carrousel (the arch resembling a smaller Arc de Triomphe). Those who already have tickets or have the Carte Musées et Monuments can use the special entrance to the Louvre at the **passage Richelieu** between rue de Rivoli and the courtyard.

Tickets are valid all day so you can enter and exit the museum as many times as you prefer. Admission is reduced after 6 p.m. on Monday and Wednesday, and free the first Sunday of each month.

The Louvre didn't need Dan Brown's bestseller *The Da Vinci Code* to attract large crowds, but the attention certainly hasn't hurt. The book, which starts off with an off-hours murder of the Louvre's curator and focuses on the painting by Da Vinci of The Last Supper (which is in the convent of Santa Maria delle Grazie in Milan), has sold more than ten million copies worldwide and is drawing crowds to all the venues mentioned in it. (Look for the movie with Tom Hanks sometime in 2006.) There is even a two-and-a-half hour private "Cracking the Da Vinci Code" tour of the Louvre given by Paris Muse for 110€ ($127) per person (www.paris muse.com).

The magnificent Louvre palace (see "The Louvre" map nearby) evolved during several centuries, first opening as a museum in 1793, and it would take you a month of visits to see the more than 30,000 treasures it houses. But a visit to the Louvre doesn't have to be overwhelming. The Louvre is organized in three wings — Sully, Denon, and Richelieu — over four floors exhibiting art and antiquities from Oriental, Islamic, Egyptian, Greek, Etruscan, Roman, Oceanic, European, and North and South American civilizations, and sculpture, *objets d'art,* paintings, prints, drawings, and the moats and dungeon of the medieval Louvre fortress.

When you're in a hurry, but want to do the Louvre on your own, do a quick, "best of the Louvre" tour on either Wednesday or Friday when the museum is open until 9:45 p.m. Start with Leonardo da Vinci's *Mona Lisa* (Denon wing, first floor); on the same floor nearby are two of the Louvre's most famous French paintings, Géricault's *The Raft of Medusa* and Delacroix's *Liberty Guiding the People.* Next, visit the *Winged Victory* and Michelangelo's *Slaves* (both Denon wing, ground floor) before seeing the *Venus de Milo* (Sully wing, ground floor). After that, let your own interests guide you. Consider that only Florence's Uffizi Gallery rivals the Denon wing for its Italian Renaissance collection, which includes Raphael's *Portrait of Balthazar Castiglione* and Titian's *Man with a Glove.* And the revamped Egyptian antiquities department is the largest exhibition of Egyptian antiquities outside Cairo.

 If you want to purchase tickets in advance while in Paris, you can order tickets by phone from Fnac ☎ 08-92-68-46-94 (0.34€/min.), and pick them up at any Fnac store (except Fnac photo shops). A 1.30€ ($1.50) commission is charged by Fnac. A nearby branch is at Forum des Halles, 1 rue Pierre Lescure.

Rue de Rivoli. ☎ *01-40-20-50-50 for recorded message, 01-40-20-53-17 for information desk;* www.louvre.fr. *Métro: Palais-Royal–Musée du Louvre. Admission: 8.50€ ($9.80) adults; 6€ ($6.90) after 6 p.m. on Wed and Fri; free first Sun of month, Bastille Day (July 14) for disabled visitors and for children younger than 18. Open: Fri and Wed 9 a.m.–9:45 p.m.; Thurs–Mon 9 a.m.–6 p.m. Closed Tues.*

Mange with Mona Lisa

There are plenty of places to refuel at the Louvre from the gastronomic Le Grand Louvre to a cafeteria serving plenty of ethnic eats. Note: The museum and its restaurants are closed Tuesdays.

Beneath the Pyramid:

✔ **Le Grand Louvre:** (☎ 01-40-20-53-41). Open Wednesday to Monday noon to 3 p.m. and 7 p.m. to 10 p.m. Friday and Wednesday.

✔ **Café du Louvre:** Open 9 a.m. to 7 p.m. Thursday to Sunday, until 9:45 p.m. Friday and Wednesday.

✔ **Café Napoléon:** Open Wednesday to Monday 10 a.m. to 6 p.m.

✔ **Cafétéria:** Open Wednesday to Monday 11.30 a.m. to 3 p.m.

In the Denon Wing:

✔ **Café Mollien:** (first floor) Open Thursday to Sunday 10.30 a.m. to 5:00 p.m.; open until 9 p.m. Friday and Wednesday.

✔ **Café Denon:** (mezzanine) Open Thursday to Sunday 9 a.m. to 5 p.m.; open until 7 p.m. Friday and Wednesday.

In the Richelieu Wing:

✔ **Café Richelieu** (first floor) Open Thursday to Monday 10.30 a.m. to 5:00 p.m.; open until 9 p.m. Wednesday.

In the Cour de Napoléon (facing the Pyramid):

✔ **Café Marly:** (☎ 01-49-26-06-60) Open daily 8 a.m. to 2 a.m.

See Chapter 10 for restaurant reviews.

Musée Jacquemart André
Champs-Elysées (8e)

Talk about having interests in common: Edouard André, the heir of a prominent banking family, and his wife, Nélie Jacquemart, a well-known portraitist, commissioned architect Henri Parent to build their "house," then traveled the world to find French, Flemish, and Italian paintings, furniture, and tapestries to fill it. They had no children, so Nélie willed the house and its treasures to the French government, giving the city of Paris one of its best museums. This is very much worth a visit for the Italian and Flemish masterpieces by Bellini, Botticelli, Carpaccio, Uccello, Rubens, Rembrandt, and van Eyck and to see how very rich Parisians lived in the

19th century. Highlights of the collection include Rembrandt's *Docteur Tholinx,* Van Dyck's *Time Cutting the Wings of Love,* a fresco by Jean Baptiste Tiepolo, Domenico Ghirlandaio's naturalistic *Portrait d'un Vieillard,* and a portrait of *Catherine Skavronskaia* by Elisabeth Vigée-Lebrun, one of Marie Antoinette's favorite artists. As you wander the ornate gilt-ridden rooms, pause in the "winter garden," a tour de force of marble and mirrors flanking an unusual double staircase. Take advantage of the free audio that guides you through the mansion with fascinating narrative. Visit at 11 a.m., allow at least an hour, then take a break in what was Madame Jacquemart's lofty-ceilinged dining room, now a pretty tearoom serving light lunches (the salads are all named for artists) and snacks.

158 bd. Haussmann. ☎ *01-45-62-11-59. Métro: Miromesnil. Bus: 22, 28, 43, 52, 54, 80, 83, 84, 93. Admission: 8.50€ ($9.80) adults; 6€ ($6.90) students and children younger than 18. Open: Daily (including Dec 25) 10 a.m.–6 p.m. Le Café is open 11:45–6 p.m.*

Musée Nationale d'Auguste Rodin
Eiffel Tower/Les Invalides (7e)

How times have changed. Auguste Rodin, often regarded as the greatest sculptor of all time, lived and worked here from 1908 until his death in 1917, an era when his legendary sculptures were labeled obscene. This collection includes all of his greatest works. In the courtyard, *Burghers of Calais* is a harrowing commemoration of the siege of Calais in 1347, after which the triumphant Edward III of England kept the town's six richest burghers as servants. Also in the courtyard is *The Thinker.* The *Gates of Hell* is a portrayal of Dante's *Inferno.* Intended for the Musée des Arts Decoratifs, the massive bronze doors were not completed until seven years after Rodin's death. Inside the most popular attraction is *Le Baiser (The Kiss)* which immortalizes in white marble the passion of doomed 13th-century lovers Paolo Malatesta and Francesca da Rimini. Studies done by Rodin before he executed his sculptures take up some of the 16 rooms. Particularly interesting is the evolution of his controversial nude of Balzac rising from a tree trunk. Don't miss the room devoted to the works of Camille Claudel, a top-rate artist and Rodin's student and lover for many years. The museum is in the 18th-century Hôtel Biron, which was a convent before it became a residence for artists and writers. Matisse, Jean Cocteau, and the poet Rainer Maria Rilke lived and worked in the mansion before Rodin moved there at the height of his popularity. Count on spending at least an hour and a half in the museum.

If you don't have much time or money, pay the 1€ ($1.15) admission to visit just the gardens, where Rodin's works stand among 2,000 rosebushes. Allow at least an hour to visit the garden, longer if you want to break for coffee in the garden café. *Note:* The museum is undergoing construction of a new two-story glass wing looking out on the garden. It will house some of the permanent collection and temporary exhibits. The museum will remain open through construction which is expected to last through 2005.

Hôtel Biron, 77 rue de Varenne. ☎ *01-44-18-61-10; www.musee-rodin.fr. Métro: Varenne. Bus: 69, 82, 87, 92. Admission: 5€ ($5.75) adults; 3€ ($3.45) ages 18–24 and* *seniors and on Sun; 1€ ($1.15) for garden only; free for children younger than 18. Open: April–Sept Tues–Sun 9:30 a.m.–5:45 p.m.; Oct–March Tues–Sun 9:30 a.m.–4:45 p.m. Garden closes at 6:45 p.m. in summer, 5 p.m. in winter, last admittance one hour before closing.*

Musée Picasso
Le Marais (3e)

Located in the Hôtel Salé, a renovated Marais mansion built in the mid-17th century for a salt tax collector (hence the name which translates as the salted mansion), the Musée Picasso houses the world's largest collection of Spanish master Pablo Picasso's art. The museum was created in 1973 by Picasso's heirs, who donated his personal art collection to the state in lieu of paying outrageous inheritance taxes after his death. You can pay a visit to the Musée Picasso on each trip to Paris and see something different each time because the works are rotated. The spectacular collection includes more than 200 paintings, nearly 160 sculptures, 88 ceramics, and more than 3,000 prints and drawings. Every phase of Picasso's prolific 75-year career is represented. Works can be viewed chronologically; particularly interesting is seeing how his paintings were influenced by the women he loved at the time: his first wife, Olga; Marie-Thérèse Walter, mother of his daughter, Maya; Françoise Gilot, mother of Paloma and Paul, and Dora Maar, among others. Budget at least two hours here, if not more. The museum also displays works by other artists collected by Picasso, including Corot, Cézanne, Braque, Rousseau, Matisse, and Renoir. This museum is worth every minute!

Hôtel Salé, 5 rue de Thorigny. ☎ *01-42-71-25-21;* www.musee-picasso.fr. *Métro: Chemin-Vert, St-Paul, or Filles du Calvaire. Bus: 29, 69, 75, 96. Admission: 5.50€ ($6.30) adults; 4€ ($4.60) ages 18–25 and on Sun; free for children younger than 18. Free the first Sun of each month. Open: April–Sept Wed–Mon 9:30 a.m.–6 p.m.; Oct–March Wed–Mon 9:30 a.m.–5:30 p.m.*

Panthéon
Latin Quarter (5e)

Is it a church? Is it a tomb? Perhaps the best description would be: the Panthéon is to France what Westminster Abbey is to England: a final resting place for many of the nation's greatest men — and one woman, Marie Curie. Few other monuments in Paris have had as versatile a career as the neoclassical Panthéon, whose huge dome is one of the landmarks of the Left Bank. Inside the domed church's barrel-vaulted crypt are the tombs of Voltaire, Rousseau, Hugo, Braille, and Zola. French writer, politician, and adventurer André Malraux was the last to be entombed here in 1996. Louis XV originally built the Panthéon as a church in thanksgiving to St-Geneviève after his recovery from gout. Construction started in 1755, but after the French Revolution, the church was renamed the Panthéon, in remembrance of ancient Rome's Pantheon, and rededicated as a burying ground for France's heroes. All Christian elements were removed and windows were blocked. From 1806 to 1884, officials turned the Panthéon back into a church two more times before finally declaring it what it is today. A pendulum suspended from the central dome recreates Jean-Bernard Foucault's 1851 demonstration proving the rotation of the earth. The views from the top here are some of the best in Paris.

Place du Panthéon. ☎ *01-44-32-18-00. Métro: Cardinal-Lemoine or Maubert-Mutualité. Bus: 21, 27, 83, 84, 85, 89. Admission: 7€ ($8.05) adults; 4.50€ ($5.20) ages 18–25; free for children younger than 18. Open: April–Sept daily 10 a.m.–6:30 p.m. (Oct–March until 6 p.m.).*

Père-Lachaise Cemetery
Montmartre and beyond (20e)

Cresting above a high hill overlooking Paris, this landmark cemetery is the final resting ground for some of the world's most illustrious composers, poets and philosophers. Chopin, Bizet, Proust, Balzac, Corot, Delacroix, Pissaro, Modigliani, Molière, Oscar Wilde, Isadora Duncan, Simone Signoret, Yves Montand, and of course, Jim Morrison (framed pictures of him grace the walls of neighboring brasseries, but his bust has been removed due to vandalism). This, the world's most visited cemetery, is more outdoor museum than place of mourning. No wonder Parisians have always come here to stroll and reflect; with its winding, cobbled streets, park benches, and street signs, the 110-acre Père-Lachaise is a mini-city unto itself. Many visitors leave flowers or notes scrawled on Métro tickets for their favorite celebrity residents. The tombs are artistic works, decorated with exquisite marble and stone statuettes or chiseled around diminutive stained-glass windows.

Legends abound. The 18th-century bronze tomb of murdered journalist Victor Noir is reputed to make women fertile when rubbed (the polished sheen of certain parts of his statue is testament to its lore!). The tragic love story of Abélard and Héloïse (she was his student and her uncle castrated him when he found out about their affair) has faded, but in the 19th century, their tombs were magnets for disappointed lovers. You can obtain a free map from the gatekeeper at the main entrance, but the better map is one sold outside the entrance for 2€ ($2.30). Or you can just use the "Père-Lachaise Cemetery" map provided in this chapter. Allow at the very least two hours to visit.

16 rue du Repos. Main entrance on bd. du Ménilmontant. Métro: Père-Lachaise. Bus: 61, 69, 102. Admission: Free. Open: March 16–Nov 5 Mon–Fri 8 a.m.–6 p.m., Sat 8:30 a.m.–6 p.m., Sun and holidays 9 a.m.–6 p.m.; Nov 6–March 15 Mon–Fri 8 a.m.–5:30 p.m., Sat 8:30 a.m.–5:30 p.m., Sun and holidays 9 a.m.–6 p.m.

Place des Vosges
Le Marais (3e)

You wouldn't guess that the most beautiful square in Paris got its name from the first region of France to completely pay its taxes, the Vosges. The place des Vosges sits right in the middle of Le Marais — a symmetrical block of 36 rose-colored town houses, 9 on each side, with handsome slate roofs and dormer windows. At ground level is a lovely arcaded walkway that's now home to galleries, cafés, antiques dealers, and smart boutiques. In the early 17th century, Henri IV transformed this area into the most prestigious neighborhood in France, putting his royal palace here, and the square quickly became the center of courtly parades and festivities. After the Revolution, it became place de l'Indivisibilité. Victor Hugo lived at No. 6 for 16 years (see "Finding More Fun Things to See and Do" later in this chapter.) Allow 30 minutes to walk all the way around the square under the arcades and a brief stroll in the park.

Métro: St-Paul. Bus: 69, 76, 96.

Sacré-Coeur
Montmartre (18e)

The white Byzantine-Romanesque church dominating Paris's highest hill — the one that you can see from all around the city — is Basilique du Sacré-Coeur. Built from 1876 (after France's defeat in the Franco-Prussian War) to 1919, the church's interior is not as striking as its exterior and is, in fact, vaguely depressing. The best reason to come here is for the city-spanning views from its Dome — visibility is 30-miles across the rooftops of Paris on a clear day. Conserve your pre-Dome climbing energy by using the *funiculaire* to take you to Sacré-Coeur. Simply take the Métro to the Anvers station, then ride the elevator to exit the station. Walk the short distance from rue Steinkerque and turn left onto rue Tardieu, where, for the price of a Métro ticket, the *funiculaire* whisks you from the base of the Montmartre butte to an area right below the church.

To reach the dome and crypt, face the church and walk around to its left side, following signs for the Dome and Crypte. You walk down a set of stairs and follow a walkway about 50 feet to an iron gate. The entrance and ticket machine are on your right.

The climb from church floor to dome is up a flight of nail-bitingly steep corkscrew steps.

On the other side of Sacré-Coeur is the **place du Tertre,** where Vincent van Gogh once lived; he used it as a scene for one of his paintings. The place is usually swamped by tourists and quick-sketch artists in the spring and summer. Following any street downhill from the place du Tertre leads you to the quiet side of Montmartre. The steps in front of the church come alive around dusk, when street musicians entertain the crowd that gathers to watch the city's lights come on. Be alert: Pickpockets love Montmartre.

25 rue du Chevalier-de-la-Barre. ☎ *01-53-41-89-00. Métro: Anvers. Take elevator to surface and follow signs to funiculaire, which runs to the church (fare: 1 Métro ticket). Bus: The only bus that goes to the top of the hill is the local Montmartrobus. Admission: Basilica free; dome and crypt 5€ ($5.75). Open: Basilica daily 6 a.m.–10:30 p.m.; dome and crypt daily 10 a.m.–5:45 p.m.*

Père-Lachaise Cemetery

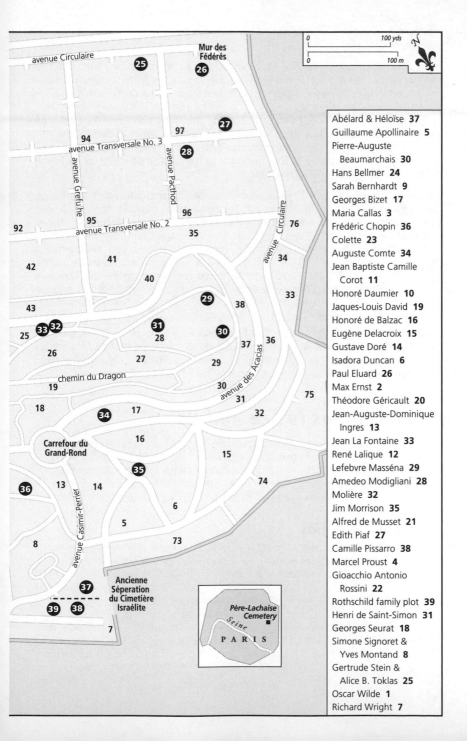

avenue Circulaire

Mur des
Fédérés

25

26

0 — 100 yds
0 — 100 m

avenue Transversale No. 3

94

97

27

28

avenue Pacthod

avenue Greful he

95

avenue Transversale No. 2

96

92

35

76

avenue Circulaire

42

41

40

34

43

25 **33** **32**

31

28

30

37

36

avenue des Acacias

33

38

29

26

27

29

chemin du Dragon

19

30

31

75

18

17

34

32

Carrefour du
Grand-Rond

16

15

35

74

36

13

14

avenue Casimir-Perrier

6

5

73

8

37

Ancienne
Séperation
du Cimetière
Israélite

39 **38**

7

Père-Lachaise
Cemetery

Seine

PARIS

Abélard & Héloïse **37**
Guillaume Apollinaire **5**
Pierre-Auguste
  Beaumarchais **30**
Hans Bellmer **24**
Sarah Bernhardt **9**
Georges Bizet **17**
Maria Callas **3**
Frédéric Chopin **36**
Colette **23**
Auguste Comte **34**
Jean Baptiste Camille
  Corot **11**
Honoré Daumier **10**
Jaques-Louis David **19**
Honoré de Balzac **16**
Eugène Delacroix **15**
Gustave Doré **14**
Isadora Duncan **6**
Paul Eluard **26**
Max Ernst **2**
Théodore Géricault **20**
Jean-Auguste-Dominique
  Ingres **13**
Jean La Fontaine **33**
René Lalique **12**
Lefebvre Masséna **29**
Amedeo Modigliani **28**
Molière **32**
Jim Morrison **35**
Alfred de Musset **21**
Edith Piaf **27**
Camille Pissarro **38**
Marcel Proust **4**
Gioacchio Antonio
  Rossini **22**
Rothschild family plot **39**
Henri de Saint-Simon **31**
Georges Seurat **18**
Simone Signoret &
  Yves Montand **8**
Gertrude Stein &
  Alice B. Toklas **25**
Oscar Wilde **1**
Richard Wright **7**

Sainte-Chapelle
Ile de la Cité (4e)

Save Sainte-Chapelle for the early afternoon on a sunny day, because the effect of its 15 perfect stained-glass windows soaring 50 feet high to a star-studded vaulted ceiling is purely kaleidoscopic. Louis IX, the only French king to become a saint, had Sainte-Chapelle, the "Holy Chapel," built as a shrine to house relics of the crucifixion, including the Crown of Thorns that Louis bought from the Emperor of Constantinople. Building Sainte-Chapelle certainly cost less than the outrageously expensive Crown of Thorns, which was said to have been acquired at the crucifixion and now resides in the vault at Notre-Dame.

Built between 1246 and 1248, Sainte-Chapelle consists of two chapels, one on top of the other. Palace servants used the *chapelle basse* ("lower chapel"), ornamented with fleur-de-lis designs. The *chapelle haute* ("upper chapel," accessed by 30 winding steps) is one of the highest achievements of Gothic art. If you spend the time (which can take hours or even a day!), you can see that the 1,134 scenes in the stained glass windows trace the Biblical story from the Garden of Eden to the Apocalypse. St. Louis is shown several times. Some evenings, when the upper chapel becomes a venue for classical-music concerts, the effect of its chandelier lights dancing off the windows is magical. *4 bd. du Palais, Palais de Justice.* ☎ *01-53-40-60-97. Métro: Cité or St-Michel. RER: St-Michel. Bus: 21, 27, 38, 85, 96. Admission: 6.10€ ($7) adults; 4.10€ ($4.70) students over 18 and seniors; free for children younger than 18. Open: March–Oct daily 9:30 a.m.–6 p.m., and Nov–Feb 9 a.m.–5 p.m. Closed major holidays.*

More Fun Things to See and Do

After you hit all of the city's top attractions, you may want to search out some of its lesser known but still captivating sights. This section introduces you to some of those spots. Organized with specific interests in mind, it gives you ideas about how to make Paris truly your own. The "More Fun Things to Do in Paris" map can help you locate the fun zones.

Especially for kids

You can have a fabulous time with your kids in Paris just seeing the traditional sights. But there are so many more things to do and see! Steep them in the Parisian tradition of *les guignols* (puppet shows). Even though the shows are in French, it's pretty easy to figure out what's going on. You can find the shows in the Jardin du Luxembourg, the Champ de Mars, and the Jardin des Tuileries. All Parisian parks, in fact, are wonderful for children, even without the puppet shows; One of the best is the **Bois de Vincennes,** located at the most eastern edge of the city. You can rent a boat for a leisurely row on the lake, or a bike to ride on the park's miles of bike paths, or visit the great zoo with 1,200 animals. Wander the wonderful maze at the more centrally located **Jardin des Enfants aux Halles,** 105 rue Rambuteau (☎ 01-45-08-07-18; Métro: Chatelet). The French love well-behaved children and are happy to welcome them, especially in the following locations which have been designed with kids in mind.

Aquarium Tropical de la Porte Dorée

This is a fascinating place to visit either before or after a visit to the nearby parc Zoologique de Paris (see the last entry in this section). Located in the beautiful Art Deco building that once housed the Musée des Arts d'Afrique et d'Océanie, aquatic life is grouped by theme and by oceanographic region in 80 aquariums. Your kids will love the circular aquarium where the Nile crocodiles live. A recent exhibit displayed piranhas in a re-creation of their natural habitat in the rapid rivers of Guyana. Allow at least an hour and a half.

293 av. Dausmenil, 12e. ☎ 01-44-74-84-80. Métro: Porte Dorée. Admission: 5.50€ ($6.30) adult, 4€ ($4.60) ages 5–26, free for children younger than 4. Open: Summer daily 9 a.m.–6 p.m. (Sun till 6:30 p.m.); winter 9 a.m.–5 or 5:30 p.m.

Cité des Sciences et de l'Industrie/Parc de la Villette

You and your kids will find this enormous, modern science complex with interactive exhibits on everything from outer space to genetically manipulated plants incredibly cool! With a planetarium, movie cinemas, ten themed gardens, and an aquarium, as well as an adventure playground designed specifically for 3- to 12-year-olds, it's hard to decide what to do first. On the complex's east side is **Explora,** which features exhibits, models, robots, and interactive games, demonstrates scientific techniques, and presents subjects that include the universe, the earth, the environment, space, computer science, and health (in one experiment, you can test your sense of smell). The **Children's City** is divided into exhibits for 5- to 12-year-olds, including: Machines and Mechanisms, the Living Species, and Techniques of Communications (in one demonstration, kids can be part of a weather broadcast). A separate exhibit on electricity will stand your kids' hair on end. A small section of the Children's City is reserved for 3- to 5-year-olds. Organized around a stream, children learn about themselves in relation to the world around them (in one activity, they get to wear a tortoise shell). The gigantic **Géode** sphere, on the complex's south side, is a wonder, with a huge hemispheric IMAX screen on which six or so films are shown daily. Another theater, the **Cinaxe,** is a simulator that projects movies on a screen while accelerating and moving the audience in different directions (children younger than 3, pregnant women, and the disabled are not allowed). Kids can climb aboard an actual submarine in the **l'Argonaute** exhibit (on the complex's south side next to Géode) and participate in technology demonstrations at the **Technocité.**

More Fun Things to Do in Paris

Aquaboulevard **4**
Aquarium Tropical de la Porte Dorée **33**
Brasserie Lipp **13**
Cabinet des Médailles **15**
Café les Deux Magots **14**
Cité des Sciences et de l'Industrie/
  Parc de la Villette **18**
Cluny Museum **29**
Conciergerie **26**
Fondation Cartier pour l'Art
  Contemporain **10**
Harry's New York Bar **16**
Jardin d'Acclimatation **1**
Jardin des Plantes/Museums
  of Natural History **31**
La Closerie de Lilas **11**
La Crypte Archéologique **27**
La Grande Arche de la Défense **1**
Les Catacombes **9**
Les Égouts **5**

Maison de Balzac **3**
Maison de Victor Hugo **23**
Maison Européenne de la
  Photographie **24**
Musée Carnavalet **22**
Musée Cognacq-Jay **21**
Musée d'Art et d'Histoire du Judaïsme **19**
Musée de la Curiosité et de la Magie **25**
Musée de la Sculpture en Plein Air **30**
Musée de l'Histoire de France/
  Archives Nationales **20**
Musée de l'Orangerie des Tuileries **7**
Musée Gustave Moreau **17**
Musée Maillol **8**
Musée Marmottan Monet **2**
Musée Zadkine **12**
Palais de la Découverte **6**
Parc Zoologique de Paris **34**
Promenade Plantée **32**
Shakespeare and Company **28**

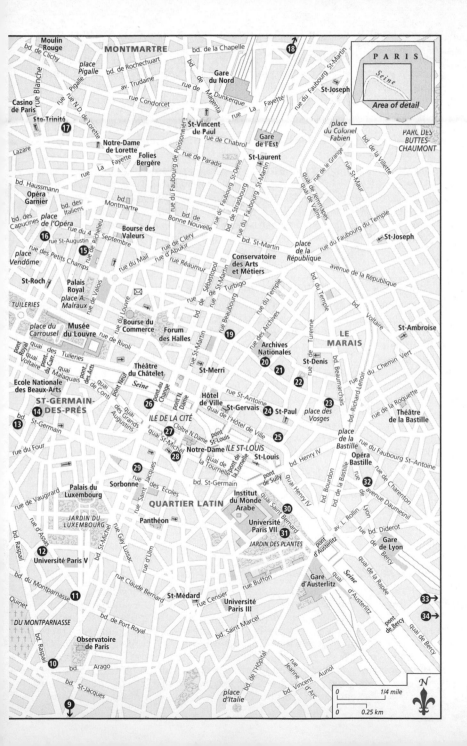

After the visit, let your kids run wild in the expansive, green **parc de la Villette** where they can play in one of the ten gardens — especially neat is the **Garden of Childhood Terrors,** a blue spruce and silver birch "forest" where eerie music plays and the **Dragon Garden** where kids and adults can cruise down the tongue of a dragon, an enormous slide. There are restaurants in the complex and food stands in the park. This could easily be an all-day visit. The Cité des Sciences et l'Industrie is bordered by the La Villette canal basin. Directly across is another smaller complex, the **Cité de la Musique,** accessible by a bridge. Its exhibits, museums and concerts are also worth a stop.

30 av. Corentin-Cariou, 19e. ☎ 01-40-05-80-00; www.cite-sciences.fr. *Métro: Porte-de-la-Villette. Admission: Explora exhibitions (including l'Argonaute submarine) 7.50€ ($8.60) adults, 5.50€ ($6.30) seniors and students under 25, free for children younger than 7. Admission to Cité des Enfants 5€ ($5.75); to Géode 8.75€ ($10) adults, 6.75€ ($7.75) 25 and under and per person in large families or groups; to Cinaxe Theater 5.20€ ($6), or combined with another ticket (Explora or Géode) 4.50€ ($5.20). Open: Tues–Sat 10 a.m.–6 p.m.; Sun 10 a.m.–7 p.m.*

Jardin de l'Acclimatation Bois de Boulogne

After a half-day at this 25-acre amusement park, your children will sleep well! The park's layout is simple: Just follow its circular road in either direction, and it eventually gets you back to where you started. Attractions include a house of mirrors, an archery range, a miniature golf course, a petting zoo and farm, an American–style bowling alley, a playground, pony rides, paddle boats, and a "City of Merry-Go-Rounds," where young "citizens" can drive cars, fire trucks, and planes, try their hand at carnival games, and ride the carousel. The park also has an "enchanted river," a lake bordered by a bright blue-topped Korean pavilion, a restaurant, and snack and ice cream stands. The most fun way to get here is to take the Petit Train from the Métro's Porte Maillot exit (5€/$5.75 adults round-trip, 3.75€/$4.30 kids round-trip.)

16e. ☎ 01-40-67-90-82. Métro: Les Sablons, exit on rue d'Orléans, entrance is about 50 feet away. Bus: 43, 73, 82, or 174. Or take the open-air Petit Train from the Bois de Boulogne's Porte Maillot exit; 5€ ($5.75) round-trip adults, 3.75€ ($4.30) round-trip children and students. Admission to the Jardin d'Acclimatation: 2.50€ ($2.90) adults and children ages 3 and older. Free for children younger than 3. Open: Daily 10 a.m.–7 p.m. June to Sept; daily 10 a.m.–6 p.m. Oct to May.

Jardin des Plantes/Museums of Natural History

The rows of trees, beds of herbs and flowers, 17th-century maze, carousel, greenhouses, zoo, and specialized gardens are just the sights on the outside of these former royal medicine gardens and museums of natural history. Indoors, children stare in awe at the bugs, bones, minerals, meteorites, dinosaurs, fossils, and endangered species in the galleries of the Jardin's Musée National d'Histoire Naturelle. Here, the Grand Gallery of Evolution traces life and humankind's relationship to nature. Don't miss the endangered and extinct species room, which displays (stuffed versions of) Gabonese monkeys, Sumatran tigers, lemurs of Madagascar, and a mock-up of the dodo bird. English explanations of some exhibits are available. Also part of the natural history museum in separate buildings are the Mineralogical Gallery (1,800 minerals, meteorites, and precious stones), the Entomological Gallery (1,500 insect specimens for bug-loving kids), and the Paleobotanical Gallery (plant evolution and specimens of fossil plants). Save for last the medium-sized menagerie (zoo), one of the oldest in the world, containing live bears, buffalo, big cats, apes, antelope, reptiles (including an alligator found in a room at the Hôtel de Paris), tortoises, and birds. Don't overlook the Vivarium — the spiders and insects are remarkable, especially the bugs that look like living tree branches! — or the Microzoo, where kids use microscopes to get a look at the life of the tiniest animals. A small restaurant on the zoo's premises offers pick-me-ups for the tired and cranky — and their children. Allow at least two hours.

57 rue Cuvier, 5e. ☎ *01-40-79-30-00. Métro: Gare d'Austerlitz. (Exit from the rue Buffon side; you're right next to the Gallery of Anatomy and Paleontology.) or Jussieu (Walk up rue Geoffroy St-Hilaire to the Grande Galerie de l'Evolution.) Admission: Grande Galerie 7€ ($8.05) adults, 5€ ($5.75) students, seniors, and children 5 and under; other galleries 5€ ($5.75) adults, 3€ ($3.45) students, seniors, and children; ménagerie (zoo) 6€ ($6.90) adults, 3.50€ ($4) students, seniors, and children. Admission to gardens is free. Open: Park dawn–dusk; galleries April–Oct Wed–Mon 10 a.m.–6 p.m., Oct–April till 5 p.m.; zoo April–Sept 9 a.m.–6 p.m. Mon–Sat, until 6:30 Sun and holidays, Oct–March daily 9 a.m.–5 p.m.*

La Grande Arche de la Défense

This 35-story cube provides a spectacular vista down avenue Charles-de-Gaulle to the Arc de Triomphe, the Champs-Elysées and the Louvre, and kids will love the cool outdoor elevator to the top. The Grand Arche de la Défense is the centerpiece of a very futuristic Paris suburb rife with glass and chrome skyscrapers lending their height to surreal sculptures. Built in 1989 to commemorate France's bicentennial, the arch completes a continuous line of perspective running from the Arc de Triomphe du Carrousel in the courtyard of the Louvre, down the Champs-Elysées, and through the Arc de Triomphe to the suburb of La Défense. The netting you see here is for catching any pieces of the façade that may fall down — several chunks have already. This is a popular destination with about 500,000 visitors a year. There is a restaurant on the premises, but I suggest bringing snacks to stave off any hunger pangs and enjoying a better meal back in Paris. Allow about two hours for the round-trip journey from central Paris, including the climb to the top.

1 parvis de la Défense, 92040 Paris-La Défense. ☎ *01-49-07-27-27. Métro, RER: Grande Arche de la Défense. Admission: 7.50€ ($8.60) adults, 6€ ($6.90) ages students and seniors, free for children younger than 6. Open: Daily 10 a.m.–7 p.m., until 8 p.m. Sat and holidays.*

Musée de la Curiosité et de la Magie

You might just walk past this small museum the first time; don't give up, just look up — for a sign reading Académie de Magie. Bona fide magicians escort you through vaulted rooms containing a collection of trick mirrors, animated paintings, talking genies, and the history of illusion in general. While they won't disclose any secrets, you and your kids will have your senses tickled through many interactive displays. Who amongst you is brave enough to stick his hand in the open mouth of a lion and see if it really is an illusion? Live magic shows performed throughout the afternoon are also highly entertaining. The museum shop sells all the tools your kids need to cast (benevolent) spells back home.

11 rue St-Paul, 4e. ☎ *01-42-72-13-26. Métro: St-Paul. Admission: 7€ ($8.05) adults, 5€ ($5.75) children younger than 13. Open: Wed, Sat, and Sun 2–7 p.m.*

Palais de la Découverte

Here, you can explore a planetarium, a room devoted to the earth's geology from its beginnings to the future, a mathematics atelier that promises a fun experience, and lots of live experiments on weekends. Within the Art Nouveau metal and glass confines of the Grand Palais you find the Palais de la Découverte a full funhouse of science brought to life for kids. Their hair will stand on end in the electrostatics room; they can light up displays, test their muscle reactions on special machines, see experiments about electromagnetism in annex off the Electricity Room and learn about DNA in the Life Sciences wing. Count on spending at least two hours here.

Grand Palais Av. Franklin-D-Roosevelt, 8e. ☎ *01-56-43-20-21. Métro: Franklin-D-Roosevelt. Admission: 6.50€ ($7.50) adults, 4€ ($4.60) students and children 5–17. Planetarium supplement 3.50€ ($4). A family of two adults and two children older than age 5 is 13€ ($15), each additional child older than 5 years is 2.50€ ($2.90). Open: Tues–Sat 9:30 a.m.–6 p.m.; Sun 10 a.m.–7 p.m. Closed major holidays.*

Parc Zoologique de Paris

Most animals live in settings that closely resemble their natural habitats in this modern zoo big enough (1,200 animals) to keep your kids occupied for an afternoon. A cool climbing tower (*Le Grand Rocher*) offers a great view of the lions, tigers, bears, elephant, and more, and you can even watch while some are fed lunch (bears at 11:30 a.m., pelicans at 2:15 p.m., seals and sea lions at 4 p.m.). The zoo has picnic areas on-site as well as a snack bar. It's located in the middle of the Bois de Vincennes, on Paris's far eastern side.

53 av. de St-Maurice, Bois de Vincennes, 12e. ☎ *01-44-75-20-10. Fax: 01-43-43-54-73. Métro: Porte Dorée. (Take av. Daumesnil past the Square des Combattants Indochine to av. de St-Maurice and turn right; it's a 5- to 10-minute walk.) Admission: 8€ ($9.20) adult, 5€ ($5.75) ages 4–27, free for children younger than 4. Open: Summer daily 9 a.m.–6 p.m. (Sun till 6:30 p.m.); winter 9 a.m.–5 or 5:30 p.m.*

Especially for teens

The kid-friendly sights in the previous section are appropriate for teenagers, as well. But here are a few more suggestions for kids who are a bit older.

Aquaboulevard

If could happen: Your teens say they're bored. Send them to Aquaboulevard. It may not be the beach, but its seven water slides, wave pool, against-the-current river, indoor and outdoor pools, spas and Jacuzzis, whirlpool, geysers, water cannons, walls of water, waterbed with bubbles, and waterfall make it a fun substitute, and it's safer than swimming in the Seine. A McDonald's, an Oh! Poivrier!, a pizza place, and a first-run movie theater are located on the premises as well.

4 rue Louis-Armand, 15e. ☎ 01-40-60-10-00. Métro: Balard, head down av. de la Porte de Sèvres; just after you walk under the overpass, you will see Aquaboulevard straight ahead. Admission: 20€ ($23) people ages 12 and older, 10€ ($12) children 3–11, who must be accompanied by an adult. Open: Mon–Thurs 9 a.m.–11 p.m., Fri–Sat 8 a.m.–midnight, Sun 8 a.m.–11 p.m. Children under three are not admitted.

Champs-Elysées

If it's the mall they're missing, your teens can shop to their hearts' content on Paris's most famous street in clothing stores like O'Neill, Quiksilver, Zara, Naf Naf, and Kookaï, and music stores Virgin and Fnac. They can catch movies in French or English (look for "v.o." for *version originale* on the marquee or in newspaper listings for U.S. releases that aren't dubbed into French) in one of the many movie theaters and eat familiar fast food at McDonald's or KFC. Many of the stores on this street are open Sunday, and plenty of teens — both residents and tourists — hang out here.

Métro: Concorde, Champs-Elysées, Clémenceau, Franklin-D-Roosevelt, George V, Charles-de-Gaulle–Étoile. Many bus lines cross the Champs, but only the 73 travels its entire length.

Les Catacombes (The Catacombs)

"Arrête, c'est ici l'Empire de la Mort" (Stop, here is the empire of death) reads the inscription over the door to what has to be Paris's most macabre attraction. The Catacombes are truly not for the faint-hearted, and are thus perfect for hardy kids older than ten, because its tunnels are dark, damp, and spooky. A former quarry, Les Catacombes began housing bones in 1785 from the Cimetière des Innocents and an assortment of other overstocked Parisian cemeteries. Now Les Catacombes are the final resting place for about 6 million skulls and skeletons stacked in thousands of yards of tunnels (a visit is bound to provoke at least a little bit of fear, even among the bravest adults).

Those prone to claustrophobia should think twice about entering. The deep, dark tunnels close in rapidly and tightly. Equip yourself with a flashlight to navigate the poorly lit corridors and read the inscriptions, and wear proper shoes (such as hiking boots) to avoid a misstep on the rocky, often slippery passageways. Wear a hood to protect yourself from the water dripping overhead. Les Catacombes earned the nickname *place d'Enfer* ("Hell Square"), which later became *place Denfert-Rochereau,* and you can take Métro line 4 or 6, or RER B to the stop of the same name.

1 place Denfert-Rochereau, 14e. ☎ 01-43-22-47-63; Métro: Denfert-Rochereau. The entrance is an unassuming small door on which a plate reads Entrée des Catacombes. Admission: 5€ ($5.75) adults; 3.30€ ($3.80) ages 8–26 and seniors; free for children younger than 8. Open: Tues–Sun 10 a.m.–4 p.m.

Les Égouts

Granted, this subterranean labyrinth is not as beautiful as the city, but the tour of the city's sewers is so popular that you sometimes have to wait as long as a half-hour in line. The tour starts with a short film about the history of sewers: The tunnels here were laid out in the 1850s during the reign of Napoléon III, at the same time that Haussmann was designing the grands boulevards, but the history of the sewers goes all the way back to Roman times. The film is followed by a visit to a small museum, and finally a short trip through the maze. Paris's sewers are laid out like an underground city, with streets clearly labeled and each branch pipe bearing the name of the building to which it's connected. Don't worry; you won't trudge through anything *dégoutant* (disgusting), but the visit may leave your clothes smelling a bit ripe. Make this the last of the day's attractions, and wear something you don't plan to wear again until after the next wash day. Plan on spending an hour and a half to two hours.

7e. ☎ 01-47-05-10-29. Fax: 01-47-05-34-78. Métro: Alma-Marceau, then walk across the bridge to the Left Bank. RER: Pont de l'Alma. The entrance is a stairway on the Seine side of the Quai d'Orsay, facing no. 93. Admission: 3.80€ ($4.40) adults; 3.05€ ($3.50) students and adults older than 60; free for children younger than 5. Open: May–Sept Sat–Wed 11 a.m.–5 p.m.; Oct–April 11 a.m.–4 p.m. Closed three weeks in Jan.

Especially for history buffs

Paris resounds with history. Blue plaques on buildings tell you the names of famous people and the dates that that they lived there. Brown-and-orange signs in French give you an overview of an area's particular story. The city is filled with wonderful museums to satisfy even the pickiest buff's thirst for knowledge. This section lists a few of the particularly good ones.

Cluny Museum

This is one of the jewels of Paris museums, home to the famous tapestry series *The Lady and the Unicorn* (with a great gift shop to boot!). Officially called the Musée National du Moyen Age/Thermes de Cluny, it houses ancient Roman hot and cold baths, the original statues that furious revolutionaries tore from Notre-Dame in 1790 (thinking they represented royalty), and one of the most beautiful tapestry series in the world. You also find remnants of clothing that royalty wore in the Middle Ages, coins, leatherwork, and gothic furniture, as well as church art — jeweled crosses, statues, sculptures, clothing, tapestries, and paintings of saints.

In the 19th century, the Hôtel de Cluny belonged to a collector of medieval art; upon his death in the 1840s, the government acquired the house and its contents. You enter through a medieval cobblestone courtyard, the

Cour d'Honneur (Courtyard of Honor) — be sure to take in the turreted building and its gargoyles; this is one of the only medieval residences left in Paris. After paying for admission in the tiny lobby, turn left past the gift shop (save it until last) and try to take it all in. The fascinating Roman baths and the Notre-Dame statues are one floor down; One floor up is *The Lady and the Unicorn*. The tapestries hang in a dimly lit room by themselves. You can sit in one of the cushioned seats and try to figure out the meaning of the sixth tapestry. (The first five are an allegory representing the five senses; the meaning of the sixth tapestry remains a mystery.) The gift shop here is a wonderful place for souvenirs, and the renovated gardens are an oasis of calm off one of the Latin Quarter's busiest streets. Every plant (except two) in *The Lady and the Unicorn* tapestries was extensively researched and tracked down to be planted here.

6 place Paul-Painlevé, 5e (between rue du Sommerard and rue des Écoles). ☎ *01-53-73-78-00. Métro: Cluny-Sorbonne. Admission: 5.50€ ($6.30) adults; 4€ ($4.60) ages 18–26, seniors older than 60 and on Sun; free for children younger than 18. Free for all the first Sun of every month. Open: Wed–Mon 9:15 a.m.–5:45 p.m. Closed Christmas, New Year's Day, and May 1st.*

Conciergerie

Though the building dates from the Middle Ages, the Conciergerie is probably most famous for its days as a prison during The Terror years of the French Revolution, when 4,164 "enemies of the people," including Marie Antoinette and her husband, Louis VXI, passed through. Built in the 14th century as part of the administrative offices of the crown, the Conciergerie was turned into a prison in the 15th century. Visitors pass through the Tour d'Argent, where the crown jewels were once stored, and the Tour César to the Salle des Gardes (Guard Room) entrance. Probably the most popular exhibit is the 11-square-foot cell of Marie Antoinette, who was kept here in squalor to await her fate. More than 4,000 of those imprisoned here headed for the guillotine on the place de la Révolution (now the place de la Concorde), including revolutionary ringleaders Danton and Robespierre, assassin Charlotte Corday, and the poet André Chenier. The far western tower, the Tour Bonbec, came to be known facetiously as the Tower of Babel because of the frequent screams from the many prisoners tortured there. Marie Antoinette's cell is now a chapel, and the other cells have been transformed with exhibits and mementos designed to convey a sense of prison life in a brutal era. Plan on spending two hours both here and in Sainte-Chapelle, the high-Gothic chapel and one of Paris's top sights (mentioned earlier this chapter) with 15 spectacular stained glass windows that are simply awe-inspiring.

Palais de Justice, Ile de la Cité, 1er. ☎ *01-53-73-78-50. Métro: Cité, Châtelet–Les Halles, or St-Michel. (Exit the Métro at Cité, which is between rue de la Cité and bd. du Palais; the Palais is directly across bd. du Palais.) RER: St-Michel. Admission: 6.10€ ($7) adults; 4.10€ ($4.70) ages 18–25; free for children younger than 18. The better deal is the combined Sainte-Chapelle and Conciergerie ticket for 9€ ($10). Open: April–Sept daily 9:30 a.m.–6:30 p.m.; Oct–March daily 10 a.m.–5 p.m. Closed Christmas, New Year's Day, and May 1st.*

La Crypte Archéologique

In 1965, excavations for a new parking lot under the parvis (a portico in front of the church) of Notre-Dame revealed Gallo-Roman ramparts, third-century Gallo-Roman rooms heated by an underground furnace system called a *hypocaust,* and cellars of medieval houses. The parking lot project was abandoned, and the excavations were turned into this neat archaeological museum. When you descend into the crypt, you are at the Ile de la Cité's original level. Over the centuries, builders erected new structures over the ruins of previous settlements, raising the island about 23 feet. To help you visualize the buildings that once stood here, scale models show how Paris grew from a small settlement to a Roman city, and photographs show the pre-Haussmann parvis. Allow about 45 minutes, longer if you're a history buff.

Place du parvis Notre-Dame, 4e (about 200 feet directly in front of Notre-Dame, accessed by downward-leading stairs). ☎ *01-43-29-83-51. Métro: Cité, RER: St-Michel-Notre-Dame. Admission: 3.30€ ($3.80) adults; 2.20€ ($2.50) 25 and younger. Open: daily 10 a.m.–6 p.m.*

Musée Carnavalet

If you prefer to see history rather than read about it, this is the museum for you. Housed inside two beautiful Renaissance mansions, Paris history comes alive through an incredible selection of paintings, reassembled rooms in all their period glory, and other items from daily life long ago. The blue-and-yellow rooms of Louis XV and Louis XVI are here in all their ornately furnished glory. The chess pieces that Louis XVI played with while awaiting his beheading are here, as are Napoléon's cradle and a replica of Marcel Proust's cork-lined bedroom. The *Cabinet Doré de l'hotel La Rivière* room has a spectacular gilded, ceiling painting of Apollo and Aurora by Charles Le Brun; his other ceiling painting is of Psyche with the Muses. Many salons depict events related to the Revolution, and the paintings of what Paris used to look like are fascinating. In 2000, the museum opened a 1.6 million dollar wing devoted to the archaeology of Paris's earliest settlements (some artifacts, such as the fishing boats used by settlers, date back to between 2200 and 4400 B.C.). Visitors can even touch some of the exhibits here. You may want to buy an English-language guidebook in the museum's gift shop, because audio guides are in French.

23 rue de Sévigné, 3e. ☎ *01-44-59-58-58. Métro: St-Paul. (Turn left on rue de Sévigné.) Admission: Free for permanent collections; temporary exhibits 6€ ($6.90) adults, 4.50€ ($5.20) students. Open: Tues–Sun 10 a.m.–6 p.m.*

Musée d'Art et d'Histoire du Judaïsme

The beautiful 17th-century mansion Hôtel de St-Aignan houses this enormous collection tracing the development of Jewish culture in France and Europe, from life in the Middle Ages to the 20th century. In addition to beautifully crafted religious objects, including copies of the Torah, shofars, menorahs, ark curtains, and spectacular velvet cloaks reflecting both the Sephardic and Ashkenazi traditions throughout Europe and North Africa, the museum has medieval gravestones and 20th-century paintings and sculptures. The museum also presents newly available documents relating to the Dreyfus affair, the notorious scandal that falsely accused a Jewish army captain of providing secret military information to the German government in 1894. The free audio tour is very informative. The exhibits end with a collection of works by Jewish artists, including paintings by Modigliani, Soutine, Zadkine, and Chagall. A recent exhibition here included stunning portraits Polish artist Zber (Fiszel Zylberberg) painted in the French internment camp Beaune-la-Rolande where he was held for three months in 1942 before his deportation to Auschwitz. He died there on Oct. 26th. Allow at least two hours. Security is tight here.

71 rue du Temple, 3e (between rue Rambuteau and rue de Braque). ☎ *01-53-01-86-60. Métro: Rambuteau, Hôtel de Ville. Bus: 29, 38, 47, 75. Admission: 6.10€ ($7) adults; 3.80€ ($4.40) ages 18–26 and seniors; free for children younger than 18. Open: Mon–Fri 11 a.m.–6 p.m.; Sun 10 a.m.–6 p.m.*

Cabinet des Médailles

For those who love treasure, this is your museum. Housed in France's original national library, still referred to as the Bibliothèque Nationale de France, the museum shows an impressive display of archaeological objects, cameos, bronzes, medals, and money originally amassed by French kings. Among the more exceptional objects are the Treasure of Berthouville, a collection of Gallo-Roman money; the Cameo of Sainte-Chapelle, a huge multicolored cameo dating from the first century; and the Treasure of Childéric, one of the oldest remnants of the French monarchy. Take a peek into the Salle Labrouste, a lovely reading room built in 1868, which now echoes sadly without its book collection (Ten million books were removed in 1998 to the new Bibliothèque Nationale de France in the 13e). The garden, a virtual mini-Versailles, also merits a stop. Security is tight here. Plan to spend at least an hour.

Bibliothèque Nationale de France, 58 rue de Richelieu, 2e (between rue des Filles St-Thomas and rue Colbert). ☎ *01-53-79-83-30. Métro: Palais-Royal–Musée du Louvre or Bourse. Bus: 20, 29, 39, 48, 67, 74, 85, 95. Admission: Free. Open: Mon–Fri 1–5:45 p.m.; Sat 1–4:45 p.m.; Sun noon–6 p.m.*

Musée de l'Histoire de France/Archives Nationales

In January 2004, the Musée de l'Histoire de France transferred its collection from the spectacular Hôtel de Soubise (which is to undergo a renovation) to the Hôtel de Rohan. In 1808, Napoléon ordered the acquisition of the Rohan-Soubise estate to house Empire archives; the palace also contains the National Archives. The Hôtel de Rohan will now display some of the most important documents that pertain to the country's history, as well as personal papers of some famous French citizens. Exhibits include Henry IV's Edict of Nantes (a document that guaranteed religious liberty); the wills of Louis XIV, Louis XVI (along with his diary), and Napoléon; the

Declaration of Human Rights; Marie Antoinette's last letter; and the French constitution. Rooms are devoted to the Middle Ages, the French Revolution, and other themes.

Hôtel de Rohan, 87 rue Vieille du Temple, 3e. ☎ *01-40-27-60-96. Métro: Rambuteau. Bus: 29, 75, 96. Admission: Museum 3.05€ ($3.50) adults; 2.30€ ($2.65) ages 18–25; free for children younger than 18. Open: Mon, Wed–Fri 10 a.m.–12:30 p.m. and 2–6:30 p.m.; Sat–Sun 1:45–5:45 p.m.*

Place de la Bastille

Ignore the traffic and try to imagine the place de la Bastille just more than 200 years ago, when it contained eight towers rising 100 feet. It was here, on July 14, 1789 (now commemorated in France as Bastille Day), that a mob attacked the old prison, launching the French Revolution. Although the Bastille had long since fallen into disuse, it symbolized the arbitrary power of a king who could imprison anyone for any reason. Prisoners of means could buy a spacious cell and even host dinner parties, but the poor disappeared within the prison's recesses and sometimes drowned when the Seine overflowed its banks. The attack on the prison was therefore a direct assault on royal power. The Bastille was razed in 1792. In its place stands the Colonne de Juillet, a 171-foot bronze column built between 1830 and 1849 to commemorate Parisians killed in civil uprisings in 1830 and 1848.

11e. Métro: Bastille. (The Colonne de Juillet is across from the Métro.)

Especially for art lovers

From galleries in the Marais, Bastille, St-Germain-des-Prés, and near the Champs-Elysées, to the Egyptian, Assyrian, and Greco-Roman art at the Louvre, through realism, Impressionism, and Art Nouveau at the Musée d'Orsay, to the modern international masters at the Centre Pompidou, it is an understatement to say that Paris offers a vast wealth of art. And art in Paris is not merely French art. Many French movements began or developed here, but generations of artists from all parts of the world have thrived in Paris, and the city's museums and galleries hold enough art for several lifetimes of daily viewing.

Each October, Paris also presents the overwhelming *Foire Internationale d'Art Contemporain* (`www.fiac-online.com`), one of the largest contemporary art fairs in the world with stands from more than 150 galleries, half of them foreign. You may find the following museums often less crowded than their larger and more famous counterparts, but each is still capable of wowing you.

Fondation Cartier pour l'Art Contemporain

One of *the* art exhibits of the year 2004 had to be designer Jean Paul Gaultier's Pain Couture, a display of fashion made entirely of bread, displayed in this trendy museum with works that reflect the main trends of contemporary art since the 1980s. Art is displayed in a gorgeous building, designed by architect Jean Nouvel, that is too striking to miss. Its glass-and-metal screen stands between the street and the glass-and-metal building, creating an optical illusion that makes the courtyard greenery appear as if it is growing indoors. The offices for the Cartier jewelry empire are upstairs, and most of the first-rate contemporary art exhibits that the foundation hosts are in the basement. The collection is built around large groups of work by living artists and includes paintings by artists such as Vija Celmins, Sam Francis, and Matthew Barney, as well as photography, sculpture, huge installations, and video works. Reservations are necessary for the très cool performance art and music of Les Soirees Nomades (Nomadic Evenings) every Thursday night at 8:30. Plan to spend at least an hour and a half here.

261 bd. Raspail, 14e (200 meters from the Raspail Métro stop, past Passage d'Enfer and rue Boissonade). ☎ 01-42-18-56-50, 01-42-18-56-72 for Nomadic Evenings reservations. www.fondation.cartier.fr. *Métro: Raspail. Admission to exhibits and Nomadic Nights: 6.50€ ($7.50) adults; 4.50€ ($5.20) students younger than 25; free for children younger than 10. Open: Tues–Sun noon–8 p.m.*

Maison Européenne de la Photographie

This museum's goal is to make the three fundamental mediums of photography — exhibition prints, the printed page, and film — accessible to all, and it succeeds on all fronts. A first-floor gallery exhibits original period prints (see Irving Penn's photo of Colette), the vaulted 18th-century basement displays cutting-edge photography, film projections, and installations. There is a space for young photographers to show their work, and the Roméo Martinez library displays some 12,000 titles spanning the last 50 years of photography. Martinez was editor-in-chief of *Camera* magazine for 20 years. There are permanent collections of Polaroid art and an excellent video library that allows you to look up thousands of photographs. The museum was created from two restored 18th-century mansions. Allow at least an hour and a half including a pick-me-up in the cozy vaulted basement cafe.

5–7 rue de Fourcy, 4e. ☎ 01-44-78-75-00; www.mep-fr.org. *Métro: St-Paul or Pont-Marie. Bus: 67, 69, 96, 76. Admission: 5€ ($5.75) adults; 2.50€ ($2.90) ages 8–26 and older than 60; free for children younger than 8. Free admission Wed 5–8 p.m. Guided tours 7.55€ ($8.70) adults, 5€ ($5.75) reduced; reservations necessary. Open: Wed–Sun 11 a.m.–8 p.m.*

Musée Cognacq-Jay

La Samaritaine department store founder Ernest Cognacq and his wife amassed at the turn of the 20th century this collection of 18th-century rococo art that features works by François Boucher, Jean-Honoré Fragonard, Peter Paul Rubens, Louis-Michel van Loo, Jean-Antoine Watteau, Elisabeth Vigée-LeBrun, and Giambattista Tiepolo displayed in elegant Louis XV and Louis XVI paneled rooms. There is a collection of everyday objects, such as dance cards, and snuff and candy boxes, shelves of porcelain and porcelain figures, rich wood cabinets, and furniture. The building housing it all is the beautifully preserved Hôtel Donon, built in the 16th century. You can walk through a little manicured garden, open May to September, and enjoy sunny days. Temporary exhibits are presented two to three times a year.

8 rue Elzévir, 3e (between rue des Francs Bourgeois and rue Barbette). ☎ *01-40-27-07-21. Métro: St-Paul. Admission: Permanent collections free; temporary exhibits 6.10€ ($7) adults; 3.05€ ($3.50) students 14–26 and seniors; free for children younger than 14. Open: Tues–Sun 10 a.m.–6 p.m.*

Musée de la Sculpture en Plein Air

Displayed here are the sculptures of 29 artists, including César, Ossip Zadkine, and Stagio Stahly. Located on the banks of the Seine, you may pass it on one of your strolls without realizing that this graceful waterside park is really a museum.

Quai St-Bernard, 5e (on the quay of the Seine between the Institut du Monde Arabe and the Jardin des Plantes). Métro: Sully-Morland or Gare d'Austerlitz. Admission: Free. If you go on a summer Thurs evening around 8 p.m., you can see outdoor dancing nearby.

Musée de l'Orangerie des Tuileries

Will this museum in the Tuileries ever reopen? It's been closed for renovations since the late 1990s, and its reopening dates are regularly estimated and then pushed back. At press time, the museum was slated to open in early 2006. If you're lucky enough to be in Paris when the Orangerie again admits the public, pay it a visit. The highlight is its two oval rooms wrapped nearly 360 degrees with Monet's *Nymphéas,* the water lily series he painted especially for the Orangerie. (It's partly to improve their presentation that the museum is undergoing the overhaul.) Since 1984, the museum has also housed the remarkable John Walter and Paul Guillaume art collection, comprising works by Cézanne, Renoir, Rousseau, Matisse, Dérain, Picasso, and Soutine. Check with the Paris Tourist Office (www.parisinfo.com) for an official update on the museum.

Jardin des Tuileries, 1er. Métro: Concorde.

Musée Gustave Moreau

The artist himself established and designed this duplex museum studio so that his symbolist work could be displayed the way he wanted long after his death. More than 6,000 of Moreau's works — which are not to everyone's taste — can be found here. The teacher of Henri Matisse, Gustave Moreau was a symbolist painter influenced by the English Pre-Raphaelites. He created fantasies of a mythological world, embracing the bizarre and painting mythological subjects and scenes in a sensuous, romantic style that look to be encrusted with jewels. Among the works displayed are *The Pretenders, The Life of Humanity, The Apparition, Orpheus by the Tomb of*

Eurydice, and *Jupiter and Semele.* Moreau taught at the École des Beaux-Arts; his museum's first curator, Georges Rouault, was his favorite student. The artist's apartment is also preserved here. An hour and a half should be plenty.

14 rue de la Rochefoucault, 9e (between rue la Bruyère and rue St-Lazare). ☎ *01-48-74-38-50. Métro: Trinité d'Estienne d'Orves. Bus: 68 or 74. Admission: 3.05€ ($3.50) adults; 2.30€ ($2.65) students, ages 18–25, seniors older than 60, and for adults on Sun; free for children younger than 18. Open: Wed–Mon 10 a.m.–12:45 p.m. and 20–5:15 p.m.*

Musée Maillol

Curvaceous, bold, and graceful bronze statues of Aristide Maillol's favorite model, Dina Vierny, are on vibrant display as well as the works of Impressionist and Postimpressionist artists in this renovated 18th-century convent. Outside is the sculpted fountain of the four seasons by Edme Bouchardon. But it is the important modern art collection inside that rightly draws the most notice. The elegant upper floors of the museum display crayon and pastel sketches of Vierny who Maillol discovered at 15. He believed her voluptuous figure was the personification of femininity and she served as his exclusive model for ten years. Maillol's personal collection includes the work of his friends, Matisse and Bonnard, as well as two sculptures by Rodin, works by Gauguin, Dégas, Rousseau, Odilon Redon, Maurice Denis, Kandinsky, and Renoir. Vierny, who collected art most of her life, has an important collection of modern primitives that include Douanier, Rousseau, and Camille Bombois, as well as drawings by Suzanne Valadon, Dégas, Picasso, and Foujita. The museum features splendid temporary exhibits; a recent exhibit was Francis Bacon's "The Sacred and Profane."

59–61 rue de Grenelle, 7e. ☎ *01-42-22-59-58;* www.museemaillol.com. *Métro: Rue du Bac. Admission: 8€ ($9.20) adults; 6€ ($6.90) students 18–26; free for children younger than 16. Open: Wed–Mon 11 a.m.–6 p.m. (last ticket sold at 5:15 p.m.)*

Musée Marmottan Monet

If you can't get enough of Claude Monet, this museum is for you; the Marmottan Monet celebrates the painter and contains an outstanding collection of his water lily paintings, as well as his more abstract representations of the Japanese Bridge at Giverny. The painting *Impression: Sunrise,* is located here; it was from this painting that the term *Impressionism* was coined to describe the painting style and subsequent artistic movement. Also on hand is Monet's personal collection, which includes works by his contemporaries Pissarro, Manet, Morisot, and Renoir.

The museum, located between the Ranelagh garden and the Bois de Boulogne, is in a 19th-century mansion that belonged to the art historian Paul Marmottan. He donated the mansion and his collection of Empire furniture and Napoleonic art to the Académie des Beaux-Arts upon his death in 1932.

When Claude Monet's son and heir bequeathed his father's collection to the Marmottan, the museum paid permanent homage to Monet's unique vision. Subsequent donations have expanded the collection to include more Impressionist paintings and the stunning Wildenstein collection of late medieval illuminated manuscripts. Allow at least an hour and a half for a visit.

2 rue Louis-Boilly, 16e. ☎ *01-42-24-07-02;* www.marmottan.com. *Métro: La-Muette. Admission: 6.50€ ($7.50) adults; 4€ ($4.60) ages 8–25; free for children younger than 8. Open: Tues–Sun 10 a.m.–6 p.m. Closed Christmas, New Year's Day, and May 1st.*

Musée Zadkine

If you have time to spare after wandering in the Jardin du Luxembourg, exit the garden's west side and head approximately a block south on rue d'Assas to this serene place, the perfect spot to view the works of Ukrainian sculptor Ossip Zadkine. The small sculpture garden is sheltered within walls of Virginia creeper, and Japanese cherry, maple, and birch trees lend shade to the garden's changing sculptures. The garden and museum are free, and the temporary exhibits don't cost much more, and it's worth a visit if you like contemporary sculpture or are familiar with the artist's work. Zadkine lived and worked in this house and studio until his death. His art, books, tools, and furniture are all on display, as well as many of his works in brass, wood, and stone. His bronze, *Destroyed City* (1953) is considered a masterpiece; the model is exhibited here (the original is in Rotterdam). The museum is accessed through an alleyway.

100 bis rue d'Assas, 6e. ☎ *01-43-26-91-90. Métro: Notre-Dame-des-Champs or Vavin. Bus: 38, 82, 83, 91. Admission: free for permanent exhibits. For temporary exhibits: 4€ ($4.60) adults; 3€ ($3.45) children and students ages 7–26 and adults older than 60; 2€ ($2.30) for children younger than 7. Open: Tues–Sun 10 a.m.–5:30 p.m.*

Especially for the literary

Paris's literary landmarks aren't all connected to Ernest Hemingway, F. Scott Fitzgerald, and the "Lost Generation," as many of the listings in this section testify.

An important WWII memorial

Behind Notre-Dame is a small fenced-in park, which on closer look, reveals a set of stairs leading down. This is the Mémorial des Martyrs de la Déportation honoring more than 200,000 Jews, who, during World War II were sent to concentration camps. Architect G.H. Pingusson created a most moving tribute, from the walls etched with sayings and poetry to the solemn corridor inscribed with the names of the deported and lit with an eternal flame. A barred window looks out onto the Seine, a reminder of how precious — and easily taken away — is freedom. Square de l'Isle de France 7, quai de l'Archevêché, 75004. (☎ 01-46-33-87-56; Métro: Cité.) Admission: free.

Brasserie de l'Ile St-Louis

If you're a fan of *From Here to Eternity* or *The Thin Red Line,* pay a visit to this brasserie (see also Chapter 10 for a review of the food), where novelist and regular customer James Jones kept his own *chope* (mug) at the bar. Not only is the location excellent — the building is situated directly off the footbridge from Ile de la Cité to Ile St-Louis with an unparalleled view of the eastern tip of Ile de la Cité (including the back of Notre-Dame) — but this eatery is one of the last remaining independent brasseries in Paris. Jones lived with his family around the corner on Ile de la Cité, and the film about their lives, *A Soldier's Daughter Never Cries,* was filmed in the neighborhood.

Ile St-Louis, 55 quai de Bourbon, 1er. ☎ *01-43-54-02-59. Métro: Pont Marie.*

Brasserie Lipp and Café les Deux Magots

You can't talk about literary Paris without mentioning Ernest Hemingway, and two of his favorite hangouts are just across the street from each other on boulevard St-Germain-des-Prés. Brasserie Lipp is where Hemingway lovingly recalls eating potato salad in *A Moveable Feast,* and the Café les Deux Magots is where Jake Barnes meets Lady Brett in *The Sun Also Rises.* Tourism has driven up prices, so just go for a glass of wine or a coffee (and remember that it's cheaper standing up at the bar than sitting down at a table).

Brasserie Lipp: 151 bd. St-Germain, 6e. ☎ *01-45-48-53-91. Open: Daily 9–1 a.m. Café les Deux Magots: 170 bd. St-Germain, 6e.* ☎ *01-45-48-55-25. Open: Daily 7:30– 1:30 a.m. Both are less than 50 yards from the St-Germain-des-Prés Métro stop.*

Café de Flore

Next door to Les Deux Magots is this other infamous St-Germain-des-Près cafe. Sartre is said to have written *Les Chemins de la Liberté (The Roads to Freedom)* at his table here, and he and Simone de Beauvoir saw people by appointment here. Other regulars included André Malraux and Guillaume Apollinaire.

172 bd. St-Germain, 6e. ☎ *01-45-48-55-26. Métro: St-Germain-des-Prés.*

Harry's New York Bar

This place is still going strong all these years after — guess who? — Ernest Hemingway and F. Scott Fitzgerald went on a few famous benders. Unfortunately, Harry's has pretty high prices, so peek in for the ambience and maybe one drink. They do make great martinis and it's said that the Bloody Mary was invented here.

5 rue Danou, 2e. ☎ *01-42-61-71-14. Métro: Opéra; head down the rue de la Paix and take the first left. Open: Daily 10:30–4 a.m.*

La Closerie de Lilas

Author John Dos Passos and painter Pablo Picasso hung out here, and Soviet revolutionary Leon Trotsky played chess here. But the true claim to fame is that Hemingway completed *The Sun Also Rises* on the terrace here in just six weeks. Much of the novel also takes place at Closerie des Lilas, which means "the courtyard of lilacs." Lilac bushes still bloom here, and the place is just as crowded as it was in the 1930s, although its high, high prices are geared toward an American tourist crowd.

171 bd. du Montparnasse, 6e. ☎ *01-40-51-34-50. RER: Line B to Port-Royal. Exit onto bd. du Port-Royal and walk west. Cross av. de l'Observatoire. Bd. du Port-Royal turns into bd. du Montparnasse. The restaurant is on the north corner of av. de l'Observatoire and bd. du Montparnasse. Open: Daily noon–1 a.m.*

Maison de Balzac

The very modest Honoré de Balzac lived in this rustic cabin in this very posh residential Passy neighborhood from 1840 to 1847 under a false name to avoid creditors, only allowing entrance to those who knew the password. He wrote some of his most famous novels here, including those that make up his *La Comédie Humaine (The Human Comedy)*. His study is preserved, and portraits, books, letters, and manuscripts are on display. You can also see his jewel-encrusted cane (why spend on bills when you can have jewels?) and the Limoges coffeepot that bears his initials in mulberry pink. Expect to spend about 45 minutes here.

47 rue Raynouard, 16e. ☎ *01-55-74-41-80. Métro: line 6 to Passy; walk 1 block away from the river and turn left into rue Raynouard. Bus: 32, 50, 70, 72. Admission: Permanent collections free; temporary exhibits 3.30€ ($3.80) adults, 2.20€ ($2.50) seniors and students to age 26, free for children 13 and younger. Open: Tues–Sun 10 a.m.–6 p.m. Closed holidays.*

Maison de Victor Hugo

Here's your chance to explore one of those gorgeous place des Vosges apartments! Of course, if you or your kids have read *The Hunchback of Notre-Dame* or *Les Miserables,* you may want to visit here anyway. Victor Hugo lived on the second floor of this town house (built in 1610) from 1832 to 1848. The museum was designed to reflect the way Hugo structured his life: Before Exile, During Exile, and After Exile. (He fled the country after an unsuccessful revolt against President Louis Napoléon [who later became Napoléon III], and returned to Paris 16 years later after the collapse of the Second Empire.) You can see some of his furniture, samples of his handwriting, his inkwell, first editions of his works, and a painting of his 1885 funeral procession at the Arc de Triomphe. Portraits of his family adorn the walls, and the fantastic Chinese salon from Hugo's house on Guernsey (where he was exiled) is reassembled here. The highlight is more than 450 of Hugo's drawings, illustrating scenes from his own works. Plan to spend an hour here.

6 place des Vosges, 4e (between rue des Tournelles and rue de Turenne, nearer to rue de Turenne). ☎ *01-42-72-10-16. Métro: St-Paul. Bus: 20, 29, 65, 69, 96. Admission: Free. Open Tues–Sun 10 a.m.–6 p.m. (ticket window closes at 5:15 p.m.). Note: Though admission is free, you still must stand in line for a ticket from the cashier in the gift shop (enter on the right).*

Shakespeare and Company Bookstore

This is *not* the original Shakespeare and Company, even though it looks old and dusty enough to be. The original opened in 1919 at 6 rue Dupuytren (take the Métro to Odéon, walk through the square there, and turn left) by Sylvia Beach. Two years later, Beach moved the shop to 12 rue de l'Odéon (the building is no longer there) and stayed until the United States entered into World War II (in German-occupied Paris, Beach was considered an enemy alien and was forced to abandon shop). The newest of the Shakespeares was opened by George Whitman in the mid-1960s and named in honor of Beach. It serves as a haven for Americans and English speakers, playing the dual role of gathering place and bookstore. Poetry readings take place on Sunday nights, and Whitman will give lodging to a (debatably) lucky few writers or poets in exchange for work in the store.

37 rue de la Bûcherie, 5e. ☎ *01-43-26-96-50. Métro or RER: St-Michel.*

Especially for nature lovers

Most parks are open until sunset, unless otherwise noted. Count on spending at least one hour (much of that relaxing in the beautiful surroundings).

Bois de Boulogne

This huge park on the west side of Paris was once a royal forest and hunting ground. Napoléon III donated it to the city and Baron Haussmann transformed it, using London's Hyde Park as his model. Today the Bois is a vast reserve of more than 2,200 acres with jogging paths, bridle trails, bicycling (bike rental available April–Oct near the Les Sablons entrance to the park) and boating on its Lac Inférieur and Lac Supérieur (boat rental available at the northern edge of the Lac Inférieur). Also here are the **parc de la Bagatelle** (see the listing later in this section); the famous **Longchamp** and **Auteuil** racecourses; the **Stade Roland Garros,** where the French Open is held; the **Musée National de des Arts et Traditions Populaire** (documents French every day life from the year 1000 to the present); and the beautiful **Pré Catalan,** a lovely park in which it is said the copper beech here has a span wider than any other tree in Paris. The Pré Catalan contains the **Jardin Shakespeare** in which you can find many of the plants and herbs mentioned in Shakespeare's plays and the Pré Catalan restaurant, one of Paris's prettiest and most expensive restaurants. The **Jardin d'Acclimatation** (see "Especially for Kids" earlier in this chapter) is one of Parisian children's favorite amusement parks. **Les Serres d'Auteuil** at the southeastern edge of the Bois are the municipal greenhouses and gardens that supply Paris with its flowers and plants. Open to the public, the greenhouses are especially nice to visit in winter; they provide a taste of the Caribbean with orchids, tropical plants and palm trees. As the sun sets, prostitutes in parked cars and vans line the road on each side of the Porte Dauphine entrance, so the Bois is best enjoyed in daylight. This park is so big, you can spend an entire afternoon here.

16e. Métro: Porte Dauphine or Les Sablons.

Bois de Vincennes

Once a hunting ground for kings, this is the largest green space in Paris. You can rent a boat at the two lakes here: **Lac Daumesnil,** on the west side of the park has two islands connected by a bridge; **Lac des Minimes** is located on the northwestern edge of the Bois. The Bois de Vincennes is home to the **parc Zoologique** (see "Especially for kids" earlier in this chapter); a **Buddhist center** right next to the bridge at Lac Daumesnil, complete with temple and Buddha effigy; and the **Château de Vincennes,** in which early monarchs Charles V and Henri III sought refuge from war and where Mata Hari was executed in 1917. The Bois de Vincennes houses the spectacular **parc Floral de Paris** (see the next listing), the **Hippodrome de Vincennes** for harness racing, and the **Aquarium Tropicale de la Porte Doree** (see the "Especially for kids" section). This is also a big park you can spend an entire afternoon enjoying.

12e. Métro: Porte Doree or Chateau de Vincennes.

The Center for Nature Discovery, Garden in Memory of Diana, Princess of Wales

The city of Paris is trying to get Diana fans to bring their messages and bouquets here instead of to the flame at place de l'Alma (Métro: Alma-Marceau), near the entrance to the tunnel where the princess, her friend Dodi Fayed, and driver Henri Paul were killed in an automobile accident on August 31, 1997. In this small park that opened in 2002, children discover how to grow flowers, vegetables, and decorative plants and learn about nature. Plan on spending at least a half-hour here.

21 rue des Blancs-Manteaux, 3e. Métro: Rambuteau.

Parc de Belleville

This park is a tranquil place to watch the sun set over western Paris and has wonderful views of the city — without the lines. Topped by the Maison de l'Air, a museum with displays devoted to the air that we breathe, you can enjoy fountains, a children's play area, and an open-air theater with many concerts during the summer. Rock formations and grottoes evoke the days when the hill was a strategic point for fighting enemies such as Attila the Hun. Access the park by taking the rue Piat off rue de Belleville and enter through an iron gate spelling out the words Villa Ottoz. A curved path leads you to tree-lined promenades (more than 500 trees are here), with the first of the magnificent Left Bank views peeping through the spaces between pretty houses. Beds of roses and other seasonal flowers line walks, and views of the city's Left Bank become more pronounced the higher up the terraced pathways you go.

20e. Métro: Pyrénées (walk down rue de Belleville and turn left onto rue Piat where you see arched iron gates leading into the park) or Courrones (cross bd. de Belleville and turn left onto rue Julien Lacroix to find another entrance).

Parc de la Bagatelle

Contained in the Bois de Boulogne, the parc de la Bagatelle is known for its rose gardens and the thematic gardens that reveal the art of gardening through the centuries. A water lily pond pays homage to a certain famous painter (think Monet) because the park was designed by Monet's friend, Jean-Claude-Nicolas Forestier, whose claim to fame was as designer of the Champs de Mars and other gardens. Forestier was inspired by the Impressionists and their way of showing flowers by species and emphasizing the effects of mass planting. The rose garden here remains his major work with 10,000 roses of 1,200 varieties, most of them peaking in June. You can also enjoy bulbed plants (tulips, hyacinths, and so on) in March, peonies, clematis, and irises in May, water lilies in June, dalhias and autumn foliage in October; and winter-flowering trees, shrubs, and snowdrops during the cold months. The Orangerie here is home to the Festival Chopin à Paris from mid-June to mid-July. The château here, which you can view from the outside only, was built by the Comte d'Artois in 1775, after he made a bet with his sister-in-law, Marie Antoinette, that he could do it in less than 90 days. It took 66 days. Under Napoléon, it was used as a hunting lodge.

16e. Métro: Porte Maillot. Exit at av. Neuilly. Bus: 244 to the Bagatelle-Pré-Catalan stop.

Parc de la Villette

In the summer, you can catch an outdoor movie or listen to a concert, and your kids can play on a giant dragon slide. You can also visit the children's museum, the Cité des Sciences et de l'Industrie, and the Musée de la Musique, which are all located on the grounds separated by the La Villette canal basin. This modern park has a series of themed gardens, including an exotic bamboo garden and a garden featuring steam and water jets. Scattered throughout the park are playgrounds and other attractions. (See "Especially for Kids" earlier in this chapter.)

You can get to the parc de la Villette by Métro, but a fun, alternative route worth trying is the guided canal trip to the park from Pont l'Arsenal or Musée d'Orsay with **Paris Canal** (☎ 01-42-40-96-97; Métro: Bastille) or with **Canauxrama** (☎ 01-42-39-15-00; Métro: Jaurés). See "Seeing Paris by Guided Tour" later in this chapter.

19e. Métro: Porte de la Villette.

Parc des Buttes-Chaumont

Featuring cliffs, a suspension bridge, waterfalls, a lake, and a cave topped by a temple, this former gypsum quarry and centuries-old dump is one of four man-made parks Napoléon III commissioned to resemble the English gardens he grew to love during his exile in England. This is worth a stop if you're in the area.

19e. Métro: Buttes-Chaumont. (The station is located within the park.)

Parc Floral de Paris

The Bois de Vincennes houses the spectacular parc Floral de Paris, with a butterfly garden, library, and miniature golf course, as well as the parc Zoologique de Paris. You can rent bikes here and ride around the extensive grounds, or row a rented canoe around a winding pond. (You can even rent *quadricycles* — bicycles built for four (around 10€/$12).

12e. ☎ 01-55-94-20-20. Métro: Château de Vincennes. Exit at cours des Maréchaux and walk south; the chateau is on the right. Cross av. des Minimes into the park. Admission: 0.75€ (90¢)adults, 0.35€ (40¢) seniors and students 7 and older.

Parc Monceau

The oddities abound in this park in Paris's ritzy 8e, including a Dutch windmill, a Roman temple, a covered bridge, a waterfall, a farm, medieval ruins, and a pagoda, all designed by Carmontelle. It was a favorite place for Marcel Proust to stroll, and it contains Paris's largest tree, an Oriental plane tree with a circumference of almost 23 feet. Have a picnic on a bench here with supplies from the rue de Levis (open Tues–Sun; Métro: Villiers) and watch the English nannies from the nearby palatial apartment buildings guard their charges.

Boulevard de Coucelles, 8e. Métro: Monceau. (The Métro station is at the edge of the park.)

Promenade Plantée

This old railroad bridge was converted into a clever 5-kilometer-long garden that begins behind the Opéra Bastille, runs along the length of avenue Daumesnil, the Reuilly Garden, and the Porte Dorée to the Bois de Vincennes (it makes a great jogging path). Beneath the promenade, artisans have built boutiques and studios into the bridge, collectively known as the Viaduc des Arts. Check them out for eclectic, unusual gifts.

12e. Métro: Bel Air or Dugommier. Walk from the Métro to av. Daumesnil. The elevated railroad bridge above av. Daumesnil is the Promenade Plantée.

Houses of the holy

Paris has had a tradition of worship since the first settlers on the Isle of Parisii in the third century B.C. In fact, many of Paris's churches were built on the ruins of pagan temples. Today Paris's churches are treasure troves of fine art, stained glass, and architecture. Included here are some of those worth a visit.

Église St-Etienne du Mont

Standing directly behind place du Panthéon, this is one of Paris's most extraordinary churches. Completed and consecrated in the 17th century, on the site of a 13th-century abbey, the church is a unique blend of late Gothic and Renaissance styles. Preserved near the chancel and set in an ornate copper-trimmed shrine is the sarcophagus stone for Paris's patron saint Geneviève, who saved the city from the Huns in the fifth century. The most impressive attraction here, however, is the 16th-century rood screen, embraced by twin spiraling marble staircases — a stunning display of Renaissance design. The tombs of Pascal and Racine are also here.

1 place St-Geneviève, 5e. ☎ *01-43-54-11-79. Métro: Cardinal Lemoine. Open daily Sept–June Mon–Sat 8:30 a.m.–noon and 2–7 p.m., Sun 9 a.m. noon and 3:30–7:30 p.m.; July and Aug Tues–Sun 10 a.m.–noon and 4–7:15 p.m.*

Église St-Eustache

This massive church at the heart of Les Halles was built between 1532 and 1637, combining a Gothic structure with Renaissance decoration. Molière and Mme. de Pompadour were baptized here, and Molière's funeral was held here in 1673. This was the first church to contain the tombs of celebrated Parisians, most notably Louis XIV's finance minister, Colbert. The organ is one of the finest in Paris and has been entirely restored and modernized. Franz Liszt used to play the organ here, and there is a free concert every Sunday at 5:30 p.m. There are also free jazz and piano concerts here Tuesdays from 7:30 to 8:30 p.m.

2 impasse St-Eustache, 1er. ☎ *01-42-36-01-05;* www.st-eustache.org. *Métro: Les Halles. Open: Daily 9 a.m.–7:30 p.m., until 8:30 p.m. in summer.*

Église St-Germain-des-Près

This is the most famous church in the 6e and one of the most important Romanesque monuments in France. Built in the 11th century, St-Germain-des-Près was an important abbey and center of learning during the Middle Ages. At the time of the French Revolution, the monks were expelled and the church was vandalized. But much still remains, including the large tower, the oldest in Paris. King John Casimir of Poland is buried at the church, as is the heart of René Descartes. A small square at the corner of place St-Germain-des-Près and rue de l'Abbaye contains's Picasso's small sculpture of the head of the poet . Guillaume Apollinaire.

3 place St-Germain-des-Près, 6e. ☎ *01-43-24-41-71 Métro: St-Germain-des-Près. Open daily 8 a.m.–8 p.m.*

Église St-Julien le Pauvre

One of the oldest churches in Paris, this small example of Gothic splendor sits in the lovely square René Viviani. Originally constructed in the 12th century, it lies on the original pilgrimage route of St-Jacques de Compostelle to Spain. The oldest tree in Paris, an acacia reputedly planted in 1602, still stands in its garden. The church contains a stunning wooden screen, which encloses a beautiful chancel. Many classical concerts take place here throughout the year.

79 rue Galande, 5e. ☎ *01-43-54-52-16. Métro: St-Michel. Open Mon–Sat 9:30 a.m.–noon and 3–6:30 p.m., Sun 9:30 a.m.–6:30 p.m.*

Église St-Roch

This 17th-century church has the richest trove of painting and sculpture in Paris outside a museum. Beginning on the right aisle, notice the bust of *Maréchal François de Créqui* by Geneviève, *Cardinal Dubois and Priests* by Coustou and paintings by Louis Boulanger in the fourth chapel. The celebrated statue by Falconet, *Le Christ au Jardin des Oliviers* is at the entrance to the choir, and other highlights include *La Nativité* by Anguier (on the altar), the bust of Le Nôtre by Coysevox, and the monument to the painter Mignard by Girardon (both on the left side).

296 rue St-Honoré, 1er. ☎ *01-42-44-13-19. Métro: Tuileries or Palais-Royal-Musée du Louvre. Open Mon–Sat 8 a.m.–7:30 p.m., Sun 8:30 a.m.–7:30 p.m.*

Église St-Severin

A religious building has stood here since the sixth century. The current building, begun in the 13th century, is in flamboyant Gothic style. The west portal came from the church of St-Pierre-aux-Boeufs on the Ile de la Cité before it was demolished in 1837. The dramatic palm-tree shaped vaulting only serves to enhance the brilliant stained glass windows behind the altar depicting the seven sacraments. Also notable is the chapel to the right of the altar, which was designed by Mansart and contains an intensely moving series of etchings by Georges Rouault and an extraordinary rendering of the crucifixion by G. Schneider.

1 rue des Prêtres-St-Severin, 5e. ☎ *01-42-34-93-60. Métro: St-Michel. Open Mon–Sat 11 a.m.–7:30 p.m., Sun 9 a.m.–8:30 p.m.*

Église St-Sulpice

This church, unfinished since the funds ran out in the mid-18th century, houses three of Eugène Delacroix's greatest masterpieces: *Jacob Wrestling with the Angel, Heliodorus Driven from the Temple,* and *St. Michael Vanquishing the Devil*. And that's not all: during both equinoxes and at the midday winter solstice, sunlight hits the bronze meridian line running along the north-south transept, climbs the obelisk to the globe on top and lights the cross. The organ here is one of the grandest in Paris, built in 1781.

Place St-Sulpice, 6e. ☎ *01-42-34-59-65. Métro: St-Sulpice. Open daily 7 a.m.–7:30 p.m.*

La Madeleine

Resembling a Roman temple, the Madeleine is one of Paris's minor landmarks. Although construction started in 1806, the Madeleine wasn't consecrated as a church until 1842. The building was originally intended as a temple to the glory of the Grande Armée (Napoléon's idea, of course). Climb the 28 steps leading to the façade and look back: You'll be able to see rue Royale, place de la Concorde and the obelisk, and, across the Seine, the dome of Invalides. Inside, Rude's *Le Baptême du Christ* is on the left as you enter.

Place de la Madeleine, 8e. ☎ *01-40-07-03-91. Métro: Madeleine. Open daily 8:30 a.m.–6 p.m.*

La Mosquée de Paris

Built from 1922 to 1926 in the Hispano-Moorish style and overlooked by a green and white minaret, this is one of the newer religious establishments in Paris. The complex is divided into three sections for study, leisure, and worship. At the heart is a patio surrounded by finely carved arcades, modeled on the Alhambra in Granada, Spain. The Salon du Thé here is a lovely place for refreshment, as popular for its Arabian Nights décor as it is for its mint teas and baklava. Fountains, North African music, plush banquettes, and mosaics create an exotic but casual hangout for the local student population. The *hammam* (steam baths) are a popular place with trendy types who get massaged and exfoliated here (I hear it's pretty painful!).

39 rue Geoffroy-St-Hilaire, 5e. ☎ *01-43-31-18-14. Métro: Monge. Open daily 10 a.m.–10 p.m.*

Paris's Bridges

When you buy Métro tickets, have a look at the logo. What looks like the profile of a woman in a circle is actually an artistic rendering of the Seine as it meanders through Paris. What the logo doesn't depict are the 35 bridges that Parisians refer to as the river's soul. Here are just a few.

Pont Neuf

The 12-arched Pont Neuf (New Bridge) is probably Paris's most famous bridge, and its design marks the end of the Middle Ages. Started in 1578, it was finally completed in 1603 and opened to the public by Henri IV in 1603. A statue of Henri IV astride a horse divides the bridge into its two spans, which are anchored on the tip of Ile de la Cité.

Métro: Pont Neuf.

Pont St-Michel

The Pont St-Michel has three arches and is decorated with a large letter N which causes some to mistake it for the Pont Neuf. The N in fact refers to Napoleon III who had it built in 1857 to replace the crumbling bridge that preceded it that, up until 1808, still had people living in the houses on the bridge.

Métro: St-Michel.

Petit Pont

The Petit Pont (Little Bridge) crosses the Seine from the Left Bank to the Isle de la Cité. The current one-arched bridge was constructed in 1853 but a bridge has spanned the Seine here since the times of Julius Caesar, who wrote about one in his Commentaries. The Petit Pont crosses the Seine from the Left Bank to the Isle de la Cité. This current incarnation dates from 1853.

Métro: St-Michel.

Pont des Arts

The Pont des Arts is one of Paris's prettiest bridges. This seven-arched pedestrian-only footbridge connecting the Louvre and the Acadèmie Française was opened in 1804, the first iron bridge on the Seine. It suffered much bomb damage during World Wars I and II, and barges often ran into it. It finally collapsed in 1979 and was replaced with this steel version in 1984. You see plenty of artists painting the views of the northern tip of Ile de la Cité, the Louvre, and the Acadèmie Française, as well as pedestrians navigating the potted plants on their way to the Louvre.

Paris by Guided Tour

If you're a newcomer to the wonders of Paris, an orientation tour can help you understand the city's geography. But even if you've been coming to Paris for ten years or more, one of the various tours can introduce you to sides of the city you never knew existed. As you see in this chapter, you have many good reasons for taking a guided tour. Being lucky enough to be shown around by guides whose enthusiasm makes the city come to life can be the high point of your entire trip.

Embarking on a bus

Paris is the perfect city to explore on your own, but if time is a priority, or your energy is at low ebb, consider taking an introductory bus tour. The biggest company is **Cityrama** (4 place des Pyramides, 1er. ☎ 01-44-55-61-00; www.cityrama.fr; Métro: Palais-Royal–Musée du Louvre). The two-hour orientation tour is a bit pricey at 24€ ($28), but kids younger than 12 ride free. Also available are full-day art or history tours (the major artistic and historic sights including a Seine cruise) for 86€ ($99) adults, 43€ ($50) children. Tours to Versailles (from 56€/$64 adults, 28€/$32 children) and to Chartres (51€/$59 adults, 25.50€/$29 children) are a better bargain because they take the hassle out of visiting these monuments. Nighttime illumination tours include a Seine boat cruise and start at 34€ ($39) for adults, 17€ ($20) for children.

Paris L'OpenTour, 13 rue Auber, 9e(☎ 01-42-66-56-56; www.paris-opentour.com; Métro: Havre-Caumartin), from Paris's public transportation system (the RATP), has quickly come to rival Cityrama. Its bright yellow and green convertible double-decker buses take you to four different areas, and you listen to recorded commentary in English through a set of headphones given to you when you board. The *Paris Grand Tour* covers Paris's most central sights, minus the Islands: the Madeleine, Opéra, the Louvre, Notre-Dame, St-Germain-des-Près, Musée d'Orsay, place de la Concorde, Champs-Elysées, Arc de Triomphe, Trocadéro, Eiffel Tower, and Invalides. The *Montmartre tour* goes to the Montmartre funiculaire (but not up the Montmartre hill), the Gare du Nord, Gare de l'Est, and the Grands Boulevards. The *Bastille-Bercy tour* goes east to Notre-Dame, Gare de Lyon, and parc Bercy. The *Montparnasse–St-Germain-des-Près* tour goes to the Jardin du Luxembourg, the Observatory, the Catacombes, Invalides, and St-Germain-des-Près.

L'OpenTour makes its stops at regular city bus stops marked with the L'OpenTour logo. You can board at any of these stops and buy a pass right on the bus. The pass is also on sale at any branch of the Paris Tourist Office, L'OpenTour kiosks near the Malesherbes (8e) and Anvers (9e) bus stops, the RATP office at place de la Madeleine (8e), the Montmartre tourist office (21 place du Tertre), the main Batobus docks on the Seine, and the offices of Paris l'Open Tour at 13 rue Auber.

A one-day pass costs 24€ ($28), 12€ ($14) for children aged 4–11; a two-day pass costs 27€ ($31) for adults, 12€ ($14) for children 4 to 11, and 20€ ($23) for holders of the Paris Visite pass. You can get on or off the bus as many times as you want, which, in my opinion, makes this the more worthwhile tour. The buses run daily every 25 minutes throughout the year from about 9:30 a.m. to 6:30 p.m.

The **RATP** also runs the **Balabus** (☎ 44-68-43-35), a fleet of orange-and-white buses that only runs on Sundays and holidays, noon to 8 p.m. from April to September. Routes run between the Gare de Lyon and the Grand Arche de La Défense, in both directions, and cost just one Métro ticket. Look for the *Bb* symbol across the side of the bus and on signs posted along the route.

Touring by boat

One of the most romantic and beautiful ways to see Paris is by taking a sightseeing boat cruise up and down Paris's waterways. In addition to the Seine River cruises (see the "Paris's top attraction: The Seine river cruise" sidebar earlier this chapter), try a longer and more unusual tour with **Paris Canal** (☎ 01-42-40-96-97; www.pariscanal.com; Métro: Bastille). Its three-hour cruises leave the Musée d'Orsay at 9:30 a.m. and end at parc de la Villette. The boat passes under the Bastille and enters the Canal St-Martin for a lazy journey along the tree-lined quai Jemmapes. You cruise under bridges and through many locks. The boat leaves the parc de la Villette at 2:30 p.m. for the same voyage in reverse. Reservations are essential. The trip costs 16€ ($18) for adults, 12€ (14) for ages 12 to 25 and older than 60, and 9€ ($10) for children 4 to 11.

If you have restless young children, the wait for the water to rise at each lock may prove too long. You may want to consider one of the shorter Seine boat trips mentioned in Chapter 17.

Canauxrama (☎ 01-42-39-15-00; www.canauxrama.com; Métro: Jaurès) offers two-and-a-half-hour tours similar to Paris Canal's at 9:45 a.m. and 2:30 p.m., leaving from Port l'Arsenal in the 12e and ending at the parc de la Villette in the 19e. The cost is 14€ ($16) for adults, 11€ ($13) for ages 12 to 25, 8€ ($9.20) for children 6 to 11, and free for children younger than 6. Reservations are required.

Horsing around — a guided tour at two horsepower

The Citroën 2CV (meaning two *chevaux,* or two horsepower) was to France what the VW Beetle was to the United States, and it was France's most popular car from its debut before World War II up to 1990, when Citroën stopped production. Now you can tour Paris in its best-loved car with this new outfit, **4 Roues Sous 1 Parapluie** (Four Wheels Under an Umbrella, ☎ inside France **08-00-80-06-31;** outside France 33-6-67-32-26-68; www.4roues-sous-1parapluie.com). Run by twenty-something Florent Dargnies, one to three people can take one of three tours around the City of Light: the 75€ ($86) Essential Tour, a circuit of the most popular monuments; the 130€ ($150) Magic Tour, which goes to the Essential Tour sites then visits the most beautiful neighborhoods of the city and, if traffic permits, stops by the Moulin Rouge; or a 150€ ($173) design-your-own three-hour minimum tour (the company suggests a trip out to Versailles). Every driver speaks English and French. Cost is per vehicle, not per person, but note these are small cars and a three-hour three-person (adult) tour could get uncomfortable. Reservations required by e-mail at info@4roues-sous-1parapluie.com or by telephone.

Walking your way across Paris

WICE (20 bd. du Montparnasse, 15e. ☎ **01-45-66-75-50,** outside France, 01-45-66-75-50, inside France; Fax: 01-40-65-96-53; www.wice-paris.org; Métro: Duroc or Falguière), a nonprofit cultural association for Paris's English-speaking community, gives comprehensive walking tours of Paris. The walking tours are in-depth tours for travelers who want to do more than skim the surface. Recent tours included: *Renaissance* and *Classical Paris: The Marais,* and tours of *Belleville-Ménilmontant* and *Montmartre.* The commentary is always excellent, and the guides are experts in their respective fields.

Tours vary in length and cost, but most start at 18€ ($21) for a two- to three-hour tour. Paris residents and returning visitors love these tours, so book a few weeks ahead to reserve a spot. Unfortunately, the Web site does not handle online payments, so you have to send in payment or pay in person at the WICE office in Paris.

Paris Walks (☎ **01-48-09-21-40;** www.paris-walks.com) was founded by Peter and Oriel Caine and has become a popular English-language outfit whose two-hour guided walks cost 10€ ($11.50) for adults, 7€ ($8.05) for students younger than 25, and 5€ ($5.75) for children. Specific tours concentrate on a single neighborhood *(The Village of Montmartre, The Historic Marais, St-Germain-des-Près),* a particular theme *(Hemingway's Paris),* or perhaps a single sight *(Les Invalides, the Paris Sewers).* Check the Web site or call for the designated meeting place.

Paris à Pied (☎ **800-594-9535** in the United States; www.parisapied.com) has three three-hour tours geared to first-time visitors to Paris. Tours cost $45 (they prefer to be paid in dollars) and are made up of no more than six people. Tours take in the heart of Old Paris, the Latin Quarter, Montmartre, and the Marais.

French Links (☎ 01-45-77-01-63; www.frenchlinks.com) lets you cus-
tomize your tour from a two-hour walking tour, to a full-day cultural tour.
Trained, experienced guides with degrees in art and history lead you on
such walks as *Paris in a Basket Gourmet Market Tour, Parisian Art Nouveau,
The Liberation of Paris, Photographer's Walking Tour,* and many others. And
they're happy to help you design your own tour. The talks are entertaining
and fun, geared to everyone from high school and college-age students to
retirees. Tours start at $225 for one to six people for two hours. All tours
must be pre-booked and prepaid with a U.S. bank check or by credit card
using their secure server.

Seeing Paris by bike

The banks of the Seine are closed to cars and opened to pedestrians and
cyclists March to November each Sunday from 10 a.m. to 5 p.m. It may
not make much of a dent in the air quality, but bicycling is a fun and
healthy way to do some sightseeing. For a bike map of Paris, pick up
the *Plan Vert* from one of the branches of the Paris tourist office.

The RATP (which runs the city's buses and subways) in partnership with
the mayor's office rents bikes through its *Roue Libre* program. To rent a
bike, you need to put down a 150€ ($173) deposit per bike by traveler's
check or with cash and show a passport or driver's license. Costs are 7€
($8.05) per weekday, 15€ ($17) for five days, 30€ ($35) for the week.
On weekends you pay 4€ ($4.60) per hour, 10€ ($12) for a half day, 15€
($17) for the eight hours between 9 a.m. and 5 p.m. and 25€ ($29) for the
weekend. A Roue Libre location is at 1 passage Mondétour, in front of
120 de la rue Rambuteau, 1er (☎ 08-10-44-15-34; Métro: Les Halles);
open daily 9 a.m. to 7 p.m. Roue Libre also gives 24€ ($28), three-hour
guided tours of Paris (see Chapter 11.) There are rumors that this company may shut its doors in the near future; it's a good idea to call before
you go.

It's not just bike tours you can take with **Fat Tire Bike Tours** (24 rue
Edgar Faure, 15e ☎ 01-56-58-10-54; www.fattirebiketoursparis.
com), formerly Mike's Bike Tours. This American-accented outfit conducts tours on the Segway scooter, the first of its kind in Paris (70€/$81
for a four-hour day or night tour). Day tours leave daily March 1 through
November 30 at 10:30 a.m. Night tours run from April 1 through October
31 at 6:30 p.m. There are no night tours on June 21st and July 14th.

Look for the yellow meeting-point sign in front of the Pilier Sud (South
Pillar) of the Eiffel Tower (*Pilier Sud* is spelled out above the ticket
booth) for the bike tour; look for the guide on the Segway in the same
place for the Segway tour. Friendly guides take you on day or night bike
tours of the city (22€/$25 day students, 24€/$28 adults; night tours are
26€/$30 students, 28€/$32 adults, 44€/$51 and 48€/$55 both tours). The
tours last three to four hours. Day tours are at 11 a.m. and 3 p.m. May 15
through July 31, and 11 a.m. only March 1 through May 14 and August 1
through November 30. Night tours, which are beautiful (especially the

ride past the Grand Pyramid through the courtyard at the Louvre), take place at 7 p.m. nightly April 1 through October 31, and at 7 p.m. Sunday, Tuesday, and Thursday in the months of March and November . Reservations are optional for day tours but required for night and Segway tours. Bike rental is available at 2€ ($2.30) per hour, 15€ ($17) for 24 hours, 25€ ($29) for a weekend, and 50€ ($58) per week.

Fat Tire has its own tourist office, where owner Dave Mebane says English-speakers from all over Paris like to congregate. The office has bathrooms, free daily storage for bags and luggage, snacks, drinks (including Starbucks coffee), computers, CD burner, and low-cost Internet access, as well as Air France bus tickets and telephone cards for sale. If you're homesick for the United States, or English-speakers in general, this is the place to be!

Paris à Vélo C'est Sympa (☎ 01-48-87-60-01; www.parisvelosympa.com; Métro: Richard Lenoir; meeting place 22 rue A Baudin, 11e) has three-hour *Heart of Paris* tours of Paris at 10 a.m. Friday through Monday from April to November, and Saturday and Sunday at 10 a.m. from November to March. Reservations are required, and most tours are in French (call or stop in for times of English-speaking tours). The company also has night *(nocturne)* bike tours Saturday at 8:30 p.m. May to September. Other tours include *Paris Contrasts, Unusual Paris, Strange Paris,* and *Paris at Dawn.* Prices for all tours are 32.50€ ($37) for adults, 28€ ($32) for ages 12 to 26, and 18€ ($21) for ages 10 and 11. Children younger than 10 are not permitted. Daylong tours for groups can also be arranged; call for information. Bike rental is available at 12.50€ ($14) a day, 9.50€ ($11) for a half-day, and 24€ ($28) for the weekend. Tandem bike rentals are 25€ ($29) a day, 19€ ($22) for a half-day, and 48€ ($55) for the weekend. A 250€ ($288) deposit is required for bike rentals, 600€ ($690) deposit for tandem bikes. Note: There are rumors that this outfit may be going out of business; call before you go.

Chapter 12

Shopping the Local Stores

*P*aris simply has some of the best shopping in the world, and every first-time visitor to Paris should set aside a little time for it. Even the window-shopping is exquisite: enticing goods are arranged just so in windows — and the prices are listed! Believe it or not, bargains DO exist here. From the toniest haute couture shop, to the hidden *dêpot-vente* (resale shop) selling last year's Yves Saint Laurent at fabulously reduced prices, even nonshoppers find something. This chapter gives you an overview of the Parisian shopping scene, providing hints about where to find the bargains, how to get it all home, and even how to get some of your money back.

Surveying the Scene

The cost of shopping in Paris isn't always astronomical. If you plan only to buy haute couture clothing, then yes, you'll pay top prices. However, Paris has many stores that sell clothing and goods at prices comparable to what you'd pay in the United States. And some items in Paris are cheaper even than they are in your hometown, including some French and European brands of perfume and cosmetics, shoes, clothing from French-based companies such as Petit Bateau and Lacoste, and French-made porcelain, cookware, and glassware. You'll obviously pay more for any name brand imported from the United States, such as Donna Karan and Calvin Klein, and for any souvenirs in areas heavily frequented by tourists.

 Keep in mind that a 19.6% value-added tax (VAT) is tacked on to the price of most products, which means that most things cost less at home. (For details on getting a VAT refund, see the next section "Getting the VAT back.") Appliances, paper products, housewares, computer supplies, electronics, and CDs are notoriously expensive in France, but

Paris Shopping

Jacques Papin **59**
La Chaise Longue **80**
La City **31**
La Clef des Marques **69**
Lafayette Gourmet **32**
La Maison du
  Chocolat **22**
La Maison du Miel **20**
La Maison Ivre **63**
La Marelle **41**
La Samaritaine **55**
Le Bon Marché **26**
Le Depôt-Vente de Buci,
  Le Depôt-Vente de
  Bourbon **64**
Legrand Filles et Fils **44**
Le Drugstore **9**
Le Jardin des Vignes **84**
Le Louvre des
  Antiquaires **46**
Le Mouton à Cinq
  Pattes **28**
Le Village St-Paul **76**
Les Caves Augé **11**
Librarie La Hune **62**
Lumicristal **35**
Madelios **15**
Mango **58**
Marché aux Puces de la
  Porte de St-Ouen **29**
Marché aux Puces de la
  Porte de Vanves **1**
Mi-prix **3**
Monic **77**
Morgan **70**
Natalys **9**
Nicolas **16**
Nip Shop **5**
1-2-3 **47**
Passage Brady **38**
Passage Choiseul **42**
Passage des
  Panoramas **37**
Passage du Caire **40**
Passage du Grand Cerf **50**
Passage Jouffroy **36**
Passage Verdeau **33**
Pylones **74**
Réciproque **6**
Rodier **7**
Rue d'Alésia **2**
Rue Paradis **34**
Rue St-Placide **27**
Shakespeare and
  Company **73**
Shoe Bizz **67**
Talmaris **4**
Tartine et Chocolat **10**
Tati Or **78**
Ted Baker **81**
Verrerie des Halles **48**
Viaduc des Arts **75**
Village Voice **65**
Why? **83**
Zara **53**

Alessi **21**
Anna Lowe **19**
Annexe des Créateurs **13**
Antoine et Lili **39**
Au Nain Bleu **23**
Au Printemps **12**
Baccarat **34**
BHV **79**
Biche de Bère **57**
Bijoux Burma **8**
Bonpoint **60**
Cacharel **66**
Cedre Rouge **25**
Colette **45**
Comptoir des Cotonniers **82**
Conforama **56**
Cop-Copine **51**

Corinne Sarrut **61**
Déhillerin **49**
Du Pareil au Même **54**
Eric et Lydie **57**
Etam **72**
Façonnable **18**
Fauchon **17**
Fnac Junior **68**
Galerie Colbert **41**
Galerie Vivienne **43**
Galeries Lafayette **32**
Gelati **71**
Gibert Joseph **72**
Guerrisold **30**
H&M **52**
Hédiard **14**
Jacadi **24**

checking out prices of French products before your trip can help you
recognize a bargain.

Probably the best time to find a bargain in Paris is during the government-
mandated twice-annual sales (*soldes*) in January and July when merchandise gets marked down 30% to 50% or more. Parisians line up outside their
favorite stores the first days of the sales. If you can brave the crowds, you
just may find the perfect designer outfit at a fraction of its retail price.

Generally, store hours are Monday through Saturday from 9:30 a.m.
(sometimes 10 a.m.) to 7 p.m., and later on Thursday evenings, without
a break for lunch. Some smaller stores are closed Monday or Monday
mornings, and break for lunch for one to three hours, beginning at
around 1 p.m., but this schedule is becoming increasingly rare. Small
stores also may be closed for all or part of August and on some days
around Christmas and Easter. Sunday shopping is gradually making
inroads in Paris but is limited mostly to tourist areas; try the Carrousel
du Louvre at the Louvre, rue de Rivoli across from the Louvre, rue des
Francs-Bourgeois in the Marais, and the Champs-Elysées. The department
stores are open the five Sundays before Christmas, and occasionally one
or two Sundays during the annual sales.

Politeness is imperative when you shop in Paris. Always greet the sales-
people with *"Bonjour, madame"* or *"Bonjour, monsieur"* when you arrive
(the Glossary in Appendix B can help with pronunciation). And regardless of whether you buy anything, say, *"Merci, au revoir"* (Thank you,
goodbye) when you leave.

Clothing sizes are different around the world. In French men's trousers,
for example, add 10 to the waist size you wear in U.S. clothing to get
the French size. To determine what size you need to look for, check
out Table 12-1, which lists conversions for U.S. and Continental sizes.

Table 12-1   The Right Fit: Size Conversions

U.S.	Continental	U.S.	Continental
Women's Clothes		Women's Shoes	
4	36	5	36
6	38	6	37
8	40	7	38
10	42	8	39
12	44	9	40
14	46	10	41

U.S.	Continental	U.S.	Continental
Men's Clothes		*Men's Shoes*	
14½	37	7	39½
15	38	8	41
15½	39	9	42
16	41	10	43
16½	42	11	44½
17	43	12	46

Getting the VAT back

Whenever you spend more than 175€ to 182€ ($201 to $209) in a single store, you're entitled to a partial refund on the value-added tax (VAT), also referred to in France as TVA. The refund, however, isn't automatic. Food, wine, and tobacco don't count, and the refund is granted only on purchases that you take out of the country — not on merchandise that you ship home. The amount of the refund varies; it's 12% in Galeries Lafayette and Printemps, and it may be anywhere from 15% to 18% at smaller boutiques.

When applying for a refund, you must show the store clerk your passport to prove your eligibility. You're then given an export sales document (in triplicate — two pink sheets and a green one), which you must sign, and usually an envelope addressed to the store.

 When you're shopping in a store that participates in the Europe Tax-Free shopping program (indicated by the *Tax-Free* sticker in the store's windows), you're given a Tax-Free Shopping Cheque that shows the amount of refund owed to you when you leave the country. Have this check stamped by a customs officer in the airport, then take it to the special Global Refund counter for an instant refund. Global Refund offices are located within the American Express Bureaux de Change in the Charles de Gaulle airport: Terminal 1 departures level at Gate 26, Terminal 2A Gate 5, Terminal 2B Gate 7, Terminal 2C Gate 5, Terminal 2F Gate 6. In Orly Airport, there is only one Global Refund office in Orly South near the international baggage claim on the departures level. For more information, contact Global Refund (www.globalrefund.com).

Department stores that cater to foreign visitors, such as Au Printemps and Galeries Lafayette, have special *détaxe* areas where clerks prepare your invoices for you. You must present your passport. Otherwise, when you leave the country, bring all documents to the airport's *détaxe* booth and have a Customs official stamps them. To receive an immediate cash refund, you pay a fee of about 4.60€ ($5.30). Make sure you get the refund in euro, which offer the best rate when you exchange them back to your own country's currency. If you prefer to wait for your refund, enclose the appropriate document (the pink one) in the store envelope the clerk provided when you bought your merchandise and mail it from the airport from which you are leaving the European Union. The wait for a refund is anywhere from one to three months. Travelers leaving from Charles-de-Gaulle Airport can visit the *détaxe* refund point in Terminal 1 on the departure level between Gate 14 and 16; in Terminal 2, Hall B between Doors 6 and 7 near the baggage claim area or in Hall A between Doors 5 and 6; and in Terminal T9, near the departure gates. At Orly, the *détaxe* booth is in Orly West between Halls 3 and 4 on the departure level.

 Whenever you're claiming a tax refund, try to arrive at the airport as early as possible because you must show everything you're declaring to a Customs official, and you may have to wait in line. Plus, after you finish with *détaxe*, you must stand in line again to check your luggage.

If you're traveling by train, go to the *détaxe* area in the station before boarding because you can't have your refund documents processed on the train. Give the three sheets to the Customs official, who stamps them and returns a pink and a green copy to you. Keep the green copy and mail the pink copy to the store.

Your reimbursement is either mailed as a check (in euro) or credited to your credit-card account, which is better, as you may find it difficult to cash a check for euro in your own country. If you don't receive your tax refund within four months, write to the store, giving the date of purchase, and the location where the forms were given to Customs officials. Include a photocopy of your green refund sheet.

Getting your goodies through Customs

Returning **U.S. citizens,** who've been away for 48 hours or more, are allowed to bring back, once every 30 days, $800 worth of merchandise duty-free (a *duty* is a tax). You're charged a flat duty of 2% on the next $1,000 worth of purchases; on gifts, the duty-free limit is $100 (any item that costs more than $100 is subject to the full tax). You can't bring fresh food into the United States (ignore what the people in duty-free tell you, fresh meats and cheeses are NOT allowed); canned foods, however, are allowed.

Citizens of the United Kingdom and **Ireland** who are returning from a European Union country have no limit on what they can bring back from an EU country, as long as the items are for personal use (including gifts), and the necessary duty and taxes have been paid. Limits are set at: 3,200 cigarettes, 200 cigars, 3kg smoking tobacco, 10 liters of spirits, 90 liters of wine, and 110 liters of beer.

Canada allows its citizens a once-a-year C$750 exemption after spending seven days out of the country, and you're allowed to bring back duty-free: 200 cigarettes, 1.5 liters of wine or 1.14 liters of liquor, and 50 cigars. In addition, you can mail gifts to Canada from abroad at the value of C$60 a day, provided they're unsolicited and don't contain alcohol, or tobacco, or advertising matter. Write on the package *Unsolicited gift, under $60 value.* All valuables need to be declared on the Y-38 form before your departure from Canada, including serial numbers of valuables you already own, such as expensive foreign cameras.

The duty-free allowance in **Australia** is A$400 or A$200 for those younger than 18. Upon returning to Australia, citizens can bring in 250 cigarettes or 250 grams of loose tobacco, and 1.125 liters of alcohol. If you're returning with valuable goods that you already own, such as foreign-made cameras, you need to file form B263.

The duty-free allowance for **New Zealand** is NZ$700. Citizens older than 17 can bring in 200 cigarettes or 50 cigars or 250 grams of tobacco (or a mixture of all three as long as the combined weight doesn't exceed 250 grams), plus 4.5 liters of wine or beer or 1.125 liters of liquor.

Checking Out the Big Names

Two of Paris's major department stores, Au Printemps and Galeries Lafayette, offer visitors a 10% discount coupon, good in most depart-ments. If your hotel or travel agent doesn't give you one of these coupons (they're sometimes attached to a city map), you can ask for it at the stores' welcome desks; the clerks speak English.

Check out the "Paris Shopping" map for the locations of the stores listed here.

Au Printemps

Au Printemps is one of Paris's largest department stores, and a recent ren-ovation costing millions of euro has made it one of Paris's best. Merchandise is sold in three different buildings: Printemps de l'Homme (menswear), Printemps de la Maison (furniture and accessories), and Printemps de la Mode (women and children's fashion). Designers include Dolce & Gabbana and Burberry. Fashion shows take place under the 1920s glass dome (7th floor) at 10 a.m. every Tuesday year-round, and every Friday from March to October. You can easily spend a day here, and there are eight restaurants scattered throughout the store's three buildings. The beauty department in the main building is, according to Printemps, the largest in the world. There is a fabulous selection of lingerie in the base-ment level of the main building, as well. Détaxe is offered at 12% here. *64 bd. Haussmann, 9e.* ☎ *01-42-82-57-87. Métro: Havre-Caumartin. Open Mon–Sat 9:35 a.m.–7 p.m.; open until 10 p.m. Thursdays.*

BHV

Near the Marais, BHV (*Bazar de l'Hôtel de Ville*) sells the usual clothing, cosmetics, luggage, and leatherware at decent prices, but it's really worth a visit because of its giant basement-level hardware store with everything you need to fix up your home plus Café les Bricollations, decorated like your grandfather's old workshop and serving light lunches and snacks. *52 rue de Rivoli, 1er.* ☎ *01-42-74-90-00. Métro: Hôtel de Ville.*

Galeries Lafayette

Merchandise here ranges from good to excellent with lots of deals during the sales. Look for women's clothing from Sonia Rykiel, Comptoir des Cotonniers, and agnès b. And check out the gourmet grocery store, Lafayette Gourmet, in the men's store. Main store restaurants include: Häagen-Dazs, Lina's gourmet sandwiches, Fauchon tea room and restaurant, McDonald's, Café Sushi, and Lafayette Café, which has great views of Paris (it's a self-serve cafeteria and my personal favorite). If you don't already have one, ask at the front desk for the 10% discount coupon, good in most departments. All the advertising has only benefited Galeries Lafayette: this store gets downright crowded, and if you visit during the sales, pace yourself or you can become thoroughly fatigued. Détaxe is 12% here.

40 bd. Haussmann, 9e. ☎ *01-42-82-34-56. Métro: Opéra or Chaussée-d'Antin.*

La Samaritaine

The department store Samaritaine also sells, clothing, stationery, accessories, jewelry and beauty items but has long suffered an inferiority complex to the overrun Galeries Lafayette and Aux Printemps. Not for much longer, however: LVMH (Moet Hennessy Louis Vuitton), the owner of such ultra-luxury stores as Le Bon Marché, and Sephora, is the new owner, and renovations are already underway. Look for signs in its main building to the *panorama,* a free observation point with a wonderful view of Paris that actually takes in the Eiffel Tower. (Catch the elevator to the 9th floor, then climb two flights of stairs to the 11th floor panorama. On the 10th floor is a terrace, also with good views, where meals are served.) Located between the Louvre and the Pont Neuf, La Samaritaine is housed in four buildings with Art Nouveau touches, and has an Art Deco facade on quai du Louvre. The fifth floor of store No. 2 has a nice, inexpensive restaurant.

19 rue de la Monnaie, 1er. ☎ *01-40-41-20-20. Métro: Pont-Neuf or Châtelet–Les Halles.*

Le Bon Marché

This is Paris's only Left Bank department store, and a recent renovation expanded its clothing department for women in the space above its huge supermarket next door, once home to an antiques market. Elegant, but small enough to be manageable, much of the store's merchandise is exquisite and includes designers such as Sonia Rykiel, Bensimon, Vivienne Westwood, Burberry, and Yohji Yamamoto. The main store's third floor is particularly renowned for its large shoe selection and grand lingerie department (where dressing rooms have phones to summon your salesperson!). But it isn't cheap. Make sure to visit Le Grand Épicerie next door, where you can buy everything from toilet paper to truffles. A new café, Delicabar in the space above Le Grand Épicerie, has a menu divided into tasty sweet and salty offerings.

24 rue de Sèvres, 7e. ☎ *01-44-39-80-00. Métro: Sèvres-Babylone.*

Le Drugstore

This stunningly modern glass landmark on the Champs-Élysées closed for two years for a facelift by French and American architects that cost millions of euro. Though not a department store (it's more a mini-mall), it's included here because it was an important part of Parisian culture in the 1960s, and its owner, ad giant Publicis, is hoping to regain that status again. Inside is a brasserie run by a disciple of multi-starred French chef Alain Ducasse (wait staff is clothed by French designer Jean-Charles Castelbajac), an invitation-only restaurant, Privé Marcel, an international newsstand, gift shop, a drug store (naturally), gourmet food, wine and cigar stores, and a Shu Uemura beauty products shop. Also here are movie theaters and a cool bar with a terrace overlooking the Champs and the Arc de Triomphe. Owned by Publicis since the late 50s, Le Drugstore was the height of cool in the 1960s when it was one of the few places in Paris you could pick up a pack of cigarettes or a magazine at 2 a.m. Publicis is hoping its new revamping will make it the hip place it once was while helping to push the Champs-Elysées into the 21st century.

133 av du Champs-Elysées, 8e. ☎ *01-44-43-79-00. Métro: Georges V, Charles-de Gaulle-Étoile.*

Monoprix

This is the Target of Paris, where you can find wonderful clothing at reasonable prices along with accessories, low-priced cosmetics, lingerie, and housewares. Many locations also have large grocery stores. The Champs-Elysées branch at number 52 is open until midnight Monday to Saturday.

Various locations. ☎ *01-40-75-11-02.*

Tati

For the most part, Tati (originally opened to cater to budget-conscious shoppers) is frankly tacky, but where else can you find the occasional funky top for 2€ ($2.30)? Or wear-for-one-season shoes at 10€ ($12)? In fact, you never know what you may find here If you dig; the occasional gem rewards those who are persistent. Tati also has a jewelry branch called Tati Or (see "Gifts and Jewelry" later in this chapter, eyewear (Tati Optic) and a travel agency (Tati Vacances). At press time, there were rumors of Tati's demise due to large losses in all its branches, so you may want to call ahead to see if the store is up and running when you visit.

4 bd. Rochechouart, 18e. ☎ *01-55-29-50-00. Métro: Barbés-Rochechouart. Other branches are located at 106 rue Faubourg du Temple, 11e (*☎ *01-43-57-92-80; Métro: Belleville), and 76 av. Clichy, 17e (*☎ *01-58-22-28-90; Métro: La Fourche).*

Taking It to the Street (Markets)

The huge **Marché aux Puces de la Porte de St-Ouen**, 18e, purportedly the largest flea market in the world, is a real shopping adventure and although you probably won't snag a bargain, it's still well worth the visit! Open Saturday, Sunday, and Monday, it features several thousand stalls, carts, shops, and vendors selling everything from vintage clothing (see if you can find the vendor whose specialty is wearing her merchandise from the mid-1800s) to antique chandeliers, paintings, furniture, and toys. You need to arrive early to snag the deals — if you can find any. The best times for bargains are right at opening time and just before closing time. To reach the market, take the Métro to the Porte de Clignancourt stop; exit onto avenue de la Porte de Clignancourt. (You can also exit onto boulevard Omano, which turns into avenue de la Porte de Clignancourt.) Head north a block and cross beneath an underpass; the markets begin on your left. Open Saturday through Monday 9 a.m. to 8 p.m.

 Starting at the underpass just past the Clignancourt Métro stop, you'll see stalls selling cheap junk, but don't stop here! Turn left onto rue des Rosiers, the market's main street. Be alert; pickpockets roam the markets, especially the stalls on the periphery.

 Don't pay the ticketed price or the price the vendor first quotes you; always haggle. You can usually get at least 10% off.

Visitors to Paris usually choose the Clignancourt market over the convivial market at **Porte de Vanves**, 14e, a gem waiting to be discovered. Probably the smallest of the fleas, it's nevertheless a good place to browse among friendly dealers. To reach the market, take the Métro to the Porte de Vanves stop; exit at boulevard Brune; follow it east to avenue Georges Lafenestre, and turn right. Open Saturday and Sunday 8:30 a.m. to 1:00 p.m. A cheap clothing market takes its place after 1 p.m. Other flea markets include one at **Porte Montreuil** (Métro: Porte de Montreuil) and another at **place d'Aligre**, 14e (Métro: Ledru-Rollin, open 9 a.m. to noon). Much more downscale, these markets give the term "junk" a whole new meaning.

Scoring Bargains in Paris

The savvy Parisian waits for sales, knows the addresses of discounters, and knows that some of the best fashion deals are found in resale shops that deal directly with designer showrooms for half-price designer clothing that has been worn on a runway or used in a fashion shoot. And four words are the key to her world: *soldes* (sales), *dégriffés* (designerwear with the labels cut out), *stock* (overstock), and *dépot-vente* (resale). Most *dépôts-vente* are on the Right Bank in the 8e, 16e, and 17e arrondissements. If you're itching for a bargain after shopping for full-price items, visit one of the streets where discount stores abound:

✔ **Rue d'Alésia,** 14e (Métro: Alésia), is filled with French designer discount outlets selling last year's overstock at up to 70% below retail. These stock boutiques are more downscale than their sister shops; be prepared to rifle through the racks to find the gems. Outlets include **Chevignon** at No. 12, **Sonia Rykiel** at No. 54, **Cacharel** at No. 114, **Sergent Major** at No. 82, **Toute Compte Fait** at No. 101, **Jacadi** at No. 116, and **Naf Naf** at No. 143.

✔ **Rue Paradis,** 10e (Métro: Poissonnière), is filled with wholesale china and porcelain stores such as **Paradis Porcelaine** at No. 56 and **La Tisanière Porcelaine** at No. 21.

✔ **Rue St-Placide,** 6e (Métro: Sèvres-Babylone), is also a street of dreams with many discount stores, including **Le Mouton à Cinq Pattes** (8 rue St-Placide, 6e) and **Kookaï** (15Ter). Discounted no-name shoes and housewares are also sold here.

✔ **Boulevard de Rochechouart,** 18e (Métro: Anvers or Barbès-Rochechouart), It's certainly not the prettiest of Paris's boulevards and it can get awfully crowded, but this is a street of deep discounts with multiple branches of **Tati** (at 4 and 18) and resale shop **Guerrisol,** among others. If you have time to spare after visiting Sacré-Coeur, head south from the cathedral down rue Steinkerque or rue Seveste and make a left onto boulevard de Rochechouart.

You can also try these discount stores spread throughout the city.

Anna Lowe

If you consider only the very best designers, this store is for you. It carries Yves Saint Laurent, Chanel, and Giorgio Armani at a steep discount — at least 50%. The clothes may be overstock or last year's models with samples from the runway. Most of the staff speaks English.

Keep in mind that a steep discount off an incredibly expensive couture price can still mean an expensive item.

104 rue du Faubourg-St-Honoré, 8e. ☎ *01-42-66-11-32 or 01-40-06-02-42. Métro: Miromesnil or St-Phillippe-de-Roule.*

Annexe des Créateurs

This is made up of two stores — one devoted to selling gently worn designer daywear, the other to barely worn evening wear. If you don't mind wearing resale togs, you could save yourself between 40% and 75% off the retail price of the items. The store has been described as an Ali Baba's cave entirely devoted to luxury, and the description is apt. You find names like Chanel, Dior, Thierry Mugler, Louis Vuitton, Hermès, Vivienne Westwood and Jean-Paul Gaultier.

19 rue Godot de Mauroy, 9e. ☎ *01-42-65-46-40. Métro: Hauvre-Caumartin or Madeleine.*

Bonpoint

These are the kind of clothes you see royalty wearing — hand-smocked dresses, lace collars, velvet — and the prices usually reflect this level of craftsmanship. However, this Bonpoint branch sells end-of-season clothes at reduced prices; it's particularly good during the yearly sales in January and July.

42 rue de l'Université, 7e. ☎ *01-40-20-10-55. Métro: Rue-du-Bac.*

Guerrisol

If you're in the area, this large resale shop, comparable to Goodwill or the Salvation Army, is worth a peek. There are loads of clothes and accessories for men and women that will look just great after they're cleaned up. Note: there are two #17s, this is located next door to a Marionnaud shop.

17 bd. de Rochechouart, 9e. ☎ *01-45-26-38-92. Métro: Anvers.*

La Clef des Marques

If you're missing the Doc Martens you left home, you can buy a pair at this large store that also sells baby clothes, lingerie, and end-of-series couture items. Racks are overfull so you have to hunt a bit for a bargain.

124 bd. Raspail, 6e. ☎ *01-45-49-31-00. Métro: Notre-Dame des Champs.*

La Marelle

Located in the wonderful Galerie Vivienne, this store resells clothing from some of the top designers in very good condition.

21 Galerie Vivienne, 2e. ☎ *01-42-60-08-19. Métro: Palais Royal.*

Le Depôt-Vente de Buci Bourbon

This resale store is actually two shops right next to each other with vintage and not-so-old clothing and accessories for men and women along with gently used furniture.

4 and 6 rue Bourbon Le Chateau, 6e. ☎ *01-46-34-45-05. Métro: St-Germain-des Prés or Mabillon.*

Le Mouton à Cinq Pattes

Visit "the sheep with five legs" when you're feeling energetic — racks are simply packed and the store is often crowded. It carries extremely well-known designer names (most of the tags, though, are ripped out) on women's, men's, and children's clothing, shoes, and accessories. The stock changes constantly, and if you see something you like, grab it; it won't be there the next time.

8 and 18 rue St-Placide, 6e. ☎ *01-45-48-86-26 for all stores. Métro: Sèvres-Babylone. Another branch is located at 138 bd. St-Germain (☎ 01-43-26-49-25).*

Mi-prix

Karl Lagerfeld, Alaia, Missoni, and Gianfranco Ferré are just some of the labels that are steeply discounted in this men's discount store. *27 bd. Victor, 15e.* ☎ *01-48-28-42-48. Métro: Balard or Porte de Versailles.*

Nip Shop

Yves Saint Laurent, Sonia Rykiel, and Guy Laroche are big labels here, but lesser-known designers are also represented. It's in the same neighborhood as Réciproque (see the next listing), but much more intimate. *6 rue Edmond-About, 16e.* ☎ *01-45-04-66-19. Métro: Rue de la Pompe.*

Réciproque

This series of *depôt-ventes* (resale shops) on rue de la Pompe is the largest in Paris for men, women, and children. Exhaust yourself among the jewelry, furs, belts, antiques, and designer purses (Hermès, Gucci, and Vuitton are just a few of the names I've seen). This store is for shoppers willing to spend upwards of $1,000 on a gently-worn Chanel suit, less for other designers. Mid-range labels are also well represented. *89–123 rue de la Pompe, 16e.* ☎ *01-47-04-30-28. Métro: Rue de la Pompe. Closed Monday.*

Hitting the Great Shopping Neighborhoods

The shopping in Paris is terrific, and you don't need *beaucoup* (lots of) bucks (except in the 8e) to afford it. Great deals for every taste and dollar amount can be found. Read this section to get a significant head start in the hunt.

The land of luxe: The 8e

When people around the world need a luxury-shopping fix, they go to Paris, and all you have to do is head for the 8e to see why. Nearly every French designer is based on two streets — **avenue Montaigne** (Métro: Alma-Marceau, Franklin-D-Roosevelt) and **rue du Faubourg St-Honoré** (Métro: Concorde) — where prices more than 1,000€ ($1,150) are normal, and snooty sales clerks are par for the course. You can still have a good time window-shopping here, even if you don't have a platinum card.

Although avenue Montaigne and rue du Faubourg St-Honoré boast some of the same big designer names, they are completely different in temperament. Avenue Montaigne is wide, graceful, lined with chestnut trees, and undeniably hip, attracting the likes of **Dolce & Gabbana** at No. 22 (☎ **01-42-25-68-78**) and **Prada** at No. 10 (☎ **01-53-23-99-40**). Other designers on this street include **Céline**, 36 avenue Montaigne (☎ **01-56-89-07-92**); **Chanel**, 42 avenue Montaigne (☎ **01-47-23-74-12**); **Christian Dior**, 30 avenue Montaigne (☎ **01-40-73-54-44**); **Escada**, 53 avenue

Montaigne (☎ 01-42-89-83-45); **Ferragamo,** 45 avenue Montaigne (☎ 01-47-23-36-37); **Gucci,** 60 avenue Montaigne (☎ 01-56-69-80-80); **Ungaro,** 2 avenue Montaigne (☎ 01-53-57-00-00); and **Valentino,** 17 avenue Montaigne (☎ 01-47-23-64-61).

Rue du Faubourg St-Honoré is jammed with shoppers walking along the small, narrow sidewalks. **Prada** is located at No. 6 (☎ 01-58-18-63-30); **Yves St-Laurent** for women is at No. 38 (☎ 01-42-65-74-59). Begin at the rue Royale intersection and head west. Other designer stores you run across here include **Ferragamo,** 50 rue du Faubourg St-Honoré (☎ 01-43-12-96-96); **Gianni Versace,** 62 rue du Faubourg St-Honoré (☎ 01-47-42-88-02); **La Perla,** 20 rue du Faubourg St-Honoré (☎ 01-43-12-33-60); **Chloé,** 54 rue du Faubourg St-Honoré (☎ 01-44-94-33-00); **Sonia Rykiel,** 70 rue du Faubourg St-Honoré (☎ 01-42-65-20-81); **Christian Lacroix,** 73 rue du Faubourg St-Honoré (☎ 0142-68-79-04), and **Missoni,** 1 rue du Faubourg-St-Honoré (☎ 01-44-51-96-96).

Arty and individual: The 3e and 4e

Divide your time between culture (15 museums are here alone)and commercialism in the Marais (3e, 4e), a beautiful neighborhood crammed with magnificent Renaissance mansions, artists' studios, secret courtyards, and some of the most original shops in the city. **Rue des Francs-Bourgeois** (Métro: St-Paul or Rambuteau), the highlight of the area, is full of small shops selling everything from fashion to jewels. And its stores are open on Sunday! Don't miss **Rue des Rosiers** (Métro: St-Paul), a fashion destination in its own right, with white-hot designers standing shoulder-to-shoulder with Jewish delis. Everything is really close in the Marais, so don't be afraid to ramble down the tiniest lane whenever whim dictates. Part of the fun of this neighborhood is that it's such a mixed (shopping) bag.

Marais highlights include **Paule Ka,** 20 rue Mahler (☎ 01-40-29-96-03), for the sort of 1960s clothing made famous by Grace Kelly, Jackie Onassis, and Audrey Hepburn; **Autour du Monde,** 8 rue des Francs-Bourgeois (☎ 01-42-77-06-08), a clothing/housewares store with everything from relaxed and sporty cotton dresses by Bensimon to delicate linen sheets and inventive tableware; and **Issey Miyake,** 3 place des Vosges (☎ 01-48-87-01-86), for loose, structured clothing that screams "artist." Fans of Spanish shoe brand **Camper** can find a store at 9 rue des Francs-Bourgeois (☎ 01-48-87-09-09). **Plein Sud,** 21 rue des Francs-Bourgeois (☎ 01-42-72-10-60), sells sexy, curve-hugging women's fashion; and check out **Zadig et Voltaire,** 1 rue Guillemites (☎ 01-42-72-15-20), for casual clothes with a flair from new and established European designers.

BCBG chic: The 6e

Stylish young professionals with old family money are called BCBG *(Bon Chic Bon Genre)* and call this area home. Here you can shop among them amid art and antiques galleries, high-end designer clothing shops, decently priced shoe and accessories stores, and sophisticated and trendy boutiques. This is one the prettiest neighborhoods in Paris. You won't go thirsty with famed literary hangouts such as **Café de Flore, Les Deux Magots,** and **Brasserie Lipp** nearby, and you may not even go broke — all price ranges are represented here.

Louis Vuitton has a huge store behind Les Deux Magots on 6 place St-Germain (☎ 01-45-49-62-32), and **Christian Dior** is nearby at 16 rue de l'Abbaye (☎ 01-56-24-90-53). **Emporio Armani** is at 149 boulevard St-Germain (☎ 01-53-63-33-50); **Céline,** 58 rue de Rennes, (☎ 01-45-48-58-55); **Christian Lacroix,** 2 place St-Sulpice (☎ 01-46-33-48-95); or **Prada,** 5 rue de Grenelle (☎ 01-45-48-53-14). Much more pleasing price-wise are **Stefanel,** 54 rue de Rennes (☎ 01-45-44-06-07), **Comptoir des Cotonniers,** 59T rue de Bonaparte (☎ 01-43-26-07-56), **APC Surplus,** 45 rue Madame (☎ 01-45-48-43-71), and **Tara Jarmon,** 18 rue de Four, (☎ 01-46-33-26-60).

Gap and other international chain stores have taken up residence in the Marché St-Germain at 14 rue Lobineau, a modern shopping mall that's a bit out of place in a neighborhood known for bookstores and upscale boutiques. Visit if you need to experience air conditioning, otherwise don't waste your time; prices are higher, and the styles are the same at home.

Young and branché: The 2e

Branché is a high compliment among Paris's younger set, meaning "plugged in," or "hip," and the 2e is where you head if you are. The area sells a mix of high fashion and discount, with Jean-Paul Gaultier in the pretty **Galerie Vivienne** on one end and Kookaï le Stock on the other. The cheapest shopping is in the **Sentier area,** around the Sentier Métro stop, which is Paris's garment district, overlapping parts of the 3e and 1er. The best — but not the cheapest — shops are found within a square formed on the south by rue Rambuteau, on the west by rue du Louvre, on the north by rue Réamur, and on the east by rue St-Martin. This area is where you can find hip secondhand clothes, funky clubwear, and *stock boutiques* selling last season's designs at a discount.

The neighborhood is rapidly gentrifying, but prostitutes still frequent the area later in the afternoon and evening.

For last year's unsold stock of women's and teen's clothing visit **Et Vous Stock,** 15 rue de Turbigo, 2e (☎ 01-40-13-04-12), and **Kookaï Le Stock,** 82 rue Réamur, 2e (☎ 01-45-08-93-69). **Kiliwatch,** 64 rue Tiquetonne, 2e (☎ 01-42-21-17-37), sells the cool looks of up-and-coming designers mixed in with vintage clothing, none of it a bargain, while the Paris branch of London store **Kokon To Zai,** 48 rue Tiquetonne, 2e (☎ 01-42-36-92-41), sells funky designerwear in a small store that dazzles with mirrors and neon. **Le Shop,** 3 rue d'Argout, 2e (☎ 01-40-28-95-94), sells two floors of clubwear, skateboards, and CDs — all to tunes spun by a DJ. Those with a more sophisticated palate can go to **Barbara Bui,** 23 rue Etienne-Marcel, 1er (☎ 01-40-26-43-65), for elegant, contemporary

The arcades

Shopping in the 19th century was a bit less pleasant than it is today: People, horses, and carriages crowded unpaved, dirty, badly lit streets. In the rain, everything turned to mud. But one 19th-century shopkeeper looking for innovative ways to draw crowds to his store proposed displaying wares in pretty covered passageways with other merchants. The first malls were born. These days, the charming iron and glass arcades are still shopping havens, and the 2e has Paris's greatest concentration, each with its own character.

✔ **Passage Choiseul,** 44 rue des Petits-Champs (Métro: Quatre-Septembre), dates from 1827 and is the longest and most colorful arcade selling discount shoes and clothing and used books. French writer Céline grew up here and included it in his books *Journey to the End of Night* and *Death on the Installment Plan.*

✔ **Passage des Panoramas,** 11 boulevard Montmartre and 10 rue St-Marc (Métro: Grands Boulevards), opened in 1800 and was enlarged with the addition of galleries Variétés, St-Marc, Montmartre, and Feydeau in 1834. Its stores sell stamps, clothes, and gifts, and it's the passage with the largest choice of dining options: Korean food, a cafeteria, tea salons, and bistros.

✔ **Passage Jouffroy,** across the street at 10 boulevard Montmartre (Métro: Grands Boulevards), was built between 1845 and 1846. It became an instant hit as Paris's first heated gallery. After an extensive restoration of its tile floors, the gallery now houses a variety of arty boutiques, including a dollhouse store.

✔ **Passage Verdeau,** 31 bis rue du Faubourg-Montmartre (Métro: Le Peletier), was built at the same time as its neighbor, Passage Jouffroy. You can find old prints, books, and postcards here.

✔ **Galerie Vivienne,** 4 place des Petits-Champs, 5 rue de la Banque, or 6 rue Vivienne (Métro: Bourse), is hands down the most gorgeous of all the arcades. Its classical friezes, mosaic floors, and graceful arches have been beautifully restored. Built in 1823, this neoclassical arcade is now a national monument that attracts upscale art galleries, hair salons, and boutiques, including Jean-Paul Gaultier.

✔ **Galerie Colbert** is linked to the adjoining Galerie Vivienne. It was built with a large rotunda and decorated in Pompeian style in 1826 to capitalize on the success of Galerie Vivienne.

✔ The pretty **Passage du Grand Cerf,** 10 rue Dussoubs (Métro: Etienne-Marcel), has more of a modern bent, with jewelry designers, trendy clothing stores, and an ad agency.

For a complete change of pace, head over to the following arcades, but keep in mind that the neighborhoods aren't the nicest. The **Passage Brady,** 46 rue du Faubourg St-Denis (Métro: Strasbourg St-Denis), has become an exotic bazaar where Indian restaurants and spice shops scent the air. The passage opened in 1828. The **Passage du Caire,** 2 place du Caire (Métro: Sentier), is one of the oldest arcades built in 1798 to commemorate Napoléon's triumphant entry into Cairo. It reflects the Egyptomania of the time with fake columns and death masks of pharaohs on its exterior. In the heart of Paris's Sentier garment district, it's home to clothing wholesalers and manufacturers.

fashion. (She also has a trendy cafe two doors down.) For sophistication with an edge, head to **Jean-Paul Gaultier,** 6 rue Vivienne (☎ **01-42-86-05-05**). Find men's, women's, and children's clothes at **agnès b** at 2, 3 and 6 rue du Jour (☎ **01-40-39-96-88,** 01-42-33-04-13, and 01-45-08-56-56 respectively). The stores are minimalist and designs are timelessly chic with plenty of black clothes for the whole family.

Shopping in Paris from A (ntiques) to W (ine)

Listed here are some of the best stores representing both economy and first-class shopping in the City of Light.

Antiques

Le Louvre des Antiquaires

This is an enormous mall filled with all kinds of shops selling everything from sketches by Jean Cocteau to Louis XIV furniture. Items are pricey, but rumors have it that some good deals exist here. A cafe and toilets are located on the second floor.

2 place du Palais-Royal, 1er. ☎ 01-42-97-27-27. Métro: Palais-Royal-Musée du Louvre.

Le Village St-Paul

This secluded 17th-century village (it's in a courtyard) has been turned into an indoor-outdoor arts and antiques fair with shops that display paintings, antiques, and other items, both inside and in the courtyard. It's easy to walk past the entrances, so look for the signs just inside the narrow passageways between the houses on rue St-Paul, rue Jardins St-Paul, and rue Charlemagne. Keep in mind that this is a very popular destination on the weekend. Closed Tuesday and Wednesday.

23–27 rue St-Paul, 4e. No telephone. Métro: St-Paul.

Bookstores

Bouquinistes

These booksellers hawking posters, postcards, and used books from green wooden boxes on some of the Seine's quays are worth a browse. Many of these merchants come from a long line of booksellers dating back to the time of Henri IV in the 17th century.

Quai de Montebello, Quai St-Michel, and various other locations.

Gibert Joseph

Gibert Joseph is *the* Parisian students' bookstore, selling new and secondhand books, records, videos, and stationery on several floors and in several branches on boulevard St-Michel.

26 and 30 bd. St-Michel, 6e. ☎ *01-44-41-88-88. Métro: Odéon or Cluny-Sorbonne.*

Librarie La Hune

Sandwiched between cafes Les Deux Magots and de Flore, this bookstore has been a center for Left Bank intellectuals since 1945 when Sartre was among its clients. Most books are in French. It's open until midnight every night except Sunday.

170 bd. St-Germain, 6e. ☎ *01-45-48-35-85. Métro: St-Germain.*

Shakespeare and Company

No, this *isn't* the original, but English-speaking residents of Paris and backpackers still gather in this wonderfully dark and cluttered store, named after Sylvia Beach's legendary literary lair. There is a selection of new books, but most books are used. *Note:* Poetry readings are held on Sundays.

37 rue de la Bûcherie, 5e. ☎ *01-43-26-96-50. Métro or RER: St-Michel.*

Village Voice

Owner Odile Hellier has been hosting free poetry and prose readings with celebrated authors and poets since 1982, and this is a wonderful place to attend an English-language reading. (Check *Paris Free Voice* for readings.) Quality fiction in English is the highlight of this small two-level store in St-Germain-des-Prés, along with an excellent selection of poetry, plays, nonfiction, and literary magazines.

6 rue Princesse, 6e. ☎ *01-46-33-36-47. Métro: Mabillon or St-Germain.*

Ceramics, china, and glass

Baccarat

The prices at Baccarat are the same at all its branches — except for this one, which sells discontinued items.

30 rue de Paradis, 10e. ☎ *01-47-70-64-30 or 01-40-22-11-00. Métro: Château-d'Eau, Poissonnière, or Gare-de-l'Est.*

La Maison Ivre

The Left Bank between St-Germain-des-Prés and the Seine is the unofficial antiques and art gallery district, and this store sits right in the district's heart. It carries an excellent selection of handmade pottery from across France, with emphases on Provençal and ceramics from southern France.

You can purchase beautiful, well-made pieces of ovenware, bowls, platters, plates, pitchers, mugs, and vases are here.

38 rue Jacob, 6e. ☎ *01-42-60-01-85. Métro: St-Germain-des-Prés.*

Lumicristal

For discounted crystal by Daum, Limoges, and Baccarat, Lumicristal is the place to shop.

22 bis rue de Paradis, 10e. ☎ *01-47-70-27-97. Metro: Château-d'Eau, Poissonnière, or Gare-de-l'Est.*

Clothing for children

Du Pareil au Même

Du Pareil au Même is *the* place to buy clothes for every child on your list — clothes are practical, *très mignons* (very cute), and very reasonably priced.

1 rue St-Denis, 1er ☎ *01-42-36-07-57. Another branch is at 14 rue St-Placide, 6e* ☎ *01-45-44-04-40.*

Jacadi

When BCBG women (see the "'BCBG Chic: The 6e" section earlier in this chapter) have children, Jacadi is where they buy their very proper children's clothes that feature rich fabrics and such gorgeous touches as hand-done smocking.

256 bd. St-Germain, 7e. ☎ *01-42-84-30-40. Many branches are located throughout the city, including 17 bd. Poissonière, 2e* ☎ *01-42-36-69-91.*

Natalys

Part of a French chain with a dozen stores in Paris, Natalys sells children's wear, maternity wear, and related products.

92 av. des Champs-Elysées, 8e. ☎ *01-43-59-17-65. Métro: Franklin-D-Roosevelt. Other branches include 69 rue de Clichy, 9e* ☎ *01-48-74-07-44, and 47 rue de Sèvres, 6e* ☎ *01-45-48-77-12.*

Tartine et Chocolat

This store features more typically French, precious, and pricey clothes.

105 rue du Faubourg-St-Honoré, 8e. ☎ *01-45-62-44-04. Métro: Concorde. Another branch is located at 266 bd. St-Germain, 7e* ☎ *01-45-56-10-45.*

Clothing for men

Façonnable

For quality shirts in nearly every color and casual pants, in addition to jackets, suits, and other men's furnishings (all a bit on the conservative side), Façonnable is the place. In the United States, Nordstrom carries Façonnable, but this store has the entire line.

9 rue du Faubourg-St-Honoré, 8e. ☎ *01-47-42-72-60. Métro: Madeleine or Concorde. Another branch is located at 174 bd. St-Germain, 6e tel 01-40-49-02-47.*

Madelios

This huge store offers one-stop shopping for men, selling everything from overcoats to lighters. If companions get bored waiting, the store is part of a small mall that has some nice stores for browsing.

23 bd. de la Madeleine, 1er. ☎ *01-53-45-00-00.*

Ted Baker

This is the Paris branch of the London designer and sells relaxed dressy and casual clothes with little details (like large French cuffs or a wild pattern lining the collar) that set this brand apart.

20 rue des Francs Bourgeois, 3e. ☎ *01-44-54-02-98.*

Clothing for teens and the young at heart

Antoine et Lili

If you're strolling the quays of the newly hip Canal St-Martin, have a peek into this candy-colored store selling fun bohemian-style clothes and accessories, and decorations that look great in dorm rooms. A garden and small canteen also are located here.

95 quai Valmy, 10e. ☎ *01-40-37-41-55. Métro: Gare de l'Est. Another branch is at 51 rue des Francs Bourgeois, 4e* ☎ *01-42-72-26-60.*

Cop-Copine

Cutting-edge and flattering, Cop-Copine makes great youthful clothes that enhance your good parts and disguise your not-as-good ones.

80 rue Rambuteau, 1er. ☎ *01-40-28-03-72. Métro: Les Halles, RER: Châtelet-Les Halles. Another branch is located at 37 rue Etienne-Marcel* ☎ *01-53-00-94-80.*

H&M

Hennes & Mauritz, the Swedish "IKEA of fashion," has a large selection of up-to-the-minute men and women's fashion at very low prices. This is where you run to get the latest Prada copy. Quality can be poor; count on your outfit lasting about a season.

120 rue de Rivoli, 1er. ☎ *01-55-34-96-86. Métro: Hôtel-de-Ville, Louvre-Rivoli.*

Mango

With locations throughout the city, this store is popular with young Parisian women for its inexpensive, fashion-conscious, body-hugging clothes.

82 rue de Rivoli,1er. ☎ 01-44-59-80-37. Métro: Hôtel-de-Ville, Louvre-Rivoli.

Morgan

Form-fitting suits, dresses, and casual wear in synthetics and blends can be found at low prices for young women at Morgan.

92 av. Champs-Elysées, 6e. ☎ 01-43-59-83-72. Métro: George V.

Zara

Zara offers well-made copies of today's hottest styles for women, men, and children at extremely low prices. Expect bargains galore during the January and July sales.

128 rue de Rivoli, 1er.☎ 01-44-82-64-00. Métro: Hôtel-de-Ville, Louvre-Rivoli. Locations all over the place, including 44 av. Champs-Elysées ☎ 01-45-61-52-81, and 45 rue de Rennes, 6e ☎ 01-44-39-03-50.

Clothing for women

Cacharel

Beautiful women's, children's, and men's clothes are featured at Cacharel, some in pretty Liberty-flower printed fabrics. A Cacharel overstock boutique is at 114 rue Alésia, 14e (☎ 01-45-42-53-04).

64 rue Bonaparte, 6e. ☎ 01-40-46-00-45.

Colette

This is Paris's most cutting-edge clothing store, and everything from designer clothes to cameras to beauty products is on sale here arranged in *très* artistic displays. You can also find artsy chotchkes, art magazines, and art exhibits. Even if you don't buy (the prices are astronomical), just looking is fun and you can break for a snack or drink one of the extensive selection of waters at the basement Water Bar.

213 rue St-Honoré, 1er. ☎ 01-55-35-33-90. Métro: Tuileries.

Comptoir des Cotonniers

This reasonably-priced designer has branches in the major department stores, as well as its own boutiques scattered around the city. Clothes are fashionable without being too cutting-edge and made well from cotton, wool, or silk. Styles, though not timeless, will last a few seasons at home.

33 rue des Francs-Bourgeois, 4e. ☎ 01-42-76-95-33. Métro: St-Paul.

Corinne Sarrut

If you loved those charming outfits with nipped-in waists and swingy skirts worn by Audrey Tautou in the film *Amélie,* you simply must visit this boutique from the woman who designed them.

4 rue de Prè aux Clercs, 6e. ☎ *01-42 61-71-60. Métro: École Militaire. An overstock boutique is located at 24 rue du Champ de Mars, 7e* ☎ *01-45-56-00-65.*

Etam

Women's clothing at Etam is made mostly from synthetic or synthetic-blend fabrics, but the fashions are recent, and the stores are simply *everywhere.* Etam's lingerie, sold in regular Etam stores and separately at Etam Lingerie, has the best deals on pretty and affordable nightclothes and underwear.

67 rue de Rivoli, 1er. ☎ *01-44-76-73-73. Métro: Pont Neuf. There's an Etam Lingerie at 47 rue de Sèvres, 6e* ☎ *01-45-48-21-33, across the street from Bon Marché.*

Gelati

Paris is home to exquisite shoe designers like Christian Louboutin, Robert Clergerie, and Maude Frizon, but if you can't afford their high, high prices, come to this fun shoe store that carries styles inspired by top designers but doesn't reflect their couture prices.

6 rue St-Sulpice, 6e. ☎ *01-43-25-67-44. Métro: Odéon.*

La City

The clothes sold here are perfect for work or for going out to dinner and young women are the target audience. Although everything is synthetic, the prices are reasonable.

37 rue Chaussée d'Antin, 9e. ☎ *01-48-74-41-00. Métro: Chaussée d'Antin. Other branches are located at 18 rue St-Antoine, 4e* ☎ *01-42-78-95-55, and 5 bis rue St-Placide, 6e* ☎ *01-42-84-32-84.*

1-2-3

Like La City, 1-2-3 targets young women looking for stylish suits, blouses, and sweaters to wear to work and après (after). Most clothes are synthetics or synthetic blends; clothing and accessories are sold at moderate prices.

146 rue de Rivoli, 1er. ☎ *01-40-20-97-01. Métro: Louvre-Rivoli. Other branches include 116 rue de Rennes, 6e* ☎ *01-45-80-02-88.*

Rodier

For quality, stylish knitwear, Rodier is the upscale choice. Prices are high for ready-to-wear, but you can often find good bargains during the sales.

72 av. Ternes, 17e. ☎ *01-45-74-17-17. Métro: Ternes. Other branches include 47 rue de Rennes, 6e* ☎ *01-45-44-30-27.*

Shoe Bizz

You can find the latest well-made fashions for your feet at budget-friendly prices.

42 rue Dragon, 6e. ☎ *01-45-44-91-70. Métro: Ternes. Another branch is at 48 rue de Beaubourg, 3e* ☎ *01-48-87-12-73.*

Crafts

Viaduc des Arts

When the elevated railroad cutting across the 12e was transformed into the Promenade Plantée, the space beneath was redesigned to accommodate a long stretch of artisan shops, galleries, furniture stores, and craft boutiques. If you plan to visit the Bois de Vincennes via the Promenade Plantée, duck in for a look on any day except Sunday, when it's closed. The Viaduc Café here (43 avenue Daumensil) is a pleasant place for a light bite or a glass of wine.

9-147 av. Daumensil, 12e. Métro: Bastille, Lédru-Rollin, Reuilly-Diderot, or Gare-de Lyon.

Food

Fauchon

Paris's original gourmet store is still going strong, opening small branches all over the city. This is its flagship store, and you find pink-labeled cans of coffee, caviar, foie gras, biscuits, wines, oils, candy, pastries, and on, and on. If you're in the area, take a peek inside if only for its long history. But save your shopping for other, cheaper grocery stores, that carry, incidentally, some of Fauchon's products. Its tea salon is next door.

26 place Madeleine, 8e. ☎ *01-47-42-91-10. Métro: Madeleine.*

Hédiard

Across the street from its rival, Fauchon, is Hédiard, a gourmet food shop that sells most of the same products as Fauchon, but packaged in red and black stripes. Hédiard is slightly cheaper than Fauchon and has good prepared hot and cold food. Branches are located throughout the city.

21 place Madeleine, 8e. ☎ *01-43-12-88-88. Métro: Madeleine.*

Jacques Papin

If you're visiting the rue de Buci market, have a look inside this store, if only to salivate over some of the most exquisite foods you may ever see, including trout in aspic, fine patés and salads, lobsters, and smoked salmon.

Prestige et Tradition, 8 rue de Buci, 6e. ☎ *01-43-26-86-09. Métro: Odéon.*

Lafayette Gourmet

They keep this large, well-stocked supermarket well hidden in the men's building at Galeries Lafayette. Once you find it, you'll discover it's a terrific spot to browse for gifts or for yourself. It has a good selection of wines, and the house-brand merchandise, often cheaper than other labels, is of very good quality. Eat at the prepared-food counters or sit at the small bar for a glass of wine.

40 bd. Haussmann, 9e (Enter through the men's dept. of Galeries Lafayette. It's on the mezzanine level, accessed by an escalator.) ☎ *01-42-82-34-56. Métro: Chaussée-d'Antin.*

La Grande Epicerie de Paris (at Le Bon Marché)

This is one of the best luxury (meaning it's not cheap) supermarkets in Paris and a great place to look for gourmet gifts, such as olive oils, homemade chocolates, and wine. Food is artfully arranged in glass cases and the produce is some of the freshest around. It makes for wonderful one-stop picnic shopping, too, offering a wide array of prepared foods and cheeses.

38 rue de Sèvres, 7e. ☎ *01-44-39-81-00. Métro: Sèvres-Babylone.*

La Maison du Chocolat

Each candy here is made from a blend of as many as six kinds of South American and African chocolate, flavored with just about everything imaginable. All the merchandise is made on the premises. If the smell doesn't lure you in, the windows will.

225 rue du Faubourg-St-Honoré, 8e. ☎ *01-42-27-39-44. Métro: Ternes. Another branch is at 52 rue François Premier, 8e* ☎ *01-47-23-38-25.*

La Maison du Miel

For an unusual but very welcome gift, try bringing back some French honey from this little shop. It has more than 40 varieties of honey you never dreamed possible (pine tree or lavender), identified according to the flower to which the bees were exposed.

24 rue Vignon, 9e. ☎ *01-47-42-26-70. Métro: Madeleine or Havre-Caumartin.*

Gifts and jewelry

Biche de Bère

Chunky and unusual jewelry in sterling silver and gold plate can be found here.

15 rue des Innocents, 1er. ☎ *01-40-28-94-47. Métro: Châtelet.*

Bijoux Burma

To make others whisper "Are they real or aren't they?" visit Bijoux Burma for some of the best costume jewelry in the city. (To what else did you think I was referring?)

50 rue François 1er, 8e. ☎ *01-47-23-70-93. Métro: Franklin-D-Roosevelt. With branches at 8 bd. Des Capucines* ☎ *01-42-66-27-09 and 23 bd. Madeleine, 1er* ☎ *01-42-96-05-00.*

Eric et Lydie

This shop in the arty Passage du Grand Cerf, contains unusual, beautiful, and reasonably priced costume jewelry, hair ornaments, and other accessories.

7 passage du Grand Cerf, 2e. ☎ *01-40-26-52-59. Métro: Etienne-Marcel.*

La Chaise Longue

This bi-level gift shop is open on Sunday (when it gets very crowded) and is simply bursting at the seams with cool gifts such as silver cufflinks in the shape of computer mice, dinnerware, designer teapots, three-dimensional picture frames, patterned drinking glasses, children's straw hats with a cat face and ears, bath towels with fun prints, among many, many other things. It's very reasonably priced and definitely worth a visit.

20 rue des Francs Borgeois, passage du Grand Cerf, 2e. ☎ *01-48-04-36-37. Métro: St-Paul.*

Monic

There's so much to look at in this store in the Marais — open Sunday afternoons — that it's overwhelming! Here you find a wide range of affordable costume jewelry and designer creations, many at discount prices.

5 rue des Francs-Bourgeois, 4e. ☎ *01-42-72-39-15. Métro: St-Paul.*

Pylones

This boutique sells Simpsons collectibles, children's umbrellas that stand on their own, bicycle bells shaped like ladybugs, and a variety of other unusual gift items. It's a fun place to browse.

57 rue de St-Louis-en-l'Ile, 4e. ☎ *01-46-34-05-02. Métro: Cité. Branches at 7 rue Tardieu, 18e* ☎ *01-46-06-37-00, and rue Ste-Croix de la Brètonnerie, 4e* ☎ *01-48-04-80-10.*

Tati Or

Eighteen-carat gold jewelry for up to 40% less than traditional jewelers, and more than 3,000 bracelets, earrings, necklaces, rings, and pins are offered, with about 500 items selling for less than 75€ ($86). Tati is in financial difficulty and rumors are that it might close, so call before you visit.

57 rue de Rivoli, 1er. ☎ *01-40-41003-26. Métro: Hôtel de Ville.*

Why?

If you're a teenager at heart (or just appreciate dirty jokes) Why? is for you. Inflatable chairs, shower curtains, dirty cards and jokes, Tintin figurines, notebooks, and T-shirts are highlighted.

41 rue des Francs-Bourgeois, 4e. ☎ *01-44-61-72-75. Métro: St. Paul.*

Home and housewares

Alessi

Alessi offers bright and affordable kitchen implements, such as magnetized salt and pepper shakers and wine openers that look a tad, well, *human.* You can find some cutlery, dishes, and linens, too. Check out the Mr. Suicide drain plug — a yellow man chained to a blue stopper floats to the surface when you take a bath.

31 rue Boissy d'Anglas, 8e. ☎ *01-42-66-14-61. Métro: Madéleine or Concorde.*

Cedre Rouge

Cedre Rouge is a little like American company Smith and Hawken — it sells that urban rustic look made with natural materials for the garden or terrace, apartment or country home. It isn't cheap, but you can find some unusual gifts (like cute, but tiny, snail candleholders for 20€/$23). Finds include Tuscan pottery, Irish linen tablecloths and napkins, Murano glass, teak and wicker furniture, and beeswax candles.

116 rue du Bac, 6e. ☎ *01-42-84-84-00. Métro: Sèvres-Babylone or Rue du Bac.*

Conforama

This huge store sells everything for your home at reasonable prices: furniture, appliances, garden tools and accessories, and everyday china and glass.

2 rue de Pont-Neuf, 1er. ☎ *01-42-33-37-09. Métro: Pont Neuf.*

Déhillerin

Filled with high-quality copper cookware, glasses, dishes, china, gadgets, utensils, ramekins, pots, and kitchen appliances, this place makes cooks go wild — especially because the prices are discounted.

18–20 rue Coquillière, 1er. ☎ *01-42-36-53-13.* www.e-dehillerin.fr. *Métro: Les Halles.*

Talmaris

Vintage and modern, expensive and reasonable are all mixed up in this store that the owner, 30-something Alain-Paul Ruzé, likes to call the world's smallest department store. Ruzé, a true collector, travels the world for special vintage items (an 18th-century American flag anyone?). You'll find mostly home-decor pieces like Herend porcelain or Biedermeier chair reproductions, funky colorful tablewear from Too Beautiful for You and beautiful patterned glass from Vitreluxe. The stock is constantly changing as Ruzé brings in his most recent finds.

61 av. Mozart, 16o. ☎ *01-42-88-20-20. Métro: Ranelagh.*

Verrerie des Halles

The restaurant industry buys its china, glassware, furniture and other supplies here, and you can, too, at discount prices.

15 rue du Louvre, 1er. ☎ *01-42-36-80-60. Métro: Louvre-Rivoli.*

Toys

Au Nain Bleu

F.A.O. Schwartz in Manhattan emulated this, the world's fanciest toy store. Translated as "at the blue dwarf's," for more than 150 years Au Nain Bleu has been selling toy soldiers, stuffed animals, games, and puppets in a gorgeous space. More modern toys are also on hand, including airplanes and model cars. Obviously, this is a terrific place to bring your kids — expect to walk out with a very light wallet!

408 rue St-Honoré, 8e. ☎ *01-42-60-39-01. Métro: Concorde.*

Fnac Junior

An outpost of the Fnac chain, Fnac Junior sells books, videos, and music for children, and has story hours and other activities for its young guests.

19 rue Vavin, 6e. ☎ *01-56-24-03-46. Métro: Vavin.*

Galeries Lafayette

Floor 4 of the Galeries Lafayette main store is devoted to toys and children's clothing, and there's a play area kids love.

40 bd. Haussmann, 9e. ☎ *01-56-24-03-46. Métro: Havre-Caumartin, Chaussée-d'Antin-La Fayette, Opéra, or Trinité.*

Le Bon Marché

The basement of Le Bon Marché is a children's wonderland filled with adorable clothing and loads of toys, both educational and purely fun.

24 rue de Sèvres rue Vavin, 6e. ☎ *01-56-24-03-46. Métro: Vavin.*

Wine

Legrand Filles et Fils

In addition to fine wines, this store stocks brandies, chocolates, coffees, and oenophile (which means "wine lover," in case you're not one) paraphernalia. It also conducts wine tastings one night a week.

1 rue de la Banque, 2e. ☎ *01-42-60-07-12. Métro: Bourse.*

Les Caves Augé

This is the oldest wine shop in Paris with a sommelier (wine steward) on site who can advise you on the vintage French and international wines this store carries.

116 bd. Haussmann, 8e. ☎ *01-45-22-16-97. Métro: St-Augustin.*

Nicolas

Nicolas is the flagship store of the wine chain that has more than 110 branches in and around Paris, and it offers good prices for bottles you may not be able to find in the United States.

31 place de la Madeleine, 8e. ☎ *01-42-68-00-16. Métro: Madeleine.*

Chapter 13

Following an Itinerary

*P*aris offers so much to see and do that first- and even second-time visitors to the city can feel overwhelmed just trying to figure out where to begin. When you're short on time, or have young children with you, you want to maximize your opportunities to see the best Paris has to offer in the most efficient way possible. The itineraries in this chapter help you figure out where to start and what to do. But please feel free to branch out and explore those interesting alleyways and pretty green spaces you encounter all around you. That's what's so much fun about Paris; it reveals itself in all kinds of ways, making the trips of each individual visitor different — and special.

Making the Most of Paris in Three Days

On **Day One,** start early by having coffee and croissants at a cafe. Then begin at the true center of Paris: **Notre-Dame** on the **Ile de la Cité.** The cathedral is *the* starting point for any tour, and it's Paris's starting point, as well; you're at Kilometre Zéro, from which all distances in France are measured. From there, take a short walk to the island's other Gothic masterpiece — **Sainte-Chapelle** in the **Palais de Justice.** Afterward, cross the Seine to the **Louvre.** Select just a few rooms in a particular collection for your first visit — this is one of the world's largest and finest museums, and it would take months to see everything. Take a well-deserved lunch break in the museum's comfortable **Café Marly** (see Chapter 10 for a description).

From the museum, stroll through the beautiful **Jardin des Tuileries** to the **place de la Concorde,** with its Egyptian obelisk and fountains. Walk up the **Champs-Elysées** to the **Arc de Triomphe** and browse the stores (**Fnac** and **Virgin Megastore** are good places to buy music, and each has a café on the premises for a break; **Zara** is good for the latest fashion at low prices). Walk south on avenue Marceau or take bus 92 to Alma

Marceau and board the **Bateaux-Mouches** for a **Seine boat ride** (see Chapter 11). After you disembark, have dinner at the friendly and reasonably priced **L'Assiette Lyonnaise,** 21 rue Marbeuf, 8e (from Pont L'Alma walk down avenue George V to rue Marbeuf and make a right; L'Assiette Lyonnaise is on your right).

Explore the **Left Bank** on **Day Two.** Take the Métro to LaMotte-Picquet-Grenelle and stop into **Monoprix** just across the street for cheap picnic food from its grocery store. Walk down avenue de Suffren until you reach the **École-Militaire.** Facing it is the **Champs-de-Mars** where you can spread out to have a picnic after visiting the **Eiffel Tower.** After you climb the tower (and have lunch), visit the **Église du Dôme** (which contains the **Tomb of Napoléon**) on the other side of the École-Militaire. Admission also includes entrance to the **Musée de l'Armée.** Across boulevard des Invalides is the **Musée Rodin,** where you can enjoy a slow walk around the beautiful gardens before gazing at the artwork inside. Then walk down boulevard des Invalides to the Seine, and head east for quay Anatole France (this is a long walk) and the **Musée d'Orsay** to spend a few hours with the Impressionist masters. (Instead of tackling this leg of your journey on foot, you can hop on the Métro at Varenne, at the corner of boulevard des Invalides and Varenne, change to RER Line C, and arrive at Musée d'Orsay.) Afterward, walk over to the Métro's **Assemblée Nationale** station at the intersection of boulevard St-Germain and rue de Lille. Take the Métro two stops to rue du Bac and exit onto boulevard St-Germain, making sure to walk in the direction traffic is heading, all the while browsing in upscale shops and art galleries. At place St-Germain-des-Près, look for one of the famous cafes, **Café de Flore, Les Deux Magots** (see Chapter 10), or **Brasserie Lipp** and have a drink. When you finish, take rue Bonaparte (which intersects St-Germain-des-Près) to Parisians' favorite park, the **Jardin du Luxembourg.** Stroll through the park and exit at the boulevard St-Michel gates. Walk down boulevard St-Michel toward the river. You'll be in the **Latin Quarter.** The **Panthéon** is at the top of the hill on rue Soufflot. Many inexpensive restaurants where you can enjoy a nice meal are located behind the Panthéon on rue Mouffetard.

On **Day Three,** get up early and hop on the Métro to St-Paul, in the heart of the **Marais.** Walk over to Paris's oldest square, the aristocratic **place des Vosges,** bordered by 17th-century town houses. Then head over to rue Thorigny for the **Musée Picasso.** Try to arrive when it opens at 9:30, and allow two hours for your visit. Afterward follow rue du Vieille du Temple to rue des Rosiers and pick up lunch from **Florence Finkelsztajn** or **Jo Goldenberg.** Browse the stores here and on rue des Francs Bourgeois, which turns into rue Rambuteau. Follow rue Rambuteau to rue Beaubourg, where you'll face the back of the wonderful **Centre Georges Pompidou.** Spend two hours exploring it. Afterward, jump on the Métro and head for Père-Lachaise. Spend the afternoon searching out **Cimitière Père-Lachaise's** famous residents with the 2€ ($2.30) map (it's the best one) sold outside the gates on boulevard de Ménilmontant. Afterward, take the Métro's Line 2 to the Anvers station. Walk down rue Tardieu to the base of **Sacré-Coeur.** Take the funicular (one Métro ticket) to the top and then spend 15 to 20 minutes inside Sacré-Coeur before climbing to its dome. After climbing down, head behind the church to the **place du Tertre,** which still looks like an old-fashioned Parisian square, despite artists begging to paint your picture (some can be quite persuasive, but they're too expensive, and it's better to just politely tell them *"non, merci"*). Even though the cafes are picturesque — and more expensive — save your appetite for **Au Poulbot Gourmet,** 39 rue Lamarck (follow rue Lamarck down the hill to No. 39) for dinner.

Planning a Five-Day Visit

Spend the first three days as outlined in the "Making the Most of Paris in Three Days" itinerary. Add the **Conciergerie** to your tour of Ile de la Cité on Day One; the entrance is on the Seine side of the Palais de Justice.

On **Day Four,** visit **Versailles.** On **Day Five,** take the Métro to Opéra to visit the stunning and newly renovated **Opéra Garnier** with its mural by Marc Chagall. Cash the last of your traveler's checks at nearby **American Express** and then head over to boulevard. Haussmann to shop the rest of the afternoon away at department stores **Au Printemps** and **Galeries Lafayette.** The sixth-floor cafeteria at Galeries Lafayette offers plenty of lunch or dinner choices — from a salad bar to grilled steaks and dessert.

Doing Paris in Just One Day!

Friends at the Bonjour Paris (BP) Web site (www.bonjourparis.com) say that one of the most frequently asked questions they get is "I only have one day in Paris, can I see all of it?" BP president Karen Fawcett, Pat Brien, and Sarah Gilbert Fox say "yes," but you'll have to don your most comfy shoes and have a strong heart, because this itinerary is simply is jam-packed!

Okay . . . you have 24 hours to find the fun. Not exactly a challenge, right? I mean, this is Paris: the most beautiful town in the world, the City of Light, the place where even the rain is romantic. Anyone could do it. But alas, so many get it wrong. What about all that intimidating French culture? All that history! All that intellectualism and philosophy! And the Parisians! How do you deal with all *that* in a day?

A word to the wise: don't panic!

Here's a plan:

> ✔ **7–9 a.m.:** Greet the early morning with the shop owners as they sweep their storefronts and the sweet French ladies as they roll their *charrettes* (carts) to get the morning paper and baguettes. Bask in the quiet glow of Paris. Grab a coffee and an exquisite *pain au chocolat* (chocolate-filled croissant) for breakfast. Yum.

Start on the Champs-Elysées (and snag a couple of the 20 famous flavors of macaroons for later in the day from **Ladurée** (75 avenue des Champs-Elysées) then *dépéches-toi* (hurry up) to the top of the **Arc de Triomphe** for the best view of Paris as well as the greatest traffic jam *à la Français* below.

✔ **9 a.m.–12 p.m.:** Don't miss **Place de la Concorde,** your second best view of the City: You'll have in your sights the Egyptian Obelisque, the Louvre, the Eiffel Tower, the Jardin des Tuileries, the Madeleine, the Seine, the Assemblée Nationale, l'Orangerie, and the Arc de Triomphe.

Head to the **Louvre,** three blocks away. Do not miss: *The Winged Victory of Samothrace* or *Venus de Milo,* undoubtedly the two most exquisite pieces of artwork there. It is, of course, illegal to visit the Louvre without seeing what's-her-name, but feel free to miss her. We always do. The way in? There's a HUGE PYRAMID, but look around. There are better options. (*Hint:* Buy a ticket in advance off-site from any Fnac store, except their photo stores, and head for the Cour Richelieu entrance in the courtyard).

✔ **12–1 p.m.:** If it's the weekend, take *Métro* line 13, Champs-Elysées-Clemenceau: direction Chatillon-Montrouge. Purchase a one-day Mobilis pass that allows you to jump on the bus or metro endlessly. Exit at Porte de Vanves for the **Porte de Vanves Market** to hunt for the perfect Paris souvenir. Find Madame Béatrice de Laigue's Stall (rue Marc Sangnier no. 1) for three reasons:

1. She'll drop your purchases off at your hotel, free.

2. She specializes in items that can fit in your luggage.

3. This is where you'll find Paris celebrities looking for treasures (you may well spot Deneuve or Depardieu).

If it's a weekday, spend the hour at the **Parc Montsouris** walking among the copses and winding paths, throwing bits of leftover baguette to the swans and ducks on the pond.

✔ **1–3 p.m.:** Back on Métro line 13, head in the opposite direction, change lines at Montparnasse Bienvenue and hop on Métro 4 toward Porte de Clignancourt. Get off at St-Germain-des-Prés, view the church and the Café Flore (172 boulevard St-Germain-des-Prés) to see and be seen. Buy nothing. It's overpriced!

Instead, trot over to **FISH - La Boissonerie** (69 rue de Seine) for lunch. You're likely to see expatriate cookbook authors Dorie Greenspan, or Patricia Wells, and the food is fantastic. After you eat, walk north towards the **Musee d'Orsay.** Don't miss the Impressionists. Next, go see the **Eiffel Tower.** But why stand in line for hours, only to be herded up like buffalo to see a view in which the Eiffel Tower is missing? Doh!

✔ **3–5 p.m.**: Getting *fatiguée?* Hop on a Segway at **Fat Tire Bike Tours** (24 rue Edgar Faure, 15e), the mode of transport of the moment; a space-age technological marvel shaped like a hand-pushed lawn mower that rides you around effortlessly. At first you'll feel as if you should be wearing alien-block tin foil on your head, but, hey, you ain't the one walking everywhere! Segway over to **Notre-Dame**, through the hip-squeezing **Marais**, around the newly-hip **Canal Saint-Martin**, glide through the **Jardin du Luxembourg**, and end at the **Opéra**, where you'll need to dodge being a hit-and-run so you can get one of the best snapshots in all of Paris.

✔ **5–7 p.m.**: Around **Pigalle** you'll realize that there's still a sense of the *Oooh, la! la!* alive in Paris. But it's pretty tacky. The **Moulin Rouge** is still there, living off its legend, offering expensive dinner-and-show formulas, but moving around there, you may sink in sleaze. Still, you have to hand it to the French, they love museums so much that there's actually a **Musée de l'Erotisme** (72 bd. Clichy, 75009), giving a highly cultural account of the expression of sex via art from Asia, Africa, and Latin America. Exhibitions for those without inhibitions, *peut-etre* (perhaps)?

✔ **7–9 p.m.**: After Pigalle, and depending on where you stand or kneel on the big religious questions, you may wish to head straight for confession. Easily arranged. The magnificent church of **Sacré-Coeur** rises above the flesh-peddlers and tack-shacks of Pigalle like a sacred vision; the crowning point of Montmartre, it is not only one of the highlights, but one of the *high points* of Paris. Nearly as high as the Eiffel Tower itself, clamber up the infamous, seemingly endless steps of its Dome for a great night view of the city. Or, if you're smarter, take a quickie round trip on the strange little *funiculare* that rides up the butte (hill) to just under the church. Work started on the Sacré-Coeur in the 1870s and the building is a pastiche of Romanesque and Byzantine styles. A cause of some controversy amongst critics, two experts once met on the steps of the church to hold a fierce 12-hour debate about which style should have won out during the planning stages. Unfortunately, the whole audience fell asleep after the first three minutes and nobody knows what was said. Amen. Renoir, Picasso, Seurat, Degas, Van Gogh, and Zola all hung out in Pigalle and Montmartre. And there was no keeping Toulouse-Lautrec away, of course. Museums, tourist traps, and quiet, pretty little streets abound.

✔ **9–11 p.m.**: Time for dinner, so go BIG with it. My recommendation: Call at least three months in advance to get a seat at the **Jules Vernes Restaurant**, on top of the Eiffel Tower; or ask a French friend (preferably known to the establishment) to call at least a month in advance to get a reservation at **L'Ambroisie** (9 pl des Vosges); or catch a **Seine Dinner Cruise** and be amazed at the twinkling lights of Paris reflecting off the river.

You must be exhausted, and Paris is winding down, too, so walk back in the night air to your hotel and rest assured that you've conquered more of Paris in one day than most people do in a week.

Or . . . if your little Segway has saved you enough energy, hit a jazz club such as **The Duc des Lombards** (42 rue des Lomards). After all, the only proper way to end a truly Parisian day out is to stay out.

Playing in Paris with the Family

These itineraries take into account short attention spans, so the restaurants listed tend to be on the fast-food side. These outlines aren't broken down into day-by-day schedules because your kids probably have varying (and, if more than one, probably competing) interests. So feel free to mix-and-match.

Taking a magical history tour: Version 1

Climb the **Eiffel Tower,** then cross over the Champs-de-Mars to visit **Napoleon's Tomb** and the **Musée de l'Armée** at **Invalides.** Afterward cross the Pont Alexandre III and pay a visit to the kid-friendly science museum, **Palais de la Découverte.** You'll be more than ready to eat, and you have your pick of places on the Champs-Elysées. **Lina's Sandwiches,** 8 rue Marbeuf, is a nearby inexpensive (and delicious) choice. After lunch, continue walking up the Champs-Elysées until you face the **Arc de Triomphe.**

Never cross the traffic circle to get to the Arc; make sure you use the pedestrian tunnel.

Climb the nearly 300 steps or take the elevator to the top of the Arc. Watch 12 lanes of traffic converge around the circle below, and take in a view that includes the Eiffel Tower. Afterward take bus No. 83 from the Friedland-Haussmann stop across the traffic circle to the **Jardin du Luxembourg,** Parisians' favorite park. Exit the park on boulevard St-Germain or boulevard St-Michel for some quick shopping before having dinner at one of the many restaurants in the area. (Check out eateries in Chapter 10.)

Sampling science, slides, and stalagmites: Version 2

Take a one-way ride on a **Canauxrama** boat excursion (if they're restless or very young, your kids won't stand for more) to **parc de la Villette** and cross over the pedestrian bridge to visit the **Cité des Sciences et de l'Industrie.** Try to catch one of the six short films shown on the giant **Géode** IMAX screen on the grounds. Afterward, grab lunch in the complex's cafeteria, at restaurant chain **Quick,** or from one of the vendors in the park grounds and watch your kids tackle the giant-dragon sliding board and explore the submarine. Then, cross the pedestrian bridge to the other side where your small kids can enjoy kiddie rides, and your bigger ones can enjoy the **Musée de la Musique.** Afterward, take the Métro to the Buttes-Chaumont stop; you'll be at the edge of the **Buttes-Chaumont** park. Admire the waterfalls, cross the suspension bridge, gape at cliffs and the cave with stalactites and stalagmites (all of it man-made).

Picnicking through the parks: Version 3

Bring a picnic lunch with you, then take the Métro to Porte Dorée and follow the signs for the **Bois de Vincennes.** Rent a bike in the park to explore the extensive grounds, or rent a canoe and lazily take in the lush surroundings. Spread out near the cave crowned by a pseudo-Greek temple. Afterward walk over to the **parc Zoologique** on avenue St-Maurice and spend a few hours observing the animals in very natural settings. Your kids may want to climb the neat futuristic observation tower from which they get a great view of the animals, park, and surrounding city. Afterward, hop on the Métro for the Château de Vincennes stop. After a tour of the **Château,** head over to the **parc Floral,** which has a great playground, a butterfly garden, and a large amphitheatre where jazz musicians play on summer Saturdays. Then get on the Métro and shoot over to Hôtel de Ville. Walk over the Pont d'Arcole onto **Ile de la Cité** and stroll over the Pont St-Louis, which connects the two islands. Ile St-Louis's best ice cream shop, **Berthillon,** is right down the street at 31 rue St-Louis en l'Ile. If you have any energy left, try taking one of the nearby **Seine boat tours** from Vedettes Pont Neuf, moored next to Pont Neuf, or take a **Batobus** from the Notre-Dame stop.

Chapter 14

Going Beyond Paris: Five Day-Trips

In This Chapter

▶ Enjoying the excesses of Versailles
▶ Reliving French history at Fontainebleau
▶ Basking in the stained-glass light at Chartres's cool cathedral
▶ Hanging out at Disneyland à la français
▶ Lingering at the water lilies in Monet's gardens

*W*ith so much to see and do in Paris, it may be hard to tear yourself away for one of the day trips I outline in this chapter. But all are worth the short excursions. And don't worry; you'll be back in the city in time to enjoy a nightcap in a cafe. The "Day-Trips from Paris" map can help you plan your excursions.

The Château de Versailles

There's more to Versailles (☎ 01-30-84-74-00; www.chateauversailles.fr) than its incredible château, of which the words awe-inspiring don't begin to do justice. This is a small city on more than 2,000 acres that houses formal and fanciful gardens, meadows (with sheep), a mile-long Grand Canal modeled on the one in Venice, the Grand and Petit Trianon mansions, a hamlet where Marie Antoinette played peasant, the restored royal stables, a coach museum, fountains, and woods. All this attests to the power royalty once had and to one king who truly believed he deserved it: Louis XIV. The king hired the best to build Versailles: Louis Le Vau and Jules Hardouin-Mansart, France's premier architects; André Le Nôtre, designer of the Tuileries gardens; and Charles Le Brun, head of the Royal Academy of Painting and Sculpture, who fashioned the interior. Construction got underway in 1661.

In 1682, Louis XIV transferred the court to Versailles to live with him and thus prevent plots against him. (Because his taxes on citizens paid for Versailles, he was a little paranoid.) Historians estimate that anywhere from 3,000 to 10,000 people, including servants, lived at Versailles in the

Day-Trips from Paris

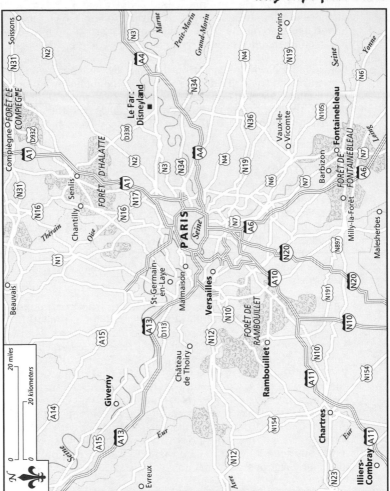

100 years between the rules of Louis XIV and Louis XVI, and court etiquette grew to be absurd. (Sometimes attendants engaged in power
struggles about who ranked high enough to dress Marie Antoinette while
the young queen waited, shivering.) When you see all this over-the-top
magnificence and try to estimate the cost, you may have a better understanding of the anger of the revolutionaries a century later.

Louis XIV enjoyed an incredibly long reign of 72 years (though he was
just a boy when he inherited the title). When he died in 1715, he was
succeeded by his great-grandson, Louis XV, who continued the outrageous pomp and ceremony and made interior renovations and redecora-
tions until lack of funds forced him to stop. His son and daughter-in-law,

Louis XVI and Marie Antoinette, had simpler tastes and made no major changes at Versailles, but by then it was too late. On October 6, 1789, a mob marched on the palace and forced the royal couple to return to Paris, and Versailles ceased to be a royal residence.

Louis-Philippe, who reigned from 1830 to 1848 and succeeded Louis XVIII, prevented the château's destruction by donating his own money to convert it into a museum dedicated to the glory of France. John D. Rockefeller also contributed to the restoration of Versailles, and the work from that contribution continues to this day. The nearby "Versailles" map shows the current configuration.

Getting there

Catch the **RER line C** to Versailles at the Gare d'Austerlitz, St-Michel, Musée d'Orsay, Invalides, Ponte d'Alma, Champ de Mars, or Javel stop and take it to the Versailles Rive Gauche station, from which there's a shuttle bus to the château. Round-trip tickets cost 5.20€ ($6) and the trip takes 35 to 40 minutes. Eurailpass holders travel free on the RER, but must show their Eurailpass at the kiosk near any RER entrance to receive a ticket that opens the turnstile leading to and from the RER platforms.

An alternative method of reaching Versailles from central Paris involves regular **SNCF trains,** which make frequent runs from two railway stations — Gare St-Lazare and Gare Montparnasse — to Versailles. Trains departing from Gare St-Lazare arrive at the Versailles Rive Droit railway station; trains departing from Gare Montparnasse arrive at Versailles Chantiers. Both stations lie within a ten-minute walk of the château, which is a wonderful way to orient yourself with the town, its geography, its scale, and its architecture. If you can't or don't want to walk, you can take bus B, bus H, or (in midsummer) a shuttle bus marked *Château* from any of the three stations directly to the château for a fee of 2.50€ ($2.90) each way per person. Because of the vagaries of the bus schedules, it may be easier to walk. Directions to the château are clearly signposted from each railway station.

To reach Versailles by car, drive west on the A13 highway from Porte d'Auteuil toward Rouen. Take the Versailles-Château exit, about 14 miles from Paris. Park in the visitors' parking lot at place d'Armes for 4.50€ ($5.15) Monday through Friday, 5.50€ ($6.30) on weekends. The drive takes about a half-hour, though in traffic it can take more than an hour.

You can also take a tour bus to Versailles. **Cityrama,** 4 place des Pyramides, 1er (☎ 01-44-55-61-00; www.cityrama.fr), has different trips to Versailles ranging from 36€ to 95€ ($41–$109) for adults, 28€ to 48€ ($32–$55) children (the higher-priced tickets also include trips to Fontainebleau and Barbizon). **Paris Vision,** 214 rue de Rivoli, 1er (☎ 01-42-60-30-01; www.parisvision.com), offers bus excursions starting from 68€ to 139€ ($78–$160); it's half price for ages 4 to 11.

Versailles

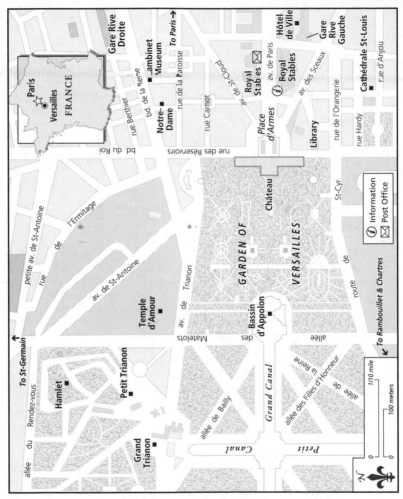

Exploring Versailles

Two words of advice — arrive early! More than three million tourists visit Versailles each year, and you'll want to have as much of a head start as possible.

The first rooms you see in the palace are the six Louis XIV–style **Grands Appartements,** which kings used for ceremonial events, and **the Petits Appartements,** where they lived with their families. Louis XV stashed his mistresses, Madame du Barry and Madame de Pompadour, in his second-floor apartment, which you can visit only with a guide. Attempts have been made to restore the original decor of the Queen's bedchamber, which Marie Antoinette renovated with a huge four-poster bed and silks in patterns of lilacs, her favorite flower, and peacock feathers.

Other magnificent rooms include the **Salons of War and Peace,** which flank the palace's most famous room, the 236-foot-long **Hall of Mirrors.** Hardouin-Mansart began work on the hall in 1678, and Le Brun added 17 large windows and corresponding mirrors. The ceiling paintings represent the accomplishments of Louis XIV's government. Jacques-Ange Gabriel designed the **Library** with its delicately carved panels. The **Clock Room** contains Passement's astronomical clock, which took 20 years to make; it's encased in gilded bronze.

Gabriel also designed the **Royal Opéra** for Louis XV. Try to imagine it the way it used to be during a concert — bearskin rugs underfoot and the light of 3,000 powerful candles. Hardouin-Mansart built the gold-and-white **Royal Chapel** between 1699 and 1710. After his father's death, Louis XVI and Marie Antoinette prayed for guidance here, fearing they were too young to run the country.

After you see the château, plan to spend at least an hour strolling through the **Formal Gardens,** spread across 250 acres. Here Le Nôtre created a Garden of Eden, using ornamental lakes and canals, geometrically designed flowerbeds, and avenues bordered with statuary. Louis XV, imagining he was in Venice, used to take gondola rides with his lover of the moment on the mile-long Grand Canal. The restored vegetable gardens (*le Potager de Roi*) are here, as well. If you visit on a weekend in the summer, try to take in **The Grands Eaux Musicales,** a show in which the fountains move in time to the classical music of Bach, Mozart, or Berlioz. Cost is 6€ ($6.90) adults, 4.50€ ($5.15) ages 10 to 26 and seniors, under 10 free. **Les Fêtes de Nuit de Versailles** is a spectacular sound-and-light show with fireworks held seven times a year between June and Septem-ber. Cost is 17€ ($20) adults, 15€ ($17) ages 10 to 26 and seniors, under 10 free. (For reservations to either show, call ☎ **08-92-70-18-92** .34€/min.)

Because of the crowds and long lines, most guests are content to visit only the château and gardens, but you can see much more at Versailles if you have the stamina. The most important of the remaining sights are the **Grand Trianon** and the **Petit Trianon.** *Trianon* was the name of the town that Louis bought and then razed in order to construct a mansion, le Grand Trianon, where he could eat light meals away from the palace. Designed in 1687 by Hardouin-Mansart, the Grand Trianon has traditionally served as a residence for the country's important guests, although former President Charles de Gaulle wanted to turn it into a weekend retreat for himself. Napoléon I spent the night here, and U.S. President Richard Nixon slept in the room where Madame de Pompadour (Louis XV's mistress) died. Gabriel, the designer of the place de la Concorde, built the Petit Trianon in 1768 for Louis XV, who used it for trysts with Madame du Barry, his mistress after La Pompadour. Marie Antoinette adopted it as her favorite residence, where she could escape the constraints of palace life.

Behind the Petit Trianon is the **Hamlet,** a collection of small thatched farmhouses and a water mill, a setting where Marie Antoinette pretended she was back at her family's country retreat in Austria. Near the Hamlet is the **Temple of Love,** built in 1775 by Richard Mique, Marie Antoinette's favorite architect. In the center of its Corinthian colonnade is a reproduction of Bouchardon's Cupid shaping a bow from the club of Hercules.

Louis XIV's stables, **Le Grande Ecurie,** are newly restored and open to the public for the first time in 200 years. Also designed by Hardouin-Mansart, the stables held as many as 600 horses owned by the king. These days, you'll see 20 ivory-colored Lusitanian horses from Portugal. A morning tour here includes a dressage demonstration with riders in costume on horses performing to music. Near the stables is the entrance to the **Coach Museum,** which houses coaches from the 18th and 19th centuries, among them one used at the coronation of Charles X and another used at the wedding of Napoléon I and his second wife, Marie-Louise. One sleigh rests on tortoiseshell runners. A ticket to the Petit Trianon also admits you to this museum. Admission to Le Grande Ecurie is 7.50€ ($8.60) adults, 3€ ($3.45) 17 and under. Open Tuesday to Friday 9 a.m. to 1 p.m., weekends 11 a.m. to 3 p.m. Admission to the coach museum is 2€ ($2.30), free for children younger than 18. It's open every weekend from April to October 9 a.m. to 6:30 p.m. and the first two weekends in November 12:30 to 5:30 p.m.

Admission to the palace is 7.50€ (8.60) for adults, 5.30€ ($6.10) for ages 18 to 24 and over 60. It's free for those younger than 18 and for all on Sunday. Combined admission to the Grand and Petit Trianons is 5€ ($5.75) for adults, 3€ ($3.45) for ages 18 to 24 and seniors, and free for those younger than 18. Admission to the gardens is 3.50€ ($4) for adults, 3€ ($3.45) for ages 10 to 17.

One-hour audio tours of the King's Chambers are admission price plus 4.50€ ($5.15), free under 10 years old. Lecturer-led one-hour tours of the palace are admission price plus 4€ ($4.60), 3€ (3.45) ages 10 to 17 and seniors; one-and-a-half-hour tours are admission plus 6€ ($6.90), 4.50€ ($4.50) ages 11 to 17 and seniors; two-hour tours are admission plus 8€ ($9.20) for adults, 6€ ($6.90) ages 10 to 17. Tours are free for children younger than 10.

From May to September, the palace is open Tuesday through Sunday from 9 a.m. to 6:30 p.m. The rest of the year, the palace is open Tuesday through Sunday from 9 a.m. to 5:30 p.m. From May through September the Grand Trianon and Petit Trianon are open daily noon to 6:30 p.m.; from October to April, the Grand Trianon and Petit Trianon are open daily noon to 5:30 p.m. The park and the gardens are open every day except in bad weather from 7 a.m. in summer, 8 a.m. in winter, until sunset (between 5:30 and 9:30 p.m. depending on the season).

Dining options

The town of Versailles has no shortage of places where you can break for lunch, but after you're on palace grounds, you may find it infinitely more convenient just to stay put — otherwise you have to hike back into town and back out to the palace again. In the château, you can eat at a **cafeteria** just off the Cour de la Chapelle. In the Formal Gardens is an informal restaurant, **La Flotille,** on Petite Venise. (To get there from the château, walk directly back through the gardens to where the canal starts. Petite Venise and the restaurant are to your right.) Finally, several **snack bars** are located in the gardens near the Quinconce du Midi and the Grand Trianon.

The Palais de Fontainebleau

Fontainebleau is a terrific day trip from Paris: After you tour the castle, you can hike the trails or rent bikes to ride in the 42,000-acre Forêt (forest) de Fontainebleau. The palace (☎ **01-60-71-50-75;** check out the nearby "Fontainebleau" map) is probably most famous as the site of Napoléon's farewell to his imperial guard before he went into exile. It also contains more than 700 years of royal history from the enthronement of Louis VII in 1137 to the fall of the Second Empire in 1873.

Getting there

To reach Fontainebleau by train, take the Montargie line to Fontainebleau Avon station; it departs hourly from the Gare de Lyon in Paris. The trip takes 35 to 60 minutes and costs about 8€ ($9.20). Fontainebleau Avon station is just outside the town in Avon, a suburb of Paris. From the station, the town bus (direction Château) makes the two-mile trip to the château every 10 to 15 minutes on weekdays and every 30 minutes on Saturdays and Sundays.

You can also reach Fontainebleau on a tour bus. **Cityrama,** 4 place des Pyramides, 1er (☎ **01-44-55-61-00;** www.cityrama.fr), combines both Fontainebleau and the nearby artist's village of Barbizon for 57€ ($66) adult, 29€ ($33) child.

Exploring Fontainebleau

It's said that Fontainebleau was built for love. François I transformed a run-down royal palace into Fontainebleau in 1528 for his mistress, and his successor, Henri II, left a beautiful memorial to the woman he loved — a **ballroom** decorated with the intertwined initials of his mistress, Diane de Poitiers, and himself.

The Mona Lisa once hung here; François I bought the painting from da Vinci himself. Stucco-framed paintings now hanging in the **Gallery of François I** include *The Rape of Europa* and depict mythological and allegorical scenes related to the king's life. Make sure to see the racy ceiling

Fontainebleau

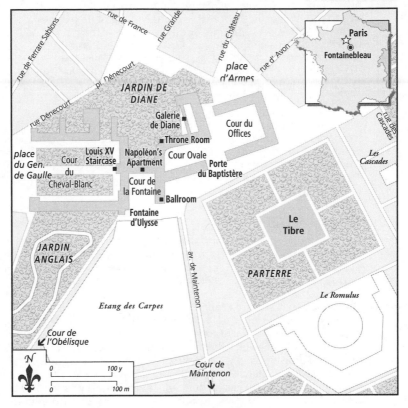

paintings above the **Louis XV Staircase,** which was originally painted for the bedroom of a duchess. The stairway's architect simply ripped out the bedroom floor, using its ceiling to cover the stairway. One fresco depicts the Queen of the Amazons climbing into Alexander the Great's bed.

When Louis XIV ascended the throne, Fontainebleau was largely neglected because of his preoccupation with Versailles, but it found renewed glory under Napoléon I. You can walk around much of the palace on your own, but most of the Napoleonic rooms are accessible only on guided tours, which are in French. Napoleon had two bedchambers; mirrors adorn either side of his bed in the grander chamber (look for his symbol, a bee), while a small bed is housed in the aptly named **Small Bedchamber.** A red-and-gold throne with the initial "N" is displayed in the **Throne Room.** You can also see Napoléon's **offices,** where the emperor signed his abdication; however, the document on exhibit is only a copy. Minor apartments include those once occupied by Madame De Maintenon, the second wife of Louis XIV; those of Pope Pius VII, whom Napoléon kept a virtual prisoner; still another was Marie Antoinette's.

After a visit to the palace, wander through the gardens, paying special attention to the lovely, bucolic carp pond with its fearless swans. If you'd like to promenade in the forest, a detailed map of its paths is available from the **Office de Tourisme,** 4 rue Royale, near the palace (☎ 01-60-74-99-99). You can also rent bikes nearby from **À la Petite Reine,** 32 rue des Sablons (☎ 01-60-74-57-57), for about 5€ ($5.75) an hour, 13€ ($15) a half day, 16€ ($18) a full day, with a credit-card deposit. The **Tour Denencourt,** about three miles north of the palace, makes a nice ride and has a pretty view.

The Palais de Fontainebleau is open daily November through February from 9 a.m. to 5 p.m.; March, April, and October from 9 a.m. to 6 p.m.; and May through September from 9 a.m. to 7 p.m. Admission to the Grands Appartements is 5.50€ ($6.30) for adults, 4€ ($4.60) for ages 18 to 26 and older than 60, free for those under 18. Free for all on the first Sunday of the month.

Dining options

If you're arriving by train and plan to visit only Fontainebleau, consider bringing a picnic from Paris. In fine weather, the château's gardens and nearby forest beckon. If you have a car, however, save your appetite for Barbizon.

On the western edge of France's finest forest lies the village of Barbizon, home to a number of noted landscape artists — Corot, Millet, Rousseau, and Daumier. The colorful town has a lively mix of good restaurants, boutiques, and antiques shops — the perfect place to while away an afternoon. For lunch, try the **Relais de Barbizon,** 2 avenue Charles de Gaulle (☎ 01-60-66-40-28). The 30€ ($35) prix fixe may feature such hearty home-style dishes as duckling in wild cherry sauce and a *tarte au citron* (lemon pie). The restaurant is open Thursday through Monday noon to 2:30 p.m. and 8 to 10 p.m. (Only lunch is served on Tuesdays.)

If you stay in Fontainebleau for lunch, try **Le Table des Maréchaux** (in the Hôtel Napoléon, 9 rue Grande (☎ 01-60-39-50-50). Its 31€ ($36) three-course Ménu de l'Empereur may include a starter of seasonal terrine with tomato chutney or gazpacho with grilled almonds and pine nuts and main courses of crispy cod with basil, mashed potatoes and a tomato sauce or breast of duckling served with honey and dried fruits. Finish up with a puff pastry of honey ice cream and chestnut cream. In warm weather, diners can eat on the outdoor terrace.

The Cathedral at Chartres

It survived the French Revolution, even though it was scheduled for demolition. It withstood two world wars, when volunteers took down all of its 12th- and 13th-century stained glass piece by piece. But for a majority of its visitors, the Cathédrale de Notre-Dame de Chartres (☎ 02-37-21-56-33; see the nearby "Notre-Dame de Chartres" map), one of the world's

Notre-Dame de Chartres

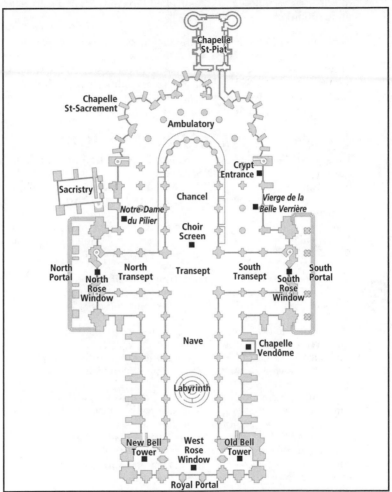

greatest Gothic cathedrals and one of the finest creations of the Middle Ages, comes second in importance to a small scrap of material housed inside. Known as the *Sancta Camisia,* it is said to have been worn by the Virgin Mary when she gave birth to Jesus — and that's the biggest draw here.

Getting there

Pick up one of the hourly SNCF trains from Paris's Gare Montparnasse to the town of Chartres. A round-trip ticket costs about 23€ ($26); the trip takes an hour.

If you'd like to drive to Chartres, take the A10/A11 highway from Porte d'Orléans and follow the signs to Le Mans and Chartres. The drive takes about 75 minutes.

Traveling to Chartres by tour bus is another option. **Cityrama,** 4 place des Pyramides, 1er (☎ 01-44-55-61-00; www.cityrama.fr), offers five-hour excursions leaving from Paris every Tuesday, Thursday, and Saturday for 47€ ($54) adult, 24€ ($28) child. **Paris Vision,** 214 rue de Rivoli, 1er (☎ 01-42-60-30-01; www.parisvision.com), also has a tour that departs the same days for the same amount.

Exploring the cathedral

Take one of Malcolm Miller's excellent 1¼-hour guided tours of Chartres Cathedral Monday through Saturday at noon and 2:45 p.m. from Easter to November; cost is 10€ ($12). Miller, an Englishman who has made the study of the cathedral his life's work, has published such books as *Chartres Cathedral* (Riverside Books Co.) and *Chartres Stained Glass* (Jarrold Publishing). Miller has been giving fascinating tours of the cathedral for 40 years. He is sometimes available in winter, too; call ☎ 02-37-28-15-58.

Sunday afternoons are a terrific time to visit, when free organ concerts (4:45–5:45 p.m.) and the filtered light coming in from the western windows make the church come wonderfully alive.

The cathedral that you see today dates principally from the 13th century, when it was built with the combined efforts and contributions of kings, princes, church officials, and pilgrims from across Europe. This Notre-Dame was among the first to use flying buttresses.

Begin at the very beginning — with the **entryway.** People say that Rodin sat for hours on the edge of the sidewalk, contemplating the portal, spellbound by its sculptured bodies draped in long, flowing robes with amazingly lifelike faces. Before entering, walk around to both the north and south portals, which date from the 13th century. The bays depict such biblical scenes as the expulsion of Adam and Eve from the Garden of Eden, and episodes from the life of the Virgin.

Next, just inside, are the **Clocher Vieux** (Old Tower) with its 350-foot steeple dating from the 12th century, and the **Clocher Neuf** (New Tower). Originally built in 1134, the new tower's elaborate ornamental tower was added between 1507 and 1513 following one of the many fires that swept through the cathedral.

You can climb to the top of the Clocher Neuf, but make sure your shoes aren't slippery — parts of the tower are without a railing and are quite steep and narrow.

The cathedral is also known for its celebrated **choir screen.** Don't let the simple term fool you; this is a carved wood structure that took nearly

200 years to complete. The niches, 40 in all, contain statues illustrating scenes from the life of Mary. The screen is in the middle of the cathedral toward the altar.

Few of the rushed visitors ever notice the screen; they're transfixed by the stained-glass windows. Bring a pair of binoculars to better focus on the panes, which cover more than 3,000 square yards. The glass is unequaled anywhere in the world and is truly mystical. It was spared in both world wars, because in both wars, the glass was removed piece by piece. Currently, the Association Chartres Sanctuaire du Monde has undertaken the considerable task of raising the millions of euro necessary for the restoration of the stained-glass windows, which have suffered on both sides from smoke from the cathedral's candles and from pollution.

Most of the stained glass dates from the 12th and 13th centuries. Many visitors find it difficult to single out one panel or window of particular merit; however, the oldest is the 12th-century **Notre Dame de la belle verrière** (Our Lady of the beautiful window, sometimes called the Blue Virgin) on the south side. The colors from the glass are such a vibrant, startling blue that many find it hard to believe that the window is 1,000 years old.

In the **nave** — the widest in France — have a look down at the 13th-century labyrinth. It was designed for pilgrims to navigate on their hands and knees as a form of penance, all 1,000 feet of it. These days, much of it is covered with folding chairs for Mass. The wooden **Virgin of the Pillar,** to the left of the choir, dates from the 14th century. The **crypt** was built over a period of 200 years, beginning in the 9th century. Enshrined is **Our Lady of the Crypt**, a Madonna made in 1976 that replaced one destroyed during the Revolution. The **Sancta Camisia,** the holy relic that some people believe Mary wore during the birth of Jesus, is behind the choir screen in a chapel to the left of the church's treasury.

The cathedral is open daily April through September from 8 a.m. to 8 p.m., October through March from 7:30 a.m. to 7:00 p.m. Ask at the Chartres tourist office (☎ **02-37-18-26-26**) outside the cathedral for information about tours in English and a schedule of masses open to the public. From April to September, the North Tower is open Monday through Saturday from 9:30 to 11:30 a.m. and daily from 2:00 to 5:30 p.m.; October through March, Monday through Saturday from 10:00 to 11:30 a.m. and daily from 2:00 to 4:00 p.m. Admission to the tower is about 4€ ($4.60) for adults, 3€ ($3.45) for seniors and students; children younger than 12 are admitted free.

Dining options

You can find plenty of restaurants, cafes, and snack bars around town, but just a stone's throw from the cathedral is **Le Café Serpente,** 2 Cloître Notre-Dame (☎ **02-37-21-68-81**). Facing the south side of the cathedral with outside tables, this restaurant serves traditional French fare at reasonable prices, with lunch priced between 10€ and 20€ ($12–$23) for two courses that may start with a dish of leeks and asparagus with foie gras and include a main course of *filet de rouget* (red fish filet). The restaurant is open daily for lunch, and Monday through Saturday for dinner.

For more upscale dining nearby, try **Le Buisson Ardent,** 10 rue au Lait (☎ 02-37-34-04-66). The restaurant serves well-prepared fare made with farm-fresh ingredients in a quaint, wood-beamed dining room. A variety of fresh fish dishes are available, and the roast pigeon with lemon juice, served with potato pancakes and fresh vegetables, is also recommended. Calvados (a cider brandy) is a specialty of the Normandy region; for dessert, try the crispy hot apples with sorbet and Calvados-flavored butter sauce. Main courses are priced between 13€ and 25€ ($15–$29); a prix fixe three-course meal is 18€ and 23€ ($21 and $26). Open Thursday through Saturday, noon to 2 p.m. and 7 to 9:30 p.m.

If you have extra time, spend it by exploring the medieval cobbled streets of the **Old Town.** At the foot of the cathedral are lanes with gabled and turreted houses and humped bridges spanning the Eure River. The turreted Norman house (it's the oldest-looking one there) on rue Chantault, dates back nine centuries.

Stop in to the **Musée de Beaux-Arts de Chartres,** 29 Cloître Notre-Dame (☎ 02-37-36-41-39), to see paintings by old masters such as Watteau, Brosamer, and Zurbarán and admire the museum's architecture, some of which dates back to the 15th century. The museum is open Wednesday through Monday, 10 a.m. to noon, and from 2 to 5 p.m. Admission is 2.50€ ($2.90), free for children under 12.

Disneyland Paris

Disneyland Paris, known locally as *Le Parc Disneyland* (☎ 08-25-30-10-30 (.15€/min); www.disneylandparis.com), is France's number-one attraction, with more than 50 million visitors a year. When it opened in 1992 the French were dead set against it; now 40 percent of its visitors are French, and half of those are Parisian. Set on a 5,000-acre site (about one-fifth the size of Paris) in the suburb of Marne-la-Vallée, the park incorporates the elements of its Disney predecessors but gives them a European flair. Allow at least a full day to see Disneyland Paris.

Information about hotels and packages is constantly changing, so your best bet for staying up to date is to obtain the Disneyland Resort Paris brochure from the Web site a few months in advance.

Getting there

To get to Disneyland Paris by train, take the **RER Line A** from the center of Paris (Invalides, Nation, or Châtelet–Les Halles) to Marne-la-Vallée/Chessy, a 35-minute ride. Trains run every 10 to 20 minutes, depending on the time of day. The station is at the entrance to the park.

 Avoid lines at the resort by buying Disneyland passes at all RER A stations, except Marne-la-Vallée, and Métro stations including Charles-de-Gaulle–Etoile, Franklin-D-Roosevelt, Gare de Lyon, Porte Maillot, Esplanade de la Défense, Anvers, Père-Lachaise, Place de Clichy, Gallieni, Havre-Caumartin, Villiers, Alésia, Barbès-Rochechouart, Châtelet, Denfert-Rochereau, and Gare de l'Est. The pass is good for either Disneyland Park or Walt Disney Studios but not both.

Within the park, a free shuttle bus connects the various hotels with the theme park, stopping every 6 to 15 minutes, depending on the time of year. Service begins an hour before the park opens and stops an hour after closing.

If you prefer to drive to Disneyland Paris, take the A4 highway east and exit at Park Euro Disney. Guest parking at any of the thousands of spaces costs 8€ ($9.20). A series of moving sidewalks speeds up pedestrian transit from the parking areas to the theme park entrance.

Exploring the park

The Disneyland Paris resort consists of two theme parks. The first, **Disneyland Park,** clusters together five "lands" of entertainment (Main Street, U.S.A; Frontierland; Adventureland; Fantasyland; and Discoveryland) and is where most of the massive and well-designed hotels, a nightlife center (Le Festival Disney), swimming pools, tennis courts, dozens of restaurants, shows, an aquarium, and the Manchester United Soccer School are located. If your kids are younger than 7, they'd be best suited for Main Street, U.S.A., Fantasyland, Sleeping Beauty's Castle, and the afternoon parade. Children ages 7 through 12 will most likely enjoy Frontierland, the Phantom Manor ghost house, the Big Thunder Mountain roller coaster, Adventureland, Indiana Jones and the Temple of Doom roller coaster, and the Pirates of the Caribbean ride. Discoveryland, the Space Mountain roller coaster, and the Star Tours simulated spacecraft ride should please your teens.

Walt Disney Studios Park is the newer of the two parks and is set up as a movie studio come to life, where children participate in the movie-making process. The entrance is called the Front Lot and resembles the Hollywood Disney studios — water tower, gates, and all. En Coulisse restaurant is located here, serving the kind of food kids like and Americans are known for — hamburgers, pizza, salads, and ice cream. In a film studio resembling a street, kids can become a part of the filming of impromptu comedy sketches as they walk around the park; later in the day, they get to see themselves on screen. In the Animation Courtyard, cartoon characters come to life via black light and mirrors, and children can play at being animators at interactive displays. The French Disney Channel has its studios here, in the Production Courtyard; kids get to see how a TV studio really works and may be asked to serve as extras.

An international buffet, Rendez-Vous des Stars, is located here. The Back Lot features the Backlot Express Restaurant, serving sandwiches and other quick fare, and the Rock-n-Roller Coaster, a very fast and very loud ride (120 speakers playing Aerosmith) that whips you through an Aerosmith rock video. Calm down afterward by watching the stunt show spectacular, which is highlighted by a high-speed car chase. Food kiosks sell popcorn, ice cream, hot dogs, and so on throughout the park.

A guide for visitors in wheelchairs gives important information about access to rides and other attractions all around the park. You can pick up a copy at City Hall in the Disneyland Park or call to have a copy sent to you (☎ 01-60-30-60-30).

Admission (subject to change) to **either** Disneyland Park or the Walt Disney Studios Park for one day is 40€ ($46) for visitors 12 and older, 30€ ($35) for children ages 3 to 11 years, and free for children younger than 3. Admission for a two-day Hopper Pass good for unlimited access to **both** the theme park and the studios park costs 89€ ($102) for adults, 69€ ($80) ages 3 to 11; a three-day Hopper Pass is 109€ ($125) for adults and 89€ ($102) ages 3 to 11. Entrance to Le Festival Disney (a consortium of shops, dance clubs, and restaurants) is free; there's usually a cover charge for the dance clubs.

Disneyland Paris is open all year. Hours vary. From January to March the parks are open Monday to Friday 10 a.m. to 8 p.m. and weekends 9 a.m. to 8 p.m. From March to May the parks are open daily 9 a.m. to 8 p.m., and from the middle of June to the end of August daily from 9 a.m. to 11 p.m. Because hours also vary with the weather, call before you go: ☎ 08-25-30-10-30 (.15€/min).

Avoid waiting in long lines with the free **Fast Pass.** After presenting the pass at the ride you want, you're given a time frame for when to come back and board the ride first upon your return. Ask for it at the ticket booth or City Hall.

Staying at Disneyland

If you want to stay at Disneyland overnight or for a few days, you need to book well in advance. Plenty of hotels are available at different price levels, and you can explore the options and book accommodations on the park's Web site at www.disneylandparis.com.

Monet's Gardens at Giverny

Monet moved to Giverny (☎ 02-32-51-28-21 for Fondation Claude Monet, which runs the museum) in 1883, and the water lilies beneath the Japanese bridge in the garden and the flower garden became his regular subjects until his death in 1926. In 1966, the Monet family donated Giverny to the Académie des Beaux-Arts in Paris, perhaps the most prestigious fine-arts school in France, which subsequently opened the site to the public. Giverny has since become one of the most popular attractions in France, but even the crowds can't completely overwhelm the magic.

Getting there

Catch an SNCF train at the Gare St-Lazare in Paris approximately every hour for the 45-minute trip to Vernon, the town nearest the Monet gardens. The round-trip fare is about 21€ ($24). From the station, buses make the three-mile trip to the museum for 2€ ($2.30), or you can go on foot — the route along the Seine makes for a nice walk.

If you're driving to Giverny, take the A13 highway from the Porte d'Auteuil to Bonnières, then D201 to Giverny. The whole trip takes about an hour.

Traveling to Giverny by tour bus is another option. **Cityrama,** 4 place des Pyramides, 1er (☎ **01-44-55-61-00;** www.cityrama.com), has two trips to Giverny: a five-hour trip on Tuesday through Saturday for 60€ ($69) adults, 30€ ($30) children; and an all-day Giverny–Auvers-sur-Oise trip on Sunday or Wednesday for 100€ ($115) for adults, 90€ ($104) for children, which includes lunch at the American Museum. Call for specific dates. **Paris Vision,** 214 rue de Rivoli, 1er (☎ **01-42-60-30-01;** www.parisvision.com), offers two trips: a Versailles-Giverny all-day trip on Tuesday and Friday that includes lunch at the **Moulin de Fourges** for 98€ ($113) for adults, 49€ ($56) for children; and a trip without lunch on Tuesday through Sunday for 58€ ($67) for adults and 30€ ($35) for children.

Exploring the gardens

Even before you arrive at Giverny, you probably have some idea of what you're going to see — but nothing prepares you for the spectacular beauty of seeing the gardens up close. The gardens are usually at their best in May, June, and July. Should you yearn to have them almost to yourself, plan to be at the gates when the gardens open or go on a rainy day. You'll probably spend at least a half-day at Giverny, longer if you plan to eat lunch and visit the American Museum.

The gardens are open from April to November Tuesday through Sunday from 9:30 a.m. to 6:00 p.m., as well as Easter Monday and Whit Monday (51 days after Easter). Admission to the house and gardens is 5.50€ ($6.30) for adults, 4€ ($4.60) for students, and 3€ ($3.45) for ages 7 to 12; admission to only the gardens is 4€ (4.60), and admission to only the house is 1.50€ ($1.70). No advanced tickets are sold.

Some say Monet's influence was responsible for the influx of American artists into the village of Giverny in the late 1880s. Others say that Monet had little contact with the Americans, and it was Giverny's beauty that captured the hearts of painters like John Singer Sargent and William Metcalf, who began spending their summers there. In any case, at one point, more than 50 American artists lived in Giverny with their families. You can see much of their work at the **Musée d'Art Américain Giverny** (☎ **02-32-51-94-65**), just 100 yards from Monet's house and gardens.

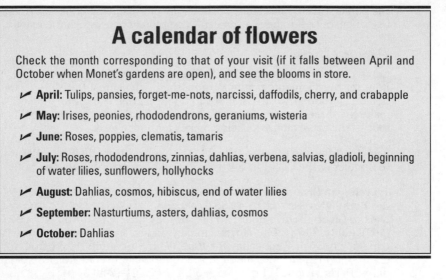

A calendar of flowers

Check the month corresponding to that of your visit (if it falls between April and October when Monet's gardens are open), and see the blooms in store.

✔ **April:** Tulips, pansies, forget-me-nots, narcissi, daffodils, cherry, and crabapple

✔ **May:** Irises, peonies, rhododendrons, geraniums, wisteria

✔ **June:** Roses, poppies, clematis, tamaris

✔ **July:** Roses, rhododendrons, zinnias, dahlias, verbena, salvias, gladioli, beginning of water lilies, sunflowers, hollyhocks

✔ **August:** Dahlias, cosmos, hibiscus, end of water lilies

✔ **September:** Nasturtiums, asters, dahlias, cosmos

✔ **October:** Dahlias

The museum is open April through November, Tuesday through Sunday from 10 a.m. to 6 p.m., as well as Easter Monday and Whit Monday (the 51st day after Easter). Admission is 5€ ($5.75) for adults, 4€ ($4.60) for students and seniors, 3€ ($3.45) for ages 12 to 18, and free for children younger than 12. Admission is free for all on the first Sunday of every month.

Dining options

Your entry ticket is no longer valid once you leave Monet's home, so think ahead about whether you want to eat lunch before or after your visit. Most people arrive in early afternoon to have a better chance of avoiding the crowds in the morning.

The square directly across from Monet's house and the adjacent street have many little cafes and crêperies. But a short walk from the gardens is **Les Jardins de Giverny,** 5 chemin du Roy (☎ **02-32-21-60-80**). This beautiful and tranquil restaurant opens its doors onto a rose garden in warm weather and serves delicious regional specialties. A *trou Normand* (cider and Calvados sorbet) aids digestion between courses that may include an asparagus-filled puff pastry and warm oysters cooked in *beurre blanc* and cider with a frothy sorell *sabayon* (sauce made of whipped eggs and wine), or monkfish and squid flavored with saffron and served in a *marmite* (small cooking pot). Main courses cost between 18€ and 25€ ($21–$29). The 26€ ($30) and 35€ ($40) menus are better deals. Open Tuesday to Sunday noon to 3:00 p.m. and 7:30 to 10:00 p.m. Closed in winter.

Another good restaurant in town is **Le Relais Normand** (☎ 02-32-21-16-12) in the Hôtel d'Evreux, an old Norman manor house with a fireplace and terrace. It serves delicious dishes like roasted Normandy oysters with house seasoning, beef filet with Livarot cream cheese, and duck filet with caramelized red fruit. The three prix-fixe menus cost 21€, 27€ and 31€ ($24, $31, and $36). The restaurant is open for lunch Tuesday through Sunday from noon to 3 p.m.

Part V
Living It Up after Dark: Paris Nightlife

In this part . . .

Paris may not be a city that never sleeps, but it's just as fabulous after the sun sets as it is during the day. There is so much to do! Take your pick of French-language, English-language, and avant-garde theater productions or ballet, opera, and symphony. But beware! Events can sell out quickly. The Ménilmontant neighborhood is a bit too trendy now — night owls are starting to head to the Canal St-Martin neighborhood in the 10e arrondissement and the dance barges on the Seine are still going strong. You can always check out the overpriced can-can cabaret spectacles at venues like the Moulin Rouge, the Lido, and the Crazy Horse — even though Parisians wouldn't be caught dead at 'em, there's still plenty of healthy business from visitors. Chapter 15 gives you the lowdown on Paris's vibrant theater scene and previews the symphony, opera, and ballet. Chapter 16 hits the bars and clubs, jumping jazz spots, live music venues, classy cocktail joints, and those naughty cabarets.

Chapter 15

Applauding the Cultural Scene

● ●

In This Chapter

▶ Getting the inside scoop on the performing arts scene

▶ Finding out what's playing and getting tickets

▶ Taking in plays, symphony, opera, and dance in Paris

● ●

*T*his is the city that gave the world playwrights Molière, Victor Hugo, Pierre Corneille, and Jean Racine; produced actors Sarah Bernhardt and Antonin Artaud; and nurtured expats Eugene Ionescu and Samuel Beckett. But you don't need to understand French to take in an evening of culture. (Mime Marcel Marceau came out of the city's still-flourishing avant-garde theater, after all!) If mime seems a little lowbrow, there are hundreds of other options: Paris has a world-class orchestra, opera, ballet companies — and wonderful venues that house them. There's a flourishing English-language theater scene, and cutting-edge theater productions with scope and visuals that make language secondary!

This chapter helps you find out what's going on and then gets you there.

Getting the Inside Scoop

Paris is one of *the* places in the world to see top-tier ballet and listen to world-renowned symphonies. Unlike New York City, where theaters are located in the area around Broadway and 42nd streets, in Paris cultural offerings are scattered around the city, from the **Opéra Bastille** in the 12th to **Théâtre National de la Colline** in the 20th. The Opéra Bastille got a new director in fall 2004, **Gérard Mortier,** who is known for being cutting edge. Some pre-Mortier highlights were Mozart's *The Magic Flute,* Wagner's *Tristan et Isolde,* and Strauss's *Elektra.* Opera buffs can't wait to see how Mortier is going to shake things up from here. The **Palais Garnier** showcased France's national ballet company performing German choreographer Pina Bausch's *Orphée et Eurydice,* and was looking forward to the March 2005 premiere of Kader Belarbi's original ballet *Wuthering Heights.* Paris is also home to a growing *early music* scene (music of the Middle Ages, Renaissance, baroque, rococo, and the early classical eras) led by an early music group, **Les Arts Florissants,** which has performed operas in Paris's biggest venues.

The musical still remains a hot ticket here: Paris audiences have been wild for *Le Petit Prince,* from the book by Antoine de Saint-Exupéry, and it will be staged for a second season. *Bob Fosse, Le Show,* ran from Christmas through Valentine's Day 2004, and *Chicago* and *Hair* played at the Casino de Paris and Palais de Sports, respectively.

On any given day, close to 100 theatrical productions may be going on in Paris and the surrounding area. Because Paris is just a hop, skip, and Eurostar train away from London, some of that city's finest actors have found their way across the Channel and into the city's English-language theater community, where they joined up with American, Australian, and even some bilingual French *confrères* (colleagues). Productions in English may not be plentiful, but quality is high, and a wide range of styles is offered.

Dinner and a show

Since performances tend to start around 8 p.m. and French restaurants tend to open at 7 p.m., with dining lasting anywhere from 1½ hours to 3 hours and more, what's a hungry show-goer to do? Have a snack before the show, and feast afterward at one of the many cafes or brasseries open late. The following are listed in Chapter 10 and plenty more can be found around the city.

✔ **La Tour de Monthélery/Chez Denise** is centrally located in the 1er and open 24 hours.

✔ **Café Marly,** 1er, in the Louvre's courtyard is open until 2 a.m.

✔ **Le Zimmer,** 1er, at place du Châtelet, serves food until 12:30 a.m.

✔ **Au Pied de Cochon** in the 1er is open 24 hours.

✔ **Bofinger,** in the 4e, is open until 1 a.m.

✔ **Brasserie Ile St-Louis,** on the tip of Ile St-Louis right across from Notre-Dame, is open until 1 a.m.

✔ You can order food at showy **Fouquet's,** 8e, on the Champs-Elysées until 11:30 p.m.

✔ St-Germain's **Vagenende,** 6e, stays open until 1 a.m.

✔ **La Coupole** on boulevard du Montparnasse, 14e, is open until 1:00 a.m., 1:30 a.m. on weekends.

✔ Trendy **Man Ray** in the 8e, serves food until midnight.

✔ The Latin Quarter's infamous **Brasserie Balzar,** 5e, stays open until 11:45 p.m.

When attending performances, arrive early. On the reverse side of Paris theater tickets is written: *Les spectateurs retardaires ne peuvant à être placés que lors d'une interruption du spectacle et en fonction de l'accessibilité.* In other words, late arrivals cannot be seated until there is an interruption (intermission) in the play, if they are seated at all. Opera tickets say: *Les spectateurs retardaires ne peuvent à être placés qu'à la fin du premier tableau, du premier acte de l'ouvrage ou à l'entracte,* meaning that late arrivals cannot be seated until the end of the first scene, the first act or between acts. Some theaters will not even seat those who arrive after the curtain rises, in many cases because the plays being performed are short with no intermission. You want to arrive at the theater or opera early anyway; the bars in these locations are generally very good and are relaxing places to unwind before the shows.

A *placeuse* (an usher, usually female) wearing a small purse around her neck will show you to your seats. Yes, that purse is for tips, which are expected; generally tip one or two euros ($1.15–$2.30) per person.

Paris audiences tend to dress up for performances, in nice jewelry and dressy pants or skirts for the women, jackets for the men. Generally, the nicer the venue, the dressier the look. Thus, for men a tie and jacket are recommended at the Palais Garnier, whereas an open collar under a stylish jacket would be the look for a performance at Bouffes du Nord.

Finding Out What's Playing and Getting Tickets

Several local publications provide up-to-the-minute listings of performances and other evening entertainment. *Pariscope: Une Semaine de Paris* (0.40€/45¢) is a weekly guide with thorough listings of movies, plays, ballet, art exhibits, clubs, and more. It can be found at any newsstand. *L'Officiel des Spectacles* (0.35€/40¢) is another weekly guide in French. *Paris Nuit* (3.05€/$3.50) is a French monthly that contains good articles and listings. You can pick up the free music monthlies, *La Terrasse* and *Cadences,* outside concert venues. The *Paris Free Voice* is a free monthly publication that spotlights events of interest to English speakers, including poetry readings, plays, and literary evenings at English-language bookstores and libraries. You can find it at cybercafes and English-language bookstores.

You can also get information on the Web from the **French Government Tourist Office** (www.francetourism.com), the **Office de Tourisme et de Congrès de Paris** (www.parisinfo.com), and the **Maison de la France** (www.franceguide.com). Likewise, try **Culture Kiosque** (www.culturekiosque.com) for excellent magazine-style sites about opera and dance, including schedules, reviews, and phone numbers for ordering tickets. The *Paris Free Voice* also has a Web site (http://paris voice.com), featuring an events calendar and reviews of current opera, dance, and theater.

Saving money on tickets

For half-price theater tickets for national theaters and other venues, go to the **Kiosque-Théâtre** at the northwest corner of the Madeleine Church (Métro: Madeleine) to buy tickets for same-day performances. The panels all around the kiosk indicate sold-out shows with a little red man; a little green man tells you that tickets are still available. The Kiosque-Théâtre is open Tuesday through Saturday from 12:30 to 8:00 p.m., Sunday from 12:30 to 4:00 p.m. A second branch of the discount-ticket counter is in front of the Gare Montparnasse. Try to arrive no later than noon, because lines are usually long.

Ticket prices in this chapter are approximate; costs vary, depending on who is performing what on which day of the week. Call the theaters for information, or consult *Pariscope* and other entertainment listings. Many concert, theater, and dance tickets are sold through **Fnac** department stores and at the box office. You can find a dozen or so Fnac outlets throughout Paris; the most prominent is 74 avenue des Champs-Elysées (Métro: George V). You can also reserve by phone at Fnac (☎ **08-92-68-36-22;** 0.45€/min.) Monday through Friday from 9 a.m. to 8 p.m., Saturday from 10 a.m. to 5 p.m. Easier is **TicketNet** (www.ticketnet.fr), in French and English, which allows you to buy tickets to cultural events online.

Raising the Curtain on the Performing Arts

The theaters listed here are national theaters supported by the government, but many private ones also exist. For full listings, consult *Pariscope: Une Semaine de Paris* (.40€/45¢), a weekly guide with thorough listings of movies, plays, ballet, art exhibits, and clubs sold at all newsstands.

Attending the theater

A good mix of modern and classic tragedies and comedies comes alive in wonderful performances in the **Salle Richelieu** of the **Comédie-Française,** 2 rue de Richelieu, 1er (☎ 01-44-58-15-15; www.comedie-francaise.fr; Métro: Palais-Royal–Musée du Louvre). Performances are in French. Tickets cost 10€ to 44€ ($12–$51). Last-minute seats for people 27 and younger are on sale one hour before the start of the performance and cost 10€ ($12). To purchase tickets up to 14 days in advance, phone daily from 11 a.m. to 6 p.m. except March 24 and 25, May 1, and July 14. For those who want to buy tickets at the theater, the ticket window is open daily 11 a.m. to 6 p.m. To order tickets 15 days to 2 months in advance, fax information to 01-44-58-14-80 or purchase online (no phone reservations are accepted). *Note:* The Web site is in French with some English; pricing and other practical information is in French.

Also a part of the Comédie-Française, the **Théâtre du Vieux Colombier,** 21 rue Vieux Colombier, 6e (☎ 01-44-39-87-00; Métro: St-Sulpice), is an intimate 300-seat venue where mostly modern works are performed. Tickets cost 8€ to 27€ ($9.20–$31) for adults, 6€ to 13€ ($6.90–$15) for people under 27, and 6€ to 20€ ($6.90–$23) for seniors. To purchase tickets up to 14 days in advance, call daily 11 a.m. to 6:30 p.m. To order tickets 15 days to two months in advance, fax information to 01-44-39-87-19 or purchase online (no phone reservations are accepted).

The Comédie-Française also has a workshop in the **Carrousel du Louvre Studio-Théâtre,** where actors perform one-hour plays and readings. Video projections of plays and films are also shown here. Tickets are sold at the ticket window one hour before the performance and cost 7€ to 16€ ($8.05–$18) for adults, 5€ to 12€ ($5.75–$14) for seniors, and 4€ to 8€ ($4.60–$9.20) for people 27 and younger.

For popular, contemporary plays, the **Théâtre National de Chaillot,** place du Trocadéro, 16e (☎ 01-53-65-30-00; www.theatre-chaillot. fr; Métro: Trocadéro), is your place. Part of the Art Deco Palais de Chaillot, the theater is located directly across the Seine from the Eiffel Tower. Tickets are 18€ to 30€ ($21–$35) for adults, 15€ to 25€ ($17–$29) for seniors, and 9.50€ to 18€ ($11–$20) for people 26 and younger. To purchase tickets by telephone, call Monday through Saturday 10 a.m. to 7 p.m. Box office hours are Monday to Friday 11 a.m. to 7 p.m., Sunday 1 p.m. to 5 p.m.

The **Théâtre National de la Colline,** 15 rue Malte-Brun, 20e (☎ 01-44-62-52-52; www.colline.fr; Métro: Gambetta), has modern drama from around the world, and the **Petit Théâtre,** located upstairs, has short plays and offerings from international theater's less famous and up-and-coming playwrights. Arrive early to have a glass of wine and admire the view from the Café de la Colline in the lobby. Tickets cost 26€ ($30) for adults, 21€ ($24) for seniors, and 13€ ($15) for people younger than 30. On Tuesdays, adults and seniors pay 18€ ($21). To purchase tickets by phone, call Monday and Tuesday 11 a.m. to 6 p.m., Wednesday through Friday 11 a.m. to 7 p.m., and Saturday 1 p.m. to 7 p.m. Box office hours are Monday through Friday 11 a.m. to 6 p.m., Saturday 1 p.m. to 7 p.m., and Sunday 2 p.m. to 5 p.m.

Because of renovations of its building at 6 place de l'Odéon, the troupe of the **Odéon Théâtre de l'Europe** has temporarily relocated until 2006 to two locations on boulevard Berthier, 17e, once home to the Opéra-Comique: 8 for the big theater and 32 for the theater annex or little theater (☎ 01-44-85-40-00; www.theatre-odeon.fr; Métro: Porte de Clichy); performances are varied and eclectic. (Lou Reed once read his poems at the Odéon.) Tickets are 26€ ($30) for adults, 20€ ($23) for seniors, and 13€ ($15) for people younger than 30. To purchase tickets by phone call ☎ 01-44-85-40-40 Monday to Saturday 11 a.m. to 7 p.m. Tickets also go on sale at the box office at each of the theaters 90 minutes before the show.

Seeking English-language theater

Summer is a good time to catch English-language theater in Paris. The
Théâtre de Nesle, 8 rue de Nesle, 6e (☎ 01-46-34-61-04; Métro: St-Michel),
and **Les Déchargeurs,** 3 rue des Déchargeurs, 1er (☎ 01-42-36-00-02;
Métro: Châtelet), sometimes stage English-language plays. Or, for comedy
in English, try **Laughing Matters,** in the historic Hôtel du Nord, 102 quai
de Jemmapes, 10e (☎ 01-53-19-98-88; www.anythingmatters.com;
Métro: Jacques Bonsergent). This company is thriving; the lineups are
always terrific, featuring award-winning comics from the United States,
the United Kingdom, Ireland, and Australia. Shows start at 8:30 p.m.;
admission varies, but count on paying 20€ to 25€ ($23–$29) at the door.

Other English-language theaters include **Dear Conjunction** (☎ 01-42-62-
35-00), known for its interpretations of Harold Pinter, and **Paris Festival
Theatre Company** (☎ 01-53-01-45-22), which performs musicals. **One
World Actors Productions** (☎ 06-07-03-83-25 or 01-48-28-09-26; www.
oneworldactors.com), founded in 2002 to promote English-language
theater and cross-cultural exchanges among English, French, and other
cultures in Paris, performs plays in French and English, with tickets aver-
aging 15€ ($17). Recent plays include Alfred de Musset's *Les Caprices de
Marianne* in French and Jim Cartwright's British comedy *Two* in English.
You can find listings for English-language productions in the *Paris Free
Voice* — just be sure to call the theater ahead of time to double-check
the curtain time.

And keep in mind that some theater isn't meant to be understood. In
fact, sometimes *not* understanding the language can actually be a bonus.
Several well-known avant-garde theater companies are located in Paris,
including **Les Bouffes du Nord** (☎ 01-46-07-34-50), run by the legendary
Peter Brook, and **Le Théâtre du Soleil** (☎ 01-43-74-24-08), known for its
stunning adaptations of both classics and original works. Even though
these performances are usually in French, the scope of these productions
is so large, and the visuals so profound, you may not even notice that you
haven't understood a single word.

Listening to classical music and the symphony

Classical music concerts occur throughout the year, and many of them
are quite affordable. Look for flyers at churches announcing schedule
times, prices, and locations.

 More than a dozen Parisian churches regularly schedule relatively inexpensive organ recitals and concerts. The most glorious, where the music
is nearly outdone by the gorgeous stained-glass windows, is **Sainte-
Chapelle,** 4 boulevard du Palais, 4e (☎ 01-42-50-96-10; Métro: Cité).
Concerts also take place at **St-Eustache,** 1 rue Montmartre, 1er (☎ 01-
45-22-58-46; Métro: Les Halles); **St-Sulpice,** place St-Sulpice (☎ 01-46-33-
21-78; Métro: St-Sulpice), which has an amazing eight-columned pipe
organ; **St-Germain-des-Prés,** place St-Germain-des-Prés (☎ 01-42-77-65-
65; Métro: St-Germain-des-Prés); the **Madeleine,** place de la Madeleine

(☎ 01-42-64-83-16; Métro: Madeleine); and **St-Louis en l'Ile,** 19 rue St-Louis-en-l'Ile (☎ 01-44-62-00-55; Métro: Pont-Marie). In a less magnificent setting, the Sunday concerts at 6 p.m. at the **American Church,** 65 quai d'Orsay (☎ 01-45-56-09-50; Métro: Invalides), are friendly and inviting.

Free concerts are staged occasionally in the parks and gardens. (See Chapter 3 for a calendar.) **Maison de la Radio,** 116 avenue du Président Kennedy, 16e (☎ 01-56-40-12-12; Métro: Kennedy-Radio France), offers free tickets to recordings of some concerts. Tickets are available on the spot an hour before the recording starts. The **Conservatoire National Superieur de Musique** at the Cité de la Musique, 209 avenue Jean Jaurés, 19e (☎ 01-40-40-45-45; Métro: Porte de Pantin), stages free concerts and ballets performed by students at the conservatory, while the **Concert Hall** here (☎ 01-44-84-44-84) plays host to all types of performances, from jazz to world music.

Paris's main concert hall, **Salle Pleyel,** 252 rue du Faubourg-St-Honoré, 8e, normally home to the Orchestre de Paris, is closed for more than 20 million € ($23 million) worth of renovations until the middle of 2006. The Orchestre de Paris has moved temporarily to the **Théâtre Mogador,** 25 rue de Mogador, 9e (☎ 01-56-35-12-12; www.mogador.net; Métro: Trinité, Chausée d'Antin, St-Lazare). Directed by Christoph Eschenbach, this is a world-class orchestra. Highlights from the 2004–2005 season included Beethoven's nine symphonies, a Brahms festival performed by up-and-coming young artists, and a series of Mendelssohn chamber music concerts. Tickets range from 10€ to 83€ ($12–$95). Reservations are best made by phone, Monday to Friday 10 a.m. to 6 p.m.

Enjoying opera and ballet

Whatever your choice of the classic arts — opera, ballet, concerts, recitals — you'll find it performed here by local and international performers of the highest caliber. Inaugurated in 1874, the **Châtelet, Théâtre Musical de Paris,** 1 place du Châtelet, 1e (☎ 01-40-28-28-40; www.chatelet-theatre.com; Métro: Châtelet), is one of the top places to take in culture in Paris. Upcoming highlights include the operas *Medea* and *La Rondine,* scheduled for July 2005. Tickets range from 10€ to 114€ ($12–$131). The box office is open daily from 11 a.m. to 7 p.m. To make reservations by phone, call between 10 a.m. and 7 p.m. daily. There is a 2€ ($2.30) surcharge for Internet and phone reservations.

You can see dazzling performances by the national opera and ballet troupes at both the radiant **Palais Garnier,** place de l'Opéra, 9e (☎ 08-92-89-90-90 at 0.35€/min for reservations; www.opera-de-paris.fr; Métro: Opéra; RER: Auber), and the ultramodern **Opéra National de Bastille** (see the next paragraph). The Palais Garnier conducts more ballet performances, and the Opéra Bastille puts on more opera. Tickets are priced from 7€ ($8.05) for seats that have little or no visibility to 300€ ($345) for the first row of the balcony. Reserve by phone up to four weeks in advance and buy at the ticket windows for performances up to 14 days in advance (including same-day tickets). Making reservations online or by phone adds a 3€ ($3.45) surcharge. The box office is open Monday through Saturday from 11:00 a.m. to 6:30 p.m.

The **Opéra National de la Bastille,** place de la Bastille, 12e (☎ 08-92-89-90-90 at 0.35€/min. for reservations; www.opera-de-paris.fr; Métro: Bastille), brings on a new director in fall 2004, Gérard Mortier, to succeed Hugues Gall. Mortier is known for cutting-edge programming. The opera house offers first-class comfort and magnificent acoustics at each level of the auditorium, although Parisians think the building is a badly designed eyesore. The opera house is located at the place de la Bastille; at night, kids crowd the steps, showing off their skateboarding moves, talking on cellphones, and flirting. Tickets are priced between 5€ ($5.75) for reduced and no-visibility seats to 150€ ($173) for the front rows of orchestra and balcony seating. Reserve by phone up to four weeks in advance and buy at the ticket windows for performances up to 14 days in advance (including same-day tickets). The cheapest seats are on sale only at the box office. Making reservations online or by phone incurs a 3€ ($3.45) surcharge; call Monday to Friday 9 a.m. to 6 p.m. and Saturday 9 a.m. to 1 p.m. to make a reservation by phone. The box office, located at 130 rue de Lyon (the side of the opera house facing the Bastille monument), is open Monday through Friday 11:00 a.m. to 6:30 p.m.

The other major venue for opera is the stunning Belle Époque **Opéra-Comique,** 5 rue Favart, 2e (☎ 01-42-44-45-47 for reservations; www.opera-comique.com; Métro: Richelieu Drouot), which offers wonderful musical theater in the Salle Favart, a more intimate venue (the auditorium is so small you can hear people whispering onstage) than its opera hall counterparts. Jérôme Savary is musical director. Tickets are priced from 7€ to 60€ ($8.05–$69) depending on the performance. The box office at 14 rue Favart, 2e, is open Monday through Saturday from 10 a.m. to 6 p.m., and Sunday from 11 a.m. to 7 p.m.

Chapter 16

Hitting the Clubs and Bars

• •

In This Chapter

▶ Getting the lowdown on the latest hot spots

▶ Searching out your kind of music and dancing

▶ Unwinding over cocktails

• •

*P*aint Paris a lovely shade of *rouge* (red) whether you want to spend the evening talking over cocktails, chatting up the beautiful people, or dancing till you drop. Bars usually close around 2 a.m., but most clubs don't open until 11 p.m., and the music doesn't stop pumping until dawn. Check the listings (in French) in *Night Life, Nova,* or *Pariscope* magazines.

Hot Spots for Cool Jazz

Since the end of WWI, when James Reese Europe and his band were a hit on a tour of Paris, the city has had a love affair with American jazz music. Paris's warm welcome to black musicians led legions of them to flee segregation at home and come to Paris to perform — and often to stay. Montmartre became home to a number of thriving jazz clubs, among them Bricktop's, run by an American singer who took a young Josephine Baker under her wing, and gave a busboy job to an aspiring poet named Langston Hughes. Cole Porter's songs debuted at Bricktop's, which eventually became a regular stop for jazz musicians on tour. A number of American musicians were more famous in Paris than they ever were in the United States; Sidney Bechet, a clarinetist, is remembered in Paris with awe. Today, as new generations develop a taste for the sound, the Paris jazz scene remains vibrant. Look through the current *Pariscope* or the free twice-monthly *Lylo* (in Fnac or Virgin Music) for the artists you admire. If you don't care who's playing, and you're just out for a night of good music, you can stop by the following clubs.

You'll find yourself having a great time jitterbugging with the noisy crowd of foreigners and locals here at **Caveau de la Huchette,** 5 rue de la Huchette, 5e (☎ 01-43-26-65-05; Métro or RER: St-Michel), a legendary club that just celebrated its 50th anniversary of welcoming jazz bands. Cover is 11€ ($13) Monday through Thursday; Friday through Sunday it's 13€ ($15) between 9 p.m. and 1 a.m. Those under 25 pay 9€ ($10) every night. Music starts at 9:30 p.m. **Baiser Salé,** 56 rue des Lombards,

1er (☎ 01-42-33-37-71; Métro: Châtelet), is a small space that gets crowded with fans of world beat. You can hear fusion jazz, funk, Afro-Caribbean, salsa, and merengue. The cover on Tuesday and Thursday through Sunday varies from 13€ to 18€ ($15–$21). On Monday and Wednesday nights, admission is free. The club is open daily from 7 p.m. to 6 a.m. with concerts generally starting at 10 p.m.

A terrific place to hear some of France's most interesting jazz in a venue crowded with casually dressed enthusiasts is **Duc des Lombards,** 42 rue des Lombards, 1er (☎ 01-42-33-22-88; Métro: Châtelet–Les Halles). Cover is 8€ ($9.20) Wednesday to Sunday; admission is free Monday and Tuesday. Your best deal at **Le Petit Journal Saint-Michel,** 71 boulevard St-Michel, 5e (☎ 01-43-26-28-59; www.petitjournalsaintmichel.com; Métro: Cluny-La-Sorbonne, RER: Luxembourg), is the 47€ ($54) menu, which includes cover charge, three-course meal, and a drink. It's a warm and relaxed French atmosphere where recent acts included the New Orleans Messengers, the High Society Jazz Band, and the Claude Bolling Trio. Cover (without a meal) is 18€ ($21), and the first drink is steep at 16€ ($18). It's open Monday to Saturday with concerts at 9:15 p.m.

New Morning, 7–9 rue des Petites-Ecuries, 10e (☎ 01-45-23-51-41; Métro: Château-d'Eau), is one of Paris's best jazz clubs, and the best from around the world perform here (Stan Getz, Miles Davis, Wynton Marsalis to name just some of them). Recent acts included Spyro Gyra, the Fred Wesley Funk Band, and James Carter. Concerts start at 9:30 p.m. Cover starts at 16€ ($18), depending on the act. With its medieval look and vaulted ceilings, **Slow Club,** 130 rue de Rivoli, 1er (☎ 01-42-33-84-30; Métro: Châtelet–Les Halles), is a vaulted dungeon filled with dancers and 30-something fans of big American and European artists who perform swing, Dixieland, and classic jazz. Cover is 9€ to 14€ ($10–$16) depending on the act. It's open daily 10:00 p.m. to 3:30 a.m. The more experimental, the better, in the cellar at **Le 7 Lézards,** 10 rue des Rosiers, 4e (☎ 01-48-87-08-97; Métro: St-Paul). Depending on the performer, entry is free to 14€ ($16). This is the place where jazz musicians go to wind down, and you can have a good meal in the restaurant upstairs beforehand. Check out the program on the Web at www.7lezards.com. Concerts start between 7 p.m. and 10 p.m.

Listening to Live Music

The Chesterfield Café, 124 rue La Boétie, 8e (☎ 01-42-25-18-06; Métro: Franklin-D-Roosevelt), an American bar known for its American beers (Coors, Budweiser) and live gigs (usually free), is the place to find up-and-coming or just-arrived rock and blues bands, and the occasional oldie. Webb Wilder, Alanis Morissette, the Spin Doctors (and, according to rumor, even tennis great John McEnroe) have played here. Concerts start at 11:30 p.m. On Sundays, a rousing gospel brunch is the feature at 2 p.m. Open daily from 10 a.m. to 5 a.m.

At press time, **Cithéa,** 114 rue Oberkampf, 11e (☎ **01-40-21-70-95;** Métro: Parmentier or Ménilmontant), promised to reveal new programming and a new sound. But its reasonable prices and eclectic mix of world, jazz, and funk bands have already made it a fun destination in Ménilmontant, not far from the Bastille. You can catch concerts Wednesday through Saturday, and a DJ spins whenever the bands aren't playing. Cover is 8€ to 12€ ($9.20–$14) depending on the entertainment and includes one drink. Open Monday to Saturday 9 p.m. to 5 a.m.

You may hear Brazilian samba or British pop or Bretagnon folk played here at the "world's sofa," where world music acts reign. **La Divan du Monde,** 75 rue des Martyrs, 18e (☎ **01-44-92-77-66;** www.divandumonde.com; Métro: Pigalle), is a hip venue (check out the round DJ booth/space-ship) that's well worth the trip. Concerts usually start around 10 p.m. Monday through Saturday and at 4 p.m. Sunday. On weekends, a DJ spins music after the concerts. Cover is 10€ to 20€ ($12–$23) depending on the act. Call for closing hours.

In another life, **La Flèche d'Or,** 102 bis rue de Bagnolet, 20e (☎ **01-43-72-04-23;** Métro: Alexandre-Dumas), was the Charonne train station, but now it's a restaurant turned music venue. Only two Métro stops from Père-Lachaise Cemetery (take the 2 to Alexandre-Dumas; see Chapter 11), it's worth a visit on the weekend when you may hear reggae, alternative rock, Celtic rock, or blues rock. Sundays at 5 p.m. a live dance band usually plays salsa, on Wednesday, a DJ spins tunes and Thursday through Saturday are live concert nights. This cavernous space pulls in a funky, artsy, racially mixed crowd. Open Tuesday through Sunday from 10 a.m. to 2 a.m. Cover ranges from free to 5€ ($5.75) depending on the act.

Avril Lavigne, Dido, and Yannick Noah (once a popular French tennis player, now a popular singer) have all played at the trendy **La Scène,** 2 bis rue des Taillandiers, 11e (☎ **01-48-06-50-70;** www.la-scene.com; Métro: Ledru-Rollin). Have a light meal in the shed-like, steel-and-white dining room before heading downstairs to the dance floor where you may be lucky enough to snag one of the tables for two scattered about. There's also a cozy lounge with caramel-colored padded walls. Restaurant open Tuesday to Saturday 7:45 p.m. to 11:00 p.m. Concerts usually start at 10 p.m. and cost 10€ ($12), nights with a DJ (check the Web site for calendar) usually cost 12€ ($14).

Shaking Your Groove Thing at the Best Dance Clubs

Whether you like dancing to techno, house, salsa, world, classic rock, or swing, you can find someplace to boogie in Paris — and legions of Parisians eager to dance if not with you, then with their mirrored reflections! Paris clubs change their programming from night to night, with house music de rigeur at many places. If you don't like house, try one of the barges along the Seine in the 13e, which attract a good mix and play everything, and you can have a fine, though often crowded, time right on the river. Check *Pariscope* magazine for barge concert schedules. Salsa, the hottest trend a few years back, is still going strong.

A word of advice: Some of these clubs have strict door policies and turn away those wearing sneakers, sweat suits, baseball caps, and shorts. Many nightclubs accept reservations, so if you're worried about getting past the bouncers, give your club of choice a call. To club on a budget, go out during the week when cover charges may be (officially or unofficially) waived. Yes, it's sexist, but women often get in free, especially if they're dressed in something slinky, low-cut, or short (or all three). Black clothes seem to be the rule for men and women, and the later you go — or earlier in the morning as the case may be — the more fashionable people get. **Barrio Latino,** 46 rue du Faubourg-Saint-Antoine, 11e (☎ 01-55-78-84-75; Métro: Bastille), is a restaurant/bar/club that delivers a terrific time — if you can get in. The lines here on weekends are enormous, and you can see why. It has three bars, private areas where you can see (but not be seen), a lounge complete with pool table, a second-floor restaurant serving Latino food, a top-floor private club with a kitschy Che Guevara mural, and energetic Latin music that sets everyone to dancing. Food ranges from hamburgers to South American specialties using Argentinean beef to tapas served from glass carts wheeled around the first and third floors. Open daily 11 a.m. to 2 a.m.

The Irish lightship **Batofar,** 11 quai François Mauriac, 13e (☎ 01-56-29-10-00; Métro: Bibliothèque François Mitterand or Quai de la Gare), promises a hot, sweaty, and ultimately fun time. Music can be anything from drum-and-bass to British pop, starting around 8 p.m., and the party can go on all night. Drinks, for which there is nearly always a line, are reasonable (4€–8€/$4.60–$9.20), the clientele are in their 20 and early 30s, and it can get crowded, but it's still worth it. Open daily 7 p.m. to 2 a.m. Cover ranges from 5€ to 12€ ($5.75–$14) depending on the band or DJ for the night. A small snack bar is onboard.

Elysée Montmartre, 72 boulevard De Rochechouart, 18e (☎ 01-42-23-46-50; Métro: Anvers), a club that serves the dual function of disco and major concert hall, is home to twice-monthly nights that pull in more than 1,000 clubbers. Moby, Björk, U2, and the Red Hot Chili Peppers have all headlined here. Dance music is usually house; the monthly *bals musettes* (dances) often have live local bands. Check *Pariscope* for events and prices. Dances are usually held 11 p.m. to 5 a.m. Cover charges vary from 12€ to 25€ ($14–$29).

If you like house music, **Le Wax,** 15 rue Daval, 11e (☎ 01-40-21-16-16; Métro: Bastille) is the place for you. The club is the premiere place for DJs who spin it all night long. Decor here is very *Clockwork Orange,* with plastic bubbles on the walls, yellow plastic couches, and lots of crimson and orange. Open Tuesday to Saturday 6 p.m. to 2 a.m. and Friday and Saturday 6 p.m. to 5 a.m. One of the best things about Le Wax is the price — it's free.

The basement dance hall at **La Coupole**, 102 boulevard du Montparnasse, 14e (☎ 01-43-20-14-20; Métro: Vavin), is a retro venue with plush banquettes and old-fashioned sounds that's a big draw for locals and out-of-towners. Tuesdays are salsa nights, with dance classes starting at 7:30 p.m. for 23€ ($26) (including a drink) and lasting two hours. Latino music is played Friday nights and garage on Saturday nights. Regular cover is 16€ ($18) on Saturday from 12:30 p.m. to 5:00 a.m., on Tuesday from 9:30 p.m. to 3:00 a.m., and Friday midnight to 5:30 a.m.

Edith Piaf made her debut at **La Nouvelle Java**, 105 rue du Faubourg-du-Temple, 10e (☎ 01-42-02-20-52; Métro: Belleville), said to be the oldest club in Paris. A diverse crowd comes to dance without restraint to mostly Cuban and Brazilian music, played by a live band on Friday and Saturday nights. If you have a taste for something fun, funky, and very authentic, and you like Latin music, this charming old dance hall may be your great night out. Cover 10€ to 20€ ($12–$23). Open Thursday to Saturday 9 p.m. to 6 a.m. and Sunday 2 p.m. to 7 p.m.

Located next door to le Moulin Rouge, the huge tri-level **La Locomotive**, 90 boulevard de Clichy, 18e (☎ 01-53-41-88-89; Métro: Place-Clichy), is popular with American students. People dance to rock, heavy metal, and techno. In the *sous-sol* (basement, the coolest of the three levels), you can even see the remnants of an old railway line (hence the name). The Bar Americain looks more Roman than Uncle Sam with fake statuary and columns crowned by lions. Drinks start at 9€ ($10). Cover Monday through Thursday is 12€ ($14) without a drink and 14€ ($16) with one drink; cover on Friday is 6€ ($6.90) for women without a drink and 10€ ($12) with one drink, 20€ ($23) for men with or without a drink. Free admission on Sundays until 1 a.m. Open 11 p.m. to 5 a.m.

Opened in 1992 and still going strong, **Rex**, 5 boulevard Poissonière, 2e (☎ 01-42-36-83-98; Métro: Bonne Nouvelle), has been one of the most popular clubs for house and techno — if not *the* club — with Paris's best sound system and its most famous DJ, Laurent Garnier, who spins with others such as Carl Cox, and even Daft Punk. Open Thursday to Saturday 11 p.m. to 6 a.m. Closed August. Admission averages 13€ ($15).

Stepping Out: The Gay and Lesbian Scene

Gay dance clubs come and go so fast that even the magazines devoted to them, such as *e-m≤* and *Illico,* both distributed free in the gay bars and bookstores, have a hard time keeping up. For lesbians, try the magazines *Lesbia* or *La Dixième Muse* for club and bar listings in their classifieds section. Also look for *Gai Guide, Gai Pied Hebdo,* and *Têtu.*

Amnesia Café, 42 rue Vieille-du-Temple, 4e (☎ 01-42-72-16-94; Métro: Hôtel-de-Ville), is a relaxed café-bar-bistro-club decorated in warm, coppery tones and furnished with comfortable leather chairs and banquettes. The atmosphere here is more friendly than cruise-y, and the drinks and food are reasonably priced. Downstairs is a vaulted dance space that can feel a bit cramped when the crowds descend after midnight on weekends. Café open daily 10:30 a.m. to 2:00 a.m.; club open daily 8:30 p.m. to 2:00 a.m.

The **Banana Café,** 13 rue de la Ferronerie, 1er (☎ **01-42-33-35-31;** Métro: Châtelet–Les Halles), is one of the most popular gay bars in Paris. Open all night, it has a street-level bar and a dance floor *sous-sol* (in the basement) that has live piano music or a DJ. After 10 p.m., things get crazy, with go-go boys dancing on the bar or on platforms in the basement.

La Champmeslé, 4 rue Chabanais, 2e (☎ **01-42-96-85-20;** Métro: Pyramides), a few blocks east of the avenue de l'Opéra, is a comfortable bar for women with singing or art exhibitions each Thursday night and tarot card readings the last weekend of each month. Cocktails start at 8€ ($9.20), beer at 5€ ($5.75). Open daily noon to 2 a.m.

There's a sound for everyone here in one of the city's largest discos, **Le Gibus,** 18 rue du Faubourg-du-Temple, 11e (☎ **01-47-00-78-88;** Métro: République). Depending on the night, you can hear trance, rock, rhythm and blues, techno, or disco. Cover ranges from 10€ ($12) for R&B nights to 20€ ($23) for classic disco. Open Tuesday through Saturday 10:30 p.m. to 5:00 a.m., Sunday 5:30 p.m. to 5:00 a.m.

Le Pulp, 25 boulevard Poissonière, 2e (☎ **01-40-26-01-93;** Métro: Grands-Boulevards), is one of Paris's hippest lesbian clubs. With decor reminiscent of a 19th-century French music hall, this venue is *très* cool, with all types of cutting-edge music. Open Wednesday to Sunday 11:45 p.m. to 5:00 a.m. Free Wednesday and Thursday, cover is 10€ ($12) Friday to Sunday.

The proprietor, Nicole, of **Les Scandaleuses,** 8 rue des Ecouffes, 4e (☎ **01-48-87-39-26;** Métro: St-Paul), sets a relaxed tone for a diverse mix of women, with styles running from pink-haired punk to denim and flannel. DJs crank up the base later in the evening. This place is simply jammed on weekends. Open daily 6 p.m. to 2 a.m.

Open Café/Café Cox, 17 rue des Archives, 4e (☎ **01-42-72-26-18;** Métro: Hôtel de Ville), are two separate side-by-side gay bars with patrons who move back and forth between them all night (the walls can't contain the crowds, who end up taking over the sidewalk at night). Basic café fare is served all day. Open Sunday to Thursday 11 a.m. to 2 a.m., Friday and Saturday until around 4 a.m.

Queen, 102 avenue des Champs-Elysées, 8e (☎ **01-53-89-08-89;** Métro: George V), used to be one of the hottest clubs in town, with nightly crowds so thick you could find it difficult to get a drink. The clientele is about two-thirds gay, but having a beautiful face and body, or at least the ability to disguise your faults with great clothes, are no longer necessary to help you get past the drag queens at the door. Cover (including one drink, with or without alcohol) is 10€ ($12) Sunday through Thursday; Friday and Saturday cover (including one drink, with or without alcohol) is 18€ ($21). Open daily midnight to 7 a.m., 8 a.m. on weekends.

Kicking Back with Classy Cocktails

If you're looking for a quiet, romantic place to unwind with a drink — or if you're on the prowl for where the hip, hot folks hang out — these places should fit the bill. Most bars and lounges in Paris open daily at 9 p.m., but no one arrives until after midnight. They generally close around 4 a.m.

At **Alcazar**, 62 rue Mazarine, 6e (☎ 01-53-10-19-99; Métro: Odéon), elements of traditional brasserie style, such as banquettes and mirrors, are slicked up and mixed with innovations such as a glassed-in kitchen theatrically installed along the left wall. The comfortable mezzanine bar is great for a view over the downstairs restaurant, once one of Paris's hottest eateries.

Bob Cool, 15 rue des Grands Augustins, 6e (☎ 46-33-33-77; Métro: Odéon or St-Michel), one of the hottest new bars on the Left Bank, has taken literary St-Germain-des-Prés by storm. Aspiring writers and artists collect around the antique oak bar and open up their laptops on the tables in the front room. The back room's banquettes play host to a cool crowd, especially during the workweek Happy Hour between 5 p.m. and 9 p.m., when two drinks go for the price of one. Clientele ranges in age from 18 to 70, and all are welcome. Open Monday to Saturday 5 p.m. to 2 a.m.

You can enjoy **China Club**, 50 rue de Charenton, 12e (☎ 01-43-43-82-02; Métro: Bastille), a popular bar/restaurant near the Bastille, for its basement piano bar, its ground-floor restaurant, or best, its first-floor bar evoking an opium den of the 1930s. The atmosphere is one of hushed, Colonial-decorated elegance. All cocktails are well made (7.50€/$8.65), but the Chinese food is overpriced.

You find French locals mingling with tourists at **Harry's New York Bar**, 5 rue Daunou, 2e (☎ 01-42-61-71-14; Métro: Opéra or Pyramides). Founded in 1911, it's been one of Europe's most famous bars, as popular today as it was in the time of that notorious Lost Generation of writers who really knew how to ring up a bar tab. The Bloody Mary was said to have been invented here, and the selection of whiskey is amazing. Make sure you step downstairs if only to look at the 1930s Piano Bar, which resembles the inside of a cozy yacht.

The très delicious specialty *flammenkeuche* — large, square, thin-crusted pizzas topped with cream, herbs, and goodies like salmon, ham, and goat cheese — draws a trendy crowd to **La Fabrique**, 53 rue du Faubourg St-Antoine, 11e (☎ 01-43-07-67-07; Métro: Bastille). This restaurant is sleek, the bar is minimalist, and the color to wear appears to be black. Although the bar is open until around 5 a.m., depending on the crowds, food is served only until midnight. Be ready to stand in line on the weekends, and look out for private parties when the restaurant is closed to the public.

Le Bar, in the Hotel Plaza-Athénée, 25 avenue Montaigne, 8e (☎ 01-53-57-49-49; Métro: Alma-Marceau), is one of the in spots in Paris, where a crowd with champagne taste sips drinks that cost more than some bottles of wine. Unless you're somebody (or on the arm of somebody), there's no guarantee you'll get in, and when you do, be prepared to withstand the once-over you'll receive from the other fabulously-dressed folk. Drinks start at 20€ ($23).

The **Lizard Lounge,** 18 rue du Bourg-Tibourg, 4e (☎ **01-42-72-81-34;** Métro: Hôtel-de-Ville), is stylish yet easygoing and a pleasant place to hang out with an arty, international crowd. The music is loud, but the heavy-gauge steel balcony overlooking the main bar offers a chance for quieter conversation. You can also come early in the evening for a reasonably priced light meal prepared in the open kitchen. A DJ spins dance music in the refurbished basement Wednesday through Saturday.

Don't visit **Man Ray,** 34 rue Marbeuf, 8e (☎ **01-56-88-36-36;** Métro: Franklin-D-Roosevelt), for dinner. Have a drink at the upstairs bar instead while listening to jazz Monday through Thursday (but do visit the enormous downstairs to see the statues of two winged Asian goddesses, who appear concerned — possibly about the food). Clubbing begins around 11 p.m. (around 15€/$17 cover) when the restaurant winds down, the music takes on a harder edge, and a sleek international crowd stands shoulder to shoulder along the curving bar. American artist and photographer Man Ray's photos adorn several walls. Celebrity owners include Sean Penn, Johnny Depp, and John Malkovich.

Spending an Evening at a French Cabaret

Parisian cabarets had a reputation for sensual naughtiness long before Josephine Baker danced in a G-string adorned with bananas at Folies Bergères in the 1920s. Although Edith Piaf and Maurice Chevalier were highlights at venues like the Moulin Rouge, today it's the topless can-can dancers who draw in the crowds. The dancers are often overshadowed by light shows, special effects, and tinny recorded music, but if you're expecting to see lots of flesh in today's Parisian revues, you won't be disappointed. The shows are highly overrated and very expensive but continue to be a huge attraction for tourists. The infamous Folies Bergères no longer exists as a cabaret; it's now a concert hall.

 When seeing a Parisian cabaret show, have dinner somewhere else and save yourself some cash. For the money you'd spend at the cabaret, you can have an absolutely fabulous meal at one of the pricier suggestions in Chapter 10. Some of the cabarets admit children, though not kids under 4. Be aware that every other member of the audience may be from another country — these are some of the least Parisian experiences you can have while still being in Paris.

2004 was a banner year at the **Crazy Horse, Paris,** 12 avenue George V, 8e (☎ **01-47-23-32-32;** www.lecrazyhorseparis.com; Métro: George V), with the production of their first DVD (on sale at music stores in France)

called *Crazy Horse, Le Show,* and a new show, *Taboo,* promising a "faster, stronger, more beautiful" striptease that highlights each dancer (who have names like Vanity Starlight, Bee Bee Opaline, and Nooka Karamel). Cover and two drinks cost from 49€ ($56) at the bar to 110€ ($127) in the orchestra with a half-bottle of champagne. Special dinner-show packages with restaurants De Vez, Chez Francis, and Fouquet's start at 115€ ($132). Two shows nightly at 8:30 and 11:00 p.m., with three shows on Saturday at 7:30, 9:45, and 11:50 p.m.

At the **Lido,** 116 avenue des Champs-Elysées, 8e (☎ 01-40-76-56-10; www.lido.fr; Métro: George V), award-winning chef Paul Bocuse designed the above-average menu, but it just isn't worth the money to dine here. Its revue, *C'est Magique,* offers "flying" and "swimming" dancers, and an ascending stage that periodically delivers feathered women, fountains, and an ice rink, as well as high-tech laser lighting and video projections. A new show, *Bonheur,* features a woman singing French *chansons* (songs), and an Indian-themed show that may be said to resemble the spectacle in the 2002 movie *Moulin Rouge.* The show with dinner and a half-bottle of champagne costs 140€ to 200€ ($161–$230); without dinner and drinks the cost is 60€ ($69) Sunday to Thursday and 80€ ($92) Friday and Saturday. Two shows nightly at 9:30 and 11:30 p.m.

And speaking of the most famous of the cabarets, the **Moulin Rouge,** place Blanche, Montmartre, 18e (☎ 01-53-09-82-82; www.moulinrouge.fr; Métro: place-Blanche), has been packing in crowds since 1889, and its signature can-can dancers, made famous in paintings by Toulouse-Lautrec, still bare breasts in the show's finale today. Edith Piaf, Yves Montand, and Charles Aznavour made their reputations at the Moulin Rouge, and even Frank Sinatra performed here. The show *Féerie* features comedy, animal, and magic acts with the requisite scantily clad women bumping and grinding around the stage. Table seats have better views than seats at the bar. A bar seat and two drinks cost 95€ ($109) for the 9 p.m. show, 85€ ($98) for the 11 p.m. show. Dinner followed by the 9 p.m. show costs 135€ to 165€ ($155–$190); you must arrive for dinner by 7 p.m.

Probably the most French of the cabarets is the **Paradis Latin,** 28 rue Cardinal-Lemoine, 5e (☎ 01-43-25-28-28; www.paradislatin.fr; Métro: Cardinal-Lemoine), designed by Gustave Eiffel. A genial master encourages audience participation during a show that's less gimmick-filled than the others. To save money, forgo dinner for the lower-priced Champagne Revue, which includes a half-bottle of bubbly and costs 75€ ($86); dinner (at 8 p.m.) plus show packages range from 109€ to 200€ ($125–$230).

Part VI
The Part of Tens

"It serves you right for requesting a lap dance from someone doing the can-can."

In this part . . .

Okay, these little extras won't make or break your trip, but they may just make it a little more fun. In Chapter 17, you can find out where to make the most of a rainy day. In Chapter 18, I give you the inside scoop on where to find spectacular views of the city — without the other tourists. And in Chapter 19, you can find out where to make like Manet and have *dejeuner sur l'herbe* — in other words, ten places to go for a fabulous picnic.

Chapter 17

Ten Things to Do in Bad Weather

● ●

In This Chapter

▶ Finding shelter during Paris's rainy season

▶ Taking advantage of *mauvais temps* (bad weather)

● ●

*I*t's bound to happen: you've had days of perfect sunshine without a cloud in the sky, and now it's teeming with rain. Rather than sink into a depression in front of CNN International, enjoy! Yes, you've read that correctly — Paris is filled with things to do inside, things you may never have done had you had perfect weather. So put on your trench coat, comfortable non-slip shoes, and don't forget your umbrella — there's exploring to do!

Spending Money at a Shopping Arcade

These indoor shopping galleries were built at the beginning of the 19th century and could be considered the harbinger of the today's mall. Most of Paris's arcades are located in the 2e, and each has its own character (see Chapter 12 for a sidebar about the arcades). From vintage clothes in the **Passage Choiseul** (44 rue des Petits-Champs, Métro: Quatre-Septembre) to the upscale galleries, boutiques and Jean Paul Gaultier showroom at the most gorgeous of them all, **Galerie Vivienne** (4 place des Petits-Champs, 5 rue de la Banque, or 6 rue Vivienne, Métro: Bourse), you'll have fun window shopping and picking up unusual gifts for the people back home. See Chapter 12 for more on shopping the arcades.

Visiting a Smaller Museum

There's no shortage of museums in Paris, but on limited time, you just can't see them all. Why not use the bad weather to check out the terrific modern exhibits at the **Fondation Cartier pour l'Art Contemporain** (261 bd. Raspail, Métro: Raspail; see Chapter 11 for more information).

A recent exhibit displayed the high fashion designs of Jean Paul Gaultier – fashioned in bread! See Chapter Or try the **Espace Montmartre Salvador Dali** (11 rue Poulbot, 18e, Métro: Abbesses) that displays over 300 works by the Spanish surrealist while his voice narrates eerily over hidden speakers.

Watching a Movie in V.O.

Parisians love the cinema, and there's no reason you can't enjoy it French style even if you don't speak the language. Pick up an issue of *Pariscope* at a newsstand and check out the listings for English-language films playing in their original version (v.o.). You'll probably be directed to the Champs-Elysées or Montparnasse. Grab some popcorn on the way in as an added treat — you can get it sugared or salty.

Sitting Beneath the Awning of a Café

With the purchase of just one cup of coffee, your time at a cafe is practically unlimited. A bad-weather day is a good time to write all your postcards as well as check out the latest French fashion — in rainwear. Try L'Étoile Manquante (34 rue de Vieille du Temple, 4e. ☎ **01-43-26-68-15.** Métro: Hôtel de Ville or St-Paul) in the Marais for just the right mix of people watching, solicitous service, and very cool décor. (See Chapter 10 for cafes.)

Strolling in the Jardin des Plantes

Amateur botanists can spend hours reading the labels on beds of herbs and flowers here in what used to be the king's medicinal gardens. There are also greenhouses, a 17th-century maze, and specialized plant beds, and a small zoo with appealing animals. If you need to head inside to get dry, visit one of the natural history museums here: the Grande Galerie de l'Evolution, the Mineralogical Gallery, the Paleobotanical Gallery, and the Entomological Gallery. See Chapter 11 for more on the garden.

Waiting in Short Lines at the Arc de Triomphe and the Eiffel Tower

At the height of tourist season when lines can be hours long at both attractions, a rainy day can be a godsend. The visibility may be compromised a bit, but, both the Tower and the Arch have small indoor museums and gift shops you may have overlooked on a more crowded day. And, hey, you get to say you've been there, done that! Chapter 11 has all the Arc and Tower info.

Getting into the Catacombes

Take in Paris's most macabre attraction, the Catacombes, which is the final resting place for about six million skulls and skeletons stacked in thousands of yards of tunnels. The remains are the18th-century overflow from local cemeteries, and the Catacombes are located far enough away to practically guarantee that you would have missed this attraction if it hadn't been raining (1 place Denfert-Rochereau, 14e, Métro: Denfert-Rochereau). See Chapter 11 for more information.

Indulging in a Long and Leisurely Lunch

If you haven't yet splurged on a meal, try to make a reservation for lunch in an upscale place such as Georges atop the Centre Georges Pompidou (sixth floor, rue Rambuteau, 4e, ☎ 01-44-78-47-99; Métro: Rambuteau). At lunch, you can eat more affordably in sumptuous restaurants that at dinner would be way over your budget. See Chapter 10 for some of Paris's best restaurants.

Shopping 'til You Tombez

Head to one of Paris's huge department stores — Galeries Lafayette and Printemps are located in the 9e, Samaritaine is in the 1er, and the 6th is home to the smaller Le Bon Marché (Chapter 12 has more shop information) — which have lots of options for eating and relaxing, too.

If you're a vintage-clothes hound and it isn't Monday (when some shops are closed), you can spend hours looking at everything from gently worn Chanel to only-a-little scuffed Hermès bags. The boutiques are located between 89 and 123 rue de la Pompe, 16e, Métro: Rue de la Pompe).

Taking a Boat Ride

Most of the boats are glassed in, and except for Bat-o-Bus versions, they all have commentary in English. If Paris is undergoing an absolute down-pour, you won't see much, but in a drizzle or light rain, you should be able to see nearly everything that's visible in the sunshine.

Chapter 18

Ten Places to See Paris — Without the Lines

● ●

In This Chapter

▶ Searching for a fantastic panorama off the beaten path

▶ Discovering some special Paris vistas

● ●

*E*veryone visits the Eiffel Tower to see the panorama of Paris spread far and wide (though the view is from behind a fence). And they climb the Arc de Triomphe to get more beautiful open-air vistas that actually include the Eiffel Tower. But with wait times at the Eiffel Tower exceeding an hour and sometimes two in high season (and not a whole lot less at the Arc de Triomphe) you may wish you could spend the time differently. Fortunately, there are lots of other places to see Paris vistas without long lines, if any. Some are even free!

Galeries Lafayette

The sixth floor cafeteria of Galeries Lafayette's main store (40 bd. Haussmann, 9e; (☎ 01-42-82-34-56; Métro: Opéra or Chaussée-d'Antin) is sleek and modern and sells fresh hot and cold food. But one of the best reasons to come here is for the views over the rooftops of Paris. If you're not hungry for a meal, at least try the delicious hand-scooped ice cream from the cart here before you go! See Chapter 12.

La Madeleine

Climb the 28 steps of La Madeleine church (Place de la Madeleine, 8e; (☎ 01-40-07-03-91; Métro: Madeleine) leading to the façade and look back: You can see rue Royale, place de la Concorde and the obelisk, and, across the Seine, the dome of Invalides. Inside, Rude's *Le Baptême du Christ* is on the left as you enter. See Chapter 11.

Panthéon

The Panthéon (Place du Panthéon, 5e; ☎ 01-44-32-18-00; Métro: Cardinal-Lemoine or Maubert-Mutualité; Bus: 21, 27, 83, 84, 85, 89) was once a mausoleum that was once a church built in honor of the patron saint of Paris. From the dome of the Panthéon unfolds a spectacular view of the Eiffel Tower and the surrounding neighborhoods. Hanging from the Panthéon's domed ceiling is also Foucault's pendulum. See Chapter 11.

Parc de Belleville

Enter this off-the-beaten track park in the 20e by a curved path that leads to tree-lined promenades (more than 500 trees are here), with the first of the magnificent Left Bank views peeping through the spaces between pretty houses. Beds of roses and other seasonal flowers line walks, and views of the city's Left Bank become more pronounced the higher up the terraced pathways you go. (Located in the 20e; take the Métro to Pyrénées, then walk down rue de Belleville and turn left onto rue Piat where you see arched iron gates leading into the park; you can also take the Métro to Courrones, cross boulevard de Belleville and turn left onto rue Julien Lacroix where you find another entrance). See Chapter 11.

Pont des Arts

This steel-and-wood, seven-arched, pedestrian-only footbridge connects the entrance to the Louvre on one end with the magnificent Institut Français on the other. Rebuilt in 1985 after the original suffered damage from barges passing beneath, the walk across offers breathtaking views all across the river, but especially of the tree-lined tip of Ile de la Cité with the spires of Notre-Dame and Sainte-Chapelle, the turrets of the Conciergerie and the fabulous curving, white apartment and judicial buildings. Métro: Pont Neuf. (Walk west along quai de Louvre or quai de la Conti. It's the bridge directly to the west of Pont Neuf.)

Restaurant Georges at the Centre Georges Pompidou

It used to be that visitors to the Centre Georges Pompidou could skip the museum entirely and ride the escalators on the outside of the building (enclosed in a plastic tube like a giant gerbil habitat) to the top for breathtaking views of the city. That's no longer permitted; you need to buy a ticket for the museum first. Unless, of course, you have drinks, lunch, or dinner at the trendy Costes brothers restaurant, Georges (you need a reservation to gain access to the floor). The entrance is to the left of the museum's main entrance (19 rue Beaubourg, 4e; ☎ 01-44-78-47-99; Métro: Rambuteau or Châtelet). See Chapter 11.

Sacré Coeur

To see the view from Sacré Coeur in the 18e (25 rue du Chevalier-de-la-Barre, 18e; ☎ 01-53-41-89-00; Métro: Anvers. Take the elevator up and follow signs to the *funiculaire,* which runs to the church; Bus: The local Montmartrobus is the only bus that goes to the top of the hill), you have two choices: The first method is the free panorama from the wall just in front of the church (use the coin-operated viewing machines); Or you can pay 5€ ($5.75) to visit Sacré Coeur's dome. To reach the dome, face the church and walk around to its left side, following signs for the Dome and Crypte. You walk down a set of stairs and follow a walkway about 50 feet to an iron gate. The entrance and ticket machine are on your right. The climb from church floor to dome is up a flight of nail-bitingly steep corkscrew steps. See Chapter 11.

Samaritaine

The free outside viewing platform at the Art Nouveau department store Samaritaine (19 rue de la Monnaie, 1er; ☎ 01-40-41-20-20; Métro: Pont-Neuf or Châtelet–Les Halles) is one of the best things about this store directly across the street from the Pont Neuf. Follow signs in its main building to the *panorama.* Catch the elevator to the ninth floor, then climb two flights of stairs to the eleventh floor. The tenth floor terrace, also with good views, serves meals. See Chapter 12.

Tour Montparnasse

That looming black skyscraper on the Left Bank is actually the Tour Montparnasse (33 av. du Maine, 15e; ☎ 01-45-38-52-56; Métro: Montparnasse-Bienvenüe) right next to the Gare du Montparnasse in the 14e. At a height of 689 feet, the Tour Montparnasse towers above Paris, and from its panoramic roof terrace on the 56th floor, you can see as far as 40 km (nearly 25 miles) in nice weather. It's a bit pricey (8.20€/$9.40 adults, 7€/$8 students 15 years and up, 5.60€/$6.40 ages 5 to 14), but the views are exceptional — you've never seen Paris like this! See Chapter 12.

The Towers at Notre Dame

Climb 387 narrow and winding steps to the top of one of the towers here for Quasimodo's view of the gargoyles and of Paris below. My advice: If you plan to visit the tower, go early in the morning! Lines stretch down the square in front of the cathedral during the summer. (6 parvis Notre-Dame, Ile de la Cité, 4e; ☎ 01-42-34-56-10; Métro: Cité or St-Michel. RER: St-Michel; Bus: 21, 38, 85, 96.) See Chapter 11.

Chapter 19

Ten Plus Great Places for a Picnic

In This Chapter
▶ Living the "a loaf of bread, a jug of wine, and thou" dream
▶ Finding that special place to enjoy a meal in *plein air* (fresh air)

*P*aris abounds with parks and green spaces for picnics. (The city is home to so many of these expanses that I couldn't limit this list to ten.) You can get delicious meats, sweets, and wine (see Chapter 12 for recommendations) from plenty of open-air markets, *traiteurs* (gourmet food shops), and grocery stores. You won't need to worry about tipping, dressing to dine, or speaking the language, and best of all, you can lay down for a snooze right after you eat.

A word of advice, however: Some parks, such as the Luxembourg Gardens or the Tuileries, jealously guard their lawns; you may have to walk a bit before you find a spot where you can spread out on the grass. But chairs are everywhere — some even have reclining backs! — and you can pull a few chairs right up to a fountain and eat amidst the spray from the water. If this seems too public, your best bet is to try the vast Bois de Vincennes or Bois de Boulogne where you can picnic nearly anywhere. Don't forget to clean up afterward.

Banks of the Seine near the Musée de Sculpture en Plein Air

Wander amid the sculptures before you spread out your meal in this waterside park that's really a museum (the name ***Musée de Sculpture en Plein Air*** translates to *Open-Air Sculpture Museum*). Twenty-nine artists created abstract works that compliment the meditative mood that the banks of the Seine inspire (kids still climb all over them). Sculptures include those by French sculptor César Baldaccini and Russian born Ossip Zadkine. (Métro: Sully-Morland or Gare d'Austerlitz)

Bois de Boulogne

A former royal forest and hunting ground, the Bois de Boulogne is a vast reserve of more than 2,200 acres with jogging paths, horseback riding paths, cycling (rentals are available), and boating on two lakes. The **Longchamp** and **Auteuil racecourses** are located here, as is the **Jardin Shakespeare** in the Pré Catelan, a garden containing many of the plants and herbs mentioned in Shakespeare's plays. (Métro: Porte Maillot, Porte Dauphine, or Porte Auteuil)

Bois de Vincennes

Rent canoes or bikes or visit the **parc Zoologique** (zoo) and petting zoo after your picnic on the extensive grounds at the Bois de Vincennes, which also has a Buddhist center, complete with temple, and the Chateau de Vincennes, where early monarchs such as Charles V and Henri III sought refuge from wars. The **parc Floral de Paris** (☎ 01-43-43-92-95) is here with its spectacular amphitheatre (and jazz concerts on summer Saturdays), a butterfly garden, library, and miniature golf. (Métro: Porte Dorée or Chateau de Vincennes)

Jardin des Tuileries

The Tuileries is a restful space in the center of Paris that houses the Orangerie and the Jeu de Paume at its western edge and plays home to 40 beautiful Maillol bronzes scattered among the trees to its east. This spot is the city's most formal garden, with pathways and fountains that invite you to sit on the metal chairs provided and munch on picnic treats while cooling off in the breezes off the waters.

The name means *tuiles* (tiles) — the clay here was once used to make roof tiles. The gardens were originally laid out in the 1560s for Catherine de Medici in front of the Tuileries Palace (which burned down in 1871). In the 17th century, landscape artist André Le Nôtre, creator of the gardens at Versailles, redesigned a large section. (Métro: Tuileries or Concorde)

Jardin du Luxembourg

The 6e arrondissement's Jardin du Luxembourg is one of the most beloved parks in Paris. You can sit on metal chairs near the boat pond or spread out on grass open to picnickers directly across from the Palais de Luxembourg, on the park's south edge. Not far from the Sorbonne and just south of the Latin Quarter, the large park is popular with students and children who love it for its playground, toy-boat pond, pony rides, and puppet theater. Besides pools, fountains, and statues of queens and poets, tennis and *boules* (lawn bowling) courts are available. See whether you can find the miniature Statue of Liberty. (Métro: Odéon; RER: Luxembourg)

Parc de Belleville

The parc de Belleville is a wonderful place to visit with children, watch the sun set across western Paris, or nosh on a baguette with *saucisson sec* (cured sliced sausage, a bit like French salami). The park has fountains, a children's play area, an open-air theater with concerts during the summer, rock formations, and grottoes that evoke the long-ago days when the hill was a strategic point to fight enemies like Attila the Hun. Beds of roses and other seasonal flowers line the walks, and views of the city's Left Bank become more pronounced the higher up the terraced pathways you go.

Access the park by taking the rue Piat off rue Belleville and enter through an iron gate spelling out the words *Villa Ottoz*. A curved path leads you to tree-lined promenades (more than 500 trees are here) with the first of the magnificent Left Bank views peeping through the spaces between pretty houses. Take the Métro to Pyrénées; then walk down rue de Belleville and turn left onto rue Piat, where you see arched iron gates leading into the park. You can also take the Métro to Courrones, cross boulevard de Belleville, and turn left onto rue Julien Lacroix where another entrance is located.

Parc de la Villette

Picnic at parc de la Villette in the summer while watching an outdoor movie or listening to a concert. Afterward, you and your kids can visit the children's museum, the **Cité des Sciences et de l'Industrie** (Museum of Science and Industry), and the **Musée de la Musique** (Music Museum), located on the grounds. This modern park has a series of theme gardens and includes an exotic bamboo garden and a garden featuring steam and water jets. Scattered throughout the park are playgrounds and other attractions (see Chapter 13). The most fun way to get here is to take a canal trip from Pont l'Arsenal or the Musée d'Orsay (see Chapter 11). You can also take the Métro to Porte de la Villette.

Parc des Buttes-Chaumont

Parc des Buttes-Chaumont is one of the four man-made parks that Napoléon III commissioned to resemble the English gardens he grew to love during his exile in England. Built on the site of a former gypsum (a mineral used to make plaster) quarry and a centuries-old dump, it features cliffs, waterfalls, a lake, and a cave topped by a temple. You have plenty of places to lay out your picnic spread here. (Métro: Buttes-Chaumont)

Parc du Champ de Mars

Once a parade ground for French troops, parc du Champ de Mars is a vast green esplanade beneath the Eiffel Tower, extending to the École Militaire (Military Academy), at its southeast end, where Napoléon was once a student. You have plenty of places to relax and contemplate the tower. After your picnic, take a boat tour of the Seine from the nearby Bateaux Mouches. (Métro: Bir-Hakeim)

Parc Monceau

The painter Carmontelle designed several structures for parc Monceau, including a Dutch windmill, a Roman temple, a covered bridge, a waterfall, a farm, medieval ruins, and a pagoda. Garnerin, the world's first parachutist, landed here. In the mid-19th century, the park was redesigned in the English style. A favorite place for author Marcel Proust to stroll, the park contains Paris's largest tree, an Oriental plane tree with a circumference of almost 23 feet. (Métro: Ternes)

Square du Vert Galant

Descend the stairs near the middle of Pont Neuf (near the Pont Neuf tour boats) to this beautiful spot commemorating Paris's favorite king, Henri IV. You're at the very tip of Ile de la Cité, in the middle of the Seine. You can spread out on a bench under the trees and enjoy the stunning views of both banks and the river stretching out ahead. The square is 23 feet lower than the rest of the island; this was the original level of Paris during the Gallo-Roman period. At sunset, this is a popular spot for romantics. (Métro: Cité)

Part VII
The Appendixes

The 5th Wave   By Rich Tennant

In this part . . .

1 tucked some really useful information into these appendixes. Appendix A — the yellow Quick Concierge section — gives you straight-to-the-point, bare-bones info on how to contact your embassy, find a pharmacy, cash a check, and generally take care of business. Appendix B is a glossary of some of the French terms you may need. It features pronunciation guides so you can at least attempt to sound like a native.

Quick Concierge

● ●

*H*ow do you use the telephones? Where can you find your embassy or consulate? This Quick Concierge offers answers to a variety of "Where do I . . . ?" and "How do I . . . ?" questions.

Fast Facts: Paris

American Express

The big Paris office, 11 rue Scribe, 9e (☎ 01-47-77-77-58; Métro: Opéra Chaussée-d'Antin or Havre-Caumartin; RER: Auber), is open weekdays from 9 a.m. to 6 p.m. The bank is open from 9 a.m. to 5 p.m. Saturday, but the mail pickup window is closed.

ATM Locations

As in big cities in the United States, ATMs are easy to find in Paris. Most bank branches have at least one outdoor machine, and there are ATMs in major department stores and in train stations. If you want a list of ATMs that accept MasterCard or Visa cards before you leave home, ask your bank, or print out lists from the following sites: www.visa.com or www.mastercard.com.

Baby-sitters

Check out Allo Maman Dépannage, 38 rue Greuze, 16e (☎ 01-47-55-15-75), or Kid Services, (☎ 0 820 00 02 30/.12€/min). Specify when calling that you need a sitter who speaks English. Also, try the American Church's basement bulletin board where English-speaking (often American) students post notices offering baby-sitting services. The church is located at 65 quai d'Orsay, 7e (☎ 01-45-62-05-00; Métro: Invalides).

Business Hours

The *grands magasins* (department stores) are generally open Monday through Saturday from 9:30 a.m. to 7:00 p.m.; smaller shops close for lunch and reopen around 2:00 p.m., but this practice is rarer than it used to be. Many stores stay open until 7:00 p.m. in summer; others are closed Monday, especially in the morning. Large offices remain open all day, but some close for lunch. Banks are normally open weekdays from 9:00 a.m. to noon and from 1:00 or 1:30 to 4:30 p.m. Some banks also open on Saturday morning. Some currency-exchange booths are open very long hours; see "Currency Exchange," later in this list.

Camera Repair

Photo Suffren, 45 av Suffren, 7e. (☎ 01-45-67-24-25) repairs camera equipment on site at this location not far from the Eiffel Tower.

Climate

From May to September you can expect clear sunny days and temperatures in the 70s and 80s (Fahrenheit). But be prepared for rainy or searingly hot summers, too. From late October to April the weather is often gray and misty with a dampness that gets into your bones. Always bring an umbrella. Temperatures average about 45 degrees Fahrenheit in winter, and the low 60s in spring and autumn. *Note:* Ignore the song "April in Paris," and pack layers for your early spring trip to the City of Light. It is often quite chilly.

Collect Calls

For an AT&T operator: ☎ 0800-99-00-11.

Credit Cards

If you lose your Visa card, call ☎ 08-00-90-11-79; for MasterCard, call ☎ 08-00-90-13-87. To report lost American Express cards, call ☎ 06-39-31-11-11.

Currency Exchange

It is so much easier to use your ATM card to get cash in Paris — you usually get a better rate of exchange than you do at *bureaux de change* (exchange offices), hotels, restaurants, and shops. Most banks in Paris have stopped cashing travelers checks and now steer tourists to bureaux de change. If you must use travelers checks, for good rates, without fees or commissions, and quick service, try the Comptoir de Change Opéra, 9 rue Scribe, 9e (☎ 01-47-42-20-96; Métro: Opéra; RER: Auber). It is open weekdays from 9:00 a.m. to 6:00 p.m., Saturday from 9:30 a.m. to 4:00 p.m. The bureaux de change at all train stations (except gare de Montparnasse) are open daily; those at 63 av. des Champs-Elysées, 8e (Métro: Franklin-D-Roosevelt), and 140 av. des Champs-Elysées, 8e (Métro: Charles-de-Gaulle–Étoile), keep long hours.

Despite disadvantageous exchange rates and long lines, many people prefer to exchange their money at American Express (see the "American Express" listing earlier in this Appendix).

Customs

Non-EU nationals can bring into France duty-free 200 cigarettes or 100 cigarillos or 50 cigars or 250 grams of smoking tobacco; 2 liters of wine and 1 liter of alcohol over 38.80 proof; 50 grams of perfume, one-quarter liter of toilet water; 500 grams of coffee, and 100 grams of tea. Travelers 15 years old and older can also bring in 183€ ($210) in other goods; for those 14 and younger, the limit is 91€ ($105). EU citizens may bring any amount of goods into France as long as it is for their personal use and not for resale.

Returning U.S. citizens who have been away for 48 hours or more are allowed to bring back, once every 30 days, $800 worth of merchandise duty-free. You'll be charged a flat rate of 10% duty on the next $1,000 worth of purchases; on gifts, the duty-free limit is $100. You can't bring fresh food into the United States; canned foods, however, are allowed.

Returning U.K. citizens have no limit on what can be brought back from an EU country as long as the items are for personal use (including gifts), and the necessary duty and tax have been paid. Guidance levels are set at: 800 cigarettes, 200 cigars, 1kg smoking tobacco, 10 liters of spirits, 90 liters of wine, and 110 liters of beer.

Canada allows its citizens a once-a-year C$750 exemption after seven days, and you're allowed to bring back duty-free 200 cigarettes, 1.5 liters of wine or 1.14 liters of liquor, and 50 cigars. In addition, you may mail gifts to Canada from abroad at the rate of C$60 a day, provided they're unsolicited and don't contain alcohol, tobacco, or advertising matter. Write on the package *Unsolicited gift, under $60 value.* All valuables need to be declared on the Y-38 form before departure from Canada, including serial numbers of valuables you already own, such as expensive foreign cameras.

The duty-free allowance in Australia is A$400 or, for those younger than 18, A$200. Upon returning to Australia, citizens can bring in 250 cigarettes or 250 grams of loose tobacco, and 1.125 liters of alcohol. If you're returning with valuable goods you already own, such as foreign-made cameras, you need to file form B263.

The duty-free allowance for New Zealand is NZ$700. Citizens older than 17 can bring in 200 cigarettes or 50 cigars or 250 grams of tobacco (or a mixture of all three if their combined weight doesn't exceed 250 grams), plus 4.5 liters of wine or beer or 1.125 liters of liquor.

Dentists

You can call your consulate and ask the duty officer to recommend a dentist. For dental emergencies, call SOS Urgences Stomatologique Dentaire (☎ 01-45-35-41-41) daily from 9 a.m. to midnight.

Doctors

Call your consulate (see "Embassies and Consulates" later in this list for numbers) and ask the duty officer to recommend a doctor, or call SOS Médecins (☎ 01-43-07-77-77), a 24-hour service. Most doctors and dentists speak some English. You can also call for an appointment at the Centre Médicale Europe, 44 rue d'Amsterdam (☎ 01-42-81-93-33). Consultations cost about 20€ ($23), and specialists are available.

Drugstores

Pharmacies are marked with a green cross and are often upscale, selling toiletries and cosmetics in addition to prescription drugs and over-the-counter remedies. If you're shopping for products other than drugs, buying them elsewhere, such as a *supermarché* (supermarket), is almost always cheaper.

A 24-hour pharmacy, Derhy/Pharmacie Les Champs, is conveniently located on the Champs Elysées at 84 avenue des Champs-Elysées, 8e. ☎ 01-45-62-02-41. Métro: George V.

Electricity

The French electrical system runs on 220 volts. You need adapters to convert the voltage and fit sockets. These are cheaper at home than they are in Paris. Many hotels have two-pin (in some cases, three-pin) sockets for electric razors. Asking your hotel whether you need an adapter is a good idea before plugging in any electrical appliance.

Embassies and Consulates

If you have a passport, immigration, legal, or other problem, contact your consulate. Call before you go: They often keep strange hours and observe both French and home-country holidays. Here's where to find them: Australia, 4 rue Jean-Rey, 15e (☎ 01-40-59-33-00; Métro: Bir-Hakeim); Canada, 35 av. Montaigne, 8e (☎ 01-44-43-29-00; Métro: Franklin-D-Roosevelt or Alma Marceau); New Zealand, 7 ter rue Léonard-de-Vinci, 16e (☎ 01-45-01-43-43; Métro: Victor-Hugo); Consulate of Great Britain, 18 bis rue d'Anjou, 8e (☎ 01-44-51-31-02; Métro: Madeleine); Embassy of Ireland, 4 rue Rude, 16e (☎ 01-44-17-67-00); US passports are issued at the Consulate of the United States, 2 rue St-Florentin, 1er (☎ 01-43-12-22-22); Métro: Concorde).

Emergencies

Call ☎ **17** for the police. To report a fire, dial ☎ **18**. For an ambulance, call ☎ **15**. The main police station, 7 bd. du Palais, 4e (☎ 01-53-71-53-71; Métro: Cité), is open 24 hours a day.

Hospitals

Two hospitals with English-speaking staff are the American Hospital of Paris, 63 bd.

Victor-Hugo, Neuilly-sur-Seine (☎ 01-46-41-25-25), just west of Paris proper (Métro: Les Sablons or Levallois-Perret), and the Hôpital Franco-Brittanique, 3 rue Barbes Levallois-Perret (☎ 01-46-39-22-22), just north of Neuilly, across the city line northwest of Paris (Métro: Anatole-France). Note that the American Hospital charges about $600 a day for a room, not including doctor's fees. The emergency department charges more than $60 for a visit, not including tests and X-rays.

Information

Before you go, contact the French Government Tourist Office, 444 Madison Ave., 16th floor, New York, NY 10022-6903 (☎ 212-838-7800; www.france tourism.com). When you arrive, contact the Office de Tourisme de Paris, 127 av. des Champs-Elysées, 8e (☎ 08-92-68-30-00; 0.34€/min. between 9 a.m. and 7 p.m.

In addition, check the "Where to Get More Information" section later in this appendix.

Internet Access

To surf the Web or check your e-mail, open an account at a free-mail provider, such as Hotmail (www.hotmail.com) or Yahoo! Mail (www.yahoo.com), and all you need to check e-mail while you travel is a Web connection, available at Internet cafés everywhere. After logging on, just point the browser to your e-mail provider, enter your username and password, and you have access to your mail.

The following Paris Web bars, listed by arrondissement, charge modest fees (4€–7€ ($4.60–$8.05 per hour):

Cybercafé de Paris, 11 and 15 rue des Halles, 1er. ☎ 01- 42-21-11-11. Métro: Châtelet.

XS Arena St. Michel , 53 rue de la Harpe, 5e (☎ 01-44-07-38-39). Métro:Mabillon, St-Michel.

Language

In the tourist areas of Paris, English is widely understood. As you move into more residential sections of the city, however, you will probably meet people who don't speak English. I suggest carrying a pocket-sized phrasebook such as *Berlitz Phrase Book: French,* available at all bookstores, (or use the glossary in Appendix B.

Laundry and Dry Cleaning

The more expensive your hotel, the more it costs to have your laundry or dry cleaning done there. Instead, find a laundry near you by consulting the Yellow Pages under *Laveries pour particuliers.* Take as many coins as you can. Washing and drying 6 kilos (13¼ lbs.) usually costs 5.50€ ($6.30). Dry cleaning is *nettoyage à sec;* look for shop signs with the word *Pressing,* and don't expect to have your clothes back within an hour; you may be able to get them back the next day if you ask nicely. The dry cleaning chain 5 à Sec has stores across Paris.

Liquor Laws

Supermarkets, grocery stores, and cafés sell alcoholic beverages. The legal drinking age is 16. Persons younger than 16 can be served an alcoholic drink in a bar or restaurant when accompanied by a parent or legal guardian. Wine and liquor are sold every day of the year. *Be warned:* The authorities are very strict about drunk-driving laws. If convicted, you face a stiff fine and a possible prison term of two months to two years.

Lost Property

Paris's Prefecture of Police runs the central Lost and Found, Objets Trouvés, 36 rue des Morillons, 15e (☎ 08-21-00-25-25. Métro: Convention), at the corner of rue de Dantzig. The office is open Monday, Wednesday, and Friday from 8:30 a.m. to 5:00 p.m. and Tuesday and Thursday from 8:30 a.m. to 8:00 p.m. (except in July and August). For Lost and Found on the Métro, call ☎ 01-40-06-75-27.

Luggage Storage

Most hotels will store luggage for you for free, and that's your best bet, especially when you plan to return to Paris after a tour of the provinces.

Maps

Maps printed by the department stores are usually available free at hotels, and they're good for those visiting Paris for only a few days and hitting only the major attractions. But if you plan to really explore all the nooks and crannies of the city, the best maps are those of the *Plan de Paris par Arrondissement,* pocket-sized books with maps and a street index, available at most bookstores. They're extremely practical, and prices start at around 9€ ($10). You can find them in Paris bookstores, at the Target-like chain store, Monoprix, (there is one in nearly every Paris arrondissement), and some of the bigger newsstands. Most Parisians carry a copy because they, too, get lost at times.

Newspapers and Magazines

Most newsstands carry the latest editions of the *International Herald Tribune,* published Monday through Saturday, and the major London papers. *Time* and *Newsweek* are readily available in Paris and so is the International edition of *USA Today.* You can also get the *New York Times* in some of the bigger English-language bookstores.

Pharmacies

See "Drugstores."

Police

Dial ☎ 17 in emergencies; otherwise, call ☎ 01-53-71-53-71.

Post Office

Large post offices are normally open weekdays from 8 a.m. to 7 p.m., Saturday from 8 a.m. to noon; small post offices may have shorter hours. Many post offices (PTT) are scattered around the city; ask anybody for the nearest one. Airmail letters and postcards to the United States cost 0.90€ ($2.05); within Europe 0.50€ ($0.60); and to Australia or New Zealand, 0.90€ ($1.05).

The city's main post office is at 52 rue du Louvre, 75001 Paris (☎ 01-40-28-76-00; Métro: Louvre-Rivoli). It's open 24 hours a day for urgent mail, telegrams, and telephone calls. It handles *Poste Restante mail* — sent to you in care of the post office and stored until you pick it up. Be prepared to show your passport and pay 0.75€ ($0.85) for each letter you receive. If you don't want to use Poste Restante, you can receive mail in care of American Express. Holders of American Express cards or traveler's checks get this service free; others pay a fee.

Restrooms

Public restrooms are plentiful, but you usually have to pay for them. Every café has a restroom, but it's supposed to be for customers only. The best plan is to ask to use the telephone; it's usually next to the *toilette.* For a 0.40€ ($0.45), you can use the street-side toilets, which are automatically flushed out and cleaned after every use (Note; these toilets do not give change for a .50€ (piece). Some Métro stations have serviced restrooms; you're expected to tip the attendant 0.50€ ($0.60).

Safety

Paris is a relatively safe city; your biggest risks are pickpockets and purse snatchers, so be particularly attentive in museum lines, popular shopping areas, around tourist attractions, on the Métro, and on crowded buses (especially in the confusion of getting on and off). Popular pickpocket tactics include someone asking you for directions or bumping into you while an accomplice takes your wallet ,and bands of children surrounding and distracting you and then making off with purchases and/or your wallet.

Women need to be on guard in crowded tourist areas and on the Métro against overly friendly men who seem to have made a specialty out of bothering unsuspecting female tourists. Tricks include asking your name and nationality and then taking advantage of your politeness by sticking like a burr to you for the rest of the day. They're usually more harassing than harmful, but if you're too nice, you may be stuck spending time with someone with whom you prefer not to. A simple *laissez-moi tranquille* (*lay*-say mwa tran-*keel*; leave me alone) usually works.

Smoking

Although restaurants are required to provide nonsmoking sections, you may find yourself next to the kitchen or the restrooms. Even there, your neighbor may light up and defy you to say something about it. Large brasseries, expensive restaurants, and places accustomed to dealing with foreigners are more likely to be accommodating.

Taxes

Watch out: You can get burned. As a member of the European Community, France routinely imposes a standard 19.6% value-added tax (VAT) on many goods and services. The tax on merchandise applies to clothing, appliances, liquor, leather goods, shoes, furs, jewelry, perfume,

cameras, and even caviar. You can get a rebate — usually 13% — on certain goods and merchandise, but not on services. The minimum purchase, depending on the store, is 175€ ($201) in the same store for nationals or residents of countries outside the European Union. Chapter 12 has more on VAT and how to deal with it.

Taxis

Alpha Taxis (☎ 01-45-85-85- 85), or G7 (☎ 01-47-39-47-39). Be aware that the meter starts running as soon as you call a cab, so they're more expensive than hailed taxis. You can hail taxis in the street (look for a taxi with a white light on; an orange light means it's occupied), but most drivers won't pick you up if you're within 200 meters (218 yards) of a taxi stand (look for the blue *Taxi* sign).

Telephone/Telex/Fax

Most public phone booths take only telephone debit cards called *télécartes,* which you can buy at post offices and *tabacs* (cafes and kiosks that sell tobacco products). You insert the card into the phone and make your call; the cost is automatically deducted from the value of the card recorded on its magnetized strip. The télécarte comes in 50- and 120-unit denominations (A *unit* is a measure of time set by the phone company issuing the card. You get more units for your money if you call during off-peak hours after 7 p.m. and before 8 a.m.) respectively costing about 7.40€ ($8.50) and 14.80€ ($17), and can be used only in a phone booth.

Cashiers almost always try to sell you a card from France Télécom, the French phone company, but cards exist that give you more talk time for the same amount of money. Instead of inserting the card into a public phone, you dial a free number and tap in a code. The cards come with directions, some in English, and can be used from public and private phones, unlike France Télécom's card, which you can use only on public phones. Look for *tabacs* that have advertisements for Delta Multimedia or Kertel, or ask for a *télécarte international avec un code.*

For placing international calls from France, dial 00 and then the country code (for the United States and Canada, 1; for Britain, 44; for Ireland, 353; for Australia, 61; for New Zealand, 64), then the area or city code, and then the local number (for example, to call New York, dial 00 + 1 + 212 + 000-0000). To place a collect call to North America, dial ☎ 00-33-11, and an English-speaking operator will assist you. Dial ☎ 00-00-11 for an American AT&T operator; MCI ☎ 0800-99-00-19; Sprint ☎ 0800-99-00-87.

For calling from Paris to anywhere else in France (the provinces, in other words, or *province*), the country is divided into five zones with prefixes beginning 01, 02, 03, 04, and 05; check a phone directory for the code of the city you're calling.

If you're calling France from the United States, the number you dial probably looks something like this: 011-33-(0)1-00-00-00-00. You must first dial the international prefix, 011; then the country code for France, (33); followed by city code and the rest of the number. When dialing from outside France, leave off the 0, which is often indicated in parentheses, in the city code.

Avoid making phone calls from your hotel room; many hotels charge at least 0.75€ ($0.90) for local calls, and the markup on international calls can be staggering.

You can send telex and fax messages at the main post office in each arrondissement of Paris, but asking at your hotel or going to a neighborhood printer or copy shop is often cheaper.

Time Zone

Paris is six hours ahead of Eastern Standard Time; noon in New York is 6 p.m. in Paris.

Tipping

The custom is to tip the bellhop about 1€ coin per bag, more in expensive (splurge) hotels. If you have a lot of luggage, tip a bit more. Don't tip housekeepers unless you do something that requires extra work. Tip a few euros if a reception staff member performs extra services.

Although your *addition* (restaurant bill) or *fiche* (cafe check) bears the words *service compris* (service charge included), always leave a small tip. Generally, 5% is considered acceptable.

Taxi drivers appreciate a tip of 0.50€ to 1€ ($0.60 to $1.15) or whatever it costs to round up the fare to the next euro. On longer journeys, when the fare exceeds 20€ ($23), a 5% to 10% tip is appropriate. At the theater and cinema, tip 1€ ($1.15) if an usher shows you to your seat. In public toilets, a fee for using the facilities often is posted. If not, the maintenance person will expect a tip of 1€ ($1.15). Put it in the basket or on the plate at the entrance. Porters and cloakroom attendants are usually governed by set prices, which are displayed. If not, give a porter 1€ ($1.15) per suitcase, and a cloakroom attendant 0.50€ ($0.60) per coat.

Transit Info

The telephone number for reservations on France's national railroads (SNCF) is ☎ 08-92-35-35-35 (0.46€/min); open daily from 7 a.m. to 10 p.m.). *Remember:* You must validate your train ticket in the orange ticket *composteur* on the platform or pay a fine. For information in English about Paris subways and buses (RATP) call ☎ 08-92-68-41-14.

Water

Tap water in Paris is perfectly safe, but if you're prone to stomach problems, you may prefer to drink mineral water.

Toll-Free Numbers and Web Sites

Major airlines

Air Canada
☎ 800-630-3299
www.aircanada.ca

Air France
☎ 800-237-2747
www.airfrance.com

Air Tahitinui
☎ 877-824-4846
www.airtahitinui.com

American Airlines
☎ 800-433-7300
www.aa.com

British Airways
☎ 800-247-9297
www.british-airways.com

Continental Airlines
☎ 800-523-3273
www.continental.com

Delta Air Lines
☎ 800-221-1212
www.delta.com

Iceland Air
☎ 800-223-5500
www.icelandair.com

Weather updates
http://europe.cnn.com/WEATHER

www.weather.com

Northwest/KLM
☎ 800-225-2525
www.nwa.com

United Airlines
☎ 800-864-8331
www.ual.com

US Airways
☎ 800-428-4322
www.usairways.com

Virgin Atlantic
☎ 800-862-8621
www.virginatlantic.com

Major car rental agencies in Paris

Avis
gare d'Austerlitz, 13e
☎ 01-45-84-22-10
www.avis.com

Hertz France
gare de l'Est, 10e
☎ 01-42-05-50-43
www.hertz.com

National
gare de Lyon, 12e
☎ 01-40-04-90-04
www.nationalcar.com

Europcar
60 bd Diderot, 12e
☎ 08-25-35-23-52/0.15€
www.europcar.fr

Where to Get More Information

The information sources listed here are the best of the bunch; dig in before you go, and you'll be well prepared for your trip.

Tourist offices

For general information about France, contact an office of the **French Government Tourist Office** at one of the following addresses:

✔ **In the United States: The French Government Tourist Office,** 444 Madison Ave., 16th floor, New York, NY 10022-6903 (☎ 212-838-7800; Internet: www.francetourism.com); 676 N. Michigan Ave., Chicago, IL 60611-2819 (☎ 312-751-7800).

✔ **In Canada: Maison de la France/French Government Tourist Office,** 1981 av. McGill College, Suite 490, Montréal PQ H3A 2W9 (☎ 514-876-9881).

✔ **In the United Kingdom: Maison de la France/French Government Tourist Office,** 178 Piccadilly, London W1V 0AL (☎ 0891-244-123).

✔ **In Australia: French Tourist Bureau,** 25 Bligh St. Level 20, Sydney, NSW 2000 Australia (☎ 02-231-5244; Fax: 02-231-8682).

✔ **In New Zealand:** You won't find a representative in New Zealand; contact the Australian representative.

✔ **In Paris: The Office de Tourisme et des Congrès de Paris,** is no longer headquartered on the Champs-Elysées, but has branches throughout the city at the following locations *Note:* These centers are closed on May 1.

- **The Opéra-Grands-Magasins Welcome Center,** 11 rue Scribe, 9e, open Mon–Sat 9 a.m.–6:30 p.m. (Métro: Chausée d'Antin or Opéra; RER: Auber)

- **The welcome kiosk beneath the modern glass-roofed terminal of the Gare du Nord,** 18 rue Dunkerque, 10e, open 7 days a week from 8 a.m.–6 p.m. (Métro and RER: Gare du Nord)

- **The Gare de Lyon Welcome Center,** 20 bd. Diderot, 12e, open Mon–Sat 8 a.m.–6 p.m. (Métro and RER: Gare de Lyon)

- **21 place du Tertre,** 18e, open daily 10 a.m.–7 p.m. (Métro: Abbesses)

- **Carrousel du Louvre, beneath the Pyramide,** 99 rue de Rivoli, 1er, open daily 10 a.m.–7 p.m. (Métro: Palais Royal/ Musée du Louvre)

- **Eiffel Tower between the North and East pillars,** 7e, open daily 11 a.m.–6:40 p.m. (Métro: Bir Hakeim, RER: Champ-de-Mars/Tour Eiffel)

Surfing the Web

You can find plenty of excellent information about Paris on the Internet — the latest news, restaurant reviews, concert schedules, subway maps, and more.

- ✔ **Aeroports de Paris** (www.adp.fr): Click the American flag on this site's home page for an English version that provides transfer information into Paris and lists terminals, maps, airlines, boutiques, hotels, restaurants, and accessibility information for travelers with disabilities.

- ✔ **Bonjour Paris** (www.bonjourparis.com): This site should be one of the first you browse before your trip; it's just full of useful information about Paris. You can find everything from cultural differences to shopping to restaurant reviews, all written from an American expatriate point of view.

- ✔ **Café de la Soul** (www.cafedelasoul.com): A sleekly designed Web site for African-American travelers in Paris. The site features articles, travelogues, and links to resources in the City of Light.

- ✔ **French Government Tourist Office** (www.francetourism.com): Here you can find information on planning your trip to France and practical tips, family activities, events, and accommodations.

- ✔ **ISMAP** (www.ismap.com): Type in a Paris address on this site, and ISMAP maps it, including nearby sights of interest and the closest Métro stops.

- ✔ **Paris Digest** (www.parisdigest.com): Paris Digest selects "the best sights in Paris" and provides photos and links to them and to restaurants with views and good decor, and information about shopping, hotels, and things to do.

- ✔ **Paris France Guide** (www.parisfranceguide.com): This site has plenty of useful information about Paris, with current nightlife, restaurant, music, theater, and events listings. This guide is brought to you by the publishers of the *Living in France, Study in France,* and *What's on in France* guides.

- ✔ **Paris Pages** (www.paris.org): So much information is on this site that you won't know where to begin. Lodging reviews are organized by area and the monuments standing nearby, and you can find photo tours, shop listings, and a map of attractions with details. Some of the information may be out of date.

- ✔ **Paris Tourist Office** (www.paris-touristoffice.com): The official site of the Paris Tourist Office provides information on the year's events, museums, accommodations, nightlife, and restaurants.

- ✔ **Parler Paris** (www.parlerparis.com): This site should be among the first you browse before your trip, or sign up for the triweekly newsletter. Editor Adrian Leeds really knows Paris, and Parler Paris is a true insider's guide to visiting and living in Paris. Her insightful commentary covers everything from visits to hidden Paris places to delicious budget dining.

🗸 **RATP (Paris Urban Transit)** (www.ratp.fr): Find subway and bus line maps, timetables and information, and routes and times for Noctambus, Paris's night buses that run after the Métro closes. Click on the word *English* for the English-language version.

🗸 **Magic Paris** (http://magicparis.com): The big attractions, such as the Louvre and the Eiffel Tower, are featured along with shop and gallery listings organized by arrondissement. Airport terminal information and click-on subway maps are also posted here.

🗸 **SNCF (French Rail)** (www.sncf.fr): The official Web site of the French railway system, this site sells seats online for trips through France. You can also find timetables and prices here. Click on the Union Jack on the upper-left corner of the screen for English.

🗸 **Subway Navigator** (www.subwaynavigator.com): This site provides detailed subway maps for Paris and other cities around the world. You can select a city and enter your arrival and departure points, and then Subway Navigator maps out your route and estimates how long your trip will take.

Hitting the books

Most bookstores have several shelves devoted entirely to Paris-related titles, given that the city is one of the most-visited on the planet. Here are a few other books that may be useful for your trip. All Frommer's guides are published by Wiley, Inc.

🗸 *Frommer's Paris,* updated every year, is an authoritative guide that covers the city and its surroundings.

🗸 *Frommer's Paris from $80 a Day* is the guide for travelers who want to visit Paris comfortably but don't want to spend a fortune doing it.

🗸 *Frommer's Portable Paris* is the pocket-sized version of *Frommer's Paris.*

🗸 *Frommer's Memorable Walks in Paris* is for folks who want to explore the city in depth and on foot with easy directions and descriptions of important sights.

🗸 *Frommer's Irreverent Guide to Paris* is a fun guide for sophisticated travelers who want the basics without much excess.

Appendix B

A Glossary of French Words and Phrases

*W*hy **La** *Tour Eiffel* but **Le** *Tour de France?* Why **un** *cabinet* but **une** *cabine?* Simply put, in French and other Romance languages, nouns are assigned a gender. The article preceding the noun, such as *le* and *la* (which mean *the*) and *un* and *une* (which mean *a* or *one*), corresponds to that gender. *La* and *une* are feminine; *le* and *un* are masculine. Plural nouns are preceded by *les*. An extra letter is also added to the noun itself to signify feminine gender. So Dan Rather is *un journalist,* but Diane Sawyer is *une journaliste.* French schoolchildren spend years memorizing the gender of nouns; fortunately no one expects you to do the same!

Basic Vocabulary

English	French	Pronunciation
Yes/no	**Oui/non**	wee/nohn
Okay	**D'accord**	dah-*core*
Please	**S'il vous plaît**	seel-voo-*play*
Thank you	**Merci**	mair-*see*
You're welcome	**De rien**	duh ree-*ehn*
Hello (during daylight hours)	**Bonjour**	bohn-*jhoor*
Good evening	**Bonsoir**	bohn-*swahr*
Goodbye	**Au revoir**	o ruh-*vwahr*
police	**la police**	lah po-*lees*
What's your name?	**Comment vous appelez-vous?**	ko-mahn-voo-za-pel-ay-*voo*
My name is . . .	**Je m'appelle . . .**	jhuh ma-*pell*
Happy to meet you	**Enchanté(e)**	ohn-shahn-*tay*

(continued)

Basic Vocabulary *(continued)*

English	French	Pronunciation
Miss	**Mademoiselle**	mad mwa-*zel*
Mr.	**Monsieur**	muh-*syuh*
Mrs.	**Madame**	ma-*dam*
How are you?	**Comment allez-vous?**	kuh-mahn-tahl-ay-*voo*
Fine, thank you, and you?	**Très bien, merci, et vous?**	tray bee-ehn, mare-see, ay *voo*
Very well, thank you	**Très bien, merci**	tray bee-ehn, mair-*see*
So-so	**Comme ci, comme ça**	kum-*see,* kum-*sah*
I'm sorry/excuse me	**Pardon**	pahr-*dohn*
I'm so very sorry	**Désolé(e)**	day-zoh-*lay*
Do you speak English?	**Parlez-vous anglais?**	par-lay-voo-ahn-*glay*
I don't speak French	**Je ne parle pas français**	jhuh ne parl pah frahn-*say*
I don't understand	**Je ne comprends pas**	jhuh ne kohm-*prahn* pah
Could you speak more slowly?	**Pouvez-vous parler un peu plus lentement?**	poo-*vay* voo par-*lay* uh puh ploo lan-te-*ment*
Could you repeat that?	**Répetez, s'il vous plaît**	ray-pay-*tay,* seel voo *play*
What is it?	**Qu'est-ce que c'est?**	kess-kuh-*say*
What time is it?	**Qu'elle heure est-il?**	kel uhr eh-*teel*
What?	**Quoi?**	kwah
Pardon?	**Pardons?**	par-*doh*
Help!	**Aidez-moi!**	*ay*-day moi!
How? *or* What did you say?	**Comment?**	ko-*mahn*
When?	**Quand?**	cohn
Where is . . . ?	**Où est . . . ?**	ooh-eh
Where are the toilets?	**Où sont les toilettes?**	ooh-sohn lay twah-*lets*
Who?	**Qui?**	kee
Why?	**Pourquoi?**	poor-*kwah*

English	French	Pronunciation
Here/there	Ici/là	ee-*see*/lah
Left/right	à gauche/à droite	ah goash/ah drwaht
Straight ahead	Tout droit	too-drwah
I'm American/Canadian/ British	Je suis américain(e)/ canadien(e)/ anglais(e)	jhe swee a-may-ree-*kehn*/canah-dee-*en*/ ahn-*glay (glaise)*
I'm going to . . .	Je vais à . . .	jhe vay ah
I want to get off at . . .	Je voudrais descendre à . . .	jhe voo-*dray* day-son-drah-ah

Health Terms

English	French	Pronunciation
I'm sick	Je suis malade	jhuh swee mal-*ahd*
I have a headache	J'ai une mal de tête	jhay oon mal de tet
I have a stomachache	J'ai une mal de ventre	jhay oon mal de *vahn*-trah
I would like to buy some aspirin	Je voudrais acheter des aspirines	jhe *voo*-dray *ash*-tay days as-peh-*reen*
hospital	l'hôpital	low-pee-*tahl*
insurance	les assurances	lez ah-sur-*ahns*

Travel Terms

English	French	Pronunciation
airport	l'aéroport	lair-o-*por*
bank	la banque	lah bahnk
bridge	pont	pohn
bus station	la gare routière	lah gar roo-tee-*air*
bus stop	l'arrêt de bus	lah-*ray* duh boohss
by means of a bicycle	en vélo/par bicyclette	ahn *vay*-low/par bee-see-*clet*

(continued)

Travel Terms *(continued)*

English	French	Pronunciation
by means of a car	**en voiture**	ahn vwa-*toor*
cashier	**la caisse**	lah *kess*
driver's license	**permis de conduire**	per-*mee* duh con-*dweer*
elevator	**l'ascenseur**	lah sahn *seuhr*
entrance (to a building or a city)	**porte**	port
exit (from a building or a freeway)	**une sortie**	ewn sor-*tee*
ground floor	**rez-de-chausée**	ray-duh-show-*say*
highway to . . .	**la route pour . . .**	lah root por
luggage storage	**consigne**	kohn-*seen*-yuh
a map of the city	**un plan de ville**	uh plahn de *veel*
museum	**le musée**	luh mew-*zay*
no entry	**sens interdit**	sehns ahn-ter-*dee*
no smoking	**défense de fumer**	day-*fahns* duh fu-may
on foot	**à pied**	ah pee-*ay*
one-day pass	**ticket journalier**	tee-kay jhoor-nall-ee-*ay*
one-way ticket	**aller simple**	ah-*lay sam*-pluh
a phone card	**une carte téléphonique**	ewn cart tay-lay-fone-*eek*
a postcard	**une carte postale**	ewn carte pos-*tahl*
round-trip ticket	**aller-retour**	ah-*lay* re-*toor*
second floor	**premier étage**	prem-ee-*ehr* ay-*taj*
slow down	**ralentissez**	rah-lahn-tis-*ay*
store	**le magasin**	luh ma-ga-*zehn*
street	**la rue**	roo
suburb	**la banlieue**	lah bahn-*liew*
subway	**le Métro**	luh may-tro

English	French	Pronunciation
telephone	**le téléphone**	luh tay-lay-*phun*
ticket	**un billet**	uh *bee*-yay
ticket office	**vente de billets**	vahnt duh bee-*yay*
toilets	**les toilettes**	lay twa-*lets*
I'd like . . .	**Je voudrais . . .**	jhe voo-*dray*
a room	**une chambre**	ewn *shahm*-bruh
the key	**la clé (la clef)**	lah clay

Shopping Terms

English	French	Pronunciation
How much does it cost?	**C'est combien?/ Ça coûte combien?**	say comb-bee-*ehn?/* sah coot comb-bee-*ehn*
That's expensive	**C'est cher/chère**	say share
That's inexpensive	**C'est raisonnable/ C'est bon marché**	say ray-son-*ahb*-bluh/ say bohn mar-*shay*
Do you take credit cards?	**Est-ce que vous acceptez les cartes de credit?**	es-kuh voo zaksep-*tay* lay kart duh creh-*dee*
I'd like to buy . . .	**Je voudrais acheter . . .**	jhe voo-dray ahsh-*tay*
aspirin	**des aspirines**	deyz ahs-peer-*eens*
cigarettes	**des cigarettes**	day see-ga-*ret*
condoms	**des préservatifs**	day pray-ser-va-*teefs*
contraceptive suppositories	**des ovules contraceptives**	days oh-*vyules* kahn-trah-cep-*teef*
a dictionary	**un dictionnaire**	uh deek-see-oh-*nare*
a gift (for someone)	**un cadeau**	uh kah-*doe*
a handbag	**un sac à main**	uh sahk ah man
a magazine	**une revue**	ewn reh-*vu*
matches	**des allumettes**	dayz a-loo-*met*

(continued)

Shopping Terms *(continued)*

English	French	Pronunciation
lighter	**un briquet**	uh *bree*-kay
a newspaper	**un journal**	uh zhoor-*nahl*
a road map	**une carte routière**	ewn cart roo-tee-*air*
shoes	**des chaussures**	day show-*suhr*
soap	**du savon**	dew sah-*vohn*
socks	**des chaussettes**	day show-*set*
a stamp	**un timbre**	uh *tam*-bruh
writing paper	**du papier à lettres**	dew pap-pee-*ay* a *let*-ruh

Elements of Time

English	French	Pronunciation
Sunday	**dimanche**	dee-*mahnsh*
Monday	**lundi**	luhn-*dee*
Tuesday	**mardi**	mahr-*dee*
Wednesday	**mercredi**	mair-kruh-*dee*
Thursday	**jeudi**	jheu-*dee*
Friday	**vendredi**	vawn-druh-*dee*
Saturday	**samedi**	sahm-*dee*
Yesterday	**hier**	ee-*air*
Today	**aujourd'hui**	o-jhord-*dwee*
This morning	**ce matin**	suh ma-*tan*
This afternoon	**cet après-midi**	set ah-preh mee-*dee*
Tonight	**ce soir**	suh *swahr*
Tomorrow	**demain**	de-*man*
Now	**maintenant**	mant-*naw*

Index

See also separate Accommodations and Restaurant indexes at the end of this index.

General Index

• A •

Accommodations Index

Restaurant Index

BUSINESS, CAREERS & PERSONAL FINANCE

0-7645-5307-0   0-7645-5331-3 *†

Also available:

- Accounting For Dummies †
  0-7645-5314-3
- Business Plans Kit For Dummies †
  0-7645-5365-8
- Cover Letters For Dummies
  0-7645-5224-4
- Frugal Living For Dummies
  0-7645-5403-4
- Leadership For Dummies
  0-7645-5176-0
- Managing For Dummies
  0-7645-1771-6

- Marketing For Dummies
  0-7645-5600-2
- Personal Finance For Dummies *
  0-7645-2590-5
- Project Management
  For Dummies
  0-7645-5283-X
- Resumes For Dummies †
  0-7645-5471-9
- Selling For Dummies
  0-7645-5363-1
- Small Business Kit For Dummies *†
  0-7645-5093-4

HOME & BUSINESS COMPUTER BASICS

0-7645-4074-2   0-7645-3758-X

Also available:

- ACT! 6 For Dummies
  0-7645-2645-6
- iLife '04 All-in-One Desk Reference
  For Dummies
  0-7645-7347-0
- iPAQ For Dummies
  0-7645-6769-1
- Mac OS X Panther Timesaving
  Techniques For Dummies
  0-7645-5812-9
- Macs For Dummies
  0-7645-5656-8
- Microsoft Money 2004 For Dummies
  0-7645-4195-1

- Office 2003 All-in-One Desk
  Reference For Dummies
  0-7645-3883-7
- Outlook 2003 For Dummies
  0-7645-3759-8
- PCs For Dummies
  0-7645-4074-2
- TiVo For Dummies
  0-7645-6923-6
- Upgrading and Fixing PCs
  For Dummies
  0-7645-1665-5
- Windows XP Timesaving
  Techniques For Dummies
  0-7645-3748-2

FOOD, HOME, GARDEN, HOBBIES, MUSIC & PETS

0-7645-5295-3   0-7645-5232-5

Also available:

- Bass Guitar For Dummies
  0-7645-2487-9
- Diabetes Cookbook For Dummies
  0-7645-5230-9
- Gardening For Dummies *
  0-7645-5130-2
- Guitar For Dummies
  0-7645-5106-X
- Holiday Decorating For Dummies
  0-7645-2570-0
- Home Improvement All-in-One
  For Dummies
  0-7645-5680-0

- Knitting For Dummies
  0-7645-5395-X
- Piano For Dummies
  0-7645-5105-1
- Puppies For Dummies
  0-7645-5255-4
- Scrapbooking For Dummies
  0-7645-7208-3
- Senior Dogs For Dummies
  0-7645-5818-8
- Singing For Dummies
  0-7645-2475-5
- 30-Minute Meals For Dummies
  0-7645-2589-1

INTERNET & DIGITAL MEDIA

0-7645-1664-7   0-7645-6924-4

Also available:

- 2005 Online Shopping Directory
  For Dummies
  0-7645-7495-7
- CD & DVD Recording For Dummies
  0-7645-5956-7
- eBay For Dummies
  0-7645-5654-1
- Fighting Spam For Dummies
  0-7645-5965-6
- Genealogy Online For Dummies
  0-7645-5964-8
- Google For Dummies
  0-7645-4420-9

- Home Recording For Musicians
  For Dummies
  0-7645-1634-5
- The Internet For Dummies
  0-7645-4173-0
- iPod & iTunes For Dummies
  0-7645-7772-7
- Preventing Identity Theft
  For Dummies
  0-7645-7336-5
- Pro Tools All-in-One Desk
  Reference For Dummies
  0-7645-5714-9
- Roxio Easy Media Creator
  For Dummies
  0-7645-7131-1

* Separate Canadian edition also available
† Separate U.K. edition also available

Available wherever books are sold. For more information or to order direct: U.S. customers visit www.dummies.com or call 1-877-762-2974.
U.K. customers visit www.wileyeurope.com or call 0800 243407. Canadian customers visit www.wiley.ca or call 1-800-567-4797.

SPORTS, FITNESS, PARENTING, RELIGION & SPIRITUALITY

0-7645-5146-9   0-7645-5418-2

Also available:
- Adoption For Dummies
  0-7645-5488-3
- Basketball For Dummies
  0-7645-5248-1
- The Bible For Dummies
  0-7645-5296-1
- Buddhism For Dummies
  0-7645-5359-3
- Catholicism For Dummies
  0-7645-5391-7
- Hockey For Dummies
  0-7645-5228-7

- Judaism For Dummies
  0-7645-5299-6
- Martial Arts For Dummies
  0-7645-5358-5
- Pilates For Dummies
  0-7645-5397-6
- Religion For Dummies
  0-7645-5264-3
- Teaching Kids to Read
  For Dummies
  0-7645-4043-2
- Weight Training For Dummies
  0-7645-5168-X
- Yoga For Dummies
  0-7645-5117-5

TRAVEL

0-7645-5438-7   0-7645-5453-0

Also available:
- Alaska For Dummies
  0-7645-1761-9
- Arizona For Dummies
  0-7645-6938-4
- Cancún and the Yucatán
  For Dummies
  0-7645-2437-2
- Cruise Vacations For Dummies
  0-7645-6941-4
- Europe For Dummies
  0-7645-5456-5
- Ireland For Dummies
  0-7645-5455-7

- Las Vegas For Dummies
  0-7645-5448-4
- London For Dummies
  0-7645-4277-X
- New York City For Dummies
  0-7645-6945-7
- Paris For Dummies
  0-7645-5494-8
- RV Vacations For Dummies
  0-7645-5443-3
- Walt Disney World & Orlando
  For Dummies
  0-7645-6943-0

GRAPHICS, DESIGN & WEB DEVELOPMENT

0-7645-4345-8   0-7645-5589-8

Also available:
- Adobe Acrobat 6 PDF
  For Dummies
  0-7645-3760-1
- Building a Web Site For Dummies
  0-7645-7144-3
- Dreamweaver MX 2004
  For Dummies
  0-7645-4342-3
- FrontPage 2003 For Dummies
  0-7645-3882-9
- HTML 4 For Dummies
  0-7645-1995-6
- Illustrator CS For Dummies
  0-7645-4084-X

- Macromedia Flash MX 2004
  For Dummies
  0-7645-4358-X
- Photoshop 7 All-in-One Desk
  Reference For Dummies
  0-7645-1667-1
- Photoshop CS Timesaving
  Techniques For Dummies
  0-7645-6782-9
- PHP 5 For Dummies
  0-7645-4166-8
- PowerPoint 2003 For Dummies
  0-7645-3908-6
- QuarkXPress 6 For Dummies
  0-7645-2593-X

NETWORKING, SECURITY, PROGRAMMING & DATABASES

0-7645-6852-3   0-7645-5784-X

Also available:
- A+ Certification For Dummies
  0-7645-4187-0
- Access 2003 All-in-One Desk
  Reference For Dummies
  0-7645-3988-4
- Beginning Programming
  For Dummies
  0-7645-4997-9
- C For Dummies
  0-7645-7068-4
- Firewalls For Dummies
  0-7645-4048-3
- Home Networking For Dummies
  0-7645-42796

- Network Security For Dummies
  0-7645-1679-5
- Networking For Dummies
  0-7645-1677-9
- TCP/IP For Dummies
  0-7645-1760-0
- VBA For Dummies
  0-7645-3989-2
- Wireless All In-One Desk Referenc
  For Dummies
  0-7645-7496-5
- Wireless Home Networking
  For Dummies
  0-7645-3910-8